The Daily Telegraph

GUIDE TO

ENGLAND'S
PARISH
CHURCHES

The Daily Telegraph
GUIDE TO
ENGLAND'S PARISH CHURCHES

ROBERT HARBISON

For Esther

First published 2006 by Aurum Press Limited,
25 Bedford Avenue, London WC1B 3AT

Copyright © 2006 Robert Harbison

An earlier edition of this book was published by André Deutsch Ltd
as *The Shell Guide to English Parish Churches* in 1992.

The moral right of Robert Harbison to be identified as
the author of this work has been asserted by him
in accordance with the Copyright Designs and Patents Act 1988.

Photographs © 2006 John Damien Noonan
Designed by Damien Noonan
Maps supplied by PerroCarto Ltd
Illustrations pp. 12–14 by Sandra Oakins

A catalogue record for this book is available from the British Library.

ISBN 1 84513 066 9

Printed in Singapore

10   9   8   7   6   5   4   3   2   1

2010   2009   2008   2007   2006

Photographs:
Cover: Steeple Ashton, Wiltshire
Frontispiece: Gayhurst, Buckinghamshire
This page: Sherborne Abbey, Dorset

Contents

Key map to the regions of England as used in this guide

NORTH
*Yorkshire,
Durham,
Northumberland*

NORTH WEST
*Cumbria,
Lancashire,
Cheshire*

MIDLANDS
*Derbyshire,
Nottinghamshire,
Leicestershire,
Rutland,
Northamptonshire,
Warwickshire*

WELSH BORDERS
*Herefordshire,
Shropshire,
Worcestershire,
Staffordshire*

**EAST ANGLIA
& LINCOLNSHIRE**
*Essex, Suffolk, Norfolk,
Cambridgeshire,
Huntingdonshire,
Lincolnshire*

COTSWOLDS
*Wiltshire, Gloucestershire,
Oxfordshire, Berkshire*

HOME COUNTIES & LONDON
*Buckinghamshire, Hertfordshire,
Bedfordshire, Middlesex, London*

SOUTH EAST
*Hampshire, Isle of Wight,
Sussex, Kent, Surrey*

SOUTH WEST
*Cornwall, Devon, Somerset,
Dorset*

Note to Reader

Full names and dates of all architects and designers mentioned in the text will be found in the index.

In this book non-Anglican buildings which serve local congregations but are not in the strict sense parish churches occasionally find a place.

Abbreviations have been kept to a minimum but the following may be noted:

RC   Roman Catholic
CCT   Churches Conservation Trust

The last, set up in 1969 as the Redundant Churches Fund, looks after over two hundred of the best redundant churches, most of which can be visited.

Acknowledgements

Many people helped me during two years of intensive work on this book. I have forgotten the names of some whose kindness I remember most warmly, like the woman who showed me around All Saints, Leek and who remains a beacon of helpfulness, or the organist at Queenborough in Sheppey, the ladies at Jarrow, the couple who helped us track down the key at Roker, a man at St Margaret's, Leicester and many others.

Vicars were often well informed and ready to talk. I particularly remember those at Stanstead Abbots, Bishop's Cleeve and Sefton. People occasionally interrupted what they were doing to show me round churches that lay at some distance. The picture would not be complete without mention of a few unhelpful people: the vicar in Kent who ordered me off his property, in Northamptonshire who said there was no key, and the disagreeable sub-curate in Middlesex who had to go there himself and still wouldn't let us into the church. There are a few further churches omitted because of the unusual obstacles that present overseers erect against visitors.

I have seen every church and indeed every feature that I describe, a principle to which I cling most fiercely. The physical actuality of the project is the main point of it; this was not just an intellectual exercise, but a series of particular immersions.

So I come to my stopping places, bed and breakfasts in Titchfield, Hants (the first, where Mrs Kit Buckley was welcoming and informative) and twenty-one other places. Best of all were visits with hospitable friends, who were named in the first edition. And three people who generously lent us houses which became bases for a region: Sandra Morris and Peter Salter in Great Walsingham, Tony and Ruth Sullivan in Penmachno (when I still hoped there would be room for Wales), and Alex Stitt in Stourpaine.

Howard Davies read the manuscript with the care usual for him but rare, catching errors and suggesting many improvements. The book has also been unusually lucky in its designer, Damien Noonan, who took all the photographs.

Final thanks are due to the person who proposed it in the first place and steered me away from the fly's eye view that came naturally to me. She likes churches well enough but isn't the fanatic I am, and has nonetheless visited almost one-third of those included here, though it is only fair to say not always cheerfully. I cannot express what I or the book owe her – Esther Whitby has been the best editor, consoler and friend.

Foreword to the new edition

Much has changed in the fourteen years since the first edition. The worst loss is probably the seventeenth-century woodwork at Brancepeth, completely consumed in a fire; the most striking improvement, the cleaning of the nineteenth-century murals at Garton-on-the-Wolds. More momentous changes are rumoured, changes in the state of religious belief which in the gloomiest forecasts will leave most churches empty and uncared for in the years ahead. Revisiting many of the buildings in the book, though, I have seen exuberant signs of life, newly carved font lids, children's drawings of Biblical narratives or architectural features, sheets which explain a new theory about the pattern on the roof overhead.

Inevitably, returning I sometimes see things differently, but I have generally left the text alone unless it contained errors, not just preferences I do not share on a particular day. Two examples of this – clearly I didn't much like Beverley Minster in 1991; since then, it has become such a decided favourite that I wanted to redraft the entry but have resisted the temptation. And Bodley's chapel at Clumber was left out because I didn't like it then, a decision I would change if I started over.

Inconsistently, I have added fifteen new entries, all in Yorkshire and mainly in the North Riding. Even there, I found a church at Winteringham I should have put in, just a week too late.

Otherwise I have expanded the abbreviated style names I had picked up from Pevsner, EE for Early English and so on, and some but not all of the many contractions which peppered the text. I have also clarified or simplified a number of constructions, but mainly I have left the text alone.

There are many ways one could write a church guide; the quick and telegraphic one I settled on has something to be said for it. Among other things, it reflects the pace at which I had to travel: now I can spend half a day in Selby Abbey instead of the twenty minutes I allowed myself in 1990.

The best new feature and the one readers will notice first is the fuller photographic coverage by Damien Noonan, over three hundred and thirty pictures taken especially for this edition.

Finally, my thanks to Piers Burnett of Aurum Press for making the new edition possible.

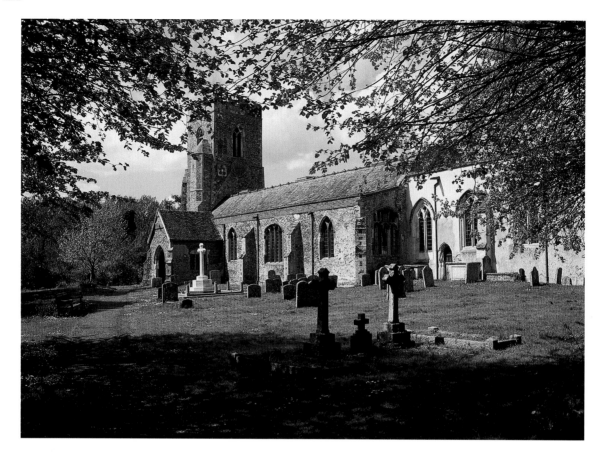

Kedington, Suffolk. A richly textured exterior which contains a treasure trove of fittings within

Introduction

There are 16,000 parish churches in England. Many are the oldest surviving buildings in their village by far, and keep a haphazard record of all the intervening centuries. This book consists mainly of short descriptions of five hundred of the best of these buildings. The intention has been to suggest quickly, without technical language, what makes each one remarkable and to point out carefully selected features.

This is a guidebook in the true sense of the term, not a history of its subject in disguise, but a tool for planning visits and journeys. The table of contents together with the maps makes clear what the mechanism of the book is. There are separate alphabetical series for each of the nine regions: the book attempts to keep buildings which are near each other in reality near in these pages too.

Interesting churches are not scattered evenly across England. Parts of Suffolk, the Cotswolds, the Fens and the East Riding of Yorkshire, for example, have more than their share. Density and dearth on the maps generally correspond to what one actually finds on the ground, but I have made an effort not to leave huge empty spaces, on the theory that at some point it will be useful to have suggestions about what to see in every area.

The criteria for selection aren't easy to codify. Some churches like Cirencester, Walpole St Peter and Patrington will probably appear in every guide. Some are pre-eminent of a certain type like Brixworth (Saxon), Kilpeck (Romanesque) or Willen (late 17c). But after those which are virtually obligatory, how does one choose?

Parish churches are wonderful almost *because* they are not important in the history of architecture, because they are unpredictable palimpsests or overlays of the efforts and preferences of different centuries. There are few pure examples of any style, and tombs and fittings often confuse the rich mixture further. So the standard cannot always be strictly architectural. I (like many visitors) am heavily influenced by setting, and have favoured churches in magnificent landscapes, by streams, or set in memorable churchyards. A chapter at least should be devoted to the tombstones, trees, walls and gates that colour so powerfully the impression these buildings make. But other things pressing in have meant I could only attend to churchyards occasionally.

All the notable classes of church art and craftsmanship like glass, roofs, fonts and effigies have entered into my calculations, and I have tried to include buildings which have the best of each. The scarcity of wall paintings in this book reflects a real scarcity.

It would be amusing but invidious to make lists of churches which were almost excluded and ones which almost got in. I have tried to give clear signs of which churches I regard as most noteworthy and which least. Some specialist interests are perhaps inordinately catered for. I have a weakness for Arts and Crafts, and some readers may find this movement represented more fully than they would like. My final check has always been 'Would a reader thank me for bringing him/her here?'

These buildings are valuable above all for the intricate physical memory of long-superseded moments in the human past, in other words for the most vivid history there is. Then how does one justify including, on equal terms, Victorian, Edwardian and 1950s churches?

In a number of ways: these later buildings are more consistent works of art, where intention not accident rules. And perhaps more important, like Picasso re-drawing Delacroix, they are intelligent commentaries on tradition, and thus another way of connecting us to the past. What constitutes a church is different in every age: plain 18c preaching boxes are replaced by Victorian dens of mystery, and those are superseded in their turn by Arts and Crafts Gothic, like someone whose memories grow indistinct.

A whole subject in itself, which crops up over and over in the entries, is how each historical moment sees the past, and what it does in consequence. Extreme responses have an interest in themselves. Thus, Shobdon church and the works of Edward Maufe (the architect of Guildford Cathedral) are far more important indicators of 18 and 20c spirituality respectively than strict aesthetic merit could ever allow.

So certain examples are included as historical curiosities, a class I have usually not identified for fear of belittling it. Oddities are important for what they reveal of normal as well as extravagant imaginations. Besides, oddity, in part a perceptual phenomenon, gives great exercise to perception, as one struggles

(one may not succeed) to assimilate it. I have also sought out surprising collisions between centuries.

I should confess another preference: an inordinate liking for medieval stone itself over any later restoration or replacement. And, semi-consciously, for 17 and 18c defacements of medieval fabric over Victorian reinstatement of Gothic regularity. I hold with Ruskin that renewed stonework isn't really there any more, or that it's like being in Disneyland rather than Venice to savour fresh carved tracery, gargoyles, etc.

Victorian tracery in a Victorian church can be enjoyed wholeheartedly. Victorian tracery in a medieval church causes a fatal drop in temperature. It is like looking at a measured drawing rather than a building. The line may not always be easy to draw, though. The subtlest restorations are hard to detect – a few are mentioned in the text – but this successful kind of camouflage occurs only two or three times in every thousand.

A friend of mine once relegated parish churches to a sub-class of the picturesque, which he called the English disease. Some writers – of whom Pevsner,

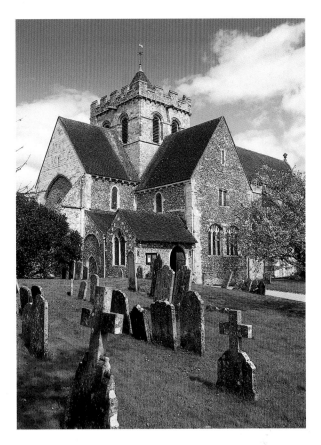

The cathedral proportions of Boxgrove Priory, Hants

9

the church visitor's best friend, is one – have regarded excessive interest in old textures as a kind of mental weakness. I cannot agree with this anti-sensuous stringency. Maybe a diagram of an old building (the round church in Little Maplestead, Essex for example) is better than nothing. Some Victorianized fabrics are wonderful blends – Algarkirk, Lincs an outstanding case. But over-zealous repair of old buildings has been the commonest cause of my omitting churches which other guides include. Probably most vulnerable to thoroughgoing rebuilding are churches in prosperous towns. It was true in the past and continues true now, that poverty is a better guardian of old buildings than wealth. You need money to build them in the first place and then a lack of it to ensure they are not maintained or improved out of recognition. It sometimes seems the past survives only through the negligence of the present, which can't be bothered to impress its own stamp on a fabric, or is content to do it in an ad hoc, piecemeal way.

One of my strongest feelings around these buildings is a reverence for dark plaster, faded colour, crumbling stone – in other words for perishable materials perishing. An old building should show its age; bright new colours on Elizabethan tombs or Gothic vaults are in this sense nonsensical – what delusion in us to pretend they are new. To my mind a well-kept church

is careful not to repress signs of age at the most intimate level. I am sure I go further than most visitors in this, and relish mottled surfaces – old render falling away from old brick – which look simply diseased to some eyes. My favourite London street, Fournier Street in Spitalfields, has often struck my students as inexpressibly squalid.

Underlying this book is a belief that the most intense contact with the past occurs at an almost molecular level. There's a mystical ingestion and transubstantiation in the presence of mouldering, lichen-besprinkled stone. In some sense the rich genuineness of oolite quarried and carved five hundred years ago is what the enterprise is all about. The individuality of the five hundred sites subsists at every scale from the building's place in land or town scape to minute variations in the colour of its skin.

Sometimes a church has wonderful features which don't quite come together, or is so awkwardly inhabited that its beauties are obscured. Many old churches are nowadays acquiring partitions of pale oak and glass which prevent heat loss or carve out a useful meeting room. Quite unintentionally, they break the spell of the whole space, not because they are literally obtrusive, just alien in spirit. Old arrangements shouldn't be absolutely inviolate; yet they should not be overridden for trivial purposes.

Little Gidding, Huntingdonshire, a place to catch the flavour of 17c piety

How can one say, though, that the whole church exists for higher functions than most of those happening in it, and that carving up its space for the best meeting rooms you ever saw is a desecration? Not just a spoliation of architecture, but an amputation of spiritual possibility.

For no matter how estranged from Christian practices someone who enters a church is, a hope always exists that the spaces will remind this visitor of higher things. I must confess that, non-attender at church rituals as I am, I cannot regard churches as just another class of building to be anatomized like pieces of anthropological hardware. What the naive church guides say is true. These buildings are great repositories of people's efforts to see beyond the immediate facts of their daily lives, to conceive themselves as playing a part in the universe, and to imagine their actions judged by a more searching standard than any local one.

They aren't pure loftiness, of course. Crowding the altar in many churches are cold and bragging advertisements of family pride. These places aren't really the safe havens of virtue that, empty, they might seem. The mixture of human motives is part of what churches, like novels, teach. One reads in them, as in ancient texts venerated though corrupt, the moral history of a settlement. It is sometimes surprising that living people are up and about in these haunted precincts. The local accents and small preoccupations of the flower ladies can come like a lightening, freshening gust of real air.

Certain principles and prejudices have influenced the arrangement of this book. It follows the more venerable counties as they were before 1974. In that year the most massive realignment of local boundaries in modern times was imposed. Rationalization of urban administration on the one hand and consolidation of over-divided rural areas on the other was the aim. New districts were then disguised by names if possible more antiquated than the superseded ones.

Three counties disappeared entirely, Rutland, Huntingdon and Westmorland. After considerable time the new amalgamates like Humberside remained unpopular with the majority who live in them and a partial reversion occurred. In 1997 Rutland and the East Riding reappeared and many of the new names were dropped. All the earlier literature including Pevsner's *Buildings of England* and the Royal Commission on Historical Monuments Inventories work to the old boundaries, which correspond to a solider historical vision of the country. Therefore, because they are more comfortable and make better historical sense, the old divisions are observed here, but the new county, where there is one, is added to the directions at the end of the entry.

Most books about churches confine themselves to Anglican examples and stop around the end of the Gothic Revival in the early 20c, perhaps making an exception for Ninian Comper. It is harder to find out more about Catholic, Non-conformist and modern buildings, and by observing the boundary, books perpetuate the dearth of information. But what, except the writers' convenience, is served by these exclusions? Anglican churches are not a consistent group. The highest ones are higher than any Roman Catholic, the lowest as low as most Non-conformist, the newest as new. If one wants a full picture of religious observance

Itchen Stoke, Hants, a Victorian variation on the Sainte-Chapelle in Paris

or architecture, clearly the others should be included. All that prevents it are practical obstacles.

I have therefore included a selection of notable Roman Catholic churches since the first purpose-built ones were allowed in the 18c. Naturally they are few compared with Anglican, and fewer than they should be, because my means of tracking them down are more fallible, but they provide unique insights into English religious observance and its physical manifestations. Chapels and meeting houses are a different case. Here I have favoured the earlier ones as more revealing. I still labour under the belief or blindness that Victorian and later chapels are generally more curious than beautiful. The recent RCHM thematic publications on this subject are very welcome.

Twentieth-century churches deserve a book to themselves. Soon someone will write one. Two impediments stand in the way: the difficulty of tracing them, and of getting in. Because they are usually in suburbs, that is in semi-urban areas, and there isn't widespread interest in them as buildings, modern churches are almost always locked without indication where a key may be found. Nonetheless I have

11

ventured further than other guides into this interesting, low-intensity territory.

Otherwise readers will notice a bias in favour of countryside and village churches over those in towns. Most of my visiting was done by car, and from that perspective a town or city is a major headache, while a village is delightfully easy. I would like to think this book will suit a cyclist just as well as a motorist. Maybe my strong bias against messy traffic makes sense for the bike-rider too. Someone depending on public transport will find my preference for remote villages frustrating, I fear. The notion of travel which underlies it takes for granted that there is a special charm in obscure locations off heavily travelled routes.

London is summarized more ruthlessly than other places because its churches are better known to begin with and visiting them is another kind of experience from the ones this book is about. The best existing guides are by Gerald Cobb (for the City) and Basil Clarke (for the whole of London).

Finding churches is greatly simplified by the Ordnance Survey 1 to 50,000 maps (pink covers with photos). Directions at the top of every entry in this book are more precise whenever there are two or more church symbols at about the right place on these maps. Difficult locations are more elaborately identified in those headnotes, but OS map and directions together should make finding any of the examples easy. Will readers please write to me care of the publisher if they find any directions unclear or any church feature not where it is said to be?

Locked churches are the bane of the casual or dedicated visitor. When I count up how many churches I found locked in the thousand or so I visited, it isn't many. But it remains an experience influential out of all proportion to its frequency, for several reasons. You cannot predict when it will happen and thus do anything to prevent it. In certain areas all churches are open. In others, just as far from main roads or urban settlement, all are locked. Many vicars and parish councils are determined to keep their buildings open for all who need or enjoy them, some don't seem to care, and a few positively relish their power to keep out strangers.

Of course it is a vexed question. There have been appalling thefts and mindless vandal attacks on churches. After more experience than I care to recall, I have come to think that much depends on the character and view of the world held by those who have charge of the church and keys. Whatever the attendant frustrations for the visitor, this is a healthy and human state of affairs. You will learn more about villages and their inhabitants chasing church keys than in more trouble-free visits.

Brief survey of historical styles

Though the book's approach is non-specialist, intricacies of ritual and the span of architectural development lead, inevitably, to a certain complexity. So a brief account or overview of historical stages of church architecture in England follows here.

This sketches the context into which all the entries fit, but it must be said that it depicts an ideal world: in reality parish churches are usually confusing overlays of different periods.

On top of this, I have tried not to load the text with frequent style names. Nonetheless, most visitors will want to carry some such scheme in their heads.

Anglo-Saxon

Whole buildings from this time are scarce. Usually isolated elements survive, particularly doors or windows which were blocked up and then rediscovered in the 19 or 20c. Spaces and openings are tall and narrow and, with a little familiarity, instantly recognizable. Architectural decoration is wonderfully irrational in Saxon buildings. Structural systems imitated from Roman examples are misunderstood.

Sculpture survives mainly in the North in the form of outdoor crosses and tombstones. These are remarkable for the high proportion of animals to men and for  dazzling vegetable interlace. Pagan and Christian themes are often mixed, probably a sign of mental confusion, not synthesis. These are some of the least polished and most moving works of art in Britain.
For examples see Escomb, Durham; Deerhurst, Glos.

Anglo-Saxon

Norman or Romanesque c1066–1200

Much greater technical sophistication, dressed masonry and more ambitious scale are found, though by later standards Norman village churches are small. Classical proportions replace the strange elongated Saxon spaces. Windows are roundheaded and infrequent. There are massive arcades with cylindrical piers. Unaltered Norman buildings tend to be heavy, dark and firmly anchored on the earth.

Sculptural decoration is concentrated on tympanums above the main entrance, nave capitals and chancel arch. Carving is rude and vigorous. The best surviving cycles of wall painting date from this period.
For examples see Adel, W Yorks; Kilpeck, Hereford.

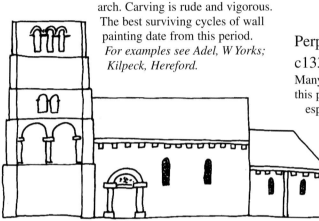

Norman, or Romanesque

Transitional late 12c

Piers are heavy with beginnings of lighter leafy trimmings on capitals. Pointed instead of round arches begin to appear, so heights and intervals can become more flexible.

Early English, also called Early Gothic c1190–1250

Encompasses a serene and collected moment, at its best a perfect balance between clarity and grace. Windows in simple lancet shapes occur in stately series. Complex mouldings and clustered piers are made of simple cylindrical elements. Springy rib vaults are seen. Decoration is rather sparing and in the form of elegant leaf sprigs simplified to systems of curves. Individual elements are solid, not attenuated or over-detailed.
For examples see West Walton, Norfolk; Skelton near York, N Yorks.

Decorated or High Gothic c1290–1350

This style is rich and elaborated. Windows become subdivided with complex geometrical figures in their upper reaches; then, instead of staying contained within circles, tracery flows into the whole space and divisions are blurred. Carved decoration becomes more obviously dynamic in bubbling, proliferating activity. Intense and detailed naturalism gives way to stylized knobbly elements.
For examples see Patrington, E Yorks; Heckington, Lincs.

Perpendicular or Late Gothic c1335–1530

Many of the best known English churches date from this period when wealth from the cloth trades, especially wool, made many towns rich and churches were rebuilt on grander scales.

Clerestories were often added to existing churches, the goal being to introduce more light. The ideal Perpendicular church is a glass house, whose walls are almost all window, whose proportions are tall and thin. Towers and arcades emphasize vertical continuities: the same moulding often runs from floor to ceiling, where wooden roofs (often of great complexity) are more common than stone vaults. Angular window tracery resembles leaf membranes. Decorative detail in this phase often seems a bit mechanical. In fact it is usually a cool style performing its technical feats somewhat automatically.
For examples see Cirencester, Glos; Walpole St Peter, Norfolk.

Tudor early 16c

This style finds Gothic forms infiltrated by Renaissance detail. Secular heraldic imagery appears, including pomegranates, roses, putti, acanthus.
For examples see Lacock, Wilts (N chapel); Warwick (Beauchamp chapel).

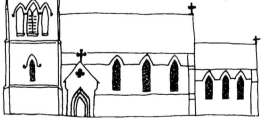

Early English, or Early Gothic

13

Elizabethan and Jacobean 1560–1620

This is English Mannerism: tombs and fittings but not church fabrics (porches and the like excepted) are exuberant, overloaded, unintentionally anti-classical in effect – with strapwork, garlands and obelisks.

17c Gothic

A stripped down and rational style; roundhead window lights in rectangular frames are found, and modest rectangular buildings domestic in feel.
For examples see Monnington on Wye, Hereford; Berwick-upon-Tweed, Northumb.

18c Classicism

The most Protestant phase in English church building. Brick frequently used as a material. Buildings are relatively modest and non-numinous with clear glass and plasterwork, not carved decoration.

The overall orientation is often changed with the focus shifted from the altar to a pulpit placed laterally, implying a move from ritual to preaching as the centre of worship. This is the age of box pews that carve the space into many private domains.
For examples see Avington, Hants; Blandford, Dorset.

Gothick 1750–1820

Gothick is an English invention and a local variant of rococo. It signals the reimportation of medieval motifs, which had migrated from churches to landscape gardens and parlours, back again to churches.

Whole buildings in the style are rare. Instead of stone, the forms are executed in wood and plaster and painted in frothy pastel colours. The agitated silhouettes abstracted from Gothic become merely picturesque.
For examples see Shobdon, Hereford; Croome d'Abitot, Worcs.

18th Century

Gothic Revival 1820 onwards

From those silly beginnings the revival style went on to become deadly serious in Pugin's hands and was linked to a liturgical revival, which tried to recover Catholic forms for the English church.

New prominence was given to the Eucharist and its setting, the chancel. Screens proliferate, and the pulpit is downgraded. Colour, rich patterning and stained glass are reintroduced. Many variations and changing preferences in the particular phase of Gothic revived.
For examples see Pendlebury, Lancs; Croydon, Surrey.

Arts and Crafts c1885–1910

Decorated

A very English strand of the previous phase, which carries on the supposed medieval interest in workmanship and materials. Forms were influenced by the vernacular (rural and domestic) as well as ecclesiastical models.
For examples see Brockhampton, Hereford; Roker, Durham.

Perpendicular, or Late Gothic

Modernism 1930 onwards

This style infiltrates English church architecture almost invisibly, but Maufe, Nicholson and Goodhart Rendel show its influence. Stripped whiteness in this context is more like an austere monasticism than a technological utopia, though.

By the postwar period a church has become the most marginal of all building types. None of the leading practitioners since Basil Spence has ever designed a church or even a church fitting (Hugh Casson's font at Greensted the only exception I know).
For examples see Coventry, Warwicks; Plymouth, Devon.

Further reading

There are vast floods of writing on churches. Many parishes produce guidebooks, an English institution not much emulated in other countries. These productions vary greatly and charmingly. The postcards sold next to them are sometimes more informative. You can usually count on locally produced guides to supply anecdotal lore about vicars, patrons, donors and other characters, which is not available elsewhere. At their best these amateur concoctions show the sturdiness of local history studies; there are outstanding ones for Youlgreave, Edington and Hailes, Glos. Sad to say, the best ones are often by scholars imported for the purpose. In this class are H. M. Taylor's Repton and a joint effort for Skelton near York. Kenneth Clark did one for Winchelsea and the architect George Pace, Tamworth. Occasionally a whole area is covered by a local enthusiast like C. L. S. Linnell, a Norfolk rector of the 1950s.

Church visiting is older than we realize. David Elisha Davy, a Suffolk antiquarian, toured local churches in the 1820s and 30s. His journal was reprinted by the Suffolk Records Society in 1982. John Sell Cotman's etchings of Norfolk churches, published 1812–18, still turn up in local print shops.

A history of guidebooks would be fascinating. Pevsner's predecessor, the *Little Guides*, which began in 1900 (spearheaded by a clergyman, J. Charles Cox), restore one's faith in natural human curiosity. The photographs in earlier editions are revealing period pieces (most buildings are shrouded in ivy).

Nikolaus Pevsner's *Buildings of England* (currently 51 volumes) are indispensable. They describe every old church and a selection of Victorian and later ones. Pevsner can be maddeningly deadpan and won't tell you whether piers, mouldings and openings add up to a building you should visit. But any serious student of architecture keeps returning to these volumes.

The old *Shell Guides* from the 1950s onwards are useful to flesh out Pevsner's data. They seem to carry on from the Bucks and Berks guides which John Betjeman and John Piper did for Murray in 1948–9. Photographs in the *Shell Guides* are splendidly evocative, and the text ventures the human judgements Pevsner often denied himself.

Probably the best popular book about churches is John Betjeman's *Collins Guide to Parish Churches* which he did in 1958 with many collaborators, revised by Nigel Kerr in 1993. It includes several thousand examples, so individual entries are exceedingly terse: mostly lists of features. It is more reliable than Pevsner on atmosphere, and wide in its sympathies. Betjeman wrote a general introduction that is the envy of all writers on this subject, and many separate county introductions which are very splendid too.

For a full recent bibliography on parish churches see Richard Morris, *Churches in the Landscape*, 1989, a book which is itself full of interest for the church visitor.

Since the first edition, Simon Jenkins' deservedly popular *England's Thousand Best Churches* has appeared, which treats more churches and gives each of them more space than I was able to do. Jenkins is often good on curious associations, like the turkeys, unmentioned by Pevsner, which make an entertaining appearance at Boynton in the East Riding of Yorkshire.

I would also recommend Stephen Friar's curious and wonderful *Sutton Companion to Churches*, packed with lore on such subjects as heraldry, yews in churchyards, archaisms in inscriptions and seventeenth-century religious practice. One could view its enticing labyrinth as an enormous glossary and thus justify the contracted dimensions of the one included in this book.

Likewise, Lawrence Jones' *The Beauty of English Churches* does a better job of recommending churches feature by feature (fonts, glass screens etc.) than I had space for in the first edition and is well illustrated.

The stream has not dried up; a charming recent example is John Kinross's *Discovering England's Smallest Churches*, which picks out a hundred and gives details of specialist organizations, like the Round Tower Churches Society, which also appears in Friar's useful list of websites.

CD-ROM to accompany this book

Readers of this guide might like to know that the author is producing a CD-ROM version in collaboration with Colin Davies, a well-known architectural historian. The first instalment of this is available from April 2006 and includes two regions: North (Yorkshire, Durham and Northumberland) and Home Counties (Buckinghamshire, Bedfordshire, Hertfordshire and Middlesex).

Eventually all the churches in the guide will be covered in more than 5,000 images. The first part includes 110 churches and 900 images. It can be sampled at www.crowstep.co.uk.

South West

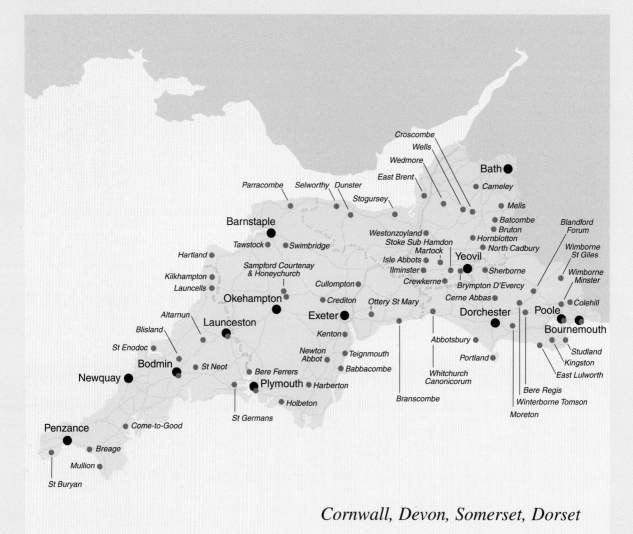

Croscombe
Wells
Wedmore
East Brent
Bath
Cameley
Parracombe Selworthy Dunster
Stogursey
Mells
Barnstaple
Batcombe
Bruton
Blandford
Forum
Westonzoyland Hornblotton
Tawstock Swimbridge
Stoke Sub Hamdon North Cadbury
Hartland
Martock
Wimborne
St Giles
Sampford Courtenay
& Honeychurch
Isle Abbots
Yeovil
Kilkhampton
Ilminster
Sherborne
Wimborne
Minster
Launcells
Crewkerne
Cullompton
Brympton D'Evercy
Okehampton
Crediton
Cerne Abbas
Colehill
Altarnun
Exeter Ottery St Mary
Dorchester Poole
Launceston
Kenton
Bournemouth
Blisland
St Enodoc
Abbotsbury
Studland
Newton
Abbot Teignmouth
Portland
Kingston
Bodmin St Neot
Babbacombe
East Lulworth
Bere Ferrers
Whitchurch
Canonicorum
Newquay
Plymouth Harberton
Bere Regis
Branscombe
Winterborne Tomson
Holbeton
Moreton
St Germans
Penzance Come-to-Good
Breage
Mullion
St Buryan

Cornwall, Devon, Somerset, Dorset

THIS REGION'S FORMER WILDNESS has been partly tamed by tourism, but you can recapture the sense of Cornwall as a separate country by entering it on a poky local train, or by wandering off-season in the empty bit north of Bude. The coast is often dramatic, of course, with towns and villages like Fowey and St Ives clinging to its sides. But inland Cornish landscape is surprisingly scruffy, the trees all low and windswept. Cross into Devon and it is immediately lusher, the slopes more generous.

Cornwall is the only district in England where granite is common as a building stone, which has memorable results in its churches. Those gritty arcades under panelled barrel vaults

are the most peculiar and striking detail. As in other remote areas, architectural styles filter through in simplified rustic variants. One of the great charms of the buildings are late Gothic bench ends.

In Devon too the woodwork is outstanding. The survival of so many rich screens is often taken as a sign of the fundamental conservatism of the county. But perhaps energy focused on such an earthbound feature reveals a taste for elaboration of an ungrandiose and even un-architectural kind.

In its rusticity Dorset belongs with these other coastal districts. It seems no accident that Thomas Hardy, chronicler of immemorial, rooted communities, was a Dorset man. But perhaps in seeing

this as one of the most unchanging though least strongly marked of English places, one is seeing it through Hardy's eyes. Still, there are plentiful signs in these chalk downlands that this is some of the oldest farm landscape in Britain.

Neighbouring Somerset is by contrast rich in golden stone and fat farmland. Its churches are among the most splendid of any county's, with many-tiered towers and complex roofs. It is notable that the outstanding features should be aspiring ones, and the proudest churches Perpendicular. The Levels, former marsh between Taunton and Yeovil, contain one of the best concentrations in the country.

Abbotsbury

St Nicholas, St Catherine's Chapel

Two buildings in remarkable situations, one with a delightful plaster ceiling, the other small and overbuilt, with a tunnel vault in stone.

Terrain is better than architecture here. Abbotsbury sits at the centre of several radiating crests of downland near the sea. The parish church of *St Nicholas* overlooks the site of a large abbey, and the tithe barn with its pond is much larger than this late Gothic church. Here the highlight is a chancel ceiling of 1638 with turtles, lotus and cherubim waving banners, a bit of real folk art, which somehow harmonizes with the 18c reredos in mahogany and gilt.

St Catherine's Chapel is silhouetted on the skyline, half a mile distant and three hundred feet higher up. Good views of the sea in front and village behind. Strip lynchets stand out clearly in surrounding fields. The chapel is a massive one-celled stone building with exceedingly thick walls. A panelled stone vault hangs far overhead, its decayed bosses like wasps' nests. Built in the 14c as the shrine of a saint of high places, the chapel was later kept in repair as a beacon to shipping.

Dorset: 9 miles NW of Weymouth on B3157; St Nicholas on SE edge of village off a sudden hitch in High Street, St Catherine reached by path running S from this street

Altarnun, Cornwall, famous for its Renaissance bench ends

Altarnun

St Nonna

Though not far from an A road, this village feels isolated and somewhat gloomy. The church sits in a hollow by the stream, approached by an old two-arch bridge, like something in the Brothers Grimm.

Mouse-coloured body, brown tower, very large interior with amazing fittings intact, such as 17c altar rail which spells out the minister's and churchwardens' names, one letter per baluster. Within the enclosure, two Communion boards with rustic paintings: the Last Supper to represent bread, the Crucifixion for wine.

Carved bench ends are common in Cornwall, but Altarnun's set is best of all. Standard Renaissance motifs like trophies and pomegranates, but there are also jesters, flocks of sheep, and a swordsman disarming his companion on an adjacent bench.

The font is a heroically primitive instance of the Bodmin type, with bearded giants and stars whose boldness would suit an early Cubist. It retains haunting traces of colour.

Cornwall: 9 miles SW of Launceston, just N of A30, before Wesley Cottage; church at N end of village

Babbacombe

All Saints, St Alban's Road

William Butterfield

A Butterfield church so dark, rich and cranky one can understand why some people do not care for this architect.

The church sits in the tattered remnant of a park-like Victorian residential development, whose villas are now hotels and nursing homes. Disappointing exterior, which plays down its size. Only a conical roof on the porch signals the eccentricity within.

Clerestory windows were an afterthought; it must have been an obscure cave without them. The overall effect is dusky richness. Cleaning would spoil the mournful power of this place; the eyes must take the time to adjust.

Above the arcades weird stone ribs cut across brick patterns. Only one of the septfoils in spandrels is inlaid with a big bauble. Money ran out before the others were filled in.

Chancel decor is the climax: profuse alabaster facing with astonishing almond windows on R, set in deep-carved frames. They are matched opposite by the same shapes filled with mosaic, not glazed. Stained glass is of a jittery and appropriate vividness. The pulpit, perched on a forest of columns, and the font are riots of coloured marble. Sloping painted ceilings in the aisles jump with fractured patterns.

Devon: part of Torquay, about 24 miles S of Exeter; church SW of Babbacombe Road in Cary Park district

Batcombe

St Mary

One of the most harmonious of all English churches, with nothing too much, and hints of grandeur in the scale.

Its gentle mound is hedged about with a few large old trees. It looks wonderful from the E, a successful marriage between Gothic and 17c vernacular. The large but square and plain E window seems just right, and has fortunately not been tampered with by anyone wishing a more conventional ecclesiastical effect.

The charming porch is a reaching-back towards Gothic of the 17c, and the tower is the most marvellous feature

of all. It lacks a fancy top edge, which seems a crowning subtlety after bell openings that approximate brocade in stone. On the W face, six angels hieratically arranged and very high up.

Inside, plain but seemly, an unrancorous compromise between pre- and post-Reformation usages. A simple but lovely wooden roof, good Edwardian glass, and an Italian painting of some interest.

Somerset: 9 miles SW of Frome, 1 mile W of A359

Bere Ferrers

St Andrew

In a strange remote location, a church with beautiful Decorated details.

Hard to reach but worth it. The road plunges down to the edge of a wide estuary and stops. The church is so near it that the water seems to lap its sides. The whole is rough-cast except for some very authentic tracery poking out. As sometimes happens, the coating gives the tower a molten Art Nouveau look.

You enter and find yourself in a Cornish church in Devon, with granite arcades which widen at the barn-like transepts. It is a marvellously irregular space. Surprising tombs here and in the chancel, especially one rising to a great clot of leafage, the founder and his wife underneath. Old glass and old benches and a font like a lump of charred wood, an enormous Corinthian capital with a belt round it.

Devon: on River Tavy estuary 2 miles N of Plymouth agglomeration as the crow flies, but laborious to reach via road; 8 miles S of A390, 7 miles W of A386

Bere Regis

St John Baptist

The 15c roof is one of the most entertaining in the country. Traditionally the gift of Cardinal Morton, a local son, it boasts many over-size hence readable details and is gaily painted in vegetable colours. There are twelve lifesize figures, all different, who have been identified

Bere Ferrers, Devon, in an evocative location on the Tavy estuary

variously as Apostles or friends of John Morton. Big braces and inner arches are so thickly cusped that the whole effect is like looking into a complicated mechanism.

On the arcades, figures in pain hold their foreheads or their jaws. In the S chapel are Turberville tombs credited with suggesting to Hardy some of the ideas for *Tess*.

A few fruits of Street's restoration of 1875 are dispiriting, namely hard tile floors and Victorian pews, but a fascinating set of Hardman windows is some recompense. In the E a Crucifixion against the night sky, in N aisle Gospel stories with figures in the last stages of neurotic decadence. It seems possible the charming folkish colours of the roof were Street's idea.

Dorset: 11 miles NE of Dorchester on A35; church at S end of village

Blisland's mellow interior by F. C. Eden

Blandford Forum

St Peter & St Paul

Bastard brothers

One of the best 18c churches outside London in one of the prettiest Georgian towns.

The fancy name, which just means Blandford Market and recalls no Roman past, suits dignified little Blandford with

Bere Regis has an entertaining roof with gaudy painted figures of surprising size

its church and Town Hall in stone and the rest in brick. Almost everything dates from an energetic rebuilding after the disastrous fire of 1731.

The church is prefaced by a little monument to this event which is, with 18c practicality, a fountain under a Tuscan canopy. It has a long inscription telling how one of the Bastards, local dignitaries and architects who rebuilt the town and church, paid for it. Their own monument lies just N of the church and is duly eccentric, an obelisk immured at the top end of a casket.

The church sits above the High Street in a yard shapely but not too big. It is built of a lovely greensand, a cool colour, with grey-white Ham stone trim. The aisle entrances are pedimented and the tower with its winsome wooden cupola (not by the Bastards, who wanted something grander) dominates both close and distant prospects of the town.

Inside, great Ionic colonnades (their Portland stone unhappily painted) under a shallow vault of smudgy white and Wedgwood blue. The round apse was moved E for a chancel to be inserted in 1895, and there is the mild outrage of not-too-garish Victorian glass. A fine display of 18c civic virtue, especially in the

Bailiff's stall with openwork carving, the organ, and the baluster font which inverts classical forms in a way that would have pleased Lutyens. Many boards record benefactions, and an apprentice-bell rung twice a day to regulate the work force survives.

Two miles SE of Blandford an early 18c remodelling of the Gothic church at CHARLTON MARSHALL was carried out by the Bastards' father. Its situation above a stream and water meadow is enchanting.

The tower has tiny pediments on every side, and fragile obelisks. A double sundial perches on the porch gable. The arcade is cased in classical arches and the E wall is filled with a carved reredos. Pulpit, font, donor's memorial and altar rail complete a perfect little place, saved recently from redundancy by the devoted energy of local residents.

Dorset: Blandford is 14 miles NW of Poole on A350 (which now bypasses town)

Blisland

St Protus & St Hyacinth*

F. C. Eden

Little Blisland has one of the most perfect interiors of any English church.

F. C. Eden, who restored it from 1894 onwards, did two other complete restorations (Elham, Kent and North Cerney, Glos: qq.v.). Of all his works, Blisland is the smallest and most intense. Inside, an immediate impression of impossible richness. Yet luxury never goes too far, its brashest bloom rubbed off. Much unevenness in wall planes and pier angles, as well as a lopsided plan. To compensate for missing N aisle, an elongated N transept retreats behind pillars out of our reach.

One column leans dramatically as a result of all the burials under the floor, we are told. Following modern notions of hygiene, Eden moved the remains to the churchyard but didn't straighten the pillar. Roof timbers have become so twisted over time that the pattern of panels is now more like zigzag than grid.

The screen running the entire width of the building is Eden's most magnificent contribution. It shimmers with gold, colour, tracery and stencilling. He borrows faded reds and greens from the old altar frontals for his painted patterns, which look like embroidery.

The church sits below the wide table of the village green. From that side the houses seem to drop beneath its edge.

The best is Mansion House in NE corner with drooping granite voluteates at the eaves' corners.

* A dedication to 3c Roman brother-martyrs unique in England

Cornwall: 6 miles NE of Bodmin, 2 miles W of A30

Bodmin

St Petroc*

St Petroc is the largest parish church in Cornwall. A harshly restored Perpendicular exterior should not deter the visitor. Some of the best sculpture and most curious glass in Cornwall lies inside. First, the Romanesque font, a wonderful combination of rudeness and clear-headedness. It consists of a great hemispheric bowl, clasped by large winged heads and adorned with vegetable scrolls cut out so deeply they are like bulky lace.

The best memorial comes from the Priory, and consists of two pieces of Catacleuse slate – a glossy effigy which looks like bronze, a dusty base which looks like wood. The subject is Prior Vivian, titular Bishop of Megara in Greece. On the base, an exhilarating variety of Renaissance ornament, which all derives from the local wood-carving tradition so that its crispness looks very odd in stone.

Two 19c windows in Pre-Raphaelite colours, one gorgeously lurid, including plenty of sunset purple.

In the churchyard at LANIVET, 3 miles SW, some of the most interesting stones and crosses in Cornwall, including two 10 feet tall.

* A Welsh prince, who was to Cornwall what Patrick was to Ireland

Cornwall: Bodmin is 31 miles W of Plymouth on A30

Bournemouth

St Stephen; St Swithun, Gervis Road; St Clement, Boscombe

This sea resort, whose great development came from 1836 onward, has an impressive set of late Victorian churches including work by Pearson, Street, Norman Shaw and J. D. Sedding.

Pearson's *St Stephen* of 1881–98 is unimpressive externally but the interior is astonishing, like a magical reduction of a cathedral to two-thirds scale. There are slim galleries the whole way round under the upper windows, double aisles and, most surprising of all, an ambulatory which threads its way behind the main altar. This is not a true aisle for it has no vault but consists of vanes generated by apse ribs. They make a series of arch-planes which add up to the

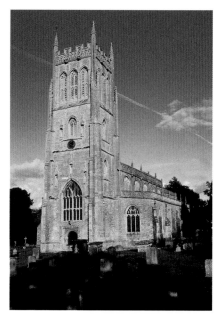

Bruton, in mellow Cotswold stone, contains a surprising 18c interior

illusion of a continuous passage. St Stephen's is one of Pearson's greatest exhibitions of spatial complexity and clarity combined, but the lavish fittings are rather dead.

Norman Shaw's *St Swithun*, begun 1876, stands among pines (a feature of many Bournemouth neighbourhoods). Unexciting externally, but the interior, cleverly approached via a narthex, is a single space of exhilarating breadth. In the W a huge clear window. Good iron screen and a painted reredos of the Shaw period, now demoted to a place near W end.

St Clement, Boscombe by **J. D. Sedding** and **Henry Wilson**, 1871–3, doesn't entirely live up to its reputation as a monument of the Arts and Crafts. Wilson's tower, added in 1890–93, an impressive asymmetric composition, rich at the top, incorporates St Clement on his anchor in the window tracery. At the SE corner an interesting set of Sedding grave markers. Inside, much richness and little vitality. Two chancel windows by Christopher Whall combine sadness and brightness.

Hants/Dorset: 30 miles SW of Southampton on A35. St Stephen at N edge of town centre, just S of bypass; St Swithun just S of A35, E of town centre; St Clement, Boscombe, 1½ miles E of town centre, N of A35 and just S of railway, on St Clement's Road at Cleveland Road

Branscombe's striking situation in a combe near the sea

Branscombe

St Winifred

Wonderfully situated, an impressive Norman building with an interesting 16c addition.

It sits deep in a combe, so its great central tower just rises above road level. There are charming rustic features like an outdoor stair to the organ loft, something you might find in a farmyard.

The screen across the chancel resembles a device for keeping animals in or out, stone wainscoting with wooden fences on top. Windows are scattered almost randomly in the walls. The space under the tower occurs after the crossing, which makes a nice amplitude in this eastward progress. Both transepts hold impressive early Renaissance monuments, especially one which shows two kneeling husbands, armed, with a helmet between them. It makes the space around them a battlefield and turns the row of children into combatants.

The village proper is further along towards the sea. Three miles E is BEER where the white stone was quarried in which so much carved detail in Devon churches is carried out.

Devon: 4 miles E of Sidmouth near coast; church W of village centre

Breage

St Breaca*

Because of its high perch this village (whose name rhymes with 'vague') is forgotten by the main road and seems pleasantly raffish and unkempt. A large churchyard, overgrown, its original circular shape still traceable.

The granite a milder grey than usual to the E of here. Hard-edged tower of same period as the vigorously battlemented S porch and transept (church entirely rebuilt 1460–66). Apparently the Irish-inspired cross-head lodged in its stepped platform is unique in this district, being a lump of imported sandstone.

Inside, arcade of the usual sand-pale granite but with rich leaf capitals. The great feature of this interior is the painting on the N wall – besides a huge St Christopher breasting the flood, a remarkable Christ of the Trades with wounds on his legs like savage tattoos. Radiating from him is a fabulous display of 15c tools: shears, saws, hooks, bladed

Breage. A remarkable wall painting of Christ of the Trades (on right)

wheels and a playing card (or inn-sign?). Apparently, it is not a celebration, but a warning. These are the things it wounds Christ for us to use on Sunday. The subject is common in (and almost confined to) Cornwall, and this is the best rendition of it.

In S transept (now the children's corner) a board with particularly well-lettered version of Charles I's thanks of 1642 to his loyal subjects, which survives in many Cornish churches.

* Reputed to have come to Cornwall as a missionary from Ireland late 5 or early 6c

Cornwall: 2½ miles W of Helston just N of A394

Bruton

St Mary

A strange Georgian implant in a rich Gothic carcase.

Bruton is an unusually beautiful small town, all stone, with a grammar school dating back to 1519. It lies atop a spine, with the church lower down, across a stream.

St Mary's has two towers, the smaller rising from the N porch. Beyond it on a hilltop stands a third, a folly-like structure which might be the scene of Elizabethan hunts or the mysteries of Udolpho. In fact it's a vanished abbey's dovecote.

Inside the church, a shock greets us. After much dark wood, including a 17c screen in the tower arch and an angel roof, comes a startling rococo chancel in light colours with fancy plasterwork, gilded garlands and thorny crowns. 19c guidebooks were appalled by the effect, but this collision of centuries is exciting. Luckily, older heraldic glass was re-set when the re-modelling was done in 1743, along with a Mannerist wall monument of a bronze bust in an oval niche.

Under the arcade, a ruined gigantesque tomb like a bit of Halicarnassus.

Somerset: about 10 miles SW of Frome on A359; church in low-lying position near the station

Brympton D'Evercy

St Andrew

A miniature building in golden stone held in thrall by the rambling manor house adjacent.

All the buildings form a single composition, which if not a little too rich in crankiness would have been an inspiration to the Arts and Crafts. For, in this late medieval house revised in a historicist spirit, asymmetry rules, and texture overwhelms structure. A few themes recur, however, as if the guiding principle is association in the memory. The most striking of such themes is the openwork pavilion, like a diminutive model of a real building. One of them forms the church belfry. Then, across the formal garden in front of the house is

Brympton D'Evercy. Mannerism in golden stone next to a beautiful manor house

another, atop a kind of ceremonial gatehouse.

Though the church is exceedingly small, a sprawling interior space unfolds, with a strange stone screen and an unexpected annex with unorthodox tombs. A compelling monk's effigy boasts some rude scenes in the spandrels over it. A kind of rusticity prevails throughout the building.

Behind the church, a family plot holds fourteen caskets made of box hedge. The whole place is uncanny – miniature overall, large in the details, like certain episodes of *Alice in Wonderland*.

Somerset: just W of Yeovil. Follow signs to Brympton House off A30 or A3088

Cameley

St James (CCT)

A humble building, wonderfully unspoiled.

The confused interior is like a palimpsest of the centuries, with the strangest assortment of benches, pews, galleries, and bits of painting on the walls peeking out from under other bits. Particularly notable are a jester and some acorn patterning on the N wall, and heraldry inside the chancel arch.

In the floor a Purbeck slab for someone who died at fifteen months, shaped like a baby's coffin. In the chancel, a rustic pedimented memorial with a single Greek word in its English inscription, and little suns atop its columns.

Somerset: about 12 miles S of Bristol off A37, 1 mile W of Temple Cloud

Cerne Abbas

St Mary

Cerne Abbas has a claim to be the most beautiful small town in Dorset, fallen from former glory. The tower makes an

Come-to-Good Meeting House. Rustic tranquillity sheltering in a hollow

impressive preface to the church, with its figures in niches and isolated pinnacles held at arm's length. The building sits right on a street full of good buildings. There is virtually no churchyard, just a tiny plot to the S with an exceedingly miserable war memorial at its centre.

You enter under the tower and then pass through charming rustic gates. The impression is light and airy, probably less atmospheric since roof and seating were renewed in the 1960s. 17 and 18c inscriptions in bold lozenges fill much of the walls. Photographs at the back show that these once extended above the screen, until Victorian improvers installed the present wide arch and thus gained a view of the chancel. It is a telling lesson that we would now like the earlier, more cramped effect back again.

North of the town is the famous CERNE GIANT, who is lying down – that is, traced on a more gradual slope than most such images – and at one time had a figleaf of gorse over his large private parts. He's been thought a Roman depiction of Hercules and forms a spiritual antithesis to the church.

Dorset: 12 miles S of Sherborne on A352; church near E edge of village, N of High Street

Colehill

St Michael & All Angels

W. D. Caröe

Among the most whimsical of its date, 1893–5.

It has been censured for being un-Dorset; perhaps it would fit better, meaning more predictably, in Cheshire, Germany or California. It is half timber, with pink brick instead of plaster infill. It has a tower like a medieval town gate in the Rhineland, and inside, a fantastic wooden roof like the Californian architect Bernard Maybeck's wildest. This is stained green, not painted, and lit in the aisle by a dormer which shows off the virtuoso carpentry. The building is perhaps absurdly variegated but carries the day by convinced enthusiasm for its rustic materials. Some fine fittings of the period, like a pearwood saint in a brick niche and a painted triptych which speaks volumes.

Next door, a church hall whose earliest rendered bit must be Caröe too, but Caröe-as-Voysey, not Maybeck. The setting remains leafy, and that is

probably the simplest justification for the woodland idiom of this delightful work.

Dorset: NE suburb of Wimborne Minster; church in Colehill Lane (at junction with Smugglers Lane), a turning N of Wimborne Road

Come-to-Good

Friends' Meeting House

The Bunyanesque name is only a corruption (though perhaps not accidental) of Cornish *Cwm-ty-coit*, combe of the house in the wood. Wonderful position down in a hollow, along the old route from Truro to Restronguet ferry and hence Falmouth. Built 1710; the lean-to on E end dates from somewhat later and was a shelter for worshippers' animals; its deep thatch roof makes a comfortable junction with the main one. Central structure is roughly rendered cob, with thick later buttresses between diamond-paned, wide-shuttered windows. Shutters are painted fresh green like a code for Nature. A new vestibule on W is fairly inconspicuous but still not an improvement on earlier weatherboard.

In the meeting room proper, a great hipped roof opens above you as you come out from under a rustic gallery

Cerne Abbas. Bold inscriptions and rustic traces remain in spite of later improvements

at W. Then you are surrounded by a timeless cleanliness, the height inspiring, the panelled benches on three sides a consoling enclosure.

George Fox, founder of the Quaker movement, visited Cornwall in 1656, and his imprisonment in Launceston jail is memorably recounted in his *Journal*.

Cornwall: 3 miles S of Truro, W of B3289, on N side of unnumbered road

Crediton

Holy Cross

One of the largest churches in the county is nicely sunken in a vast churchyard beside the rising road. Only Ottery

among Devon parish churches is more elaborate. Crediton was collegiate and has a big chapter house stuck on at the E, past the transept. The whole is unusually long with many extensions. It is made of wonderful red sandstone, tending to orange in replacement bits and to purple in older parts. This is one place where the patchwork of repair makes entertaining variety.

Colours inside are exhilarating too. This is not sandstone but Thorverton stone, in pale pink and dusky pinkish purple. Nineteenth-century restoration was tactful enough to leave this one of the finest displays of mellow stonework in the county.

Caröe's screen in the tower arch, on the other hand, is a bizarre misjudgement. Its

coloured mosaics shriek crudely. In the chancel, lovely smashed sedilia with rich recesses on the other side and original colouring. Also good Renaissance tombs, especially the resigned widow lounging between medallions of her husbands.

Devon: 8 miles NW of Exeter on A377; church near E end of High Street, to N

Crewkerne

St Bartholomew

Impressive Perpendicular rebuilding in golden Ham Hill stone.

The town has a pleasing density of cross streets at its centre. The church is immured higher up, hardly visible from the market place. There is a wonderful approach from the N where one is met by many ramifying extensions, all window and rich-hued stone. Gargoyles jut out and diversify the skyline, especially on the narrow S porch. The W end, framed by two towerlets, forms a real composition.

After all this, the interior is disappointing. Though made of the same golden stone, it feels almost undecorated, as Perpendicular buildings sometimes do. The nave roof forms a shallow tunnel in wood with one wayward beam down the centre. It rests on vivid angel corbels.

There are some good Victorian bench ends filled with vegetation. Spatially, the N parts, corresponding to those outjutting extensions, are the most interesting.

Somerset: 9 miles SW of Yeovil on A30; church on NW edge of town

Croscombe

St Mary the Virgin

Remarkable for its Jacobean woodwork.

It has an elegant stone spire and sits in a curious position up a slope from the main street. Made in part of granite-like stone, with panelled parapets and lots of gargoyles.

The screen and pulpit are the great thing – though of different vintage, they juggle a common set of motifs: obelisks on pierced bases, strapwork dotted with knobs like currants. On the screen nearly every opening has a little obelisk bisecting it. The pulpit (which is earlier) takes these same elements, alternately enlarging and shrinking them.

Overhead, a dark panelled roof of the 15c with big flat bosses, some of which

Crediton. Grand proportions, wonderful stone colours and a vivid Edwardian mosaic screen

24

refer to the weaving industry important here in those days. An interesting pseudo-Gothic roof covers the chancel, apparently 17c, with diamond lozenges stuck on here and there.

There are good chandeliers and 15c benches with jagged poppyheads of bunched leaves.

Somerset: 2½ miles SE of Wells on A371; church lies N of road in centre of village

Cullompton

St Andrew

Surprising richness in such a modest place, of carving, vaulting and wooden roofs.

The building is hidden dramatically at the end of a cul-de-sac off the High Street. Its W end presents amazing colours: a dull purple body trimmed in greenish white like Cheshire cheese. Carving is dotted on the tower with a somewhat confectionary effect.

You enter under the tower and are met by fantastic roofs, a steep barrel shape in the nave, flat in the aisles. Both are chequered in three-dimensional gingerbread; the backgrounds pale blue, the details picked out in ochre. Big faces on bosses in the aisles, angels down the central space. To some, the chancel screen, garish like Op art, suggests truly medieval richness.

In the S extension, extravagant late Perpendicular fan vaulting and carving. Funny little figures are ensconced on the pillars dividing it from the nave. At the end of this aisle fascinating graveyard scenes in wood are said to be bases of the lost rood.

Devon: 13 miles NE of Exeter on B3181, just W of M5 (exit 28); church E of High Street

Dunster

Priory Church of St George

Imposing, well-placed church in an ultra-picturesque village.

Dunster is arranged along a curving spine. The meshing of church and churchyard in the general layout is worth studying. The churchyard is almost landlocked, with only the briefest exits to the High Street, and the church is partly hemmed in by ancillary buildings – a detached gatehouse to the S and something like a farmhouse complex to the NW.

Croscombe. A curious position, gritty stone textures and remarkable woodwork

Commanding central tower in red sandstone. Good niches on porch and S transept. It is only when you get closer that the building seems a bit gone over and regularized by restorers.

The interior, stately and regular, continues surprisingly far E. The screen goes on and on: its cornice in lighter wood is particularly beautiful. In S chapel a large tomb puts the living and the dead together like passengers in a railway carriage. There's a convenient shelf for the helmet of the kneeling knight. Nearby hangs a confident Baroque painting of the Brazen Serpent by Thornhill, better than his wont. There is also an exquisite piece of effetery, a late 19c reredos in Italian primitive style; note especially St George.

Somerset: 3 miles SE of Minehead on A396; church on N side High Street, W of market

East Brent

St Mary

Remarkable fittings: above all, an early 17c plaster roof.

The church withdraws to a semi-hidden position at the end of the village. An elegant tower is topped by a spindly spire. Down its W front runs a strange tippy-pole arrangement of three figures in niches. The stone has weathered till the ashlar resembles rustication. It is the pasty grey stone native to this district.

Interior remarkable: lopsided and crowded. Never have benches been packed so densely, creating aisles so narrow. The carved ends are like gnarled tree stumps. A crooked W tower arch is partly obscured by a W gallery carved with grapevines.

Some interesting vulgar inscriptions c1840 over arches of chancel and arcade, and good garish glass in the E. N chapel window has vivid narrative in 15c glass.

Best of all is the plaster ceiling dated 1637, with ribs imitating late Gothic vaulting and huge pendants hanging down. It is creased by a single dormer, which admits welcome light to show off these intricate patterns.

Somerset: 7 miles S of Weston-super-mare on A370; church W of road

East Lulworth

St Mary (RC)

John Tasker

One of the first purpose-built Catholic churches since the Reformation looks like a gorgeous garden pavilion.

George III permitted it on the understanding it would not look like a church. It lies in parkland within sight of an earlier geometric conceit, Lulworth Castle, a piece of Jacobean medievalism with Gothick embellishments.

The church is of clover-leaf plan with three semi-circular lobes and a shallow dome. Its surfaces are a finely finished pale white ashlar, its chimneys topped with vases. Inside, much crisp woodwork in fresh colours, and painted clouds overhead.

Dorset: 5 miles SW of Wareham on B3070; church is N of the ruined Lulworth Castle, in its grounds

East Lulworth, an early Catholic church like a garden pavilion of clover-leaf plan

Harberton

St Andrew

A Perpendicular church in an enjambed position with a couple of curious and soulful Victorian accoutrements.

This village perches on a slope; the church is immured halfway up. It is made of slate with brown eyebrows over the windows and an impressive two-storey porch. Inside this, a vault with huge knobbly pendant leaves.

Impressive lightness in the interior. The screen has been re-coloured and

some very charming early 19c saints and choirs of angels added. Locals have claimed to recognize old village characters and pure local maidens in these faces.

In the N aisle an extravagant marble memorial of 1895 to Tito, a child. He wears a nightshirt, with a large thrusting lily draped across it. A garland is looped over his foot; further carved flowers, of alarming fleshiness, press into his pillow. More memorials to his family half underground in the churchyard.

Going out, notice the monster which a Victorian wood-carver has fashioned from the lock on the door.

Devon: 2 miles SW of Totnes, ½ mile W of A381; church high up on E edge of village, approached from W

Hartland

St Nectan*

At the land's edge, beyond the village (already isolated), the church is approached via a little cluster of old houses like a monastic remnant. Like Morwenstow in Cornwall it sits high on S side of a combe, exposed to winds from the Atlantic, of which its great tower has a view.

After desolate country and the low narrow streets of the village, the ambitious scale of this church is staggering. The breadth and height of the interior, which the outside hasn't prepared you for, seems a whole foreign world of grandeur. Ceilings are various and wonderful – high nave with bold folk design like Pennsylvania Dutch in yellow, black, red and light blue. The saddest exhibits in a room called the Pope's chamber, over the N porch, are a few panels of the original wooden ceiling,[†] replaced with fresh copies throughout in 1982. N aisle roof the richest, at its E end like a woven canopy; in aisle proper, recent bosses spell the donors' names in local plants and trees.

All the riches of this church cannot be told, but the unrestored screen is outstanding – both sides fully and differently decorated. Font, Romanesque on a heroic scale with wonderfully preserved scallops, spirals and face-like swirls. Its strangest features are four heads pointing down at corners (you have to bend to see them; otherwise they seem large ball-drops). Beneath them on the base are four answering heads at whom they stare.

Hartland's vast interior with varied roofs and screens, in a wonderfully remote spot

MORWENSTOW 12 miles S, in similar but even more isolated situation (nice lanes), has the best Norman carving hereabouts, some surprising heads in the arcade (look at both sides). Also a font which looks as if it is leaning in the wind, and a steep tunnel of old roof. In the bottom of the combe, an eccentric rectory built by the poet R. S. Hawker, once vicar here, who is said to have remembered churches where he had served in the many chimneys of this house. But if these are meant as copies of specific Cornish towers, they aren't very exact. Hawker has poems about both Hartland and Morwenstow churches.

* Welsh hermit, 5c

† In fact this ceiling has needed renewing every 80–90 years, so the 'original' panels are late 19c.

Devon: Hartland is 5 miles W of Clovelly on B3248; church in Stoke 1½ miles further W

Holbeton

All Saints

Remarkable for the harmonious introduction of Arts and Crafts fittings.

The starting point was a magnificently sited, mainly 15c church in an unspoiled village off the beaten track. Because of a few civic projects contemporaneous with the enrichment of the church, the whole settlement feels like a preserve of aesthetic privilege.

The great internal feature from which **J. D. Sedding** took his cue (in 1885–9) is an intricate Tudor screen, c1535, loaded with royal emblems in stylized or encrusted forms. Sedding replaced the portions which had disappeared and added a reredos in Renaissance style, framing a copy of over-ripe Correggio. Beneath this, extreme richness in the frontal of beaten metal, looking like embossed leather and enclosing panels of coloured marble. A window by Heywood Sumner adds a final note of luxury.

In the nave, stone pulpit and wooden bench ends of extremely juicy detail. Three exterior doors are also showpieces of late 19c fantasy, especially the S one, with metal filigree overlaid on an ivory-like substance. A lead rainwater box on SE angle with the patron's initials. Lovely mock-Renaissance lychgates lead into the village and out to the steep road W.

An amusing 17c monument jammed into N chapel shows, stacked up in

Hornblotton, T. G. Jackson's essay in Aesthetic Movement vernacular

several rows, twenty-three members of the Hele family of FLETE (a house 2 miles NE later improved into elephantine Gothic by Norman Shaw, now divided into flats).

Devon: 10 miles SE of Plymouth, off A379 on unnumbered road to S

Hornblotton

St Peter

T. G. Jackson

A translation of Surrey vernacular and Aesthetic Movement motifs into the sacred sphere.

The result is charming if unrepeatable. Its miniature towerlet-belfry is both tiled and shingled. Contrasted to the ruddiness of these colours is the golden local stone used in the diminutive body of this Victorian church.

Inside, a tremendous amount of mastic decoration in rust-red and cream including big Apostles, sunflowers and Morris leafage. Windows airy with leafy backgrounds. A marvellous mosaic floor in the chancel like a modern approximation of Cosmati work. In the W a whimsical spatial effect; the tower-supports create unusably small aislets at the sides.

All this was paid for by the squire's son who had travelled extensively in Biblical lands before settling into clerical life.

Somerset: 7 miles SW of Shepton Mallet, just E of A37 (½ mile N of Hornblotton Green)

Ilminster

Minster (St Mary)

This church, beautifully set above the main street, has one of the best Somerset towers.

Its churchyard is railed on three sides and approached along a walled passage on the E. From SE, the building makes a wonderfully composed group, presided over by a tower which is a masterpiece of controlled thrust and understated decoration. Bell grilles very rich, but the best touch is four plain buttresses on each side carried from top to bottom of the tower. On the N side the Wadham Chapel has battlements of oriental richness. Panelling on S porch is pleasantly eccentric.

After the satisfactions of the exterior, the inside is much less interesting. The glassed-in W gallery is probably useful but it spoils the space. The Wadham Chapel in N transept is the best part, separated by a renovated Jacobean screen or fence. Here are two great coupled brasses of very different periods – one early and one late. The second is a memorial to the female founder of Wadham College, Oxford. Here also hangs an Art Nouveau painting of the Virgin and Child asleep in a ruin.

Somerset: 12 miles SE of Taunton, S of A303; church W of market

Isle Abbots

St Mary the Virgin

A dream of what a parish church should be.

Perfect in its placement, its proportions and its state of repair. The country round about is former marsh, but the tower at the end of the village street is on you before you know it, framed between buildings. The gold of its stone is less ruddy than nearby Martock and slightly dusty in colour. There are more elaborate towers than this, but no better ones. Moderate height, rich bell openings, and most wonderful of all, original figures in the niches. Pevsner says their quality is poor; I think they're among the greatest glories of English churches, especially the Virgin with cascading cloak and hair, and Christ stepping from the tomb.

Passing under a fan vault in the porch, you come into a plain interior where golden stone contributes most of the richness. Fittings are harmonious rather than spectacular, although both piscina and sedilia are powerfully eccentric in a low-key way. The flat font has a crude monster upside down and another one behind bars.

Somerset: 9 miles SE of Taunton, S of A378; church at E end of village

Kenton

All Saints

Though this church is famous for its screen, the exterior stonework seems more remarkable still.

The main material is a deep red conglomerate with shards of darker rock fused into it in great profusion. This stone seems to have rusted onto the lighter stone used for trim, turning it from cream to orangey pink.

The S porch is best for variety of colour and carving, the W tower for sternest, darkest phases of the main stone. It is mossy in its upper stages.

Inside, Perpendicular arcades with bold leaf bands. The famous screen is magnificent, though many parts are obviously replacements. It stretches the entire distance from one wall to the other without a break, and is topped by a bulgy silver cross made by Henry Wilson for Exeter Cathedral. Interesting Renaissance panelling and monuments in the N chapel, the best one uncomfortably crowded by the screen, which was there before the tomb.

Devon: 8 miles S of Exeter on A379; church W of road

Kilkhampton

St James

In interestingly empty country N of Bude. The tower with its tall pinnacles stands high above the meander of this

Kenton's magnificent screen crowned by Henry Wilson metalwork stretches across the church

largish village. A 16c porch shields a Norman door with a grove of carved pine cones on one side and two rude heads on the other.

The great thing here is the dark and rich interior with a wonderful collection, not just of bench ends, but of complete old benches with old book rests intact. They look horribly uncomfortable, but are not. The ends have a wealth of invented heraldry including many reminders of the Passion.

Early Victorian glass in childish colours – red, blue and green. Under the tower some well-told Biblical stories. In S aisle windows, knights in bizarre, unscholarly arrangement. Next to that, a tumultuous monument to a hero of the Civil War (but only put up in 1714) with military gear stuffed in along the sides of fluted classical columns.

Cornwall: 5 miles N of Bude on A39

Launcells. Beautiful arcades of two kinds of local stone and many simple old things

Kingston

St James

G. E. Street

One of Street's best works, which makes most Victorian churches look loose and unmotivated.

In a high position with views of Corfe Castle to the N. A well-composed group with a domineering tower, its stone mottled by a purple lichen. The great W rose imposes a square on a circle. Strong latticing on the stair turret has been borrowed from Christchurch Priory on the Hampshire border. At its base

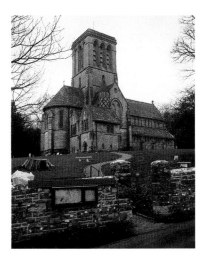

Kingston. A thoughtful Victorian design that incorporates bold medieval borrowings

there's a subtle touch, a little entrance on the diagonal.

After entry via a narthex, we meet a lavish display of different colours and scales inside. Two tones seem almost equally balanced: dark Purbeck and tan local stone. A series of bold disproportions begins with tall chancel arch matched against two storeys in nave elevations. Then a further step down to extremely small aisle windows. These have well-drawn figures by Clayton & Bell. The ironwork is exceptional: an openwork pulpit and chancel screens. It should be noted that the architect here had a very lavish budget.

Dorset: 5 miles W of Swanage on B3069; church W of road

Launcells

St Swithin

Delightful, in a sequestered position, below and almost out of sight of its tiny settlement. The porch is framed by a yucca and a cherry and, inside, the light is extraordinary.

Here the feeling is Georgian in spite of the fact that what one sees is mostly medieval. Beautiful segmental arcade, high and thin, the N granite, the S an exquisite polyphant stone, which comes from a quarry near Launceston and is blue-grey with iron flecks. A Norman

cable font with 17c lid, rustic bench ends and, most remarkable of all, some old tile floors in chancel and S chapel. These are Barnstaple ware with deeply cut patterns, uneven glaze, and mottled green-gold colouring which makes them look like facts of nature.

Not everything matches, but all is harmonious including a modest Gothick reredos of wood and marble, box pews, mellow slate floors, a languid recliner on a whitewashed monument and the biggest royal arms ever for the size of the church. These are mounted on N wall and built up in three-dimensional plaster. The thistle and rose and furls issuing from the helm jump forth with preternatural vigour.

Cornwall: 4 miles E of Bude, a short distance N of A3072

Launceston

St Mary Magdalene

Cornwall's best inland town with its most individual church, Launceston sits on a steep hill, crowned by a castle.

The church is memorable above all for repetitive ornamental carving which covers almost every inch of the external surface, like a brocade in granite. Because this hard stone won't take delicate shades of detail, it is sometimes hard to work out what the richness exactly is, though you can tell it is vegetation and that there are many rows of it. Two groups above the S door – St George and the dragon, and a Renaissance fop on horseback who cuts off something (a head?) and hands it to a lady. In fact it is St Martin, his cloak, and the beggar. Pomegranates, roses and oak trees (which look like monkey puzzles, they're so jagged) circle the building. Large feathers or ferns framing the windows are called palm branches by Pevsner.

It is all the donation of a 16c gent, Sir Henry Trecarrel, whose manor house survives half built five miles S of Launceston. He has brought the emblematic imagination of *The Faerie Queene* into a religious setting, the only earlier model for this being the aisle of St Mary, Truro, incorporated by Pearson on the S side of his Victorian cathedral.

At the E end in Launceston the patroness, Mary Magdalene, appears as an emaciated hermit, stretched out in her cave. Around her are small angel musicians playing period instruments.

Like the altar rail at Altarnun the exterior at Launceston is graced with a distended inscription. Letters, one per panel, run around the building, spelling the Ave Maria.

Inside, the lavish inscription of exterior surfaces with imagery has found an answer four hundred years later. Launceston possesses a set of Art Nouveau benches, screens and stalls which are one of the glories of Cornwall. They were designed by an unidentified designer and date from 1893–4. Perhaps the most extravagant piece is a reading desk with a goat and ram forming opposite crests, and doubtless reflecting some Scriptural text. The seventy-two

bench ends include repeats, but plenty of variety even so – crabs, otters, hedgehogs, whales, as well as innumerable fish and birds. It is all a working out of a Latin hymn about Creation.

There is also a 16c pulpit of lush carved foliage in delectable green, white and gold.

Cornwall: about 23 miles NW of Plymouth on A388

Martock

All Saints

This golden building in a town with many beautiful 17c houses has one of the best wooden roofs in England.

It sits at a bend in Church Street and makes a wonderful sight approached from the S. Many good buildings nearby; it is a district very rich in stone. The exterior consistent Perpendicular with good gargoyles and pierced parapets. The tower is modest, however, and the best things lie within.

Remarkable richness distinguishes the Martock roof from its rivals. It bears the date 1513. The entire sloping surface above the beams is divided into small panels, each filled with tracery of varied design. A local devotee has counted 768 of these panels. In intermediate sections giant pendants hang down. Something odd about the structure: alternate beams break off after two feet as if they are counterweights, not supports. Above the piers, elaborate niches, filled in the 17c by charmingly awkward painted Apostles.

There is a purple Victorian saint in a chancel window, powerful not subtle, and a yew alley running W from the church.

Somerset: 8 miles NW of Yeovil on B3165; church in centre of town on N side of High Street

Mells

St Andrew

An unusually tranquil place. Mells church has a fine tower and porch and many good 20c memorials.

The pattern of lanes is extremely obscure, making the church appear and disappear like a mirage. It lies at the end of a narrow avenue of cottages, a surprisingly formal arrangement. Below the corner pinnacles of the tower, others set diagonally and subdivided. The porch

Martock's golden exterior, rich in gargoyles and pierced parapets

Mullion in the centre of the village with notable tracery in granite

has a swoopy curve along its top edge and an impossibly tall niche in the middle.

Harshly scraped inside, but full of interesting things – a piece of silk embroidery by Lady Horner to Burne-Jones's design, whose flowers and leaves positively glitter. A peacock on a wall memorial in shallow relief, also by Burne-Jones.

The Horner Chapel is engorged by a memorial to the last heir, killed in the Great War. Lutyens and Sir Alfred Munnings collaborated on this, which is like a miniature of the Cenotaph in Whitehall with a bronze rider on top. It ingeniously incorporates the wooden marker brought back from the battlefield. Behind the monument, an eccentric St Francis window by William Nicholson, with clouds of birds and fishes.

The churchyard gives onto wide sweeps of country and contains old yews. E of church the best set of early 20c memorials found anywhere – including memorials by Lutyens and Eric Gill, memorials to Ronald Knox and Siegfried Sassoon, and another stone carved with the sun spewing flowers and a wheatsheaf on a shell. In the remote NE corner near fields, the McKenna tomb, an important work of Lutyens despite its modest scale. It resembles a primeval stone table subjected to bewildering geometrical rigours.

More work by Lutyens in the village, including a triangular pavilion over the well.

Somerset: 3½ miles W of Frome in a confusing tangle of lanes

Moreton

St Nicholas

An exquisite Gothick building of 1776 with remarkable engraved windows by Laurence Whistler.

Mells has one of the best Somerset towers and exceptional early 20c work

It sits on a sylvan mound by a stream, spider-Gothick so frail it seems a building made of paper. The internal layout resembles a drawing room, a wide centralized space, whose N extension of 1841 feels like a veranda or conservatory for taking the views.

A bomb wrecked earlier windows in 1940. This led to Whistler's engraved pictures filling fourteen windows in all. These images are like patterns materialized by your breath in the cold, which fade in certain lights or perspectives. Light is the persistent theme: flames, smoke, rain and lightning are well depicted. A pamphlet explains some surprising allegories like conceits the Baroque poet Richard Crashaw might have thought up.

Lawrence of Arabia is buried in the detached cemetery, and his eccentric cottage lies two miles to the NE near Bovington Camp.

Dorset: 8 miles E of Dorchester on unmarked road, 1 mile E of B3390

Mullion

St Mellanus*

A very pleasing church, sheltered in the centre of the village (whose street pattern forms a triangle around the churchyard and its houses). Approached from both E and W (W lychgate very low, take care). Old S door has what looks like a cat flap at the bottom, said to be for sheepdogs in this herding country.

The church was restored by F. C. Eden, who must be responsible for the chestnut-coloured rood screen, but couldn't have been given a free hand or he would have coloured it.

Bench ends are memorable and require a torch. They can partly be deciphered with the help of clear modern copies, which are mixed in. Exuberant Renaissance motifs, including a child blowing into a bag and an armed profile which in its worn state looks like a blindfolded Moor. Benches have lovely ridgy tops and knobbly leaf borders.

Outside, some charming signs of the intractability of granite in window tracery.

* Also Mellion, Melanius or Melaine – an obscure saint, spelling of whose name cannot be agreed; Breton 6c

Cornwall: 7 miles S of Helston, less than 1 mile from coast on B3296

North Cadbury. Noble Perpendicular – an especially fine porch – in an idyllic location

Newton Abbot

St Luke, Milber

An extremely eccentric design which was revealed to the vicar in a dream in 1931.

From outside (from the W), it looks like a pyx or shrine by Henry Wilson, in cement instead of silver, descending from its central cone-tower to wings at the sides. The plan is a St Andrew's cross overlaid on a long nave, resulting in a great angular snowflake.

Inside, a space which converges and splinters at once. Small triangles occur between the exploding arms, set off by low granite columns. From the nave you get views of the wing-roofs through transept windows which are tall and thin. The overall effect is a dove-grey coolness which could be the 1930s in England or Dante's empyrean with equal ease.

Many charming details and a certain awkwardness. It was actually designed by the vicar's brother, Arthur, an architect. W. Keble Martin, the vicar, is better known for another devoted and obsessive project, the *Concise British Flora*, one of the greatest amateur artefacts.

A chaste garden, with cherry trees, on rampart-surroundings; again this feels like Dante's celestial geometry.

Devon: 16 miles S of Exeter on A381; church lies SE of centre on E side of A380 (Torquay Road)

North Cadbury

St Michael

An airy Perpendicular building in an idyllic situation.

It lies between a mellow Elizabethan manor house and a wide farm vista, so it is both sheltered and liberated. The N porch looks wonderfully rich from afar, and there is the clarity of seeing straight through plain glass.

Inside, a generous supply of light, a good roof, some rather apt Victorian decor in chancel (because restrained), and dwarf-size knightly effigies under the tower.

The most interesting fitting is a set of Renaissance bench ends, including a cat robbing a mousetrap, a packhorse, a quarrelling couple, and many others more decorous but still lively.

Somerset: 6 miles W of Wincanton, N of A303; church S of village

Ottery St Mary

St Mary

Often called the most important parish church in Devon, this exceptionally lavish building has been defaced by well-meant restoration, which still continues.

Its S aspect remains very charming. The church sits like a sprawled beast on a hump at a bend in the High Street. It has two stumpy lateral towers, one of which wears a conical metal hat. Approaching, you are appalled to see that much decorative stonework at both E and W ends has been coated with tan preservative paint.

Inside, scratchy rubble walls and bright blue and red on the vaulting ribs. The chancel vault is truly remarkable and worth the trip to see. It forms a curvilinear geometrical puzzle unique in England, which has been connected with William Joy, who worked at Wells

Newton Abbot. An eccentric early 20c work revealed to its vicar in a dream

Parracombe. A gem of rusticity in slate with an unspoiled wooden interior

Cathedral in the mid 14c. The gaudy paint of recent years makes it hard to be sure, but the design is perhaps more amazing than truly satisfying.

Clerestory windows which light this vault are by Pugin (executed by Hardman), chaste in design but fresh in colour, a pleasing combination. The Lady Chapel beyond is the most surprising space of all, reached by a torturous route.

Details at Ottery tend to the bizarre. There's the Dorset aisle vault with hollow pendants, slightly twisted, and the lavish Butterfield font, which consists of a cube of variegated marble topped with a cone of wood and metal.

Devon: 11 miles E of Exeter on B3174

Parracombe

St Petrock (CCT)

A gem of an unspoiled interior, set in a humble medieval fabric. Its situation wonderfully rural, above the present

village. A simple building of slate with low tower and wide porch.

Inside, pews rise towards the back and make a complex thicket around the screen. Above, a large flat tympanum conflating Creed and royal arms. Hat pegs line the walls.

The tower shaft is now open and has a floor of flags. Stone floors throughout, and everything dim with age; then the fresh white of the plaster. The jostling of the various devices produces a dynamic result.

A national campaign which Ruskin supported saved this church from demolition when a replacement was built in 1878, more conveniently placed among the houses at the centre.

In the pleasant little resort of LYNTON nearby, St Mary's has Henry Wilson windows and fittings (especially a Benedicite series in clear glass).

Devon: Parracombe lies between Ilfracombe and Lynton just off A39; church in Churchtown E of present village

Plymouth, Crown Hill

Ascension

Robert Potter

Here hackneyed architectural forms of the 1950s are turned to expressive purpose. A large cruciform structure in which fieldstone, slate, and coloured cement panels are used decoratively.

Entered under a slender campanile. The folded plaster ceiling is painted a rich raspberry colour and held up by eccentrically shaped grey pillars. A tent-like effect, ingeniously lit by bow-headed windows in transepts and rectangles near the eaves. It feels as if the building is about to fly. Elaborate baldacchino with gilded corner posts echoes the tent form and frames an aluminium crucifix and twelve stained-glass punctures with industrial fragments lodged in them, on the rugged stone wall behind.

This exhilarating interior is difficult to reach because of recent road improvements, which have inserted flyovers and huge junctions unfeelingly into the urban fabric. You may well see the Church of the Ascension and the nearby round Roman Catholic church of *St Peter*, 1967–70 (with stained glass by Charles Norris), long before you manage to reach them.

Devon: 47 miles SW of Exeter on A38: Travelling E on A38, in the large roundabout at junction with A386, take slip road (not marked as an exit) just before exit marked Tavistock (A386 north). This slip is St Peter's Road. Turn R almost immediately into Manadon Drive, and then after 100 yds, R again. Church just ahead on L

St Enodoc, tucked into his hill, was buried in the dunes until rescued in the 1860s

Poole

St Osmund, Parkstone

E. S. Prior

This architect's last work, an eccentric fantasia on Byzantine themes.

Prior took his cue from G. A. B. Livesay's apse of 1904–5 in rendering and terracotta. The great textural innovation is handmade brick so variegated it looks like an animal's skin. This culminates in two turrets at the W end composed entirely of small columns. The resulting shimmer of brick planes is rich but unfussy.

After this somewhat sombre exterior, the festive internal space is a surprise. There's a wonderful Mediterranean mix of textures: tan and orange ceramic coating, brick and mellow plaster. Piers

and columns alternate in the aisles, and the light is set glittering by Prior's special glass, so thick it works like myriad lenses, mostly clear but with a sprinkling of subtle colour.

SE chapel closed off by screen with false perspectives and rich substances by Eric Gill's brother. Unfortunately, a new church hall will obscure that side of the church, including the little forest of columns under the chapel.

Other Prior work in Dorset: a complete church at BOTHENHAMPTON of 1887–9, dominated by a single spatial idea – the nave made from a huge Gothic arch – but sadly hard-edged in detail. Improvements c1897 to St Mary at BURTON BRADSTOCK nearby are more sympathetic, including marvellous aisle roof, painted dado, much furniture and Prior glass. Then a seaside terrace at WEST BAY (1885), a

little exercise in vernacular irregularity. Prior also designed a club and swimming bath for West Bay which wasn't built, a hump-backed and many-eyed organism in concrete.

Dorset: Poole is W of and continuous with Bournemouth; church on S side of A35 (Bournemouth Road) about ½ mile E of Parkstone station

Portland

St George, Reforne (CCT)

Among stone quarries, a notable Georgian extravaganza in fine stonework.

Portland's topography is exciting: a high, formerly detached headland, looking back along a spit of shingle to Weymouth. Human habitation here is grim and scruffy: prisoners were imported to quarry the famous stone in the 19c. The contrast with the air of gentility the material breathes in London, the main market for it, is awkward, to say the least.

St George appears to be made of finely finished geometric solids, like over-scaled children's blocks. It has many windows, but they are small: the overwhelming sensation is of stone. The main architectural emphasis is a tiered, pavilioned tower of comfortable scale. Inside, good woodwork and strong barrel vaults. A large graveyard, well packed with tombstones, stretches out to the quarry edge.

Dorset: 5 miles S of Weymouth on A354; church lies between Easton and Weston on westernmost N–S road

St Buryan

St Buryan*

A lonely, windswept but sizeable village 5½ miles from Land's End; one of those places where a crooked or stunted tree seems the right emblem for Cornwall.

Churchyard approach from S ceremonious, with triangular stone platform before the gate. Between that and S porch, one of the best Cornish crosses, an elaborate head (no shaft) marooned on high pyramid of steps. The crucified figure is clothed (not carefully) in white lichen.

St Buryan church is large, with high arcades and fine wagon roofs. It contains one of the most wonderful artefacts in Cornwall, a screen filling the whole

St Buryan's screen, preserving delicate old colour, is one of the best artefacts in Cornwall

Portland, a Georgian treasure among the quarries from which monumental London was built

width of this wide building. Its central frieze is packed with animals of all descriptions, spotted and feathered and snarled in leaves. There is a beautiful vine border above, and fragments of original tracery and coving in the most exquisite old colourings – a rusty tonality overall, like a delicate vintage.

* Variously described as 'an unknown saint' and 'Bruniec, a king's daughter of Ireland'

Cornwall: 5 miles SW of Penzance on B3283; church in centre of village

St Enodoc

Dedication unknown

One of the strangest settings of any English church – half a mile from the nearest road and approached via large suburban houses among pines and then a walk across a heathy golf course. St Enodoc's twisted slate spire is seen

some way off, poking up out of the churchyard's fringe of tamarisk. The modest building is cut cosily into the hillside; in fact it lay buried in sand c1863 and was dug out by an enthusiastic vicar. Some of its plate was recovered from a nearby farm kitchen, its Norman font from under the chancel floor. The church's most venerable fitting is the bottom half of a screen painted stark red and green.

Rows of animal drinking-bowls which line the path are actually medieval mortars from a village which lay between the church and the sea, and was probably overwhelmed in a storm.

John Betjeman's grave to E of path is marked by a slate incised (by John Piper) as if by a Victorian drawing master with flowery script and sprays of tiny flowers.

Cornwall: 6 miles NW of Wadebridge; from Trebetherick, take beach road (to SW), sign to church after 100 yds, follow path to S described above

St Germans

St Germans Priory

In pre-Norman times the Cornish bishop had his seat here, which begins to explain the odd magnificence of this church in a steep shrunken village.

The church has the air of a ruined fragment. A huge west-work, with octagonal N and square S tower, frames the best Norman portal in Cornwall: seven great fringes in elvan, a local porphyry, eroded now like an overhanging sea cliff.

The best surprise at St Germans is the Art Nouveau metalwork which adorns this door. Each nailhead is a little Celtic brooch, hinges are formed of grapes and vine leaves, and the handle is a slippery fish. They are by Henry Wilson, an outstanding late Arts and Crafts designer.

Six steps down into a vast bleak interior, with good William Morris glass to E, heavy Norman arcade, and a lavish Baroque monument in N tower cavity, like a primitive grotto. The white marble

Sherborne Abbey, showing the rich Perpendicular chancel and early fan vaults

looms spectrally in the Stygian gloom. The other tower sports an apocryphal list of the bishops of St Germans, including such mysterious personages as Athelstanus, Wolsi and Woronus – eleven in all.

Cornwall: 13 miles W of Plymouth, S of A38 on B3249 in centre of village

St Neot

St Anietus

The best old stained glass in Cornwall, most of it early 16c. There is so much of it that little space is left for monuments, so in this large church there are very few.

Start in S chapel where E window is oldest and best, and tells the story of Genesis from Creation to Noah. Next, a whole window devoted to Noah's exploits. Then a less interesting series of large saints with local donors below. The shift in mode has been explained by a change in how windows were paid for.

Narrative scenes again in NW corner, St George and St Neot windows, the first bloodthirsty and the second Celtic myth with water-magic. It is worth following these two through their twenty-four changes in the guide leaflet.

The 19c restorer Hedgeland contributed two garish 17c-ish windows in N chapel which are oddly engaging. Otherwise, colours at St Neot often seem flat, perhaps because of frequent tan glass in borders and backgrounds.

S side of exterior makes a magnificent show of squared granite and bristly battlements. Several Cornish crosses are collected near S porch.

St Neot is a pleasing place in a bowl at the edge of Bodmin moor.

Cornwall: 6 miles NW of Liskeard on unnumbered road 2 miles N of A38

Sampford Courtenay

St Andrew

Honeychurch

St Mary

A church of wonderful mellowness, and beyond it, a modest one more wonderful still.

Sampford Courtenay sits in a hollow with tall pinnacles on its tower. There is a kind of massiveness about the fabric – battlements like great stone chunks moving up and down – which ill prepares you for the fineness within. Here one arcade is granite, the other pale grey polyphant from Cornwall, a rare stone.

The roofs are very special. Bosses include the faces of old kings and queens, animals in centrifugal whirls and a sow with piglets. Manila plaster between the wooden ribs is lovely.

Honeychurch lies a little bit deeper in the country. It has all the parts of a church – tower, chancel, porch – but the tower is tiny and you must duck slightly to come in at the porch. After you pass through the bleached door you are in a world of old wood and leaning walls. The floor is wooden and uneven; the benches are almost child-size. On the entrance wall two ancient beast heads are mounted, and the space around the priest's door gives the feel of storage nooks in someone's pantry.

Devon: 5 miles NE of Okehampton, just N of A3072; church on E edge of village; Honeychurch 1 mile further N

Selworthy

All Saints

A decorous late Perpendicular building in a picturesque location near Porlock.

This wooded hilly part near the coast feels like Ambleside or the discreetly developed bits of the Lake District. Selworthy is a National Trust village and its exquisite church seems almost Comperized. Some writers take the refinement to be authentically medieval: very pretty cusped and recusped tracery, fresh white walls inside and out, and a chaste airiness under tall concave arcades.

The embossed leather reredos dates from the turn of the century; the Gothick squire's pew over the porch and the cool memorials by Chantrey from the late 18 and early 19c.

Somerset: 4 miles W of Minehead, N of A39; church E of village

Sherborne

Abbey (St Mary the Virgin)

The nearest thing to a cathedral in Dorset, a great Perpendicular abbey, saved entire as the parish church.

Sherborne is a seemly and mellow town. The E approach to the church follows a narrow, towny passage and arrives first at the Tudor grammar school, stuck on the E end and now partly reclaimed by the Abbey.

To the S and W stretches a sizeable green, ringed by pleasant old buildings. Guidebooks mention trees which are no longer there. From these angles the Abbey is certainly large, but perhaps a little heartlessly consistent. On its rough W edge, earlier traces remain, and the bottom storey of the porch is sturdy Norman.

Inside, the great feature is one of the earliest of all fan vaults. The chancel vault is earlier and unattractively coloured, while the nave is a perfected version of the idea. In spite of formidable complexity it has a tranquillizing effect. Richly panelled chancel walls make a rewarding study in the guiding principles of the Perpendicular style.

Three fittings stand out: Laurence Whistler's engraved glass reredos in the Lady Chapel with a fanciful gathering of Marian emblems, an Elizabethan tomb in S chancel aisle with interesting heraldry and female headdress, and best of all, the Digby monument of 1698 in the S transept; very large, in white and black marble. His two wives flank the Earl of Bristol – three agitated people, full of quirks in the carving.

Dorset: 6 miles E of Yeovil on A30; Abbey in centre, W of B3145

Stogursey

Priory Church of St Andrew

An unexpected building with huge Romanesque E parts.

Plastered and whitewashed outside, it looks like a German abbey, though such whiteness is also said to be a North Somerset tradition. The scale is vast and Perpendicular details look like the restorer's contribution. The original

building shows through in a powerful central tower.

Inside, the barn-like nave has little character. Beyond it, a dip down and then a long upward slope into a series of vast spaces. The E parts are complex and powerful Norman. Rugged capitals at the crossing show animals and plants of great vitality. The floor consists of large stones softened by centuries of use. One of them in N transept incorporates a huge marine fossil trailing tentacles and plumes. Two swaying fonts, one with rope and faces. On the S side, in those vast precincts where the ground rises underneath, good 18c tombs with putti, and an exquisite chest tomb with effigy, the freshness of whose carving is too good to be true.

Somerset: 9 miles NW of Bridgwater on minor road; church at E end of village

Stoke Sub Hamdon

St Mary the Virgin

A lively jumble, with wonderful relics preserved in its walls like flies in amber.

Approached through a 17c gate past a rich 15c cross. The most interesting survivor is a little Norman window-head to R of porch. It shows a warrior fighting a dragon whose tail is the floor he stands on. Below it a rich Gothic tomb or chimney arch which feels almost Rococo. Corbels at the other end of building are among the most vigorous ever, even though many are just geometrical patterns.

Interior reached through Norman door with fancy columns and riotous beast life overhead – a flying lamb, a mixture of birds, and two signs of the Zodiac thrown in. The space indoors appears twisted and impacted. Walls are scribbled with paintings and peppered with cartouches, like a jaw with too many teeth in it. There is an Elizabethan effigy, theatrically backlit, a great chancel arch with scallop capitals in various sizes, and a Norman font like a sack of grain loosely girdled with loops of carved rope.

The best part of the village lies to the W and includes the 14 and 15c 'Priory', housing chantry priests for the chapel of a manor nearby.

Somerset: 5 miles NW of Yeovil on A3088 in East Stoke; church lies on small loop just S of main road

Studland. Powerful and simple Norman overlooking the sea

Tawstock, a large and rambling building in a park, with fine carving inside

Studland

St Nicholas

Studland village, in an unspoiled bit of the Isle of Purbeck, has the best Norman church in the county.

It overlooks the sea and resembles a barn in sturdy simplicity. The bulky central tower extends beyond the sides of the nave and chancel and has a simple saddle roof. There is a crude corbel table of beast heads.

Inside, a very concentrated impression: a series of tower arches focuses our attention on the E end and its simple three-part window. You find yourself counting the elements to explain this effect of richness and strength without confusion.

The churchyard forms a wide and tranquil plateau over the sea.

Dorset: 2 miles N of Swanage on coast; church at end of lane in centre of village

Swimbridge

St James

Some of the best wood-carving in Devon is found here.

Twisting lanes to the W mislead one about the remoteness of this village swollen by recent growth. The church crouches far back in a large churchyard full of slate headstones. The low tower is slate too, capped by a lead spire. On the N pleasantly domestic windows.

The interior is a fantastic world of old wood, whose chestnut colours harmonize with the grey of the arcade and the mottled paler grey of a medieval carved pulpit.

The long screen is one of the best in Devon, and its bumpy flexible mouldings are almost entirely intact. There is also a wooden Renaissance font cover like a complex weighing device.

Devon: 5 miles SW of Barnstaple on A361; village S of new road; church in centre

Wells. St Cuthbert's fine tower, sometimes mistaken for the cathedral's

Tawstock

St Peter

In the grounds of a sham Gothic castle, Tawstock church is a surprisingly rich building with fabulous tombs.

The vagaries of the Taw cut this bit of country off from the main road to the E. The house, now a school, has interiors by Soane. Beyond it, nearer the river, lies this amazing church with a Norman central tower and a porch with divertingly panelled wall.

The interior is large and rambling and full of flavour. The main lines are 14c with large comic faces as stops in the arcade, carved in a sandy-coloured stone lighter than the tawny exterior. There are crude Renaissance motifs on the screen, Renaissance bench ends and a remarkable series of tombs.

These include a slate contraption like a wooden altar-piece with unfolding leaves of stepped overall shape, a big black casket mounted on four fierce white dogs, and a free-standing lady wistfully holding a coronet.

One of the loveliest details is painted plasterwork on transept ceilings. Grapes and bay leaves radiate delicately, tracing forgotten vaults.

Devon: 2 miles S of Barnstaple on W bank of the Taw, accessible only by minor roads

Teignmouth

St Peter, Shaldon

E. H. Sedding

A refined example of Art Nouveau, impressively perched beside the Teign.

Venetian richness of colour in the stonework, purple, grey and white outside, white and downy grey within. On the W front a canopy of stone forms itself in front of the great window. In the tracery swirling shapes merge, divide and re-combine. The whole design is metamorphic; angular bits seem about to push up above the strong line of the gable, but in the end they hesitate, a war among forms taken over from Flamboyant Gothic and smoothed out here.

The interior feels surprisingly clean, a result of light flooding from the W and the translucency of all the stone. Pulpit and screen, also stone, are among the most extravagant organicist fittings of their date. Some outstanding metalwork and glass as well.

Nearby (1½ miles W) at BISHOPSTEIGNTON is a remarkable

Romanesque tympanum, Spanish or African in its barbarity. It shows Three Kings striding forth and an angel or Herod stopping them at R.

Devon: Teignmouth is 6 miles E of Newton Abbot on A379; Shaldon on S side of Teign (pronounced 'tin') estuary; church at S end of bridge, to E

Wedmore
St Mary Magdalene

A church of impressive proportions, spatially rich and various.

The churchyard level is six feet or so above the adjacent High Street, which sets this powerfully organized building off very well. Details are mostly subordinated to the whole, but the fabric sprouts heads like personified winds over buttresses. A tall, almost three-storey porch; its inner door framed by bold Early English leaf capitals. There is good ironwork on the door and the date 1677 traced in nailheads.

You enter, subtly, through a small door in the porch side and are immediately struck by the height and ramifying variety of the space. It is a church which seems to contain not just one but a wealth of rooms. The piers are amazingly slender and the whole place flooded with light. The great W window is filled with glass on patriotic themes, and there is a good rustic memorial in the chancel.

Somerset: 9 miles W of Wells on B3139; church on N side of road

Wells
St Cuthbert, St Thomas

This small cathedral town has two outstanding parish churches, one large late Gothic, the other quirky Victorian.

St Cuthbert is one of the largest churches in the county. Many people arriving from the NW must have mistaken its tower for the Cathedral's. It has a high, slim arcade and a fancy angel roof, gaudily repainted. Over the aisles, other good roofs, especially traceried panels, recently uncovered, to the S. Against the ends of both aisles rest what is left of two wonderful stone reredoses, one of them a fascinating rendition of the Tree of Jesse.

St Thomas, at the other, poorer end of town, was designed by **S. S. Teulon** in 1856–7. Externally, bands of pink and purple stone alternate. Inside, the arcades and aisles are crazily different from one another (S added later). Unorthodox rich decoration in apse: mosaic, marble and, best of all, a rail of iron and brass.

Somerset: 22 miles S of Bristol on A39; St Cuthbert lies ten minutes' walk SW, and St Thomas ten minutes NE of Cathedral

Westonzoyland
St Mary the Virgin

The late Gothic roof at Westonzoyland is one of the great treasures of English parish churches.

The village sits in the Somerset levels, formerly marsh. The tower, built of ash-colour stone and busy with detail, is long visible over the flatland.

There are a good porch roof and gates, an old door, and then one is under the glorious wooden roof of the nave. It is of king-post construction, but the space between tie-beam and roof pitch is filled with tracery. Bulky leaf pendants hang down, and angels stick out from sides and bottoms of main timbers. Colours range unpredictably through many greys and browns. A recent rood screen does not compete, because its tawny hues are so remote from those of the roof.

Some nice concave mouldings here and there, in windows and arcade, as if the stone were trying to get out of the way.

After the Battle of Sedgemoor fought nearby in 1685, Monmouth's defeated

Westonzoyland's roof is one of the richest in England

rebels were imprisoned in the church. Some died of their wounds here, and the rest were taken elsewhere for summary execution or deportation.

Somerset: 5 miles SE of Bridgewater on A372; church on N side of road

Whitchurch Canonicorum

St Candida & Holy Cross

This church with an impressive tower might have strayed over from Somerset; it contains one of only two surviving saints' shrines with relics intact in the whole country.

Noble, though fairly plain tower; fine stone textures and lichens especially on N. Arcades are different and impressive, especially the later pointed one on N. One arch has hanging, almost detached zigzag, a holdover from the earlier Norman style.

Lovely stiffleaf carving especially where aisle meets transept. Here sits the shrine of the mysterious local St Wite. Distorted, she becomes white in the village name. Her shrine has three almond-shaped hidey-holes under the casket, which still contained her bones when opened in 1900. Like the niches in Edward the Confessor's shrine in Westminster Abbey, these holes let the

faithful get closer to the saint as they knelt here and prayed.

Dorset: 6 miles NE of Lyme Regis, about 1 mile N of A35

Wimborne Minster

The Minster

One of the county's most impressive churches in an attractive town.

Successor to a double Saxon monastery (the sexes kept separate), which became a college of secular canons. Originally it might have been rendered, which would have cancelled its most entertaining feature, walls of dark ironstone so randomly mixed through a lighter body they resemble the spots on a Dalmatian.

Another oddity: the minster's two large towers stand at an uneasy distance from each other, not so much harmonious as competitive. The central one is an impressive Norman piece, and the space under it exciting. The entire roof has only four over-sized wooden bosses.

At the E end, unorthodox windows in the form of lancets with large foiled eyes over them. The pairing creates pressure, then release, as if the round bits had been squeezed from a tube. In the central one, a very good scrambled Tree of Jesse, 16c.

The nave arcade is Norman and just too toothy; it feels almost dangerous. In the large churchyard a free-standing Jacobean sundial at the SW corner.

Dorset: 7 miles N of the centre of Poole on B3078 (N of A31)

Wimborne St Giles

St Giles

J. Ninian Comper

History takes its revenge: a fascinating de-Georgianizing by Ninian Comper of a church of 1732, which was itself a complete rebuilding, connected with the Bastards of Blandford Forum (q.v.).

Outside, all is classical decorum – a tower with rusticated quoins and stone baubles on top, in chequered flint and greensand. But inside, a riot of rich Tudor Gothic. Comper has contrived to make a clear space murky by inserting an unnecessary S arcade only a few feet from the outside wall.

His screen is a triumph of relaxed frills, and the high altar lurking within, under its canopy, is positively orgiastic.

Wimborne St Giles, whose Georgian exterior conceals a riot of Tudor Gothic within

Whitchurch Canonicorum, the shrine of St Wite with three openings for pilgrims to squeeze into

The window behind it is one of Comper's most successful. Otherwise, too much of his glass, in every window, except one containing 16c scenes, but the glass creates the correct dimness for viewing his elaborate roof, W gallery, and pseudo-Jacobean cover for a real Jacobean font.

Here Comper is the Horace Walpole of our day, enacting a kind of serious foolery not everyone will enjoy (Pevsner didn't). It may lessen the excitement to learn that Bodley preceded Comper; his Gothic improvements perished in the fire of 1908.

The famous series of Shaftesbury monuments gets swallowed up in the encasing gorgeousness. The best is one of the smallest: neo-classical of 1819 by Rudolph Schadow, with a grieving widow and the Three Fates.

The situation is idyllic: a huge green in front and a row of early 17c almshouses attached to the right shoulder of the church. Built into the churchyard wall is the most elegant war memorial in England, a diamond-shaped pier capped by a large volute like an 18c tomb.*

Nearby are two further 18c curiosities. First, the church at HORTON (5 miles S) with a powerful stone pyramid lodged against its side. This looks so much like Vanbrugh that many have turned for explanation to EASTBURY HOUSE (9 miles NW), which Vanbrugh was building a few years before Horton tower appeared. The pulpit and seating

at Horton have been moved, so that the L-shaped space now makes very little sense, but it is an interior whose oddity grows on you.

Isolated just a mile further W is the little church at CHALBURY, with a delightfully classicized interior. In place of a chancel screen is something like a Venetian window, supported by four slender columns. Linked to the pulpit and squire's pew, it makes spatial mysteries under a simple barrel vault.

* It seems this odd memorial by Comper is the result of an accident. Formerly a cross of Lorraine standing atop a shaft, it fell down and shattered. Only the tip was saved and placed directly on the base. Hence the present enigmatic form.

Dorset: Wimborne St Giles lies 10 miles N of Wimborne Minster, 1 mile W of B3078

Winterborne Tomson

St Andrew (CCT)

A precious relic of rustic faith.

This one-celled Norman building with its round apse sits next to a cowshed, and you may find yourself staring into the animals' eyes as you turn the corner. It has beautiful wooden fittings grey with age, including pews like pens or corrals of differing size. The most satisfying feature is the ribbed vault in the apse with twisted bosses at the intersections. A late Gothic font, half obscured by whitewash, looks like a garden ornament.

A sale of Hardy manuscripts paid for the loving restoration in 1931 (the church was a favourite of the novelist's, as a charming plaque recalls).

A. R. Powys, the restorer, who died that same year, is buried in the churchyard.

Dorset: 9 miles W of Wimborne Minster, ½ mile N of A31: take turning marked Anderson, bear R at T-junction; church in farmyard 100 yds or so further on

Winterborne Tomson. Simple building in a farmyard that Hardy loved

Cotswolds

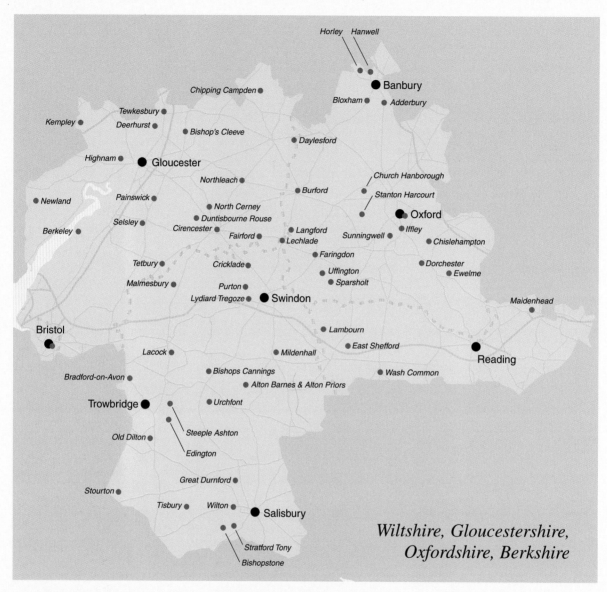

Horley Hanwell

● Banbury

Chipping Campden ●

Bloxham ●   ● Adderbury

Tewkesbury ●

Kempley ●   Deerhurst ●

● Bishop's Cleeve

● Daylesford

Highnam ●   ● Gloucester

Northleach ●   Church Hanborough

● Burford   Stanton Harcourt

Newland ●   Painswick ●

● North Cerney   ● Oxford

Selsley ●   ● Duntisbourne Rouse   ● Iffley

Berkeley ●   Cirencester ●   ● Langford   Sunningwell ●   ● Chislehampton

Fairford ●   Lechlade ●

● Faringdon

Tetbury ●   Cricklade ●   ● Dorchester

● Ewelme

Malmesbury ●   Purton ●   Uffington ●   ● Sparsholt

Lydiard Tregoze ●   ● Swindon   Maidenhead ●

Bristol ●   ● Lambourn

Lacock ●   ● Mildenhall   ● East Shefford   ● Reading

Bradford-on-Avon ●   ● Bishops Cannings   ● Wash Common

● Alton Barnes & Alton Priors

Trowbridge ●   ● Urchfont

Old Dilton ●   Steeple Ashton

Edington

Great Durnford ●

Stourton ●

Tisbury ●   Wilton ●   ● Salisbury

Stratford Tony

Bishopstone

Wiltshire, Gloucestershire,
Oxfordshire, Berkshire

EVEN IN VICTORIAN TIMES, when discovered by the Arts and Crafts movement, the Cotswolds were somewhat remote and inaccessible. Village life seemed suspended in time there, shut off from the modern world. As hills the Cotswolds are small beer, but there is a bare upland feel about the farms. These modest hills produce some of the best building stone in England, and the villages remain among the mellowest in the whole country.

In Gloucestershire and Oxfordshire the highest reaches of late Gothic village architecture occur in slightly different tones of golden stone. Cirencester, Burford, Northleach, and Chipping Campden are the grandest. There's at least one other type of Cotswold church, modest and unrestored, of which many remain in the tiny valleys north of Cirencester. Following the vein of gold stone in a north-east direction we come to a fascinating group of churches around Banbury with lively 14c carving. The same trajectory leads eventually to Stamford and the fine churches around Peterborough.

Wiltshire lies for the most part outside the spell of the golden stone, but enjoys the richest compensation. Its vast chalk downs are some of the most stirring spaces in southern Britain and convey a grander scale, geological and historical, than almost anywhere else this side of Yorkshire. Neither churches nor settlements have made much impression on this landscape, which remains basically prehistoric.

South and west of the downland are small-scale valleys dotted with interesting churches. The last of these is the Thames, and with Berkshire we are approaching London. Parts of this county are the first regions we meet where the good churches are mainly Victorian.

Adderbury

St Mary

In a gorgeous village of toast-coloured stone, a large church with a notable wealth of carving by the 14c North Oxfordshire school.

It sits raised up in its ovoid churchyard full of yews and good headstones. First, you come to the high chancel with huge gargoyles. After this, the great feature of the church: a lively row of corbels along the top of both aisles, including twisted folk with big faces who ring bells or drag horses. They're all plump, but the most plastic is a knotted dragon. On the N the exaggeration goes furthest, to the point of nightmare – what silent howls are here!

Inside, arcades of a lovely honey colour. Interesting capitals divide the transepts from the aisles – knights linking arms on one side, ladies in wimples on the other.

Oxon: 4 miles S of Banbury at junction of A4260 and B4100; church to W

Alton Priors

All Saints (CCT)

Alton Barnes

St Mary

Two simple buildings in delicious situations.

Alton Priors sits in a field half veiled by scrubby growth. Its tower is a soft grey colour and looks French. You pass the brick chancel whose clear glass gives easy views in, and enter an empty barn-like space in which the ancient chancel arch is off centre.

In the E a remarkable allegorical brass of 1590 shows someone seen from behind climbing out of a tomb towards a heaven full of words and stars.

The path between the two churches is magical: loosely laid stone setts cross a nettle-choked stream and wind towards a Saxon chapel visible a long way off.

At *Alton Barnes* is another brick chancel, notable long and short work, and an 18c tomb mounted high on the W wall.

Inside, there's a steep barn roof and much old wood, especially the W gallery, one bench of which cranes over the stair coming up until it almost hits the window.

Wilts: midway between Marlborough and Devizes, also midway between A4 and A342; Barnes church lies 200 yds SW of Priors

Alton Priors, a simple building whose tower looks French

Berkeley

St Mary

One of the most atmospheric churches in the county, mainly Early English on a grand scale.

Both approaches are wonderful in their own ways. Coming from N, you pass the detached tower and enter a vast, crowded graveyard with table tombs of later vintage than Painswick nearby (note especially an ovoid type with facet-sides). The aisle facing you is very low and mottled in texture. Simple harmonious three-light windows.

Alton Barnes, separated from Alton Priors by a magical path through a stream

Coming from W, the impression is grander, but still raffish: undressed aisles in red-purple sandstone frame the majestic W end, an Early English display of five lancets over three arches.

Inside, the Early English arcade is gorgeous and varied. Note a capital undercut until it is like a hairnet. Some 13c decorative painting, amplified by the Victorians, has fallen into wholesome decay. An open stone screen looms in the darkness, and a lady on a tomb in the nave wears a headdress like a pliable loofah.

The most complex ruffs adorn the dead in the Berkeley Chapel, inaccessible behind glass to the S. High in NW corner of nave, a fascinating fragment: the underside of a curved stair with a face on each riser.

The church stands next to the more famous castle, in a pleasing brick town. Surrounding landscape quite bizarre, flat tracts above the Severn.

Glos: 16 miles SW of Gloucester, 1½ miles W of A38, town now bypassed by B4066; church is in SE corner in an obscure location

Bishops Cannings

St Mary the Virgin

A church of astonishing scale for a small village, at the bottom of a Downs slope near Wansdyke, with a magnificent tower and stone spire.

It sits in a very large churchyard, like a common. The tower is Early English, and its simple lancets have strong roll mouldings. The design conveys the sort of force and discretion which make later Gothic feel trivial.

The S porch has a lovely, unorthodox arch, lots of broken lace, and best of all, a hollow mouchette in the gable. Maybe this excess (and the overall shape) prompted the rumour that this porch-front is a re-used tomb.

After this, the interior is a disappointment with its harshly scraped walls; but there are some lovely capitals ringed in sea-plant ruffles, and rich stranded arches in S transept.

The strange 17c penitential chair has a large Hand of Meditation painted on its high back. All the fingers and the lobes of the palm are labelled with banners reminding us of our final end. Apparently, sitting in it was a voluntary ordeal, not an imposed punishment.

Wilts: 3 miles NE of Devizes, E of A361

Bishops Cannings, an Early English tower on an ambitious church in a small Downland village

the blind arcades in this porch, interlaced (Norman), with trefoil tops (early Gothic).

At the W front, a forceful turreted design and another rich doorway. Here a dragon is kept in place by fleur-de-lys clasps. The last doorway to look at is the priest's in the chancel, a beautiful display of ballflower.

The interior shows the effects of all the various stages of growth: the space is somewhat chopped up, with transepts walled off. There's a massive 17c wooden gallery with rough classical details, and an aggressive Jacobean monument which has pulled an earlier effigy into its iron-railed compound.

Two notable eccentricities at Bishop's Cleeve: a ghoulish rood painting above the tower arch, by P. J. Crook, 1986, and a local schoolmaster's murals above the S porch, including a tiger and a battle with elephants.

Glos: 3 miles N of Cheltenham on A435; church lies to E of road

Bishop's Cleeve
St Michael & All Angels

A large Norman church encased in Perpendicular aisles like a prisoner. The large central tower is a 17c replacement.

It was from early times a manor of the Bishops of Worcester, which explains the

grand scale. The Norman parts are the grandest and have been more overlaid than defaced. A magnificent S porch is now almost hidden in the clasping embrace of the later aisle. The inner doorway is the most lavish, with two large dragons whose backs look like Eastern metalwork. Most satisfying are

Bishopstone
St John Baptist

An eccentric building with Decorated features remarkable in a church of its size.

The textures which greet the visitor are very pleasant, but one must walk around to the SE to appreciate how extraordinary this building is. On the end of the transept a low porch that holds a tomb has been attached. Further E is a curious priest's door. There are lozenges above windows and frilly panels on the parapets.

Inside, the nave is pleasantly simple and the chancel full of unexpected touches, including lavish vaults and sedilia with a forest of hefty pinnacles in different registers. Sides of the three chairs are pierced. Against the S transept wall lies an elaborate Pugin tomb. The diagonal piscina here might be his idea too.

The pulpit is a startling confection uniting high-class woodwork from at least three different centuries. The central panel displays a very Baroque *Noli me tangere*.

Wilts: 5 miles SW of Salisbury, 1½ miles W of A354; church is 1 mile E of Bishopstone village, near Throope Manor House, S of an unnumbered road which follows the River Ebble

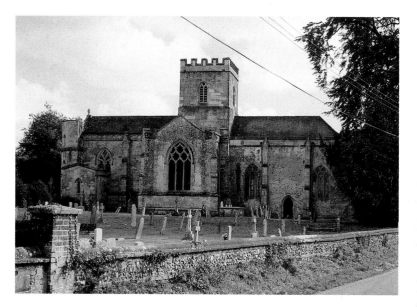

Bishopstone. A mellow building with ambitious Decorated features

Bloxham

St Mary

Less fortunate than Adderbury in its position (its W front practically in the road) but very rewarding for sculptures of the North Oxfordshire school. Some of these are hard to see (folkish scenes high on the tower), but not the earlier decoration around W doorframe: charming rows of birds, flowers and nuts.

Inside, a later SE chapel has enormous windows with free-standing cusps in the sills (also outside). Here an 18c gent lounges on books.

On many of the walls, enigmatic paintings, and in the E window William Morris glass of 1869 shows paired figures on blue grounds.

Oxon: 4 miles S of Banbury on A361

Bradford-on-Avon

St Laurence

This exceedingly beautiful small town contains one of the most evocative and complete Anglo-Saxon churches.

Gorgeous colours of stone, interesting terrain, and mellow signs of early industry make Bradford one of the most wonderful places in the Cotswolds, though ravaged by traffic.

At first it seems a mystery that a Saxon chapel survives intact next to the medieval parish church. Here is the explanation: it lay dormant for centuries – undetected, and thus untampered with – because it had been so thoroughly incorporated in a set of farm buildings.

Internally it was subdivided to provide two separate dwellings and a school. The blind arcades which run right round the exterior must have been obscured from most sides. Domestic windows had been inserted in the walls. It was Canon Jones, vicar of Holy Trinity opposite, who began to suspect around 1856 that an important relic lay hidden there. An apocryphal story has him paying a visit higher up the hill; he happened to look down on St Laurence and knew it for what it was. Another version has the crucial illumination hitting him in the Bodleian Library, where references in William of Malmesbury suddenly made sense. In any case, he masterminded the building's purchase (in 1871) and restoration.

St Laurence's proportions are striking – very high and narrow, hardly windowed at all. Internally, spaces are divided by tall doorways which give a

Bloxham, with a handsome spire and a wealth of exterior carving

sensation of squeezing through. Where the huge, worn framing-blocks survive they are extremely moving. The only internal decoration is two hovering angels on the wall many feet above eye level. The rood which stood between them has long since disappeared.

Some beautiful pattern in relief has been made into an altar in the chancel. Formerly a S porch matched the N one: its roofline is etched on the wall. Presumably then four nearly equal spaces made up the whole; there remains something enchantingly literal-minded about this plan.

Wilts: 8 miles E of Bath on A363; St Laurence lies N of parish church, N of river and W of town centre

Burford

St John Baptist

An outstanding Cotswold church in one of the best Cotswold towns.

Unlike the others, Burford is not a uniform Perpendicular remodelling, but something more inconsistent and interesting. It lies off to one side of the long High Street which plunges and then tapers down to the river.

The rich and confused impression will only be sorted out when you have gone inside, or maybe not even then: you need to know, for instance, that the vast SW chapel, built by the Merchants' Guild, used to stand apart in the churchyard, until it was hooked to the main body in the late 15c. The interior is full of such

Burford, the variegated composition of an outstanding Cotswold church

Chipping Campden

St James

One of the most imposing Cotswold wool churches in a small town many regard as the most perfect in England.

Various causes converge to make Chipping Campden a privileged place – plentiful supplies of building stone which weathers to rich gold, and a conservative building tradition which makes everything look like part of a 16 or 17c Oxford college. A walk down this gently bending High Street is one of the pleasantest in Europe.

The church lies off to the side, past old almshouses and next to the gatehouses of Sir Baptist Hicks' vanished mansion, burnt in the Civil War. St James's tower is sensational, the colour of light wheat, with stringy buttresses one of which becomes detached passing over the W window.

There is not much sculptural ornament inside or out. It is one of those late Gothic buildings which depend on scale and proportion, not detail. The arcade is amazingly high and its piers of an exaggerated concavity. The capitals with their sharp points are like something Borromini might invent.

This town is one of the shrines of the Arts and Crafts movement. C. R. Ashbee moved his Guild of Handicrafts here from Whitechapel in 1902, and it lingered on until quite recently. But the church doesn't possess the rich fittings and tombs of c1900 one might have hoped for. The nearest it comes is the E window of 1925 by Henry Payne, like a smouldering jewel of Art Nouveau. The nave becomes miraculously transparent in a window by Hardman over the chancel arch.

There are good earlier tombs, but the showiest, of the Hicks family, are frankly grotesque, in black and white marble. Sir Baptist and his wife are lying down; his daughter and son-in-law stand up in their shrouds and lean out of a cabinet with doors swung open.

Glos: 10 miles SE of Evesham on B4801; church E of High Street near its N end

Chislehampton

St Katherine (CCT)

A tiny 18c building right beside the road between a farm and the big house, with its own stone gateposts that make it a miniature world.

An airy wooden cupola sits on an oddly broken pediment at the W end,

---

anomalies which branch unexpectedly and revise our sense of the whole.

The core is Norman, and the strangest remnant of this is a crude carving stranded high on the S wall of the central tower. If this were not spotlit, you would never see it.

Late 16 and 17c tombs make a wonderful series. In SW corner a wall tablet whose two herms have leaves at their waists. On N wall a tablet with Brazilian Indians, thought to be the first intrusion of the New World into such a setting. In a railed and screened NE chapel a huge canopied tomb with lovely little statues of the Virtues.

At Burford 19 and 20c contributions tend to be rich and somewhat effete, like the large painting over the chancel arch by Clayton & Bell, and Christopher Whall's window in the S transept, pale greeny colours with briars, a dragon and flowers.

Burford churchyard is wonderful, framed by a stream on two sides and full of 'bale' tombs (a ridged half-cylinder with shells at the ends, on top of a table tomb). The eccentric novelist John Meade Falkner, a lover of the church, lies as far from it as you can get, to the E.

Oxon: 22 miles W of Oxford on A361

stone urns at the corners, and a lead urn on the E peak of roof. One enters under the W gallery (precipitous view from it, like a map) to a space lit only from the S. Pleasant segmental vault, very complete woodwork including reredos with skinny garlands and decalogue etc, twirly altar rails and railed enclosures for communicants like animal pens.

A lovely early Victorian marble monument on E wall, with garland of carved passion flowers, on which the name, Katherine, is the same one cut into the eccentric weathervane outside.

Oxon: 6 miles SE of Oxford on B480; church N of village on E side of road

Chislehampton. Well preserved rustic classicism

Bristol

St Mary Redcliffe

Bristol has one of the largest and most ambitious of all parish churches and some notable early Dissenting chapels.

St Mary Redcliffe makes a staggeringly rich impression. The tall late Gothic clerestory looks like another building perched on top. Its N porch is one of the most compelling works of the 14c, hexagonal in plan, with extraordinary features.

The door-opening resembles a mouth hung with seaweed, and the windows, hardly visible outside, make a ring of shadowy eyes or Gaudi-teardrops. Borders inside and out are so deeply cut that little spaces where creatures lurk arise within. The S porch, marginally later and much less elaborate, sports remarkable cusps around the entrances.

Inside, wonderful ribbing in the vaults – rectilinear in chancel, fractured in nave, and violently cusped throughout. The last bay of N aisle before transept has bosses with tracery studies and a little maze. It is said that the church contains 1200 different ceiling bosses. There is a series of recesses in the S aisle wall from the same wild imagination as the porch; they suggest large stars or snowflakes of which they sketch only three rays.

St Mary's immediate surroundings have become a wasteland of highways, so that you must consult old prints to guess what the original neighbourhood was like.

Across the floating harbour in the city centre, *St Stephen* has a remarkable tower with transparent battlements corbelled out like vanes at the corners, a startling effect. Passing under a miniature fan vault, you come into a large late Gothic space with interesting merchants' monuments. More of these in *St Mark's*, College Green, opposite the Cathedral. The oldest Methodist chapel in the world, the *New Room*, Horsefair, is a large tranquil cube with much white woodwork and blue-green walls. The octagonal lightwell which transfigures the space also functioned as a spy-hole for John Wesley watching his novice preachers from the living rooms above. The Room is still set back as it always was, in its own hidden courts, but now the world beyond is a late 1940s shopping precinct, not the 18c city.

Frenchay Chapel, Unitarian of 1720 (Beckspool Road, BS12, near exit 1 of M32), a diminutive redstone structure like a Scots kirk or a farm building, sits in a little yard beside a charming green, sparsely ringed by an odd collection of Georgian houses.

Glos: on S side of Severn estuary, 115 miles from London; St Mary just across floating harbour S of city centre on Redcliffe Hill

Church Hanborough

St Peter & St Paul

Isolation and precious remnants of widely different periods make this memorable.

An elegant spire, a secluded churchyard and, in it, an old quatrefoil tombchest, always more interesting when left to weather outside like this. On the way to the entrance under the tower, we pass a friendly early Norman doorway with its picture made of raised ridges like an outline drawing.

Inside are gorgeous screens with old coving and three different types of tracery and in one chapel very charming remnants of white roses on a rust ground – painted patterns which once covered more of the wall.

On the other side some modern work – a sub-Eric Gill reredos and a window of 1950 with a cat at the bottom.

Oxon: about 8 miles NW of Oxford on unnumbered road which runs between A40 and A4095

Cirencester

St John the Baptist

One of the greatest English parish churches in one of the most attractive Cotswold towns.

The church with its golden tower verges on the pleasant market place. At times the effect was more crowded: various intruders against its W walls have been removed. Nothing else like the S porch exists. From some vantage points it seems a separate building, three storeys high and three bays wide. It is latest Gothic, panelled all over in a way that dematerializes it. Like the nave and aisles, it is crowned by openwork pinnacles and emaciated battlements, which have finally lost all strength. Standing just beneath, you see tier on tier rising above you, a dazzling flicker of stone and light.

Under the porch, many bosses. The porch was built by the Abbey to house its business affairs and to keep the king's inspectors outside its precincts. Later it became the Town Hall, and a peculiar 17c entrance on the right dates from that time.

Daylesford, a vigorous early Victorian gem by Pearson

The interior is one of the best late Perpendicular spaces: very high, under rich dark roofs. Time-stained walls are very eloquent. The space branches out into grand side chapels added at various times. One, crushed between chancel and N aisle, has a gorgeous fan vault. The stone pulpit is an indoor version of papery battlements.

Plentiful old glass, but two bits stand out: the great E window and a S one with large figures. The sad fate of other glass is well recounted by W. I. Croome in a leaflet sold here. The guidebook is also instructive on how the more garish effects of Victorian restoration have been undone.

Glos: 20 miles SE of Gloucester on A417

Church Hanborough. An elegant spire, a secluded churchyard and beautiful screens within

Cricklade

St Sampson

Cricklade has an overpowering late Gothic tower and some strange 20c furnishings.

The corner pinnacles form towers in themselves and the effect is breathtaking from both far and near. The upper stage remains virtually windowless and is panelled all over. The space underneath it is magnificent. Its heraldic decoration includes the intriguing motif of a flag stuck in a plump heart.

Several windows by Martin Travers, like watercolours. But his most perplexing contribution is a reredos with young angels straight off a greetings card. He did another simpler one to the S.

Many bits of original window tracery. The large and tranquil churchyard contains an almost complete medieval cross.

Wilts: 7 miles NW of Swindon on A419; Cricklade now lies W of road, and church is W of High Street

Daylesford

St Peter

J. L. Pearson

A surprising early Pearson church, designed 1857–9, which is more vigorous and expressive than the work he is generally known for.

It is small but lavish. The massive central tower pulls the short transepts and chancel towards itself; inside, a feeling of intense concentration with spaces diverging in three directions. Transepts have wooden roofs of different heights and types, while the chancel is stone-vaulted. Only around E windows does Pearson go too far: they have Moorish cusping inside and carved birds and flowers outside which would be more at home in a French boudoir. The stained glass, by Clayton & Bell (except E and W windows by Wailes), is one of the very best Victorian ensembles – clear narratives on white, blue or red grounds. There are dozens of lively scenes to inspect.

Visible from Daylesford to the W is the charming rustic church of St Nicholas at ODDINGTON, across the Evenlode. It has a marvellous 14c Doom painting covering the whole N wall. There are also a frescoed royal arms (William IV) in carnival colours, and some nice green tendrils on the arcade, which has rudimentary composite columns: large cylinders with four little colonnettes attached.

Three miles further on (to the S) is BLEDINGTON, with two storeys of Perpendicular windows staggered along its N side, containing lovely old glass in the mildest colours. There are some lavish bits of carving on the other side of the church, and the immediate surroundings are delightful.

Glos: Daylesford is 4 miles E of Stow-on-the-Wold, just S of A436

Deerhurst

Priory of St Mary

Some of the most important Anglo-Saxon remains peek forth from later fabric, making fascinating archaeological puzzles.

Deerhurst was the site of an important monastery which flourished for several hundred years until demoted in early Norman times. The name means 'forest of wild beasts', and it is a building instinct with animal life, notably a series of carved heads. The most moving of these stretches out above the tower entrance like a battered old tortoise gasping for air. At the next stage above is a stone prong like an even more featureless face. Inside, are further fiercer beasts.

The most famous Saxon relics here are the sharply peaked window openings. For some reason these are powerfully evocative of a benighted, hence half-conscious, cruelty.

Nave walls are rich in later herringbone masonry, and outside at the E are remnants of a vanished apse. A carved angel is stuck high up in this wall. If you get as far as the E end you aren't likely to miss it: five signs with arrows point towards it.

Inside, the W end gives a powerful sensation of tall, narrow Saxon space. The font is one of the very best of its period, with repeated coils like metalwork.

From later centuries there are beautiful Early English arcades in green and white stone, old glass, especially a St Catherine, and lovely Puritanical woodwork in the chancel.

Another (late) Saxon building nearby, *Odda's Chapel*, was discovered in 1885 immured in the house to which it is still attached. Odda was a kinsman of Edward the Confessor and built this chapel to his brother's memory. The important inscription which identifies the building had been found in the orchard long before and removed to Oxford.

The chapel is a fairly unfeatured space, except for two small, deeply splayed windows. Low ground here is liable to flooding, and these two nearly adjacent Saxon buildings are sometimes cut off from each other.

Glos: 4 miles SW of Tewkesbury to W of A38 and N of B4213

Dorchester

Abbey of St Peter & St Paul

Dorchester is centred on a very pleasant curving street. Coming to the Abbey the visitor inevitably gravitates to the E end, where some of the most original medieval features in England are found. From outside, the tracery looks Gothick at first. There is a deep arcade under the S chancel window with a tiny window in each hooded bay. In N chancel, willowy rivulets of stone run across the glass.

After a good porch and many-moulded door, the interior is a disappointment, messy and vast, forming a prologue to the staggering chancel.

From inside, seen rakingly, the N side looks like a forest – the effect of a Jesse window whose branching stone tracery is inhabited by sculpted figures, which one can't usually examine head-on because of glare from the glass on

Anglo-Saxon Deerhurst, the haunt of carved beasts

either side. In each coloured panel is a further figure, and the play between carving and painting, forming a single story, is unlike any other treatment of this theme.

The great E window, bisected by a shallow buttress, contains many scenes in early glass, presided over by a starflower inserted by Butterfield c1850. The S side vies with the N in originality. Here are four canopies whose 14c stone decoration again verges on Gothick, made raffish by the unheard-of little windows hidden under the gables which are not visible until one approaches reasonably near.

In the S chapel are found the twisted effigy of a knight c1280 and the shrine of St Birinus like a tall gabled building. Further W is a lead font with Apostles.

Notable small Roman Catholic church of *St Birinus* (1849) in Bridge End.

Oxon: 9 miles SE of Oxford just W of A423; church on E side of village street

Duntisbourne Rouse

St Michael

A charming miniature building in a lovely situation.

It lies in a tiny valley tucked just over a ridge on falling ground, which allows for a little crypt under the chancel. A grassy path leads towards the cross-wise tower, half hidden by the slope and effacing itself in the nave. Its Norman slit windows are like half-closed eyes. Herringbone masonry forms flow patterns in the N wall.

The chancel arch with round mouldings is pleasantly off centre. Old painted patterns on chancel wall, and old pews. The font is a rustic Early English piece with lively leaf-sprigs.

In the churchyard stands a slender medieval cross, nearly complete.

Glos: 4 miles NW of Cirencester on unnumbered road just to W of A417; church on E side of road

East Shefford

St Thomas (CCT)

A tiny building between two farms which preserves a surprising wealth of painting and carving.

The road which follows the course of the River Lambourn is probably the most delightful in the county. In the right season the almost overflowing river passes near and seemingly under some of the oldest buildings along the way. Coming from Lambourn, one crosses and re-crosses the stream, and finally sees, in its fenced yard with a cedar and a beech, this humble building of weatherboard, tile, brick and plaster.

Inside are fragments of wall painting, among the oldest in the country: double axes (a decorative motif) and bits of kings. A huge later IHS pattern makes a commanding splash. Lovely old tiles and good modern replacements, 18c cartouches which are imitated in the inscription for a man who died in 1979.

Duntisbourne Rouse. Charming rusticity in a Cotswold valley

The highlight, off to one side, is an alabaster tomb with headless angels who wave pronged wings. It dates from c1450 and has suffered many vicissitudes.

The recovery of this church makes a fascinating story (in the splendid guide sold on the premises). E. S. Prior gave detailed advice on the repair of tomb and fabric. The Friends of Friendless Churches played an essential role, and the building has finally reached safe harbour in the Churches Conservation Trust. To a sympathetic reader, the complicated rescue is as exciting as any thriller.

Berks: 5 miles SE of Lambourn, ½ mile E of Great Shefford, reached by a N turning from road to Welford; church lies SE of East Shefford House

East Shefford. Enchanted rusticity beside the River Lambourn

Edington

St Mary, St Katharine & All Saints

A magnificent building of 1352–61, which may appear a little austere at first.

It was built by William of Edington, a local son who rose to become Chancellor of England and Bishop of Winchester. He established a monastery here whose character remains obscure.

A powerful silhouette, somewhat blockish, as if it were an early Braque townscape. There isn't much decoration here, except for three stair turrets which all point the same way (SW) and a three-storey S porch. The mouse or dun colour of the stone grows on you.

Inside, roofs and floors are outstanding. Gothic survival tracery in nave, fan vault in crossing (these picked out in mellow rose), spidery Gothick in chancel; most of the floors a refined stone lattice with tiny black marble highlights.

Passing some interesting tombs and glass and great ancient timbers in the screen, make for the chancel where there is memorable carved decoration. Niches mostly empty, but under them exquisitely graceful figures.

Among the tombs one by Sir Francis Chantrey, neo-classical but full of swooning sentiment, where a man is mourned by two females, probably allegorical as he was a bachelor. There's a wooden cherub sailing down under the heavy canopy opposite. In the transept is a gaily coloured monk's tomb peppered with sprouting barrels; and in the nave this piece of folk art – a row of kneeling

figures such as one finds on Jacobean monuments, except that these are rustic portraits in early 19c dress, looking like the assembled servants from some novel of the provinces.

The 17c poet, George Herbert, was married here.

Wilts: between Westbury and Devizes just N of B3098

Ewelme

St Mary

Of relatively modest dimensions, but with some of the richest textures and fittings of any English parish church.

It forms a wonderful group with almshouses and school endowed at the

Edington, built in one go, the resulting silhouette like 'an early Braque townscape'

same time and connected to it by a stair passage. The other buildings lie further down a pronounced slope, and the unexpected twist in the axis as one climbs into the church is enchanting. The complex was built in the mid 15c by the poet Chaucer's granddaughter and her second husband the Duke of Suffolk. It owes its preservation through the Civil War to a local Puritan landowner.

Its battlements are mellow brick, its walls flint and stone, banded in the aisles, chequered in the chancel. A nice patch of soapy whiter stone in clerestory to the W.

Inside, the font cover is a towering miracle of late Gothic woodwork with St Michael, feathered all over, on top. Above him on the hoist, a large Tudor rose, and pressing in from behind, the long stone face of a king.

The chancel lies behind old grayey screens, and the E wall is gorgeously dappled by IHS monograms, large and small, red and green. An even more enveloping effect of the same kind is repeated in S chapel. Here we find the Duchess's (Chaucer's granddaughter's) tomb, which fills an arch between chapel and chancel and is one of the best in England of its date. It continues onto the wall in borders of rich panelling and terminates in eight wooden figures on stone spindles. Beneath the effigy – with its canopy and attending angels perfectly intact – in a low recess lies an emaciated alabaster carcase, a second rendition of

Faringdon in its large churchyard above an extremely pleasant small town

The first window is full of trees. The Old Testament soon left behind, disaster again fires the designer's imagination; Christ's Descent into Limbo is a highlight. Not many scenes are mysterious, but a guidebook explains them well.

All the misericords are helpfully turned up and include domestic chores and strife. The fox with a goose in his mouth is particularly fine.

Glos: about 10 miles E of Cirencester on A417

Faringdon

All Saints

An extremely pleasant small town whose triangular market has two foci, a fancy 18c lamp standard and a market hall on stilts.

The church lies above this space in a large churchyard, its central tower comically squat. On the S door a wonderful display of ironwork; many of its loops have beast-head termini.

Inside, the arcade is glorious – bulky columns with prim leaf-capitals; delicate mouldings in arches which are yet comfortably round. It hovers unanxiously between Romanesque and the next stage. The central tower-arch, by contrast, is strongly pointed.

A fine congestion of tombs in the Unton Chapel to the N. Especially notable is the kneeling alabaster woman in a bulging headdress like a sea skate,

the deceased. She looks up at frescoes on the underside of her tombchest which only she can see.

On the other wall of the chancel, an amazing 17c monument shows the dead man emerging halfway from a bulgy urn helped by two lifting angels.

Oxon: between Wallingford and Watlington, S of B4009, an obscure location

Fairford

St Mary

Fairford has the most complete set of late medieval glass in any parish church.

The large churchyard fills part of the wide and pleasant main street. The church is a good example of Cotswold Perpendicular, with an impressive central tower. Its details are somehow blockish, as if fashioned from Cornwall granite. Halfway up are wonderfully wide-eyed grotesques. There is also a gargoyle centred over each window.

Once inside, we only have eyes for the glass, twenty-eight windows of it, the few gaps due to freak storms, not the usual malice or neglect. They were hidden in the Commonwealth and again in 1939–45. Recently they have been cleaned and covered outside with protective layers of clear glass.

The colours are weak mostly, at least from any distance. In the aisles and clerestory, large single figures. The

narrative sequence begins eastwards on the N side, but it is natural to pause at the huge W window on the way. This shows the Last Judgment, with Christ in glory at the top surrounded by ring after ring of minions. That part is all restoration. Below, and unrestored, lies a smouldering hell full of red, purple and blue horrors, with the more fortunate dead on the left.

In the smaller windows, each lancet is ordinarily a separate scene, so you cannot read them across these borders.

Great Durnford, where mixed materials combine gracefully

Hanwell where 'complex and insistent' carving decorates the arcade

who has strayed from a nearby monument onto the floor.

Berks/Oxon: 12 miles NE of Swindon on A420

Great Durnford

St Andrew

In a lovely situation, a medley of unspoiled textures and materials.

Though not far from Salisbury, this place feels very secluded next to its overflowing stream. Flint fabric with greensand buttresses, patchy plaster, then a brick porch, tiled – in other words a record of accretion which isn't random but isn't really co-ordinated either.

Inside the porch a Norman tympanum made simply of diagonal chequer in two sorts of stone, with weird faces at the springing.

Indoors, much wall painting – red patterns and a few scenes. A charming mixture of window types, and of old and oldish benches. The Norman font is ringed by tiny columns whose capitals look like big-eyed faces, the whole effect like rich embroidery. On the pulpit a green velvet cushion and fringed bath towel survive from the 17c.

Wilts: 5½ miles N of Salisbury, W of A345

Hanwell

St Peter

Perhaps the most enjoyable of all North Oxfordshire carving adorns this tiny church.

Its situation is delightful, high above the impressive remnant of a large Tudor tower-house in brick. The bumpy churchyard, like a farm field, is dotted with cherry trees, and its tombstones are overgrown with ivy.

The two corbel tables at the E end are not directly accessible from each other because of the terrain. These are the most satisfying of their kind, because

nearer to the eye and still bearing traces of whitewash. Here we see clearly that the postures are determined by the size of the stone the carvers start with. Each figure fills its stone; most are stretched out, if not literally prone. They carry vases, wave sticks and thrust shields. Again the dragon with knotted tail, the mermaid and a sprinkling of flowers.

The textures of the interior are wonderful and the whole effect of a lovely dishevelment. Decorating the arcade, complex and insistent carving. Four great columns with crouching entwined figures on the capitals. On one side smaller musicians sit in the space where normally the mouldings would meet. On the other, large heads take this place.

There is a Norman font, a good space under the tower, and a table tomb of 1693 with fat cornucopias in relief.

Oxon: about 3 miles NW of Banbury, just E of B4100 (formerly A41)

Highnam. A lavish Victorian church by Woodyer with magically slender spire

Highnam

Holy Innocents

Henry Woodyer

A lavish High Victorian church, Woodyer's first independent work, set in parkland.

The best view comes approaching from the NE, and most of the excitement is made by vestries in a jumble of forms and materials, including wooden dormers, turrets and chimneys. The spire looks magically slender from afar and on its lower stages sports many knobbly pinnacles.

Highnam is most remarkable for the richness of its interior. Despite an especially tall and narrow nave, this effect is created mainly by painted patterns, not architecture. Many of these were applied by Thomas Gambier-Parry, the client, who had invented a spirit fresco technique which makes for dusky richness. The whole space above the chancel arch is filled with a big Last Judgment.

Chancel walls resemble a dissected oriental carpet. Multiple chamfers in arches and window openings are each painted with different patterns. Excessive heights of ornament are reached at the entry to S chapel and around the font whose elongated thinness echoes the spire.

Woodyer also designed the old rectory, school and lodge-house, all to the N, for Gambier-Parry. Only five miles W at St John Baptist, HUNTLEY, **S. S. Teulon** rivalled Woodyer. The two-tone exterior in white and red stones has a strange tracery-carving on the S transept. This interior is Teulon's richest, with dramas to rival Burges.

Glos: about 3 miles W of Gloucester just N of A40, in grounds of Highnam Court, parking by village hall; church lies to SE

Horley

St Etheldreda

A church of very pleasing texture harmoniously embellished in the mid 20c.

It is known for its wall paintings of which the best is a huge, fresh St Christopher with a bold braided border and two fishermen fishing the stream the saint fords, their lines crossing in front of his legs.

In 1950 Lawrence Dale took his cue from the cartoon-like force of this image, and added a rood of Expressionist character with figures in blue, red and green (St John is said to be a likeness of the architect). Also a pulpit with primitivist scenes from the patron saint's life. There are 'moderne' light fittings and an Eric Gill-like relief of the Entombment by Edmund Ware. The overall effect is to wake the church to life. Exquisite bits of old glass, the rude Norman space under the central tower, and a lovely household organ count even more in the presence of recent artistic energy.

The church is pleasingly mounded above the road and set at the top of its attractive, isolated village.

Oxon: about 4 miles NW of Banbury, ⅔ mile W of B4100 (formerly A41)

Iffley

St Mary the Virgin

Norman, one of the most lavish of its size and date in the whole country.

Surrounded by old trees and houses, Iffley church lies in a little pocket of antiquity which feels centuries away from the bustle of Oxford. The W front is an impressive tripartite composition, though the central rose window is entirely restoration (as 19c drawings show). The main portal makes one of the greatest displays of beakhead ever – two fat rows of menacing creatures, then zigzag, and finally at the outside edge, lots of Zodiac signs.

There's also a spectacular S door, whose capitals are filled with minute scenes. On one a centaur suckles another and they float as if under water. Along this same side, interestingly awkward later windows.

Inside, after rich tower arches, you enter a chancel which offers a riot of massive toothy mouldings marking out every opening and the four ribs of the vault.

Oxon: within Oxford ring road, SE of city centre; church lies W of Iffley Road (A4158) at end of Church Way

Kempley

St Edward the Confessor, St Mary

This small and remote place has two extraordinary churches, a freakish Arts and Crafts work of 1903 and the old one with some of the best Romanesque painting in England.

The church of *St Edward the Confessor* was built by **Randall Wells**, who had worked with Lethaby at Brockhampton nearby. But if Brockhampton is mellow, Kempley is stark and aggressively rustic. Its enormous tile roof (originally large stone slates) descends to meet heavy buttresses on a windowless S wall. At the W end you find a huge clear window with criss-cross tracery, looking as if it has been rotated forty-five degrees.

Inside, effects are stark and somehow Tyrolean in flavour. The country round about is not mountainous, of course, nor is it nautical, yet the rood sculptures look much like ship figureheads. Very good glass in N chapel with Dürer ladies in starched bonnets. Notable furniture by Gimson and Ernest Barnsley but, all in all, a case of misplaced peasant style.

St Mary's, down obscure lanes, has a modest square tower with no way into it, a Norman tympanum blocked by its old wooden porch, and knights with plumes painted on nave walls. The highlight is a chancel covered in early 12c paintings, Christ at the centre surrounded by beasts and cherubim, and down below, two ranks of Apostles looking up at the vision, just as we are doing. Unlike Copford (in Essex, its nearest competitor for completeness) it hasn't been aggressively redrawn since rediscovery in the 19c.

Glos: 9 miles NE of Ross-on-Wye, equidistant between A449 and M50; St Edward in centre of village, St Mary about 1½ miles N, beyond Kempley Court, isolated

Horley. Fine wall painting with St Christopher and fishermen sharing the stream

Lacock

St Cyriac

Not large, but lavishly detailed and located in 'the loveliest village in England'.

Lacock is a National Trust preserve without a single jarring note – mellow and gorgeous, though its sepulchral calm eventually makes one uneasy.

This church was eccentrically embellished in the 15c. It has some

entertaining gargoyles, especially those clustered round the W end of the N aisle, where nichelets multiply under a canopy and strange beings climb on turrets and ledges. On the S, a 17c domestic building blends itself with the aisle. The tower under which you enter seems about to shrink to porch proportions.

Inside, a window over the chancel arch lights a row of carved bosses in its deep frame. Some exquisite cusping is drawn on the walls over the high arcade. The whole is airy and light, and then in the NE an explosion of gorgeousness in the Sharington Chapel which contains a rich 16c wall tomb and a 15c vault of Gothic form and Renaissance detail. Ribs, for example, of the easternmost vault are treated like fruit garlands bound with ribbons.

Tracery in this aisle extends beyond the glazing, an effect both elegant and astringent.

Wilts: 4 miles S of Chippenham E of A350; church on NE edge of village

Lambourn

St Michael & All Angels

At the centre of one of the best Berkshire villages, the church forms a pleasing group. Here is a central tower which really works and draws the varied whole together. The tower is stone, the rest rendered in a slightly honeyed colour.

Kempley. St Mary contains an elaborate set of 12c wall paintings

Inside, a very good Norman arcade with leaves folded down at the corners on several columns. In a strange position between transept and chapel is a twisted arch of rough-hewn multiple moulding which sports entertaining carving. It is known locally as 'the hunting arch' because, as well as two fish and three hares with ears spread wide, it shows dogs chasing a hare, then some pipers, one upside down. This drama is squeezed into a very narrow band, and one could easily miss it.

Nearby there is a brass with wonderful stripes of enamel remaining on the knight's surcoat. And across the chancel is a notable alabaster tomb. It portrays a husband and wife of the Essex family and includes entertaining emblems – a fish standing up and a griffin whose mouth emits a flame which promptly droops and heads for the ground.

Berks: 12 miles NW of Newbury on B4000

Langford

St Matthew

Rich in Saxon sculpture and unorthodox early Gothic work; its setting is idyllic.

The back road from Clanfield makes a good approach. Langford church sits square in the middle of a vast and numinous churchyard, where meaningful bumps stand forth from the general flatness.

The first thing you see are strange diamond-eyes over normal Gothic lancets in the E, disruptive but amusing. Can they really be early promptings towards plate tracery as some have proposed, or are they later attempts to admit more light and not Gothic at all?

On the S side three mysterious Saxon carvings are roughly grouped. The largest is a big headless rood which shows Christ in a long robe with drooping hands. Then there's a little Crucifixion with an almost German gnarl to it. Apparently Christ's arms twist down so expressively because they were assembled wrongly. John and Mary face outward for the same reason, errors it is too late to undo because the pieces have been trimmed to fit this conception. Then on the tower, smaller and less distinct, carvings of two workmen holding up or building something. Nearby, small Saxon windows, and bell openings with fat roll-mouldings.

One of the 17c monuments which make Lydiard Tregoze a treasure-house

Inside, a vigorous arcade which bangs down mouldings of cruciform plan on cylinders carved with stiff leaf. Amateur paintings of fiendish or Netherlandish intricacy on the screen are ruined though recent.

Oxon: 6 miles NW of Faringdon on unnumbered road, 1 mile E of A361

Lechlade

St Lawrence

Not large but rich, this is an indefinably satisfying church.

It lies just off the market place, as if in an immediately adjoining room, and lively carving is concentrated on N surfaces which are most often seen. All the gargoyles and corbels form a kind of family but fall into at least two groups, crude ones and fine ones, big boned on the tower, more delicate on the porch.

Inside, a graceful arcade with an almost Baroque curve between the colonnettes. A baffling clutter of interesting corbels at different levels in chancel, and good bosses in the roof. At Lechlade, late Gothic isn't heartless but accessible. A couple of good Baroque memorials, while outside, crushed into the narrow S part of churchyard, a little crowd of ruined table tombs.

Langford, showing its wayward early Gothic tracery, which could be later

Glos: 11 miles N of Swindon on A361

Lydiard Tregoze

St Mary

A modest Perpendicular building which is one of the great treasure houses of 17c monuments in England.

The horrible sprawl of Swindon – tract homes and endless mini-roundabouts – now forms an incongruous preface to this church like a bit of the past frozen in its tracks.

St Mary's shelters at the back of the great house which has spawned a conference centre and various leisure facilities. Nice external textures, and homey dormers on the S. The interior is a real shock. Much mural painting in soft pink, as if the walls are blushing. A 17c wooden screen to the E like fairground art. Beyond it is an amazing forest of tombs and memorials: individually the pieces are sometimes fine, sometimes not; collectively they form an apotheosis of Pride. It is one of those churches which is no longer a church but the parade ground of family glory. A 17c beautifier of the place enshrined his own name (Oliver St John) in the E window in rebus form – an olive tree and two Evangelists – like one of those allegorical title pages Rubens turned out.

There are wonderful wrought and gilded railings and gates, and a lifesize gold figure emerging from a cupboard. The best memorial shows an intricate family tree spreading over large boards, its branches like gold lace. The young heir who crowns it – his painted bust in a pediment – appears vulnerable and inadequate to the task. When these wooden doors are opened, a vast ritualized family portrait is revealed.

Wilts: about 3½ miles W of Swindon centre in grounds of Lydiard Park

Maidenhead

All Saints, Boyne Hill

G. E. Street

One of Street's most lavish churches, with a quadrangle of priests' houses, school, hall etc. attached like a set of monastic buildings.

Recent suburban houses which feebly mimic Street's have sprung up to the E. They won a prize for their good manners, I was told. In 1911 Street's son extended the nave and joined it to the tower, a great pity, diluting the jewel-like concentration of the interior and weakening the force of the marvellous tower and spire.

The material is red brick with irregular stone banding. Inside, toothy arcades and elaborate carved stations, some over the piers, others set in the walls. The high ones are identified on the capitals beneath, by inscriptions threading their leafage.

Much painting – patterns on all roofs and a scene over chancel arch darkened by candle smoke. A climax of luxury in the chancel – bands of dull and glazed bricks in bold colours, separated by wider stripes of alabaster stained light violet. Individually, some of the materials are garish; the total effect is almost Venetian and one of the high points of Victorian decoration.

Berks: W of centre of Maidenhead (27 miles W of London) and S of A4

North Cerney, one of F. C. Eden's exquisite restorations in a little Cotswold valley

Northleach. A great Cotswold wool church with thrilling windows over the chancel arch

Malmesbury

The Abbey

The S porch at Malmesbury contains the richest ensemble of Romanesque carving in England.

From afar the ruined silhouette of the Abbey, standing above the town, is most perplexing. Coming near, you find both ends sheared off, and realize that the tower belongs to another, vanished building. The present W end comes near to an 18c picturesque view – Cotman or early Turner – its interlaced arcade seems more indoor than outdoor, a lovely but disturbing misplacement.

The porch's outer arch is breathtaking, seven deeply carved bulges running clear to the ground without bases. Three of these contain roundels with scenes or figures which become more ruined lower down. Inside the porch, a lateral tympanum on either side, showing the Pentecost broken into two parts. Almost nowhere else in England does one find figures on such a scale or in such profusion: it recalls Moissac and others like it.

Outside, the Abbey's truncation is picturesque, but inside it inhibits the eye. Originally this must have been a very noble space. Outside again, pleasing, almost folkish rosettes flank S clerestory windows. These are seen again in the intriguing tympanum at Lullington, Somerset.

A set of snickets radiates from the abbey fragment into the charming town.

Wilts: 12 miles SW of Cirencester on A429, which bypasses town to E

Mildenhall *

St John Baptist

A charmed place, reached down a farm lane.

The church is a mottled record of the centuries, a mixture of stone and brick, of Norman, Perpendicular and Gothick. The first taste of the latter is iron tracery in a S window. The interior is a treasure house of early 19c woodwork, which is 'like walking into a Jane Austen novel' (Betjeman) or 'the colour of an old fiddle' (Piper). The pews retreat to leave a little circle round the font and the narrowest of aisles along the side walls. In the chancel 17c plasterwork and a spindly Gothick reredos. Along the base of the lovely altar rail are worn leather kneelers.

* Pronounced 'Minal'

Wilts: about 1 mile E of Marlborough, just S of road running along bank of River Kennet

Newland

All Saints

The largest church in the scruffy former mining region of the Forest of Dean, it is called 'Cathedral of the Forest'.

Wonderful approach across a vast churchyard lined with almshouses on the S edge. The church makes an extremely varied group in different colours of red sandstone. Most notable is the great tower with unequal pinnacles, each a rich building in itself. There is also a heroic late 19c lychgate, very over-built, with giant corbelling and a generous roof.

The church interior is vast with interestingly empty spaces, dotted here and there with old effigies, but it feels re-managed and has been severely scraped in places. There is a good 17c heraldic font and the famous brass cresting of a miner with his pick and a candle in his mouth. Plenty of Victorian glass, and nice complexity around the rood stair at the back of the chancel arch.

Glos: 5 miles SE of Monmouth on B4231; church W of road

North Cerney

All Saints

A humble building carefully beautified by F. C. Eden in the early 20c.

The church nestles in the miniature Churn valley, across the road from its mellow village. The churchyard is tended by sheep. A friendly saddleback tower dominates the variegated structure. S transept ornamented with incised depictions of monsters.

Entered through a heavy old door, the interior is barer than Eden's other restorations, but shows the same happy tolerance of different periods and styles. The old roof wonderfully dusty from traces of whitewash which remain – an effect Eden has reproduced in the frilly screen on R, with silhouetted figures in the carving.

The great spatial discovery is the squint from S chapel which has been widened to a little alleyway or street you can walk through. Borders of crowns in the glass to N, and spots of purple and blue. There are also windows by Eden. An entertaining story is told of his stumbling on the central figure of the rood in a junk shop in Italy.

Glos: about 4½ miles N of Cirencester, just off A435 to W

Northleach

St Peter & St Paul

One of the grandest Cotswold wool churches. All except the earlier tower dates from a late Gothic rebuilding.

The original settlement lay to the S, and approaching that way, you come first on the stupendous porch. It is various like a city; one pinnacle conceals a chimney. Four original images survive in niches, and occasionally the place of

niches in the pattern is taken by windows with wooden bars. The stone has a reddish cast, mottled by lichen.

Coming from the market place, you are met by the proud nave and aisles standing rank on rank. Uninterrupted displays of tracery and parapets from the N are particularly fine.

Inside, a breathtaking window over the chancel arch, even more thrilling than the one at Cirencester because it is clear glass. Remains of a painted stone reredos in aisle, and a pulpit which is a lovely, frail version of the stone vase-form. Otherwise the interior is somewhat disappointing. Glass of a greasy yellow colour does not help. A notable collection of wool merchants' brasses includes that of John Fortey who paid for the clerestory.

Glos: 10 miles NE of Cirencester on A40 (which now bypasses the village to N)

Old Dilton

The Blessed Virgin Mary (CCT)

A lovely and simple relic; the 18c inhabiting a Gothic shell.

It looks like a chapel or schoolroom and sits right alongside the road near a tiny stream. In the churchyard a little table tomb with cherubs; on the W end, a stone belfry like a dovecote.

The interior is the main thing here, a forest of wooden pew-walls which look rational enough in plan (climb to W gallery for this view), but are confusing at eye level.

Old Dilton, with a perfectly preserved 18c interior 'like a chapel or schoolroom'

From many points the altar is invisible; the pulpit on the other hand is so ingeniously placed that not many would escape its gaze.

Sparing use of curves in the carpentry, some ornament on the clockface W, but not a single religious symbol visible anywhere.

A small mystery is how one reaches the gallery over the vestry (with its fireplace, corpse-rest and mirror). This space is open to the nave, but its ladder or outside entrance has gone.

Wilts: about 2 miles SW of Westbury, between A350 and A3098, just E of railway

Oxford

St Mary, St Philip & St James, St Barnabas

Parish churches don't stand out in Oxford, which mounts one of the proudest architectural displays in England. A couple of the oldest have become college libraries and cannot be visited.

Of those which remain, *St Mary's* is one of the punctuations in the rich parade of the High (just W of All Souls). Its tower is embellished with some of the best ballflower ornament to be found anywhere. Perhaps this shows to best advantage when one approaches via the passage between All Souls and the Radcliffe Camera. On the street side, Nicholas Stone's porch forms a surprisingly congruous introduction to

Painswick. The magical churchyard with its 99 old yews

the medieval building, though when analysed it seems a crazy jumble of every misunderstood Baroque form imaginable.

Monuments in St Mary's often look learned – good ones under tower, in nave and in chancel. The W window is Kempe with all the stops pulled out.

St Philip and St James, in Woodstock Road, North Oxford (opposite Leckford Road) – a fine work of **G. E. Street** – is no longer in use as a church and looks uncared for. It is not evident how one would visit it.

St Barnabas, Cardigan Street (at junction with Canal Street, NW of centre), towers above the low streets of Jericho, not unlike an industrial building in texture. The surface is old pebbledash with dark brick trim scattered through it like stitching. The style is early Italian Romanesque. This is a zealous Tractarian building built for workers at Oxford University Press; the donor specified no-nonsense accommodation of 1000 worshippers.

Arthur Blomfield, the architect, contrived one of the most powerful and atmospheric of all Victorian interiors, with an Eastern flavour. In the apse is the Pantocrator all gold and remote. Over the N arcade runs a martyr frieze in tile. High above is a dark painted ceiling with much decorated bracing. A rich, masculine effect overall.

Fogs of incense linger in the vast space long after service time.

Oxon: 57 miles NW of London on A40

Painswick
St Mary

The churchyard at Painswick is one of the great curiosities of England.

The church forms an appropriate backdrop; within, nothing of comparable magnificence – it has all migrated outdoors. The secret of the churchyard lies in the harmony between vegetation and sculpture. Ninety-nine yews line the paths, mostly planted c1792. They have now grown large enough to form a magical shroud, disorienting the spectator like a blindfold.

At times it feels like a formal garden, at others like *Alice in Wonderland*. When paths converge or someone approaches down one of the long narrow alleys, it can be unnerving. At first glimpsed fragmentarily under the yews, the rococo tombs come in waves or clusters. There are a few main types, including high

Purton. 'Many-branched' church in an oasis near Swindon

table-forms with scrolly volutes and a pedestal variety, like a Victorian stove sitting in the middle of a room ('tea-caddy' is the local name for this type). Most date from the 18c and are covered in swags, putti, skulls and such things. The good mimeographed guide in two parts gives details about the deceased and includes maps.

Many of the best tombs memorialize clothiers and are found on the N and particularly near the NE gate (which is where you should begin). Clearly the old fear of the N side was entirely forgotten. There is a pyramid commemorating the carver of many of them SW of the church, and a fountain dedicated to two animal lovers near the war memorial.

The village is one of the loveliest, of an indescribable grey colour, which seems cool one minute and warm the next.

Glos: 6 miles S of Gloucester on A46; church S of road

Purton
St Mary

A miraculous oasis on the outskirts of Swindon: gabled manor house and stately, many-branched church fill a kink in an old lane adopted into the suburban road web.

The arcade is curious: medieval capitals on Tuscan columns with painted patterning in the arches. There are also 14c murals with angels and good Decorated tracery in SE windows. The reredos contains an interesting Baroque treatment of the Last Supper.

The large churchyard invites one to linger. Small statues turn up in niches here and there, and the church's two towers make for rich spatial play.

Wilts: about 4 miles W of Swindon centre; church is 1 mile N of Lydiard Millicent, next to Purton House, SE of Purton proper

Selsley

All Saints

G. F. Bodley

An early work of Bodley's with some of the earliest William Morris glass.

It sits on a steep slope overlooking the Frome valley. Both the site and the church's form (especially the saddleback tower) are reputedly modelled on Marling in the Tyrol. That village has subsequently been renamed Marengo and presumably wouldn't have its old appeal for Sir S. S. Marling, the patron of Selsley church.

A pleasingly simple design, the one eccentricity being a buttress which is also a railless vestry stair at the E end.

Inside, the windows compel attention, especially Morris's Ascension and Burne-Jones's Majesty in E, Morris and Philip Webb's great Creation rose in W, and – for narrative interest – the parable and preaching windows in the S. One of Rossetti's shows men with scandalously luxuriant locks.

All of them are surprisingly interesting from outside, with vigorous leading and many metallic sheens made by the colouring.

Glos: about 1½ miles SW of Stroud on unnumbered road running W from B4066; church lies N of road

Sparsholt

Holy Cross

A secluded place of great charm with three lifesize wooden effigies of the 14c.

Attractive chequer of roof heights and window sizes as one approaches. The tower looks rebuilt but to a pleasantly simple broach design. Huge old yews lean in from all sides. Within the late 18c porch is a lovely Transitional doorway, and an old door with snaky 12c ironwork.

There are interesting tombs in the nave and chancel, one of them inexplicably mossy, and a beguilingly crude font. The great sight, however, one could almost miss. Three ancient wooden figures lurk in a barny S transept behind a curtain, a space that – with its thoughtful indirect lighting – has come to feel like a museum. The male member of the trio is fully accessible in the middle of the room. There are great rents in his armour where the wood has fallen away. He lies on his helmet with a feather-crest like a toadstool. The female effigies hide in niches, their clothes a series of folded ridges, lively animals at their feet. The wood is now brown and grey, after conservation, but wonderful nonetheless.

In N wall of chancel is ensconced a nine men's morris board scratched on a stone. This was a kind of noughts and crosses for passing idle hours, mentioned in *A Midsummer Night's Dream*.

Berks/Oxon: 4 miles W of Wantage, just N of B4507

Stanton Harcourt

St Michael

A noble early Gothic chancel, fine tombs and two precious survivals.

The setting is special, next to the great towers of the manor house. A high and vast interior, wonderfully plain. Original colour has been uncovered on architectural details to the E, ochre and faded red which bring the stone to life.

Sparsholt. One of three lifesize wooden effigies of the 14c, which 'lurk in a barny transept'

Selsley, where early William Morris glass includes these roundels as well as grander narratives

Here is found one of the most remarkable memorials in England, a canopy from the shrine of St Edburg, which stood at Bicester Priory until the Dissolution. It forms a thicket of 14c carving in pale grey Purbeck, with a series of medieval faces near the top and jutting busts at the corners.

This chancel lies behind a 13c screen with cutouts like a novice's trial drawings in its solid lower half, including some drunken tracery. The transept contains a boisterous rustic Baroque monument with busts in garlanded niches.

Just behind the church, swans on a pond – and on an 18c headstone, an angel with wings like lumpy shoulder pads enclosing the whole design.

Oxon: about 10 miles W of Oxford on B4449

Steeple Ashton

St Mary the Virgin

A surprisingly splendid late Gothic church in this remote place.

The village retains many signs of an importance which was short-lived; two rich clothiers from this period paid for the aisles of the church. The steeple survives only in the name. It blew down in 1670, killing two workmen who were trying to repair a breach made by an earlier storm. A powerful tower remains. The body of the building is adorned with gigantic pinnacles and there are large gargoyles at the top of each window.

Inside, in the stone-vaulted aisles are found strong crouching figures supporting the niches from which the vault springs. The nave vault collapsed early and was replaced by an even more entertaining one of oak and plaster with fine central bosses.

Good stone floors and the remnant of an 18c vicar's library over the porch. He was an ideal country parson or a grouchy hermit, according to different reports.

Wilts: 4 miles E of Trowbridge on unmarked road

Stourton

St Peter

A modest medieval church swallowed by an 18c picturesque landscape and thus incorporated in a loose, larger work of art.

The garden at Stourhead is one of the greatest English achievements. It was developed over a long period in the later 18c by Henry Hoare, a banker who became a country gent. Stourton church and the beautiful remnants of the old village are the culmination of a route which begins at the house and circles an artificial lake whose shore is dotted with temples, bridges and a grotto.

The meaning of the church in the whole conception is somewhat as follows: classical echoes come to fruition in English history. The little graveyard with its record of generations of effort is a mine of history, and forms a continuum with the heroic past.

A medieval-Jacobean monument forms a preface to the church, the Bristol

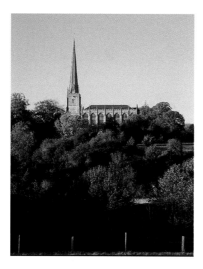

Papery Gothic Revival seen from afar at Tetbury

High Cross, discarded by the city and re-erected here in 1765. It has recently been restored by the National Trust. Its base, re-pierced as formerly, looks quite rococo. Stone figures of bearded kings (replicas since 1981) and a seated Elizabeth above them make a fascinating historical amalgam.

The church's impressive battlements are 18c embellishments, and grey-green paint on the ceiling inside has a very 18c feel.

The Hoare monuments are extremely interesting. A long congested inscription on the garden maker's tomb fails to

mention the work for which he is remembered. Instead it catalogues the deaths of sons and wives, reverses which drove him towards ideal landscapes.

Wilts: 6 miles NE of Wincanton near Somerset border, 1½ miles N of A303; church near SE corner of Stourhead estate

Stratford Tony

St Mary & St Lawrence (CCT)

In an idyllic position, this church contains an exquisite early Kempe window.

The lush watery meadow, where many streamlets are crossed by little footbridges, is the ur-form of a place of old habitation enamelled with flowers. The church stands on an eminence, lopsided from the shifting ground. Its chancel has the most lovely flinty textures and the rest is piebald from later rebuildings.

Inside, the woodwork feels 17c, but apparently the delightful balustrades at the top of wall panelling, screen and stalls are a Victorian embellishment.

Kempe's window is the highlight of this space. It shows a Crucifixion with the crown of thorns among roses at the base. Its colours and forms are somehow evanescent. Christ's loincloth is a light chartreuse and the whole effect pale as if lightly gilded. All the details, of little white flowers, or dusky blue ones below, and a diapering of oak leaves on the empty background, repay study. It is hardly there and yet world weary, apologetically rich.

Wilts: about 4 miles SW of Salisbury, 1 mile W of A354; church lies across River Ebble from the nearest road

Sunningwell

St Leonard

An eccentric arrangement. What looks like a Tudor-Gothic building, plain except for turreted tower tacked onto its N side where transept might be, has been given an ornate W porch (by Bishop Jewell, rector in 1551) in the form of a seven-sided pavilion, richly ornamented with unorthodox Ionic columns at the angles – they sit on faceted bases and a frieze juts out on top of each of them. Inside this classical frame are set Gothic windows with old-fashioned hoods. The intriguing wooden structure inside the

Stratford Tony. Piebald from rebuildings in a lovely watery situation

porch is not medieval engineering but 20c maintenance.

The interior is bare, except for oversize bench ends carved with monster plants and an interesting Pre-Raphaelitish E window dominated by shocking grass green (by J. P. Seddon, 1877).

Berks/Oxon: 2 miles N of Abingdon, N of A34 on unnumbered road, the turn easily missed

Tetbury
St Mary the Virgin

A large and papery early Gothic Revival building survives with many fittings intact in a charming small town.

Outside, thinnest, solemnest Perpendicular. Inside, cluster columns so slim you imagine they're iron, not wood. There are no aisles, and the whole space is filled up with orderly ranks of pews. In fact, the other church in Tetbury was built because the poor couldn't afford to rent seats here.

Instead of aisles, cloister-like passages N and S, from which you enter side pews like theatre boxes. The large W gallery returns halfway down the aisles.

Two miles W of Tetbury on A4135 is BEVERSTON, where the modest church overlooks a Romantic castle ruin, some of which has become a house. Leaf furls look like waves over S door, and a Transitional arcade strives towards grace. Important early carving, rather faint, mounted high on tower's S face.

Glos: Tetbury is 11 miles SW of Cirencester on A433; church S of market place on E side of road

Tewkesbury
Abbey Church of St Mary the Virgin

An abbey of cathedral scale and richness.

When abbeys became parish churches they ordinarily lost either nave or chancel and became amputees, because their village didn't want or, more

usually, couldn't afford to keep all of them. At Tewkesbury the great church survives whole, except for the Lady Chapel to the E.

From that side the display of apsidal chapels is impressive, with the Norman central tower looming over them. It is perhaps the best of its kind, with later pinnacles and parapets. The W front is substantially Norman too and consists of a single huge and – simplified by a later window – bleak arch framed by turrets.

Inside, the hefty Norman arcade has been given a fancy vault which sits rather low on it. Over the chancel, crystalline complexity in the cusped ribs, with enclosed spaces now picked out in red, blue and gold like giant flowers overhead – a disquieting, unarchitectural effect, however authentic.

The clerestory is full of old glass, one large figure per light. But the best thing here is a series of tombs and chantries built into the arcade or located opposite. These begin with an Early English one to the S, then a Decorated extravaganza with a great rectangular solid of carved

Tewkesbury. A complete Norman abbey with gorgeous High Gothic additions

foliage and animals as its final pinnacle (Robert Forthington), and, moving to the N, screen-like openwork framing a cadaver (Wakeman Cenotaph), and the best one: tiers of vaulted niches so airy you can't believe they're stone (Hugh Despenser), and finally the richest, a two-storey chantry with much miniaturized detail (Beauchamp).

Tewkesbury remains, in spite of traffic, a delightful town. It is worth seeking out the river and the *Baptist Chapel*, made from a 15c house c1690, in a back alley. A little further lies its graveyard, the width of a single house. The chapel is a high space centred on its side, not its end wall, with deep galleries of yellow wood looking down on the pulpit. The whole effect is like drawing oneself up to a table.

One can imagine the feelings of superiority bred in simple people in this simple space, as they thought of all the confusion prepared for the senses across the road in the dark abbey. Here they worshipped an immaterial God, in a place more like a schoolroom than a church.

Glos: 11 miles N of Gloucester on A38

Tisbury

St John Baptist

A charming church sprawling in a large churchyard near a 19c brewery.

It is large, low and varied, with an odd 18c top to its tower. It feels both pleasantly decrepit and comfortably inhabited. The stonework is a grey of infinite softness, and many elements, like the porch, are plain but impressive. A shrine in the N chapel shows in the external wall as a strange puncture and a partial walling up of the window.

Inside, the nave is light, the aisles dark, the overall effect spacious but homey. Its high roof, formerly panelled, has been exposed, and partly effaced details show on the tower wall to the E. Half-carved capitals under the tower.

The large chancel beyond is now a separate chapel, and almost seems another building entirely. The E window contains some of the most fetching of all Victorian glass, with blurred forms in strong chemical colours. A terracotta relief by George Tinworth has been demoted from the high altar to the N transept chapel.

Wilts: 9 miles NE of Shaftesbury, 2 miles N of A30; church W of town centre

Uffington

St Mary

A highly eccentric building with some gorgeous early Gothic features.

Not far away to the S is the famous WHITE HORSE of Uffington, one of the greatest prehistoric works of art. It is a huge drawing on a hillside 360 feet long, made by scraping vegetation away from the underlying chalk.

The church is dominated by an octagonal central tower which has a very 17c look, as do some amazing chapel extensions to the large transepts. These are the weirdest elements and hard to describe, semi-abstract exercises in angularity which Pevsner rightly likens to Lethaby's or Randall Wells's wildest reaches.

One of the most beautiful things at Uffington sits right next to this brutal geometry. It is an exquisite porchlet whose arch eats away at its canopy.

The more elaborate S porch is less bold but even more beautiful. Here, in a piece of modern bravery, the old niches are filled with a politely up-to-date St George and King Alfred of 1975. The door is adorned with vigorously irregular ironwork of 13c date. Old consecration crosses survive as punched roundels on all sides of the church.

After all this, the interior seems less exciting, though comfortably vast, with good sedilia and shafting in the

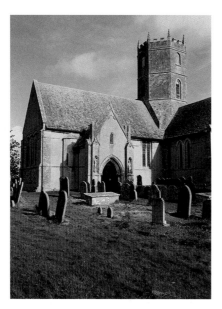

Highly individual early Gothic at Uffington, capped by a later octagonal tower

Wash Common. Eden's ascetic early Renaissance interior of 1933

windows. The odd pointy 17c chapels have interesting concave mouldings inside.

Berks/Oxon: 6 miles W of Wantage, 2 miles N of B4507

Urchfont

St Michael & All Angels

One of the mellowest in the county with distinctive traces from different periods.

There's a good approach past a green with a pond. The church presents a lovely vision of variety across the churchyard from S. The porch has nice tortured hoodmoulds, and a panelled roof. The doorframe is gorgeous Decorated with a cutaway tendril border around the arch.

Inside, the nave roof of pleasing simplicity with gold points like sharpened stakes coming down. But the eye naturally gravitates eastwards, past a remarkable chancel arch, battlemented and leaning outward, to the zigzag vault of the chancel. All these ribs make an effect of surpassing liveliness. Aisles have strainer arches at the transepts.

Externally, more unusual touches in the E – piercings near the top of the wall, fat fleurs-de-lys on the roof ridge, and a priest's door contained in a buttress.

Wilts: 5 miles SE of Devizes on B3098; church at N end of village

Wash Common

St George, Andover Road

F. C. Eden

Eden designed only two complete churches; this – of 1933 – is one.

To those who know his rich restorations of Gothic buildings, the style he chose will be a shock: it's the most ascetic early Italian Renaissance. The reason is twofold: the design had to be light and relatively cheap; and it suited a martyr of sensuality that lurked somewhere in the architect. The material is brick, lightly whitewashed except on window frames of handmade smaller bricks in mellow rose.

Only E parts follow Eden's design exactly. The nave, cloister and campanile are a sympathetic completion by John Griffin, designed thirty years later. The effect of the newer parts is to soften the severity of Eden's design. The friendly courtyard thus created has an almost Californian flavour.

Inside, Eden fittings like the rood have been completed with a baldacchino 'after Eden's design' by Dykes Bower, and other objects of great refinement by him and John Hayward, which seem very happy choices as cohabitees with Eden.

The overall effect will still feel alarmingly bare to some. I don't think Eden would have let the arcade stop so abruptly at the transepts. In fact his designs and a beautiful model (maybe someday it will find its way to the church?) survive. The space under the transepts in a restrained little forest of Tuscan columns lit by round windows (one with Hayward glass) is the nearest we come here to the generous variety of Eden's restorations.

Berks: on SW fringe of Newbury, on W side of A343 (Andover Road)

Wilton

St Mary & St Nicholas

T. H. Wyatt

An astonishing extravaganza in early Italian style dating from 1841–5.

The church was built by Sidney Herbert and his mother, daughter of the Russian ambassador. Their architect was T. H. Wyatt, and their inspiration a deep acquaintance with Italy and places further east.

Yews frame the building on both sides. The detached campanile, of unlikely slimness, is connected to the church by a narrow, gloomy cloister. Here the foreign flavour is strongest, passing over coloured marble pavements between rows of twisted columns.

The scale and richness of the interior is appalling. Much informed love of art and no expense spared, yet the result is like attending one's own funeral. We are told that two early Romanesque churches at Tuscania north of Rome were the principal models, but nothing could be further from the austere richness of that style.

Vigorously carved and overhanging capitals faintly threaten the onlooker. Mosaic, marble and painting throng together at the E end. The patrons are arranged like Renaissance princes in the form of colourless effigies on high biers near the altar. Much authentic 13c Cosmati work is embedded here and there, the bulk of it from a dismembered shrine which once formed the principal ornament of Horace Walpole's 'Chapel in the Wood' at Strawberry Hill.

Windows here and elsewhere are anthologies of ancient glass – from St-Denis and the Sainte-Chapelle among others. The RCHM* has catalogued these, but it is hard to enjoy early French Gothic in this Italianized place.

At the W end, too, many bizarre excesses, such as a Jacobean tomb as an overdoor ornament. Of all the confections the font works best. A Venetian fountain of red marble is glued to a scrolly black marble base via an inlaid shaft which resembles ivory.

* Royal Commission on the Historical Monuments of England, *Churches of South-East Wiltshire*

Wilts: 3 miles W of centre of Salisbury (with which it is practically continuous) on A30; church on S side of road

Wilton. An early Victorian extravaganza derived from Italian Romanesque in which no expense is spared

South East

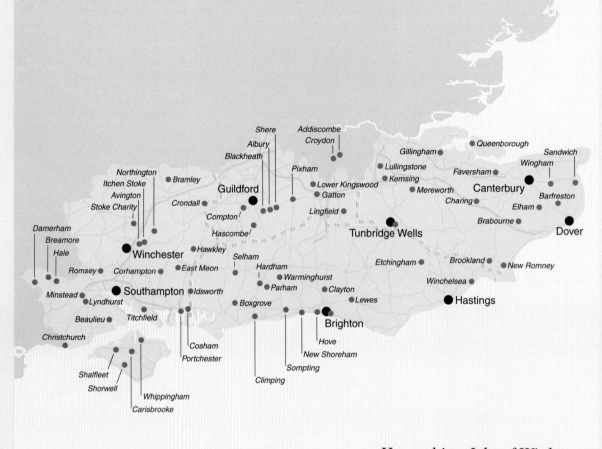

Shere
Albury
Blackheath
Addiscombe
Croydon
Queenborough
Sandwich
Northington
Bramley
Pixham
Gillingham
Lullingstone
Wingham
Faversham
Itchen Stoke
Avington
Guildford
Lower Kingswood
Kemsing
Canterbury
Stoke Charity
Crondall
Gatton
Mereworth
Barfreston
Compton
Lingfield
Charing
Elham
Damerham
Hascombe
Brabourne
Dover
Breamore
Hawkley
Tunbridge Wells
Hale
Selham
Romsey
Corhampton
East Meon
Hardham
Etchingham
Brookland
New Romney
Winchester
Warminghurst
Winchelsea
Minstead
Idsworth
Parham
Clayton
Southampton
Boxgrove
Lewes
Hastings
Lyndhurst
Beaulieu
Titchfield
Brighton
Christchurch
Hove
Cosham
New Shoreham
Shalfleet
Portchester
Sompting
Shorwell
Climping
Whippingham
Carisbrooke

*Hampshire, Isle of Wight,
Sussex, Kent, Surrey*

THE REMOTER PARTS of Kent lie on the periphery, and of Sussex, in the interior. Everyone expects these counties to be thoroughly domesticated, so it comes as a pleasant surprise to find such forlorn and forgotten places as the marshes between Thames and Medway. Just as strange, on the other side of the county is Romney Marsh. Neither of these regions is spectacular, but both are among the most gripping spots in the whole country. A few other parts of Kent are reclaimed marsh as well, and consequently characterful in spite of later despolations. It shows in various place names and in numinous flatness

like the stretch between Richborough and Sandwich.

The chain of seaside resorts along the Sussex coast is socially one of the most entertaining sequences in Britain, but few would call it a rich hunting ground for architecture. Brighton and Hove have outstanding Victorian churches, but otherwise the church hunter is mainly running counter to modern patterns of use and settlement. The dominant strains on this coast are grand Saxon and grander Norman. Inland are the best cycles of wall paintings in Britain.

Hampshire is the first county in that direction where you really get free of

London, and is therefore accorded a special value by Londoners. It is harder than most counties to characterize. One is tempted to say the county's special quality has something to do with its large square shape: Hampshire is a sound and sensible place, Jane Austen's home.

Surrey has suffered the fate, after centuries of obscurity, of being favoured by well-heeled suburbanites fleeing the city. It is probably the most troublesome county for church visiting, though there are surprising pockets of openness, usually secluded. It contains some of the greatest Victorian curiosities, sponsored by the artistic breed of early suburbanite.

Addiscombe

St Mary Magdalene

E. B. Lamb

Lamb's last and one of his wildest churches, built 1868–9.

The outside does not prepare you for the interior, partly because the SE tower dates from 1928 (post-Lamb). The nave wasn't continued to the W, and the building has an unfinished look on that side; as a result the interior is almost square. One approaches from the E, passing the vestry with its strange chimneys.

Inside, the most complex of Lamb's wooden roofs: an unvarnished rust colour, intricate and rustic at the same time. It rises to a lantern over the crossing, whose light is filtered by a web of cross-pieces.

The altar has been moved into this central space, and re-flooring has destroyed some odd symbolism. The church was built for a Jewish convert, and the number of steps to the chancel and sanctuary had a mystical significance (each set is now reduced by one).

Lamb's spatial effects are agitated, to say the least. Meetings between all that wood overhead and the stone supports are unpredictable; piers change their shape and dimension in the middle. Carved decoration looks as if it has fallen from above or sprouted in a crevice. Weirdest of all are large semi-attached columns in the transepts, which bisect rose windows and oppose to them (at right angles) demi-roses of open tracery. In the apse, a theatrical compression of different arcades. On the sanctuary arch, bosses like magnified Victorian bouquets.

Only in the apse is the stained glass garish enough to live up to Lamb's excesses.

Surrey/London: a 10-minute walk E from East Croydon station; in Canning Road which runs between Addiscombe Road and Lower Addiscombe Road

Albury

Old Church (St Peter & St Paul) (CCT)

One of the curiosities of Surrey: worship was discontinued here in 1841, so it remains suspended in time.

The Saxon tower with good paired windows is capped by a shingled dome of vaguely Eastern appearance. Entered

Avington. A landowner's 18c seemliness in Spanish mahogany

by an old door with a huge old lock. The chancel was roofless until recently, and there is a great disparity between the bare, untenanted look of most of the building and the garish opulence of the Victorian mortuary chapel decorated by Pugin around 1840: bright tile floors interrupted frequently by elaborate brasses, all enclosed in florid screens.

The history of this place is more tumultuous than you would imagine. The 18c landowner harassed his tenants until they all moved to Weston Street (now called Albury) a mile further west, so there was finally no village. Hence the peaceful parkland setting. In the next century another landowner fell under the spell of the messianic preacher Edward Irving, and built the lavish *Catholic Apostolic Chapel* a few hundred yards to the NW, kept in good repair but now disused, permanently locked and said to be 'resting'. Around the same time, he

decided he wanted to move the remaining parishioners from the old village. So, overriding some protest, he built them a new church at Weston Street and converted Albury church to the funeral chapel of his family. This is where Pugin came in. Interesting 17c monuments and a large brass survive in the nave and aisles.

Surrey: about 5 miles SW of Guildford, E of A248, in grounds of Albury Park

Avington

St Mary

Perfect of its kind, an 18c church built by a landowner adjoining his house.

In fact all but the S side is walled off and reachable only from inside the manor grounds. A strange path of creamy gravestones leads between mellow walls to a slightly harsh brick exterior. Oddly, the building is battlemented. Nice iron tracery shapes like inverted Gothic arches. Pink and blue inside, with restrained plasterwork. Box pews of Spanish mahogany have gorgeous rounded corners and discreet enrichment in squire's pew. The font is a spindle of white marble, the floor is chequered marble, and the pulpit is crowned by a wooden bird.

Hants: about 4 miles NE of Winchester, on an unnumbered road which turns S from B3047 in Itchen Abbas

Barfreston

St Nicholas

Deservedly famous for its Romanesque carving, some of the richest in England.

The approach from the E is unforgettable, the tiny church on its mound above the sunken lane like a jewel casket or shrine. There is a large wheel rose in the gable and some spun-off niches and outcrops, two lavish S doorways and various other enrichments.

Outside, these are pleasantly fragmentary and softened by weather, the E end more unorthodox and inventive, the larger doorway incredibly minute and well preserved, carved in shiny limestone like soap. Inside, the effect is more manic and not so pleasing.

Not far away is PATRIXBOURNE (about 2 miles SE of Canterbury, unnumbered turning from A2), with plentiful

Barfreston. The Romanesque doorway, teeming with creatures in soapy limestone

Romanesque carving of similar character, humble hunched tower (a creature with its neck drawn in), amusing Victorian Romanesque font and fascinating Swiss 16–17c glass patched together in the E window.

The lanes around both these obscure villages are delightful.

Kent: Barfreston is on unnumbered road between A2 and A256 about 1½ miles W of Eythorne and 3 miles S of Aylesham (8 miles NW of Dover)

Beaulieu

Abbey Church
(Blessed Virgin & the Holy Child)

A monastic refectory re-used as a church makes a strong effect.

The village of Beaulieu has a favoured position in the middle of the New Forest – here a heathy and largely treeless tract. Buildings sit low beside a reedy lake with the great house across the water.

The church can be entered from the estate, a route which misses the striking E end, divided in two by an enormous buttress.

The interior is a single space under a panelled ceiling, lit by a variety of crisp Early English windows in deeply splayed frames. The novel feature is a remarkably narrow vaulted stair-passage which climbs slowly to a balcony from which readers formerly edified the eating monks. This is presently the pulpit, supported by a stone cone covered with stiff leaf.

A large hall is now tacked at right angles to the side of this church.

Hants: 7 miles SE of Lyndhurst on B3056; church on an island site on the Beaulieu estate

Blackheath

St Martin

C. H. Townsend

A fascinating diminutive work by the architect of the Bishopsgate Institution and Whitechapel Gallery, built 1895.

Its proportions are stylized, but the materials are rustic or mock rustic. Battered concrete walls covered outside in roughcast, a pantile roof and bell turret of handmade bricks. The best detail is a snaky bulge for the pulpit in the N wall. On this same wall a craftsy war memorial like a peasant shrine.

Inside, it resembles even more a coffer or bit of jewellery. Sophisticated flavours are blended: a Venetian window, Byzantine arches, a pseudo-Renaissance screen in dark green and gold, alabaster trimming in the sanctuary lit indirectly by tiny windows. The extensive frescoes by Mrs Lea-Meritt are of poor quality but revealing.

Townsend built several houses in the mock-rustic village, including his own. The result is that unplaceable 'artistic' air we now value in turn of the century settings.

(*See also* Pixham and Lower Kingswood for nearby buildings of

Boxgrove Priory with 16c flower painting in the vault

Albury, Surrey. The Saxon tower is topped by an Eastern dome and the interior seems frozen in time

similar scale and period, and Great Warley, Essex for Townsend's most lavish church.)

Surrey: 1 mile NE of Wonersh in a clearing in the woods

Boxgrove

Priory Church of St Mary & St Blaise

An imposing building in a shrunken village now suburban except in the pleasant old cul-de-sac the Priory sits at the end of.

Though of cathedral proportions, the present building is only the chancel and crossing of the former priory church, whose nave had been reserved for parish use. At the Dissolution the villagers moved up to the monks' part, and the other elements of the complex were pulled down or fell into ruin.

Boxgrove is interesting for eccentricity, not regularity. In fact one's first impression is that whimsical use of Purbeck marble highlights in the arcade has spoiled the composure of the design. But the rich colouring of dark against light stone grows on one. In the clerestory a wonderful gawky mixing of angular and pointed arches.

Overhead the most charming eccentricity of all – painted floral heraldry covers the vault like illustrations in an old herbal, with varied leaves of outlandish scale. The painter, Lambert Barnard, also decorated ceilings in the bishop's palaces at Chichester and elsewhere.

Brabourne, where there's a rare opportunity to see 12c glass in pale old colours

Boxgrove's most surprising monument is the de la Warre chantry inserted in the S arcade. Bexhill has its DE LA WARRE PAVILION on the sea; the funeral pavilion at Boxgrove was never used for either burial or memorial masses, because the Dissolution intervened. It is a riot of Renaissance motifs coarsely carved – emblems, grotesques and scrambling figures. The hunting scene which climbs one of the columns is taken straight from a tapestry.* Recently the monument has been further vulgarized by application of garish paint.

* Actually from a printed book of hours, a copy of which is in Chichester Cathedral library

Sussex: about 3 miles NE of Chichester, between A27 and A285

Brabourne

St Mary the Virgin

A simple and moving building which contains one priceless relic.

The top stages of the Norman tower fell down in the 15c, an event which inspired pleasingly over-sized buttresses, one diagonal, the other lateral. You

69

approach an impressively windowless wall and enter through a heavy old door across a worn brick floor. The great chancel arch contains scrambled bits of Romanesque carving. Further E, a rare heart shrine and a couple of helmet trophies, one crowned with a metal bird. But the feature it is worth the trip to see is a small, roundheaded window completely filled with 12c glass – pale green, yellow, rose and white, in the old pattern. It resembles an oddly cropped bit of brocade.

Under the tower the steep stair has quarter logs for steps and a rough hewn rail. The narrow priest's door in N chancel sports a hanging keystone like a heavenly warning. On an altar tomb, large and unevadable letters proclaim that 'the name of the wicked shall rot'.

Kent: about 2 miles N of M20 and A20 between Folkestone and Ashford; church is treated as towerless on OS map and lies S of road in hamlet of Brabourne Lees

Bramley

St James

A homely domestic building full of the unexpected which includes, of all things, a Gothic chapel designed by Soane.

The visitor is met by Tudor dormers, brick tower, rendered walls and Soane's obtrusive addition in pink brick with

Bramley, rustic simplicity embellished by Soane

blue headers mixed in. Inside that chapel, a pseudo-Gothic vault with pleated-napkin effect around the cornice and a grandiloquent tomb sometimes attributed to Thomas Banks. A Virtue supports a plump man expiring on top. Beneath are two little reliefs, of War and Peace, or Fortitude and Charity.

Interesting fragmentary painting in the nave, including a huge Christopher with sprouting staff and a fancy caravel behind him; a smaller scene of Becket's murder opposite.

There is a canted wooden ceiling in the chancel, and a murky rood by

Temple Moore over the old screen. In the W, a gallery on fluted Ionic columns and an old clock ticking away.

Hants: about 6 miles N of Basingstoke between A33 and A340; church lies SW of station and present village centre

Breamore

St Mary

Important Anglo-Saxon remains in a placid setting beside an Elizabethan house.

Breamore was a large and elaborate Saxon building with a real crossing. The 'S transept' survives intact, almost as tall as a tower. Inside on the narrow arch connecting it to the main space is the largest of Saxon inscriptions, in clear, confident letters. 'Here the covenant is revealed to you,' it says. The flattened tower arches, probably 14c, are surprisingly pleasant shapes.

More may be learned about earlier phases from the external walls, made of flint pebbles with ironstone and Roman tile mixed in. Long and short work appears at intervals on nave walls. Over the S door is the hacked-off remnant of a large 11c rood. Christ's body sways dramatically, framed by the pillars of his mother and John. Light blue, ochre and oxblood colours on the background seem very Saxon, but are doubtless later. It is located awkwardly far above our heads.

Hants: about 10 miles S of Salisbury on A338; church is ¾ mile W, next to Breamore House

Brighton

St Bartholomew, Ann Street

Edmund Scott/Henry Wilson

A visionary structure, one of the most powerful 19c buildings in England.

Its height is astonishing. A long box of brick with steep gable roof, its walls remain windowless until quite high up, then yield only narrow lancets. In the W wall, one of the biggest rose windows in the country. Decoration is mainly confined to elaborate patterns in the brick.

St Bartholomew was built in a slum neighbourhood by a local benefactor and is usually seen as a prime instance of Victorian High Church fervour lavishing itself on the poor. But it provoked opposition: those living nearby claimed

Breamore. Remains of a large Anglo-Saxon building including an extra-large inscription

St Bartholomew, Brighton, turned into Byzantium with an Art Nouveau flavour by Henry Wilson

its draughts sent the smoke back down their chimneys. Even today it makes an alarming experience to enter the deep shadow on its S side, which forms a kind of wind tunnel.

Inside, it seems even more strongly Italian, brightness above and mellower light below giving an uncannily exact reminiscence of Italy. High on the E wall a cross is outlined, adorned with primitive symbols. Beneath it, a great baldacchino of the most unchurchy and mythic character, made of salmon red and sea-water green marble. Enormous candles are stuck in knots of metal on free-standing marble columns nearby.

The pulpit in coloured marble is immured in the left-hand wall, standing on marble legs which isolate it like a flooded dwelling. Each of these columns is inscribed with the name of an archangel. Further enrichment in Byzantine-primitive mode on a side altar opposite. A beaten silver frontal carries Assyrian symbols for the planets.

The brick shell was provided by a local architect, Edmund Scott, in 1872–4. The gargantuan fittings, which turn this church into a house of pre-Christian myth, are all by Henry Wilson, who also

had a plan to make a screen of the E wall, which would lead to a secretive chancel beyond. He worked here from 1897 to 1908. Altar rail, stalls, font and organ gallery are also his designs.

St Michael, Victoria Road, is an interesting union of the work of **William Burges** and **G. F. Bodley**. It contains fine early Morris glass.

St Nicholas, the old parish church of Brighton, a humble flint building in a sloping churchyard, has a Norman font with the Last Supper and St Nicholas and the ship in deep cylindrical relief. R. C. Carpenter designed its hexagonal wooden cover.

Sussex: directly S of London on S coast; St Bartholomew is visible to E from London trains entering Brighton

Brookland

St Augustine

Romney Marsh, formerly the haunt of smugglers, has now been invaded by pylons, but remains a good place for wide skies and dramatic storms. Until recently very remote, hence a rich

hunting ground for unrestored churches, four of which appear below. For others, see New Romney.

Brookland is an archetype of a building on marshy ground and one of the mellowest parish churches in England. Although tactfully repaired at various times, it seems an undisturbed palimpsest of the centuries. The building stands on a slight artificial mound, and a canalized rivulet passes very near its SW corner. Inside, arcades and walls lean outward at various angles, while many old roof trusses hold them in. Exterior buttresses of different periods do the same.

Beside the church is a startling and lightweight wooden bell-tower of three diminishing stages, like graduated conical hats. The oldest elements, formerly an unenclosed frame, have recently been dated c1260. This strange and comfortable shape announces the church from afar, which otherwise hugs the ground like a barn. Some of the aisle windows keep their great flimsy wooden shutters, and the friendly N porch has double flaps like Dutch doors.

Harmony inside comes from old floors and box pews. Residue of unassimilated functions at the W end – a schoolroom in

At Clayton Romanesque wall paintings depict the end of the world

Carisbrooke

St Mary the Virgin

One of the most unspoiled churches on the island, with an interesting memorial.

It sits above the High Street looking across to the castle ruin on a more impressive height. Arriving from the W, you see the rich late Gothic tower below you, impressive even from above.

Inside, a powerful Transitional arcade rests on huge cylinders. In the NE is a wooden memorial to an Adventurer of the East India Company, 'who died in this Isle', 1619.

IoW: in centre of island, just W of Newport; church on N side of B3401

Charing

St Peter & St Paul

Charming approach past remnants of a large archbishop's palace which filled the space N and W of church, now an airy ruin with great archways leading into an open farmyard. One of the best church towers of Kent blocks the end of this decayed passageway.

The church has many pleasing features, but the best are a nave roof with Elizabethan arabesques on the main timbers like niello inlay, and folkish 17c bench ends. They are mostly bold vegetables but include three jacks-in-the-green, faces decked with foliage.

Kent: 6 miles NW of Ashford, just N of A20; church E of High Street

Christchurch

Priory Church

Inventive late Gothic E parts of magnificent dimensions, next to a stream and near Christchurch harbour.

Outside, it is rather a pleasant hash: first an unimpressive nave, then a leap to the chancel with its great windows, followed by a further step up to the loft over the Lady Chapel. The W tower is an odd later addition of inferior scale; more truly impressive is the stair turret on the N transept with rich lattice decoration.

This is Norman, as is the nave. Beyond the crossing, a visionary burst of light: above the 14c stone reredos a supernaturally vivid recent mural. The whole effect resembles the dramatic illusions in, say, Toledo Cathedral. The reredos retains many original figures,

the NW corner now a kind of museum, and a balustraded corral in the SW where formerly the tithe measures were kept and used to collect the rector's share of corn, wine, wool, etc. Near this, the famous 12c lead font on thick base. It shows the signs of the Zodiac over labours of the months. In the SE corner, a recently discovered fresco of Becket's murder with three vivid knights.

St George, IVYCHURCH (2½ miles NE of Brookland) is another haven of pleasing irregularity. Much old tile in its disused N aisle, which feels like a farm building; good roofs and oval notice boards in nave.

ST MARY IN THE MARSH (3 miles E of Ivychurch) is set deep in the marsh.

Beautiful, slightly rustic E window: squashed quatrefoils over trefoil tops. Two primitive heads between sedilia and piscina, and a strange fragment of Italian altarpiece.

St Thomas à Becket, FAIRFIELD (2½ miles W of Brookland, a short walk N of nearest unnumbered road; kept locked). A curiosity. Tiny building of brick, tile, weatherboard and shingle sits in drained land surrounded by sheep and watery ditches. Its little island is reached by wooden foot bridges. Inside, cross beams verge near the high white pews and partly interrupt our view of chancel. Lovely painted altar rail.

Kent: about 6 miles NE of Rye on A259

Eccentric Romanesque ornament at Climping

including a large reclining Jesse. To the left a flamboyant early Renaissance chantry peppered with elaborate ornament. Wonderful fractured vaulting in chancel aisles, and even richer surfaces in the Lady Chapel, including window fringes and pendants from the vault. Back in the chancel, a lovely Flaxman memorial to a young mother shown with three children and one of the longest and most heartfelt of inscriptions.

The Catholic church in PUREWELL, E of town centre, has an Italianate fresco by the novelist Frederic Rolfe above the altar.

Hants/Dorset: E of and continuous with Bournemouth; church S of town centre

Clayton

St John Baptist

The Romanesque wall paintings here are among the most moving of all English works of art. Their survival is remarkable, and in part explained by the village's remoteness. At the foot of the South Downs, it feels secluded in spite of nearness to a main road.

At Clayton, three sides of the nave are covered with scenes in three tiers, of which the top is the best preserved. Figures are elongated and occur in throngs, swaying in a kind of dance. Particularly memorable are a crowd of Apostles high on the end wall; the Antichrist as a devil or horse pursued through the air; the central Christ over the arch, and three people in a low architectural enclosure.

Because of its fragmentary state, the scheme needs explaining to be appreciated. It forms a grand symphonic treatment of the Last Judgement framed by four angels with trumps at the corners.

It is particularly thrilling to approach the figures at eye level where white over-painting used for ridges in cloth and most interior detail gives a vivid sense of the painter's touch. The paintings were found by Kempe in 1895. Windows and memorials of intervening centuries make a series of melancholy intrusions on the best of all English wall paintings.

Sussex: just E of A273 and S of B2112, 6 miles N of Brighton

Climping

St Mary

One of the most delightful churches in the county. Three lancets in the Norman tower are framed by zigzag ornament which completely encloses the window as if it were trapped in a mouth bristling with teeth. The door under one of them employs even stranger geometry.

It is hard to say why the interior is so pleasing. The Early English phase often seems to contain a human not just an architectural secret, and the ability to express important truths compactly. The E window-arcade with quatrefoils in the spandrels is one of these moments of

expressive mastery, charmingly completed by later quatrefoil message boards on either side of the chancel arch.

In the N transept is a series of paintings by Heywood Hardy, who died in 1932, showing Christ's life on earth in our time. Though their scale is not bold enough for the setting, they represent a touching effort to bring Scouts, sportsmen and River Arun scenery into harmony with the Most High.

This church, lying next to a prison, is kept open, a lesson in trust.*

* Alas, no longer, since sale of adjacent vicarage

Sussex: about 1 mile W of Littlehampton, ½ mile N of A259 on unnumbered road

Compton

St Nicholas

The best early remains in the county: a Saxon tower and a two-storey sanctuary. Nearby, in the Watts Chapel, some of the weirdest Victorian exoticism.

Rich textures in tower masonry include herringbone, random flints and galleting. It is topped by the shingle broach spire common in Surrey.

Inside, a venerable but inexplicable arrangement: at some distance beyond the chancel arch the space is divided horizontally in two: over the lower part a

The mysterious two-storey chancel at Compton

73

massive shallow vault; in front of the upper, a rude wooden railing of arches cut from a single plank. This is an extremely rare 12c survival. No one knows what the upper chamber was for. In the low E window a bit of early glass, the Virgin and Child in two different greens and brown.

The nave arcade is impressively bulky with capitals of lively variety. On the E wall, a compelling three-dimensional box pattern in faded red, discovered in 1966.

The painter G. F. Watts lived at Compton and his wife designed a grandiose and nightmarish mortuary chapel as his memorial in 1896–1901. It

is a round building of brick, covered in rich terracotta decoration. From afar it looks Italian Romanesque but much of the detail is Celtic.

Inside, it is covered in gesso patterns painted in lugubrious colours. Angels crowd round in suffocating rings; tendrils swirl and knot themselves. The symbolic programme is based on the circle of eternity married to the cross of faith. In the graveyard a number of tombstones of the period, and a cloister also by Mrs Watts.

Surrey: 3 miles SW of Guildford on B3000

Corhampton. Beyond this Saxon chancel arch are lively Romanesque paintings

Corhampton

No dedication

A small gem, the best Anglo-Saxon building in East Hampshire. Rising right beside the road on its own mound (thought to indicate a pre-Christian ritual site) and shrouded in trees, including a yew 23 feet in diameter, which some writers judge as old as the church.

Ridges of pink quasi-coralline (or at least fossilous) stone laid vertically punctuate the S side like the bones of the building extruded past its surface. Walls are bare flint which would have been rendered. On N side, a blocked Saxon door consisting of strange imitations of columns and arch whose 'capitals' and 'bases' are non-structural.

Notice re-set Saxon sundial E of porch. Then inside, a moving Saxon chancel arch and fantastic paintings within it – reds, ochres, whites like Clayton and Hardham in Sussex. Here a decorative system is preserved of elaborate painted curtains with affronted eagles. Above this, riders, kings, bishops, ladies – a hubbub which has been explained as scenes from the life of St Swithun, including the restoration of a farm woman's broken eggs.

Hants: about 10 miles N of Fareham on A32; church half hidden on W side of road

Cosham

St Philip, Hawthorn Crescent

J. Ninian Comper

One of Ninian Comper's most imaginative works, without the cloying excess which spoils some earlier projects. It was built in 1936–7 to serve a new housing estate. The houses look Edwardian but were begun only a few years before the church.

Cost constraints spurred Comper to some of his most inventive strokes, such as fibreglass for Corinthian columns and vaults, and artificial stone for external trim, now flaking as its ill-built ancestor the Gothick folly would have done. Further discreet economies in the way colour and gilding are used in the otherwise bare interior.

It sits near a railway line (Comper insisted the rectory should come between to screen the church from noise), apparently charmless in a charmless place. Starved pinnacles and Gothic windows in concrete-colour minimally lighten dingy brick surfaces. Inside, immense quantities of daylight flood a democratic hall-church punctuated by a gold ciborium with eagles (who look like doves) bending from corners, dangling lamps from their beaks. This is fresh Italian Renaissance in style, while the font cover is Tudor and the organ gallery Jacobean. These are the only emphases in the pervasive whiteness, aside from Comperish rose-pink carpets and the beginning of a single stained glass window which there wasn't money enough to complete.

Hants: Cosham is a N district of Portsmouth; church near junction with Wembley Grove, approach via Portsmouth Road

Crondall

All Saints

One of the most exciting churches in the county.

An avenue of limes on rising ground frames the 16c porch of brick and plaster. The building is a pleasing jumble of textures: rickety wooden walkways lead from a low Norman tower to the tall 17c brick one and create momentarily the atmosphere of the Spanish inns in *Don Quixote*. Great W buttresses are tiled on top, as are smaller ones along the N side.

Inside, a riot of crisp early 13c carving in chancel, large zigzag contrasted with small dogtooth, juxtaposed to gorgeous stiffleaf capitals, all in bone-grey stone. Nave arcade unusually massive; good 16c memorials, especially one on left in chancel with kneeling-knight brass and smoke-darkened inner lip. The famous priest brass is covered by a carpet, and nearby a sampler records a local villa's Roman paving destroyed in 19c.

E of church are three interesting early 20c memorials of 1924 with Mediterranean tile roofs, and one of 1916 with bronze figure and reliefs signed H T (Hamo Thornycroft).

Hants: 1 mile S of A287 and about 4 miles NW of Farnham, Surrey

Croydon

St Michael & All Angels, Poplar Walk

J. L. Pearson

This is Pearson at his best, creating a miniature cathedral in brick – outside warm red, inside pale tan.

The setting has been brutalized by new road systems, demolition and very

Crondall. The best early Gothic in Hampshire in bone-grey stone

bad 20c rebuilding. Pearson's plan for a SW tower was not realized, so only its bulky base reminds us that the final emphasis of a carefully graded series is missing.

The hallmark of this church is restraint in the details and a great flowering of spatial intricacy, so the outside is almost bleak, the interior awe-inspiring. Inside, the mortar is faintly rose coloured, darker than the brick, and gives the whole a mysterious, fleshly warmth so that the absence of architectural ornament is not felt as a lack.

Proportions exquisitely calculated using the golden section. In the stone-ribbed brick vaults, a smaller gauge

brick is employed to give a sense that distances from the eye are larger than they actually are. The most exciting space is the narrow ambulatory, from which a series of complex vistas emanates.

The best fitting in the church is the large hanging rood which floats above the chancel threshold and subtly marks the crossing. Good small narrative windows on N, in deep brick embrasures.

Other fittings unsuitably lavish, including metal screens and a pulpit and organ case by Bodley.

Surrey/London: just S of West Croydon station

Damerham

St George

Not great architecture, but exactly what a country church should be.

It sits away from the houses, sheltered but with good views. The approach from the N is extremely pleasing; varied textures are seen piecemeal – remnants of a wall tomb, semi-rendered bits of wall. Then you turn the corner and the tower like a fortification bursts upon you, rising in gradual stages, not aspiring too high.

In the capacious porch, a Norman tympanum on a stone shaped like a loaf of bread. It shows a warrior, with his opponent lying down. Inside, a plaster tunnel vault with wooden ribs. All very spruce though mercifully unrestored.

Hants: about 12 miles S of Salisbury, 3 miles W of Fordingbridge on B3078; church is reached before village and lies up a lane SW of road

East Meon

All Saints

Built close against a hill and towering over an attractive village whose High Street meanders along an embanked stream which gives it a distinctive backbone.

Norman tower of church on heroic scale, now with lead spire. Fascinating heraldic carving on E end, where supporters are legless dragons wearing barrels around their waists.

Inside, large and relatively bare, the tower arches exceedingly powerful. Best fitting a great Tournai marble font with 12c carving on its narrow sides which looks positively Sumerian. On E and N, Adam and Eve's life; S and W filled up with animals.

Hants: 5 miles W of Petersfield, almost equidistant from A272 (which runs to N) and A32 (to W)

Elham

St Mary the Virgin

F. C. Eden

A building, originally unremarkable, which has become unique in England through the attentions lavished on it in the early 20c by F. C. Eden, a pupil of Bodley.

His improvements consist of idiosyncratic historicist fittings of his own design, humble old things (like the diamond-shaped notice boards) exquisitely placed and cared for, and continental works of art chosen for texture rather than religious expression, but integrated to a point which is almost camouflage. So the whole effect is one of rural Englishness and Popish richness at the same time. Its sensuous interior stops just short of feeling like a museum. Snowshill Manor in Wiltshire comes nearer than any church to resembling Eden's effects.

Damerham. Irregular, with a tower like a fort, but 'exactly what a country church should be'

Throughout the building one happens upon delicious interplays – between the gruff font, its frilly Jacobean cover, and the late Renaissance gilt and marble shrine behind it. Or between rustic arcades and painted testers suspended above the side altars, conditioning all the circumambient air.

Only at one moment, in the fascinating Mannerist reredos above the high altar by John Riley Wilmer, does all the beauty here become too worldly, even uncomfortably sexy.

Elham has gone on being a place which understands refinement, its market square N of the church modest but exquisite.

Kent: 5 miles NW of Folkestone on B2065; church lies E of High Street

Etchingham

The Assumption & St Nicholas

A large collegiate church built all at once in the 1360s.

Better outside than in. It forms an impressive group with stocky central tower, a nave shorter but higher than the chancel, and entertaining tracery. Old red tile goes well with the stone in which grey and tawny hues are mixed, from much iron running through it.

Old heraldic glass in tracery lights makes a strong effect. Brasses are noteworthy, especially a woman framed by two men, with canopies over them almost intact. This lies in chancel floor;

Different flavours meet harmoniously at Elham in this shrine behind the font

Gatton, 'like the castle from a model train set'

nearer the altar is the lone figure of the founder, Sir William de Echyngham.

In the set of rudimentary misericords is one intriguing motif – two keys strung on tendrils. Is it a piece of irresponsible observation or are we meant to extract a meaning from them?

Sussex: 15 miles NW of Hastings on A265

Faversham

St Mary of Charity

Not a beautiful church but a curious one. In the 18c George Dance Sr framed the nave with gigantic Tuscan arcades, which have large palm leaves and garlands in the frieze and semi-circular clerestory windows, but he left Gothic aisles, aisled transepts and chancel. Then in Victorian times Scott came along and cased Dance's work outside in flint with Gothic tracery, so now you have the odd sensation of Perpendicular mullions seen through classical frames, an unnerving palimpsest. Which way are you looking into history, forward or back?

The whole building seems infused with a divided reverence for the past: in the transepts an anthology of grotesquely various Victorian glass and a jumble of monuments and brasses. Somehow a powerful idea is conveyed of all that has gone on in these wide thoroughfares. A column to the left (entrance to N transept)

is painted with tiers of 14c scenes in red, white and green. Stalls in the chancel with vivid animal misericords.

The church's Gothick spire is of course the first element most visitors will see, eccentric openwork which seems bold and delicate at once: it wishes it were iron. Large railed churchyard and large aromatic brewery to the S and W. The church lies at edge of the old core of one of the pleasantest towns in Kent.

Kent: 9 miles W of Canterbury on A2; Church Street runs E of Abbey Street N of market place.

Gatton

St Andrew

In the 1830s Lord Monson converted a rather ordinary parish church into a dark haven of Gothic fantasy.

Outside, a crazy combination of white clunch, brick and pebbledash. The N porch looks like the castle from a model train set, and the tower is of starved proportions.

Inside, so much foreign woodwork has been inserted that it is hard to move in the space. The original nave has been made into a collegiate quire with three tiers of seats each side. The transepts are taken up with galleries, while a squire's pew is inserted in the N chapel, equipped with a sofa and a padded bench; in the corner a large fireplace. A covered way formerly led from this chapel to the house.

Surrey: just N of Redhill but difficult to find: reached from an unnumbered road (Gatton Bottom) which runs S of and parallel to the M25; turn S onto Rocky Hill Lane and church is in grounds of Gatton Hall, now the Royal Alexandra and Albert School

Gillingham

St Augustine, Rainham Road

Temple Moore

Temple Moore is an architect found more often in the North (the majority of his churches are in Yorkshire, especially E Riding). This late work of 1916 occupies an unsympathetic location, angled slightly towards the busy A2 in a continuous bit of development where Rochester, Chatham, Gillingham and Rainham run into each other.

Exterior of unattractive ragstone, but inside, notable spatial invention. A lopsided, barny N aisle (no S aisle) pulls one's eyes off course. Nave very high with surprising pierced effect: gallery runs intermittently through the wall above our heads. Arches picked out in Roman bricks. Subtle colours – sand for rendered expanses, muted red highlights. Garish E window, the only coloured glass, makes a wonderful flash behind

the big intervening rood. Two large allegorical paintings in N aisle, one a cross between Crashaw and Burne-Jones, both astonishing as 20c products.

Kent: just E of Chatham, on Rainham Road (A2); church lies on N side of road near W edge of Gillingham

Hale

St Mary

Thomas Archer

A unique curiosity, this small rustic church was incompletely transformed in 1717 by the great Baroque architect Thomas Archer, who owned the manor and lies buried inside.

The building is a bit of a hodge-podge, one side all in grey ashlar, others in brown stone with grey trim. But the mixture of colours seems witty as it does in Lutyens. The style is eccentric classicism: corner pilasters bulge in an exaggerated way, the main entrance has a Borromini-like frame, and an eyehole-window stares from above another door.

Inside, segmental arches at the crossing make an awkward space. Did Archer enjoy the sense of an incomplete conversion, or did something (expense?) inhibit him from making this entirely into his kind of space? His own memorial very pompous, with lifeless allegorical figures (his wives!) and his

Hale, a country church by the extremely sophisticated Thomas Archer

reclining self. We would prefer to think he had no hand in designing it.

Hants: about 12 miles SE of Salisbury off B3080; church W of village in grounds of Hale Park (NW of house)

Hardham

St Botolph

Romanesque wall paintings engulf the viewer completely here. All the interior surfaces of this simple whitewashed two-cell building are covered with scenes.

Although Clayton's paintings are greater works of art, Hardham is more satisfying, because the enclosing effect is more total and less interfered with by later losses. The whole space vibrates with ochre, rust and white.

Forty scenes have been deciphered, and certain ones will be quickly recognized – Eve milking, St George spearing (an infidel not a dragon, when the saint took part as an apparition in the Battle of Antioch), and the Devil riding. But the special pleasure of Hardham is that you must fight to make the faded images emerge from the walls. The longer you stay the more you are infused by these obscure meetings and struggles. Binoculars help, and show that every face bears a real expression.

Hardham church is pleasantly displaced from the London road. A few hundred yards to the S along A29 is a lovely Early English chapter house entrance, a stranded survivor of Hardham Priory.

Hardham, where the visitor is enclosed in Romanesque wall paintings

After Hardham and Clayton (q.v.), one might visit COOMBES (in farmyard 2 miles S of Steyning, on unnumbered road which follows W bank of River Adur), the humblest building of the three, with the clearest, most piecemeal bits of Romanesque painting of the Lewes school, discovered in 1949. These three churches together are like a Bible scattered in clumps with short stretches of the lanes of Sussex in between.

Sussex: Hardham is 7 miles N of Arundel, just S of A29

Hascombe

St Peter

Henry Woodyer

A supreme example of a small Victorian church on which infinite care has been lavished, and of the Ecclesiological type which saves its love for the chancel at the expense of everything else. It lies on a cul-de-sac which ends at a pond and public garden, in a region particularly good for early 20c houses (Voysey, Baillie Scott, Lutyens and others).

Henry Woodyer, the architect of St Peter's, was prolific, building much of no special character mainly in Berkshire and Surrey. At first perhaps this church looks a bit insignificant, and we fail to notice its whimsical details, like the lancet set into a buttress, or the peak of the roof-cone flattened to make a minute gable so there can be a window even there.

Woodyer was a pupil of Butterfield, but at Hascombe the interior exudes a richness only Burges has equalled. Behind a painted screen is a hard visionary dream, vaguely Eastern or maybe Slavonic – a reredos covered with angels on gold backgrounds like icons, lancets knitted in, and windowledges teeming like manuscript borders. Above, a roof structure like the skeleton of a fish. In the nave, walls are painted with nets behind which fish swim.

Surrey: 4 miles SE of Godalming just off B2130 to E

Hawkley

St Peter & St Paul

S. S. Teulon

An idiosyncratic essay in Romanesque built by Teulon in 1865.

The design of the tower is borrowed from Sompting, Sussex and the walls of

Woodyer's altar surround at Hascombe, an Eastern or Slavonic vision

crazy paving in chalk derive from local vernacular. Yet the results are quietly freakish. Low gables N and S don't quite amount to transepts, and the chalk has a subliminal greenish cast.

Inside, eccentricities are not obtrusive but nonetheless present: stylized Romanesque capitals in nave are matched by aggressive vegetable naturalism in the chancel arch. The E wall is a riot of jittery carving. Historical imitation provides the cover for formal quirks of the architect.

Near the end of N aisle a fantastic pierced screen conceals and reveals a chapel. Roof supports reputedly depict

all the trees mentioned in Scripture, and outside the W door stand ancient yews.

Hants: about 4 miles N of Petersfield, 1½ miles W of A325

Hove

All Saints, The Drive;
St Andrew, Waterloo Street

All Saints is another cathedral-scale work by **J. L. Pearson**, where the exterior is for once treated with uncharacteristic richness. The material chosen was golden stone now enhanced by a sooty black patina. S and E elevation towards street the best, where Pearson amuses himself varying tracery and pinnacles.

Inside we are surprised to find, not the expected vaulting but a wooden roof punctuated by great transverse arches in white stone. Clustered piers of the arcades impressive, chancel vaulted. A good Jesse window in the tower. Large brick vicarage by Pearson lies behind the church.

Hove also has a fascinating miniature church by **Charles Barry**, who designed the Travellers' and Reform Clubs in London. *St Andrew*, Waterloo Street, is Italianate and modest: stucco with stone dressings in front, plain brick behind. But such is the elegance and rightness of its unexpected detail that it feels like a

little work by Donatello. There's a small central belfry, with a porch under it tiled and closed by iron gates. Barry's is one of the earliest and least hackneyed Italianate buildings in England (built 1827–8), and follows oddly on the heels of his Gothic St Peter's, Brighton, of a few years before.

Sussex: W of Brighton and continuous with it

Idsworth

St Hubert

Approached up a long slope from the road. It lies at the end of a grass causeway between ploughed fields,

Itchen Stoke. An eccentric building whose architect built railways in Russia

where it sits on its own fenced island like a heroine in medieval romance.

Inside, the floors slope upward too, at three different pitches, steepest in the chancel. The crooked roof beams are limewashed, the box pews unpolished. A painted rood hangs over the simple pulpit, and a diapering of folk designs in plaster diversifies the chancel ceiling. The great surprise is extensive wall painting in two long horizontal scenes – on top what looks like a hunt, with its quarry a wild man, is in fact St Hubert healing; below, Salome's dance.

It turns out the plaster emblems are by Goodhart Rendel and belong to his restoration of the building from 1912 onwards. He also remodelled the manor house on the other side of the hill to W. Immediately to E, along the Sussex border, is remote downland with woods beautifully blended of dark firs and lighter hardwoods.

Hants: about 2 miles N of Rowland's Castle to E of unnumbered road which follows the railway line, opposite Heberdens Farm

Itchen Stoke

St Mary (CCT)

Henry Conybeare

An eccentric and effective Victorian church modelled on the Sainte-Chapelle in Paris.

The vicar was the squire's deputy in this almost feudal village. He and his architect-brother decided to tear down a building of recent vintage in order to erect this one.

A plan of amusing simplicity, coated in a rickety richness. After a strange cross-wise vestibule, you enter a tall narrow space with a peaked E end, which looks like a spiney sea-creature from outside. Windows at both ends are incredibly bright in colour. In between, a rapid succession of skinny lancets fill much of the wall space. Pulpit and pews are adorned with metal scrollwork of Eastern flavour.* Above them on the walls, tiling and panelling. The wooden roof appears to be inlaid with mother-of-pearl.

* The architect was also a railway engineer who laid out many lines in Russia, a training perhaps reflected in the church metalwork.

Hants: 6 miles NE of Winchester on B3047; church on N side of road in centre of village

Kemsing

St Mary the Virgin

A dear but unremarkable church, with memorable early 20c embellishments by Henry Wilson, Ninian Comper and Douglas Strachan.

It has a shingled spirelet and some old timbers in the porch. Comper gave the E end his full treatment: screen, rood, reredos and windows. This was done in various campaigns over the years 1894–1908. In S aisle a window designed by Wilson and executed by Christopher Whall. The two old men (Moses and Elijah) are clearly portraits, one of whom looks a lot like William Morris. The Strachan window in NW corner is rich and mythic, with a pouting expression.

More peculiar than any of this is the group of tombs by Henry Wilson for the Collets and Skarratts in extreme NE corner of the churchyard. These include a metamorphic cross with a lantern in its head and a stone table on stone legs hedged about with a carved rose-thicket.* Others have a pronounced Saxon or Celtic flavour. Incidentally, the horizontal placement of a big bronze relief on the table tomb shows that Wilson's architectural judgement sometimes faltered.

* These legs have since been stolen.

Kent: about 4 miles NE of Sevenoaks, just N of M26

Kemsing. A humble building with extraordinary 20c adornments

Lewes

A compact hill town (its name from the Saxon, *hlaewes*, hills) whose steep terrain has been its salvation. The curving High Street is one of the pleasantest in England, with many examples of a local speciality: mathematical tiles, which look like bluish glazed brick. Lewes Castle appears above the town as a magical apparition when floodlit at night.

None of the Lewes churches stands out but together they give an interesting conspectus of denominations and types. *St Michael*'s round 13c tower has an interesting large sculpture of its patron in fibreglass (by Harry Phillips, 1976) attached. *St Anne*, also in the High Street, possesses a S arcade of chunky refinement (late 12c). *All Saints*, down the hill, reached by various 'twittens' or passages, has the best churchyard, unless one prefers *St John sub Castro*'s to the N, where important Anglo-Saxon relics are embedded in the exterior walls of a crude building of 1839: in S wall a Danish prince-hermit's tomb with arched inscription in a mixture of Roman and Gothic. In an obscure NE corner an elaborate Saxon portal.*

Lewes is famous for Dissent and rich in old chapels. *Westgate*, Unitarian, in High Street, the oldest, is pleasantly tucked away, its interior chopped up before the First World War but still strong in 17c flavour. The cramped library with vertiginous views down into schoolroom is its most evocative space. Also a *Friends' Meeting House* of 1784 in Friar's Walk, and *Jireh Chapel* in Malling Street.

* This church is incorrectly orientated, with chancel facing N. All directions are therefore ritual, not actual.

Sussex: about 6 miles NE of Brighton just N of A27

Lingfield

St Peter & St Paul

For Surrey this is an impressive late Gothic church, rich in fittings.

There is a quaint approach to the churchyard between old houses, and the interior is spacious, with a large aisle like a second nave.

Behind a variety of screens some notable tombs, especially a couple of knights who rest, oblivious, on grimacing Saracens' heads. One of these is the founder and chief benefactor: his gauntlets are shown crossed on top of each other at his side. There is also a

Lingfield, with 'a variety of screens', complex spaces and notable monuments

Lyndhurst, a wild Victorian church with Morris glass and a Leighton fresco

two gorgeous capitals of enormous size, from an early Christian church at Ephesus. They sit right down on the floor. The walls are peppered with more such remains plundered from classical sites.

The baptistery is a little marble-coated cabinet focused on a huge lump of Egyptian alabaster. Over it hangs another ostrich egg.

Dr E. H. Freshfield, the patron, had travelled a lot in the Near East. His architect, Sidney Barnsley, is otherwise known for furniture in exotic woods and a few buildings in Cotswold vernacular. Barnsley executed the floral patterns on the ceiling himself.

Pines around the church came from seeds given by the King of Bulgaria.

Surrey: 3 miles N of Reigate on A217 just within M25; church on W side of road

Lullingstone

St Botolph

One of the most delightful buildings in Kent.

Reached by a circuitous route across a ford and down a rutted lane past an important Roman villa with remains of early Christian churches; then through a lavish Tudor gatehouse in brick. The church is a tiny two-celled structure to the L of a low manor house set off in wide lawns. Church appears humble with its slated towerlet and 18c plaster porch. Wide Decorated tracery in flint walls patched with brick.

Inside, a wonderful confusion of substances and flavours, including the chancel screen like a cross between German Gothic and Rococo. The entrance in its centre is a complex niche, as if a statue will be found within; along the top runs a miniature balustrade. The 17c font is a fantastic construction, like a little Tower of Babel half built into the wall.

In the brick N chapel, outlandish tombs, the oldest (1522) with rumbustious vegetable carving. Then a table tomb with allegorical figures of ill-matched sizes against a window. Opposite, a Gothick monument with marble palm trees to the 'beautifier' of the church, its inscription full of contentious politics.

Kent: about 3 miles S of M20 near its London terminus (exit 3) at M25. Leave A225 at Eynsford, going W over ford and following signs to Roman villa and Lullingstone Castle

large collection of brasses, the best in the county. Rarer and more vivid is an effigy incised on encaustic tiles like a drawing.

Surrey: 3½ miles N of East Grinstead on B2028; church lies N of this road

Lower Kingswood

The Wisdom of God

Sidney Barnsley

Arts and Crafts design married to Byzantine archaeology, with results unique in England.

The church is a simple gabled box with lean-to narthex. Nearby stands the more eccentric wooden bell tower with lead-covered Eastern dome and metal dragons jutting from the corners. This tower is modelled on a rural example in Bulgaria, the main body on St Eirene at Constantinople.

The interior is a haven of symbolism and gorgeous natural textures. In the chancel twelve different kinds of coloured marble coat walls, rails, floor and steps. In the apse a hemicircle of correctly laid gold mosaic formed of tiny pieces. All about hang large eggs, some porcelain, some genuine ostrich eggs, some plaster replacements.

Light fittings are flat rings of iron, wider than the aisle they hang over. The arcade of only two bays is wonderfully subtle. Punctuating it near the E end are

Lyndhurst

St Michael & All Angels

William White

A Victorian church of real individuality in a good position above the town, with some of the best of all 19c glass by William Morris and others.

William White, the architect, was a Hampshire man, distantly related to Gilbert White of Selborne. This church has been called his best work. He uses red and yellow brick inventively: even the spire is richly patterned. Eccentric dormers, prickly tracery and elaborate iconography in the W portal and elsewhere. The Scriptural imagination at work here is worth pursuing with the help of the church guidebook.

The interior is a shrine of Victorianness – jagged brick, faceted wood, vivid carving. Morris windows in E (New Jerusalem) and S transept (Answers to Prayer) are, as narrative, among the most interesting the firm ever did. Other main windows in the church make a telling contrast – an energetic Clayton & Bell rose in N, a luscious Kempe full of iridescent wings in W.

Behind the altar the weird, dull wall painting of 1864 is by Lord Leighton, the first fresco in England since the Reformation and consequently controversial at the time.* It shows Wise and Foolish Virgins. Marvellously fresh painting by a female Pre-Raphaelite in the S transept. In the churchyard is the grave of Alice Liddell of *Alice in Wonderland*, who lived with her husband in Lyndhurst.

* But the same technique was used at Highnam, Glos by the inventor Gambier-Parry in 1850–71.

Hants: 10 miles SW of Southampton on A35

Mereworth *

St Lawrence

A fancy Gibbsian church of 1744–6, surprising in a small village.

Its spire is elegant, perhaps too elegant. Under it, a hemicircle of columns juts out, capped by wooden eaves. The stone is a pleasing khaki colour trimmed in ochre.

Inside, a powerful Doric arcade and many painted illusions. Above the W gallery, organ pipes are depicted on slight bulges in the plaster. These look surprisingly Gothic, as Blake might have done them, a company of spectral icicles. More solid (painted) flowerets grace the aisles, and coffering fills the main vault. The great thermal window to the E is incongruously loaded with small-scale heraldry, predominantly orange-gold. It is interesting to see the effect a stodgy Gothic memorial of 1853 has in this setting: it seems more imaginative than it ordinarily would. Older tombs from the previous church are quarantined in a locked enclosure at the W end.

* Pronounced (approximately) Maryworth

Kent: 7 miles W of Maidstone, just W of A228/A26 junction

Minstead

All Saints

Minstead contains some of the oddest spaces in this or any other county.

Approaching, you get the most higgledy-piggledy welcome, different sizes and shapes of window in an assortment of extensions and outjutting parts. The effect is very domestic, brick with leaded windows and a number of dormers. The tower, in red and black brick, is the only halfway dignified bit, but even there such embellishments as dwarf pinnacles at the corners and a small wooden spike. The porch has a large white flap of a door on the outside, while within lies an Early English doorframe and a venerable medieval door.

You enter under a low gallery which swings round at right angles and is succeeded by yet another one higher up. There is also a transept like a second, higher nave at right angles to the real, first one, and only the parson in the pulpit at the pivot of the two could watch all the congregation at once. This three-decker pulpit is cosily tucked into the wall, half-obscuring the rugged 13c chancel arch, whose simple point seems heroic in these tame 18c surroundings. There are a couple of squires' pews, almost separate buildings, with their own entrances. The one nearest the altar has a fireplace and its own vestibule.

How cosy this brand of worship would have been.

A wonderful early Norman font stands under the pulpit, with a two-bodied Sumerian beast, Saxon eagles, a lamb like an ox, and three stumpy figures.

Conan Doyle, the creator of Sherlock Holmes, who chose to be remembered as 'Patriot, Physician, and Man of Letters', lies in the churchyard. His stone has a fatuous inscription which delights and appals, like his work.

Hants: 13 miles W of Southampton, 1 mile S of A31; church SE of village centre

Mereworth, a powerful 18c classical conception plunked down in a small village

83

Minstead. Some of the oddest spaces in England, mercifully untidied

New Romney

St Nicholas

A magnificent building in a shrunken town. Until the same 13c storms which overwhelmed Old Winchelsea, Romney was a major port and then this church sat at the head of the harbour, now long disappeared. The storms deposited so much soil against the N wall that you now go down a few steps into the aisle.

Inside, a powerful Norman arcade turns abruptly, but with aplomb, into a Decorated chancel. Old floors, old pews, and bold freehand hatchments in S aisle.

The E end makes a proud display – three great windows, the centre one a lattice of stacked quatrefoils over five lancets. Outside, the aisles are distinct, peaked co-equals of the nave. Inside, their ambitions have caused the Norman clerestory to be enclosed and created impressive spaces. The Norman W tower makes an unexpected vestibule, the pile of orders on its front busy with interest rather than harmonious.

1½ miles W on N side of A259 is St Clement, OLD ROMNEY. The settlement was presumably continuous once, Old Romney marking the upper end of the port. Now the church stands alone, deserted by its town – a humble and misshapen space of great power, which you step down into and can lose your way in, despite its small dimensions.

Pews and 18c gallery pinky tan with black trim. Floor of tile and tombslabs; naive saying boards in nave. A wonderful battered font with miniature capitals of diverse character.

Old photographs show this church to be a miracle of sympathetic restoration. The immemorial feeling dates from 1930, when a heavy-handed 18c functional interior was sensitively modified and more ancient bits allowed to show through without stripping away the 18c completely.

Kent: New Romney is 5 miles N of Dungeness Point on A259; church S of High Street

New Shoreham

St Mary de Haura (of the Harbour)

New Shoreham was founded by the Normans c1100 when the River Adur silted up at Shoreham (now Old Shoreham). It is a pleasantly insignificant place, and its large church in a large churchyard secluded from the High Street is the only sign of former glories. Even the church is only a magnificent fragment of what it was: sometime before 1720 the nave collapsed and a new W end was hastily patched up using old stone, so that now the W walls of the transepts appear to form part of the front.

One enters under the great tower arch, and meets the imposing vista of the choir, which iron railings prevent one from exploring. The N arcade is gorgeous Transitional, very rich, with leaves beginning to creep over the mouldings, and fancy stops.

New Romney. The east end like three distinct buildings

New Shoreham's tower is powerful though slender, and of pleasing texture (sympathetic, conservative restoration) with fruitful play between stages of different date. E end of chancel very plastic, with deep cut arcades below and pointed quatrefoils above the central lancets.

St Nicholas in OLD SHOREHAM (½ mile N) is of humbler proportions but its impressive Norman tower stump has a wonderful unobstructed opening. Entertaining mock Norman font (early Victorian) and an evocative churchyard with some good 19c memorials.

Sussex: in Shoreham-by-Sea between Brighton and Worthing; New Shoreham church just N of High Street (A259)

Northington

St John Evangelist

T. G. Jackson

In downland which begins to feel surprisingly remote, not far from the lovely medieval planned town of NEW ALRESFORD.

Wonderfully complete work by T. G. Jackson, of 1887–90, second only to his school chapel in Byzantine style at Giggleswick, W Yorks. It is now a strange anomaly, built by a landowner at the heart of his estate, where the big house (THE GRANGE: overpowering classicism by Wilkins and others) has become an unoccupied ruin, partly recovered by English Heritage (and visitable).

Jackson's church also feels untenanted though in pristine condition. It presents a powerful silhouette with its huge Perp tower, whose blended colours (flint with stone dressings) make a rich and somehow Oxford grey. Jackson has used the sloping site cleverly to create a towering French chevet in the E, enriched like the tower with over-sized blobs of grotesque carving.

Initially the interior seems bare, the idea of a church. Chancel ultra-elaborate at expense of nave. Remarkable ironwork, especially giant chandelier engulfing chancel, and Heath Robinson system for raising font cover. Earlier Ashburton memorials, mainly 18c, are relegated to the space under the tower.

Hants: 4 miles NW of New Alresford on B3046; a L turning marked Northington soon leads to church on L

Parham, serene in parkland from which the village it served has been cleared

Parham

St Peter

A dear little early Gothic remodelling (c1800–1820, just a step beyond Gothick) on its own eminence in the parkland of Parham House.

The house is a sprawling grey-white pile mainly Tudor, perhaps the model for Lutyens' LITTLE THAKEHAM nearby (3 miles W, now a hotel). The church's wonderful position is an 18c contrivance: Parham village which surrounded it was cleared in 1778–9 and the inhabitants rehoused in Rackham, out of sight of the house.

Nave walls are medieval; Tudor and 19c Gothic windows jostle each other, and a tower with miniature battlements has been added.

Inside, a demure and seemly impression – box pews in pine with rounded corners and trefoil beading, flimsy screen and railing, all stripped of their varnish in this century, with a lightening effect which makes them feel more 18 than 19c. The N transept made over into a very domestic squire's pew, with panelled ceiling, fireplace (a small stock of wood laid in), Raphaelesque painting over, and a vase of dried flowers.

Memorials in the corresponding vestry to the S, which also feels domestic. Curious lead font, 14c, decorated with inscriptions at right angles to each other, on a gimcrack stone base, capped by a wooden lid.

In the park miniature deer shelter in the dwarf forest of hawthorns. Nearby are two modest countrified churches at GREATHAM and WIGGENHOLT.

Sussex: about 10 miles NW of Worthing, in grounds of Parham House (which are entered from E); church is S of house, in sight of it

Portchester, in a unique position within a Roman harbour-fort

Pixham

St Martin

Edwin Lutyens

A small Lutyens dual-purpose building with a few delightful features.

The combination of hall and church in one explains certain eccentricities like three asymmetrically located fireplaces, which exit through chimneys concealed in the belfry.

The exterior of brick and pebbledash very domestic, except for the frontispiece with wonderful patterning and a huge hunk of Reigate stone now unfortunately rotting.

The main space has a simple barrel vault with a row of dormers on one side only. The chancel is a delight. It is capped by a saucer dome in chalk, Reigate stone and Roman tile. Here the banding of these materials makes a rich little enclave which is positively Byzantine.

Surrey: on the E outskirts of Dorking, on E side of a road which slices off a corner at the meeting of A25 and A24; church lies just S of railway which runs between Reigate and Guildford

Portchester

St Mary

One of the most interesting church situations in England. It sits in the SW corner of an immense Roman fortified enclosure at the top of Portsmouth Harbour. To reach it you drive down a charming Georgian High Street, another (like Titchfield: q.v.) of the surprising historical survivals of the Portsmouth area. Just beyond the church, passing through a gatehouse of dark ironstone, you find yourself in a vast watery landscape of reeds and tidal flats with grey warships in the middle distance.

This church is the lonely survivor from a peculiar past, remnant of an Augustinian priory that co-existed uneasily for twenty years in the 12c with the surrounding military establishment in the Castle. The W front is more tightly ordered than most things of its period in England and consists of three ornate windows above a portal.

Inside, a severe aisleless nave with high clifflike walls and great tower arches sparingly decorated with leaves and stems. Remarkable royal arms of Queen Anne, but the proudest element is a Romanesque font of bold design – on top, wild tendril medallions with a beast or bird caught in each; beneath, a miniature arcade of architectural firmness.

Hants: in Castle compound at SE tip of Portchester peninsula which fills N end of Portsmouth Harbour

Queenborough

Holy Trinity

Sheppey is a separate country, a place where one would like to linger. Kent has its former islands, like Thanet, but Sheppey still is one, with only one way across, the druidical bridge of 1960, whose four concrete piers form the frame of a great building which isn't there.

The western, inhabited end of Sheppey is scruffy, with notable churches in Queenborough and Minster. Queenborough is a decayed port where before the war grass grew in the cobbled High Street; the sea lies at the end of it. Its churchyard, full of naval tombs, is steeped in history and sinks under the burden. You go down into the church porch. The building feels almost domestic with its Tudor dormers in wood. The kindly organist, unable to open the door because the lock had been changed that morning, described the naive painted ceiling rapturously: it shows the Angel of the Apocalypse sounding the last trump, cherubim at the corners, sun and moon and stars overhead. Queenborough has caught a vision of the end in its little church.

Queenborough, Sheppey, domestic flavour in an evocative churchyard

The grander building at MINSTER (St Mary and St Sexburga; follow one-way system from B2008 up hill to Minster Abbey) sits on a sudden mound with extensive views of the marshes all around. At its W end a powerful tower base without a tower. Inside, fine effigies including a knight with graffiti in the vertical ridges of his armour as if they were ruled lines on a page. The graveyard at Minster was cleared to make a lawn twenty years ago. In Queenborough a less glorious history is savoured more reverently, but at Minster it is obliterated even now, by the awful recent construction that rises beside the palimpsest of the minster's N wall, and blocks it from view.

Kent: on W end of Isle of Sheppey; Queenborough church lies between High Street and B2007 to Sheerness

Romsey

Abbey Church of St Mary & St Elfleda

A large Norman abbey which survives more complete than usual because it was bought by the town after the Dissolution.

Though its impressive scale is evident from all sides, there is no satisfactory angle of approach, and nothing which feels like a main entrance. The S side has interesting relics but much harsh recent stonework; the N, more ragged and authentic textures.

The interior space is the great thing here, a three-storey Norman nave with

Romsey. A large abbey with beautiful arcades moving from Norman to Gothic

lovely Early English bays to the W. The W end is one of the most satisfying features of the church. Three equal lancets of enormous height and slimness fill the space. Fortunately the glass is clear. At the other end, effective Victorian glass by Powell, rich images which come apart like objects seen through heat haze.

The pale tones of the stone are very enjoyable throughout, and there is much diverse carving on capitals at the E end. Two venerable monuments – a small Saxon rood which was once gilded and bejewelled, and a large Norman one mounted outside on the transept wall. While touching as survivors, each of these is disappointing as a work of art. The little Saxon piece looks pasty like plaster. All but its outlines and minimal contour has been rubbed away; the composition is interesting for crowding figures on top of each other. In the outdoor image, the hand of God appearing in the clouds and the Sufferer's ruined arms have real dramatic impact, but the modelling of the torso seems flaccid. Nearby an interesting Norman doorway of irregular design,

Pixham, a Lutyens curiosity with amusing Byzantine features including a domed chancel

recently renewed. Also here, an eccentric Waterloo obelisk raised by 'a young architect of the town' in 1815.

Hants: 10 miles SW of Winchester on A31

Sandwich

St Clement

Sandwich, another of the decayed ports of Kent, is one of the most interesting towns in England. Though small it is baffling because few of the kinks in its medieval street plan have been ironed out. Its three medieval churches are wonderfully folded into the settlement on a hill beside a silted river – once a wide channel when this end of Kent was more watery, when Richborough fort sat on an island and Thanet lay across a considerable stretch of marshy land.

St Peter (CCT) lies at the centre, sitting angled in its churchyard. *St Mary* (also CCT) juts into the street at what used to be the edge of dry land (Strand Street).

St Clement (the best) is found at the end of a cul-de-sac overlooking Lutyens' whimsical town house The Salutation.

Sompting. A Saxon tower unique in England and many Saxon spaces and carvings within

It has an imposing Norman tower, wide Perp nave and aisles full of light with good ceilings. In NE pier of the tower arch is tucked a miniature Romanesque tympanum with tiny deer and a bird squeezed into a corner. In the S wall is a curious memorial with a frame and Dutch gable of small bricks.

Incidentally, St Peter's tower was rebuilt in brick after a bad storm by Dutch immigrants, a pleasing motley effect.

Kent: Sandwich lies between Ramsgate and Deal; Church Street St Clement runs E at top of High Street

Selham

St James

This tiniest of buildings contains extremely precious Anglo-Saxon elements which survived Victorian tinkering. In N wall recent repointing reveals, like a diagram, herringbone stonework where yellow fieldstone, dark ironstone and an occasional Roman brick seem to run in excited motion.

Coming in, after a tiny Victorian porch, the thrill of a narrow Saxon door. Inside, a chancel arch whose ornamented imposts are miracles of barbarism and depict a large snake-dragon biting its flowery tail and a smaller snake emitting flowers from its mouth. As usual the two sides of the arch do not match, and the richness and scale of the sculpture are too much for the space.

Note the squattest font in the world, and obscuring Victorian glass which makes the early features hard to see.

Sussex: 3 miles E of Midhurst, 1 mile S of A272; church at W end of village on S side of road

Shalfleet

St Michael Archangel

A church of charming rusticity with a Norman tympanum.

This is the Isle of Wight at its best, friendly and unpretentious. Under the figure in relief wrestling with two lions at once are wooden doors painted a homely mud or earth colour. Inside, a vivid arcade of grey cylinders and 17c tracery in the single aisle like three droopy eyes per window. A tombchest dated 1630 has been elevated above the S altar as if it is a shrine. A good graveyard beside the road, under the square W tower.

IoW: at W end of island, 4 miles E of Yarmouth on A3054; church on S side of road

Shere

St James

A prime example of Surrey picturesque in one of the most famously quaint villages in the county.

Gatehouses by Lutyens in the main road and a stream running through. The church lies at the end of a quiet cul-de-sac and is entered through a charming half-timbered porch. Its big square Norman tower, nicely rendered, wears a shingled broach spire.

Inside, good photographs of the crooked inner workings of the spire. Tower arches are rough but expressive in their various angles. Interesting Purbeck arches to the S, where the great width of the aisle makes the whole space feel lopsided. The squat Early English font is a pleasant dingy grey, and the nave piers are monstrous blocks, but in spite of everything there is a tidied feel about it, the whitewash too fresh, etc. The church guide gives the crucial clue to how this came about: an architect purified the impression around 1968 and did his job too well.

Surrey: 6 miles W of Dorking, just S of A25; church lies E of Middle Street which runs perpendicular to through road

Shorwell

St Peter

In a charming position, this church has the best interior on the island.

Along inland lanes, the Isle of Wight is picturesque in a way of its own, with a pronounced roll in the terrain like mild seasickness.

Shorwell is not especially promising outside, though mellow, with pierced stone plates in its bell openings. Inside, though, it is an exciting warren of spaces, with two wide, low arcades and many interesting memorials. Behind one altar is a complicated narrative brass. Behind another, a primitive Last Supper from Iceland. Beneath it are photos of the bleak island country from which it comes.

On the N wall are painted scenes from the life of St Christopher who appears, unusually, in a brocaded cloak. These occur in some nice river scenery and include lively fish.

IoW: in SW of island on B3323, 5 miles SW of Newport; church at crossroads

Sompting

St Mary

Its position now unfortunate, separated by a busy road from its village. Traffic noise never dies out here, but this is one of the most exciting churches in Sussex.

First of all, the unique Saxon tower with its Rhenish helm – from close to, a geometrical puzzle like an Escher drawing, confusing us over which surface is flat and which sloped, until roof and wall approach equality. The mouldings bisecting each side are perfect half-rounds, an un-Saxon-seeming refinement.

Selham. A tiny church with barbaric Saxon monsters on the chancel arch

Stoke Charity. Wonderful old textures in a Norman interior

Internally, a complex space, with changes of level; a place in which the visitor always feels off-centre. Part of the explanation is that the S 'transept' or porch was a separate and finally ruinous building until Victorian times. How fortunate the improvers didn't impose greater consistency when this mysterious spatial fragment was incorporated into the rest.

The tower arch includes fascinating Anglo-Saxon decoration – carving like a freehand sketch of pomegranate or pine cone, so naive we cannot tell which. Further Saxon bits embedded here and there: an abbot in the transept made entirely of bulges; Christ and the Evangelists in the N nave wall, a nobler kind of work where all the lobes are nicely organized. Rudest of all, the lattice frieze re-used to make a piscina in sanctuary. Further bits have come to rest near the altar.

Sussex: just N of A27 between Lancing and Worthing. NW of Sompting proper, church signposted

Stoke Charity

St Mary & St Michael

Surrounded by beautiful lanes and reached across a field. The humble exterior does not prepare you for the wonders within. Rich but crude Norman

arch and squint give views sideways through chancel into N chapel; from here tombs spill out and are cobbled into rest of church, a pleasing congestion of brass, wall plate and table tomb. Old tile floor in chapel and irregular old roofs throughout. Suns and stars of old glass intensify the daylight even on dark days.

From N the exterior proportions are almost Lutyens-like; high chapel, low ground-hugging nave, a thrilling contrast. Here too a Norman extravagance – the tiny priest's door with huge carved detail.

Hants: 6 miles N of Winchester, between A33 and A34

Titchfield

St Peter

This village is a miraculous survival, constantly threatened with development, but defended by vigilant residents. It is a decayed port and former market town only a mile or two from Fareham (which has outstripped Titchfield, only to be destroyed by traffic and shopping complexes).

The church sits back in a large churchyard. Sadly an adjoining orchard is now full of houses which should have been built anywhere but here. The W tower greets you from the High Street with a rich and venerable surface of irregular courses and differing sorts of stone. In the Anglo-Saxon building it was not a tower but a high and narrow porch. The church is entered through it, passing 17c iron gates which complement the heroic arches.

Interior sadly smooth and Victorianized after this, but two marvellous Jacobean tombs in SE chapel – a big one, many-tiered, in the middle, with small heraldic animals starting up from it like over-active finials (crowned heifers with chains from their noses; large heifer heads too at W corners); also some pink obelisks. This one commemorates the 2nd Earl of Southampton and his parents. The other, attributed to Epiphanius Evesham, is small – a child's wall monument of elegant shape with a touching effigy and a putto in a niche on top of its gentle arch, all in white and black marble.

Hants: 9 miles NW of Portsmouth, S of A27; follow signs to Titchfield village, which the road system makes hard to reach

Tunbridge Wells

King Charles the Martyr

A curiosity, this humble 17c building has been decked out in a magnificent plaster ceiling like a visitor to the baths with ideas above his station.

After taking the waters here became fashionable, a simple chapel was knocked up, which was soon enlarged, and then finally doubled in size. So the present building is awkward: its gabled roofs run cross-wise, and the internal space is unimpressively flat. The famous ceiling is wonderful in detail, but like a display of jelly moulds, which doesn't necessarily form up into a whole.

There are dark old galleries and two elegant columns in the middle, with carved bases which are salvaged portions from the former pulpit. The building sports a wooden cupola and sits sideways to surrounding streets, near the chalybeate spring which brought the courtiers here in the first place. From it also radiates the Pantiles – named for the surface underfoot, since replaced with flagstones – one of the first recreational shopping complexes in the world.

Kent: 12 miles SE of Sevenoaks on A26; church lies to SW of present town centre on S side of A26

King Charles the Martyr commemorated in fancy plasterwork at Tunbridge Wells

Warminghurst

Holy Sepulchre (CCT)

Remote and unspoiled. Modest medieval fabric made over in the 18c, apparently using some Tudor doorframes from William Penn's seat nearby (at COOLHAM, 3 miles SW, a

Wingham, an Oxenden monument with oxen and putti in attitudes of grief

Quaker meeting house which Penn frequented). Wonderful bleached wood of 18c pews and graceful three-arch screen. Above it, the great feature of the church – a grandiose folk painting of the royal arms, on a bold blue ground under a red-violet canopy in many swags – an exceedingly cheerful effect. In chancel (N wall), an entertaining brass in a well-carved wall plate, where the little figures, spouting Trinitarian sentiments on brass mouth scrolls, have bled most charmingly on greyish-yellow stone. Those commemorated are 16c ancestors of the poet Shelley, between whom and Penn another owner of the manor intervened.

Sussex: 8 miles N of Worthing, 1 mile W of A24 in direction of Thakeham

Whippingham

St Mildred

Prince Albert and A. J. Humbert

The nearest church to Osborne House, designed by Prince Albert, is a fascinating Victorian hodge-podge.

The style is basically Romanesque with certain unhistorical frills and embellishments. The strong central tower for example has silly pinnacles and a picturesque peaked lantern. On the way in you pass the fantastically elaborate porchlet with a door leading to the royal pew. It is marked VR. The pew contains Victoria's own chair and emotional memorials to the Consort and two children who predeceased her.

Albert had the help of an architect, A. J. Humbert, who is not mentioned in the prominent inscription. A main principle of their design is inclusion – discordant materials and techniques jostle each other: carved stone, painted wood and plaster. The inscription over the chancel arch is suitably large and unbuttoned in its sentiment.

Opposite the royal pew is the Battenburg Chapel with an Art Nouveau grille by Alfred Gilbert and sexy glass in the E window. It also contains a crucifix designed by Princess Louise in which the cross is swarmed over by a large angel.

Nice glimpses of the Cowes estuary from the churchyard.

IoW: about 1½ miles S of East Cowes, ½ mile W of A3021

Winchelsea

St Thomas the Martyr

Like other towns along this coast, Old Winchelsea, which lay on the other side of Rye, fell victim to caprices of the sea. A few fierce late 13c storms nearly obliterated it, and the new town was planned atop a steep hill six miles away. The River Brede became in its turn unusable, and by the late 16c merchants had deserted New Winchelsea for Rye. What remains is unlike anything else in England, a perfect 13c planned town, significantly depopulated and as a result unnervingly like Hampstead Garden Suburb. Streets are wide and sparsely built, with handsome 18c-looking houses, an ambiance which attracted artists and writers in the early 20c (Stephen Crane and Joseph Conrad, among others).

The church is a fragment like the town, partly ivy covered, lacking its nave, which may have disappeared in the brutal French raids of the 14c. It sits in the centre of a huge churchyard. Astonishingly cusped tracery in chancel windows contrasts with pink stone of the fabric.

Inside, the richness is overwhelming and not exactly pleasant. Douglas Strachan's windows of 1928–33 (late Art Nouveau) dazzle and confuse but make a rare ensemble predominantly rich blue (subtler ones at RYE, of similar date, donated by E. F. Benson the novelist). The walls are lined with florid niches, and there is plenty of evidence of the town's 20c wealth in some neo-Gothic fittings.

Two famous 14c effigies along S wall are entertaining. One, usually identified as first Admiral of the Cinque Ports, holds his extracted heart and turns towards us. Remnants of an angel fluffing his pillow and an obedient lion at his feet. (Millais used this tomb for *The Random Shot*, 1854, which shows a small child asleep on it covered by a soldier's cloak.) The second, possibly a later admiral, pushes a quartered shield towards the spectator.

Sussex: about 2 miles SW of Rye, in centre of Winchelsea

Wingham

St Mary

Wingham High Street combines the formality of a town with the scale of a village. Turning out of it towards this

Warminghurst. Remote and unspoiled, with bold folkish painting and old bleached wood

church of surprisingly grand proportions, you pass remnants of canons' houses dating from the time the church was collegiate.

Tower with good bell openings and copper spire; nice Perpendicular window frames on N where the aisle has disappeared. Inside a pleasantly lopsided effect from this loss, and a surprising wooden arcade, the columns being great tree trunks. The story behind this oddity is that the builder absconded with the money collected for the stone arcade, so it could only be afforded in this cheaper material.

St Mary's great feature is the Oxenden Chapel at the end of the S aisle, behind light frilly 17c iron screens. The space is engorged by a marvellous obelisk draped with carved garlands and flooded with light. At the four corners are lively putti in exaggerated attitudes of grief; beneath them four black marble oxheads placed diagonally. Other monuments here too, including one with exquisite Virtues languidly dangling books. Altarpiece from Troyes (15c) with squashed narratives of monkey-like figures in an unattractive pasty stone retaining traces of colour. There are unfortunate plans afoot to erect wood and glass screens towards the W end of church, as has been done to such bad effect at Chartham.

Kent: midway between Canterbury and Sandwich on A257; church lies just N of this road

Home Counties & London

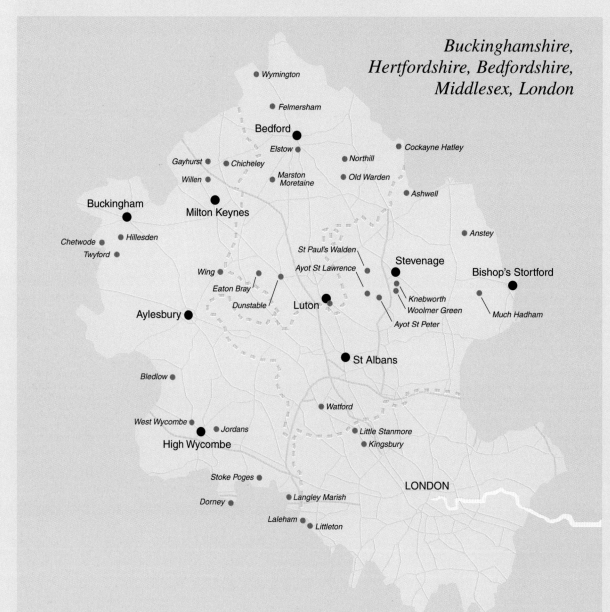

Wymington

Felmersham

Bedford

Elstow · Cockayne Hatley

Gayhurst · Chicheley · Northill

Willen · Marston Moretaine · Old Warden

Buckingham · Ashwell

Milton Keynes

Chetwode · Hillesden · Anstey

Twyford

St Paul's Walden

Wing · Stevenage

Eaton Bray · Ayot St Lawrence · Bishop's Stortford

Dunstable · Luton · Knebworth

Aylesbury · Woolmer Green · Much Hadham

Ayot St Peter

St Albans

Bledlow

Watford

West Wycombe · Jordans · Little Stanmore

High Wycombe · Kingsbury

Stoke Poges · LONDON

Dorney · Langley Marish

Laleham · Littleton

WHO CAN BE SURE whether 'Home' Counties is a term of affection or contempt? There are various Home Counties flavours, but it always means small scale with bounded horizons. Some of the most enchanting rural spots in these parts resemble countryside kept as a tasteful park. Even the Chilterns seem hills framed with Sunday walks in mind. For those who like amiable landscapes though, Bucks and Herts at their best are hard to improve on.

On the whole these counties are hunting grounds for curious and surprising rather than truly ambitious churches. A fair number of 18c (and later) pranks are found here: a notable class is the church as an attic full of fancy imported woodwork (Cockayne Hatley, Old Warden).

Middlesex has been swallowed by London, but its memory is preserved in this book because it harbours a few former village and estate churches, reminders of the pre-urban past.

London possesses the richest concentration in the whole country of 18c and later churches, which are widely known and mostly locked. In the face of these huge numbers, well covered elsewhere, I have opted for the most summary treatment.

Anstey

St George

Worth a long detour – the most lovable building in the county. Approached from the W it stands up proud on its mound, and the angle buttresses on its tower look heroic.

The Early English or perhaps just folkish decoration in the chancel is beyond praise for its vigour and clarity, including bulgy mouldings like limbs and the stop on the priest's door of a radiating heart-leaf fern. Every detail contributes to the impression of simple force – the clerestory quatrefoils with deep reveals, triple lancets in the transept with overhanging hoods, and above all the much earlier font, formed from four mermen holding their tails up like swags of cloth.

The whole place breathes a spirit familiar in certain modern sculptors, Lipschitz say, of refinement relinquished in pursuit of strong plastic statement. Over many centuries little Anstey has been lucky in the number of workers it has spawned with something authentic to say; much else by contrast is schoolroom or library work.

This church has a collection of old graffiti which unlike Ashwell's (see below) are mostly pictures not words, and inspired in the way children's drawings are.

Behind the church a moated earthwork. Apparently there were never masonry defences. Now this land-art forms a nice complement to the innocently unconventional church.

Herts: near Essex border ENE of Buntingford and 5 miles E of A10

Mermen holding their tails on the Anstey font

Ashwell. The barn-like interior with old screens and uneven floors

Ashwell

St Mary

Ashwell lies in a little northern arm of Hertfordshire which feels remote. Around here more chalk in the soil gives the fields a silvery cast. There is a marvellous first glimpse of the church tower as you come down from the W towards the village in its declivity. Although it is below you, the tower seems enormous – mottled, but mainly white, and tapering upwards.

The building is hidden from the High Street, reached through a rustic double lychgate at SW corner of churchyard, or down a snicket from the S, which leads towards windows like misremembered late Gothic. On this side it is extremely mellow and the interior truly barn-like. A farm wagon would not be unexpected in the aisle. There are old screens and uneven floors: almost nothing to break the spell except a spot of garish Victorian glass.

Under the tower and on various pillars in the nave you find the building's great popular claim to fame, an extensive set of early graffiti, including a surprising rendition of Old St Paul's in London.

But after this there is another side to the church and the village. The ingenious Tudor N porch has, sad to say, acquired harsh new parapets. Old photographs show that the tower has received the same treatment. And this village is not as innocent as it wants us to think. A little to the E is the railway station with lines of commuters' cars.

Herts: 4 miles NE of Letchworth, 2 miles from A1

Ayot St Lawrence

St Lawrence

Nicholas Revett

A curiosity or landowner's prank designed in the 1770s by Nicholas Revett, not long back from collecting material in Greece for his *Antiquities of Athens*. It is a papery design more like garden ornament than church. The miniature classical temple is extended by airy screens at both sides, each ending in an open pavilion filled by an 'altar' with a pineapple finial – tombs of the founder and his wife.

Inside, unclogged and chaste – all the paraphernalia of the medieval past swept away by the 18c purist, leaving a vase-like font, garden bench seating and a memorial urn suspiciously like a patent stove. Nearby in the village is the ruin of the outmoded Gothic church, which the landlord was tearing down when the bishop got wind of it and stopped him. Its churchyard is now locked, with

Ayot St Lawrence. A design by an 18c antiquarian which sweeps aside the medieval past

amusing recent gates of Etruscan inspiration standing guard.* Bernard Shaw spent his last years in Ayot St Lawrence (his house now run by the National Trust), which lies at the centre of a tangle of narrow lanes.

* These gates have since been stolen.

Herts: about 3 miles W of Welwyn on unnumbered roads, well signposted. Church is best approached by the footpath just W of old church ruin, N of road

Ayot St Peter

St Peter

J. P. Seddon

A gem by the proto-Arts and Crafts designer J. P. Seddon, in a wonderfully obscure location.

It puts its complex apse towards the road. This includes an impossible profusion of miniature forms. The sense of abundance is increased by elaborate patterning in the brick. On the N, white bricks are covered in a chartreuse growth.

Inside, the double-hipped roof is notable, with a rose window in the W and a working out of Seddon's fascination with the circle in a half-sphere of roof at the E end. Under it, a complete circle of mosaic on the floor. Windows, designed by Seddon, have figures too big for their spaces. Another surprising rose appears opposite the organ.

The chancel arch looks like Purbeck marble; it is in fact glazed ceramic. Nice ironwork, a curious font and lovely tile floors, the only jarring note being a Byzantine heaven full of ill-drawn angels painted on the chancel ceiling.

Former school by Seddon next door.

Herts: 1–2 miles NW of Welwyn Garden City, just W of A1

Bledlow

Holy Trinity

In mellow seclusion, it has some charming early Gothic features.

The path towards it leads between raised banks and rises before falling gently. An attractively plain porch has Early English doorways inside and out.

Lovely old plaster in the interior and a chaste arcade with clear leaf forms. The screen by a local craftsman is perfect, reticent Arts and Crafts. Traceries and window frames are outstanding: in the chancel round mouldings and irregular sexfoils; in S aisle a complex frame on whose sill sits a wooden candlestick with a wooden flame. There's also a painting of a winged figure given by a famous aviatrix.

Bucks: 2 miles W of Princes Risborough, about ½ mile S of B4009; church on the cross street

Chetwode

St Mary & St Nicholas

An entertaining jumble, where an Early Gothic fragment of noble power (remains of an Augustinian priory) is approached through a domestic and rustic prologue so that it feels like pieces haphazardly joined. Its low barny tower is off-centre and the whole is attached to an adjoining farmyard, now undergoing conversion.

You come in under the tower through a humble door with original iron-mongery. A primitive message board with cherubs greets you, and ahead appear incongruously grand lancets with

Seddon's apse in patterned brickwork at Ayot St Peter anticipates Arts and Crafts

detached columns between and generous window splays. On S wall a tranquil series of sedilia with a priest's door forming one of the series.

Gorgeous bits of 13 and 14c glass above these, single figures in mandorlas against grisaille ground. Opposite, comic-book memorial windows, post-Second World War. Branching off the nave, like a distended transept, is a large manor pew, with fireplace, hipped Gothick vault and gas lighting.

Bucks: 5 miles SW of Buckingham near Oxfordshire border in good lanes

Chicheley

St Laurence

A charming miniature – an early 18c chancel added to a Gothic church, with blind niches and cryptic heraldry on the E end. Inside, a delightful contrast between Comper's frilly Rococo-Gothic rood in rich walnut and the 18c fittings, including a plaster wreath on the chancel ceiling. In N aisle a remarkable tomb of 1576, whose cool sexiness comes straight from Fontainebleau. It shows a naked cadaver stretched between two free-standing caryatids.

CHICHELEY HALL, behind a screen of shrubbery to the E, is of course much more striking than the church. The old attribution to Thomas Archer has been abandoned, but the house, of brick with stone trim, remains a fascinating building, which borrows from Borromini and pushes him still further. It has some of the most bizarre doorframes in England and an unorthodox frieze with jutting rams' heads at the corners.

Bucks: 6 miles NE of Milton Keynes, just S of A422

Cockayne Hatley

St John the Baptist

At the end of a cul-de-sac of several miles. A former road system running E from Cockayne Hatley has disappeared. In the past fifty years the estate which this church is linked to has had a chequered history. The surrounding fields, now planted in corn, rape and peas, have been successively orchards, and a chicken farm housed in a fleet of old London buses.

The fabric is mainly brown cobbles, in all different sizes, so that it looks like a pebble or gingerbread building. The proportions are odd too – the tower too large for the rest which, especially from inside, seems a bit accordioned as if all the regulation parts are squeezed into too little space. Gothicky pinnacles and long bell openings increase the effect of a toy church.

The imported fittings, mostly of wood, are incredible – unrustic and of recent insertion – but an overwhelming success. The estate had been unoccupied for sixty years when Henry Cockayne Cust took over as squire and rector in 1806. On Christmas of that year snow fell on the altar during a service. Cockayne Cust set about a lengthy restoration which was finished by 1830. He bought the woodwork of various dates from churches in Malines, Louvain, Antwerp, Ghent and Aulne and created an overall effect of crazy and agreeable richness.

There is the organ with carved garlands like streamers or windblown Spanish moss, a marvellous set of gates in the huge tower arch before the organ, a screen for the N chapel (incorporating lattices from confessionals), then pews collegiate-wise in the nave, a swelling altar rail with Eucharistic emblems and, best of all, the chancel stall-backs. These are richest 17c Baroque and show a series of sixteen recent saints and fathers of the Roman Catholic Church: each a characterful bust, many dyspeptic in mitre or biretta, surrounded by juicy

Cockayne Hatley. A brown cobble exterior conceals a wealth of woodwork within

garlands and divided by putti wielding diverse emblems of the Passion. It is like stumbling into the deliberations of an outmoded learned body. Willement's garish glass (of 1829) in E window looks 17c (it meant to look older) and shows a real knack for narrative. Some lovely bits of 13c glass were rescued from a Yorkshire church and set in N chapel window. There is an entertaining Elizabethan monument on S wall (reset by Cockayne Cust). A descendant was instrumental in getting the real life model of Peter Pan's Wendy buried in the churchyard.*

Like many village names, this one seems to produce meaning from purely fortuitous collocations. It was Hatley Port at least as late as the 15c (from the de Port family, owners in the 12 and 13c), then became *Cockayne* Hatley (Sir John Cockayne purchased the manor in 15c) to distinguish it from East Hatley and Hatley St George nearby. *Hatley* may contain the old name of a local hill, or may be a personal name, *Haetta's leah* (or glade). So the suggestion of cocked hats, or hats askew in the Land of Cocaigne (or cocaine) which lend the name its raffish poetry have no historical warrant at all.

* Nearby are the ashes of her father, the model for Stevenson's Long John Silver.

Beds: about 5½ miles NE of Biggleswade. Leave B1040 in Potton and follow unnumbered road E (past Potton church) for 2 miles

Dorney

St James

Fascinating setting – the church is locked in among farm buildings and a grand old rectory, like a fragment of urban space deep in the country, one of those places where time unexpectedly stands still.

It is much more ancient than the most obvious features suggest; a wonderful assemblage, whose highlights are the chewed out space created by a 17c gallery – the floor drops precipitously to make room for it – a Jacobean chapel of brick with its own screen tied together by old ironwork like string, and an 18c squire's pew.

It is at this point that textures really bring the history of the place alive. To its walls are attached some 18 and early 19c memorial plaques of hammered metal, the latter smooth like slate, the former battered to leathery consistency. The font is a Norman fragment on which a repeated fleur-de-lys resembles the strapwork of a much later time.

Bucks: about 3 miles NW of Eton; church is W of village and B3206, on S side of the road to Dorney Reach

Dunstable

Priory Church of St Peter

Remnant of a large Augustinian priory which survives because it was taken over by townspeople after the Dissolution. In part this must have been a satisfying revenge, because the local folk had originally been relegated to the N aisle while the canons kept the larger precincts for themselves.

The interestingly confused W front reflects attempts to patch up after a storm which made ruins of both corner towers. Now the front is an anthology of motifs which includes rich Norman arcading, Decorated niches higher up, and plenty of interesting carving: vivid capitals with demons attacking rich men and taut vegetable webs on the central door (there is no S door now, but one is implied in the design) and marvellous decorative mouldings in the N door's hood, taking the form of geometrical solids (cones, flattened cones, cylinders) reduced to lacework by carving and separated by bands of string moulding.

Insignificant SW tower, post-Dissolution. E end shows truncation (chancel of the priory church is gone), and aisle walls give signs of Victorian tampering.

Immured among farm buildings, Dorney includes early brickwork in a wealth of different textures

Inside, hefty Norman arcades and dark screen which though late Gothic in style echoes its Norman surroundings in massive proportions and wide openings. All is much easier to see because obstructive Edwardian stained glass has recently been replaced by a lavish set of John Hayward windows, rich bits of colour on a white field. Other modern works have also been discreetly introduced.

Beds: just W of Luton on A5; church is E of main crossing, along A505

Eaton Bray

St Mary the Virgin

A peculiar building, from outside bleakest Tudor, like a Methodist chapel, in pleasant whitish stone. Inside, modest proportions but gorgeous carving, especially N arcade which seems to have wandered in from somewhere else. Twelve rolls of moulding (six from each side) meet over each clustered pier, and instead of attached columns against the walls there are lavishly carved stops, elongated like stone horns. Later S arcade is cruder. All stone has been painted an unpleasant cream colour.

Otherwise, the interior seems unfinished and raw, except for one of the most beautiful fonts in England, an Early English variation on a Norman theme, a spheric bowl trapped by four small columns at the corners.

The explanation of how this fineness came to inhabit this place so incompletely: after a prolonged quarrel and before his plans were finished, the lord of the manor was forced to yield the church to a nearby priory.

Beds: about 4 miles SE of Leighton Buzzard, E of A4146. Turn at Edlesborough church (full of interesting features, but generally locked)

Elstow

Abbey Church of St Mary & St Helena

Although Elstow is now on the outskirts of Bedford, it preserves an old precinct around the impressive fragment of an abbey. Just S of the church, interesting remnants of the early 17c house built from stones of the abbey by Thomas Hillersdon. Here a lavish frontispiece like a Mannerist engraving is in the last stages of decay.

Eaton Bray's multiplied mouldings on early Gothic arcades

Like Marston Moreteine's (q.v.), Elstow's tower is detached, and nearby there is Norman carving in a strange, gaunt style (over N door, but not a tympanum).

Inside, the walls have been viciously scraped. A huge Norman arcade ends abruptly with an E wall inserted after the Dissolution. Its awkward windows are now filled with Victorian glass like cheap jewellery. Some good bits of older carving have been embedded in it, along with a demure late 16c tomb in place of a reredos. In the floor nearby are lodged two elegant brasses showing nuns from the old nunnery.

Windows at both aisle-ends commemorate John Bunyan, who was baptized in this church and wakened to his sins by its bells. These are not high art, but very entertaining. Note the militant inscription under the N window.

Architecturally, the vestry is probably the most interesting space. Certainly it is the oddest – a low vaulted room with a central Purbeck column. The pattern of the vault is hard to describe. Main ribs are interrupted by sub-members, making a string-bag or honeycomb effect. The motive seems to be to produce finer wall divisions than the single vault would accommodate, or perhaps to achieve complexity for its own sake.

Beds: just S of Bedford; church in cul-de-sac at N end of village

Felmersham

St Mary the Virgin

Small but lavish Early English, the best in the county.

It lies near the River Ouse which is frequently flooded. Sadly, Felmersham has been too officiously looked after, so that most external stonework is renewed (a wonderful punched out window in S transept the latest casualty), and plush runner carpets cover too much of its floor.

Thus, to a certain extent, one is greeted with reminiscences of early Gothic rather than the thing itself. Lovely internal mouldings survive, however, especially those around the three W windows. Huge and entertaining corbels support the roof. One of them looks at us upside down and threatens a rude unveiling. In the serene chancel there is a post-war window like an illustration from a children's book, with a saint in a turquoise halo.

The church's proudest display is its W front, made to feel narrow and high by its situation above the road, and also by crowded tiers of motifs. The main door has one of those miraculously multiplied mouldings which early Gothic loves, and exquisite trefoils and quatrefoils dotted in the flanking arcades. The system of this front would yield up many of the secrets of the Gothic marriage of awkwardness and grace. Ruskin could have founded a whole morality on its rhythms.

Other good churches along the river include mellow ODELL, and the diminutive PAVENHAM, adorned in the 19c with assorted Jacobean woodwork.

Beds: Elstow about 7 miles NW of Bedford, 2 miles W of A6

Gayhurst

St Peter

An amusing early 18c church, lavish but ignorant in its classical detail.

It has a lovely situation in the grounds of a large Elizabethan house, to which William Burges made some eccentric additions including a monastic kitchen.

The proportions of the church could have inspired Burges. On N and S sides are stretched pediments (a heating flue runs up the centre of the N one). It is hard to believe this isn't the later recasing of a medieval building, because its parts and proportions stay so slavishly close to Gothic norms. The tower finishes with a comical lead bauble, and the low chancel has an empty niche instead of a window.

Inside, the plasterwork makes an instructive comparison with Willen nearby: this is much cruder. Books and mitres alternate over the capitals; at the corners big plaster books disappear into the wall as if returning to the shelf. On the right of chancel arch, and falling

Gayhurst. The squire's pew with two bewigged occupants in marble

within the squire's pew, is a large theatrical monument with two standing wigged figures. Many nightmares must have been started by these ancestors looming so near.

Very near to the SE is one of John Soane's most perfect works, a gatehouse, bridge and house at TYRINGHAM, in a relation to each other which is truly Elysian. Unfortunately the house was given a Second Empire dome by its crass Edwardian owner, but the gatehouse remains a work of surgical incisiveness.

Bucks: Gayhurst church about 2½ miles NW of Newport Pagnell, near M1 and just W of B526 in grounds of Gayhurst House

Hillesden

All Saints

Surprising to come upon a perfect late Gothic church in this remote location, and a special thrill as one approaches to see right through a clerestory of almost continuous glass. The structure is skewed towards the NE and an exuberant towerlet with open crown top (more familiar in Scottish examples), an effect which will be better understood from inside.

Lavish panelling in chancel and N chapel, and a frieze of angels up under the roof, which is painted teal blue with ribs picked out in white. The arcades are golden Cotswold stone, and much of the old screen survives. In SE window a complete 16c narrative of St Nicholas. Next to it (to W), fairly good Victorian pastiche (Prodigal Son, etc).

In N chapel, which seems to pull the church towards a vanished manor house (and into which there is a squint to allow the squire's family to attend service unobserved), are three interesting tombs: a knight and lady in alabaster with fine detail (1560), a scrolly cartouche whose triple fringe looks like some part of fish anatomy, and a comical strapwork tomb with two tubby caskets, one stuck under the pediment and looking like a frieze out of control. The present organ gallery with its powerful carved ornament must be the 17c manor pew. Two bits of vivid folk art under the tower – Moses and Aaron in integral, pedimented, marbelized frames.

Bucks: 3 miles S of Buckingham, in hamlet at end of cul-de-sac among farms

Jordans

Friends' Meeting House

A peaceful place of associational value. William Penn, Proprietor of Pennsylvania, lies buried here.

The spreading brick building of 1688 sits in a garden with a scattering of recessive gravestones. There are treey vistas to the W.

Inside, at the end of the room, panelling rises to a kind of pediment under a window and behind a raised bench. Otherwise, little emphasis, but a precise decorum and a homely brick floor. A serious fire in March 2005 caused damage it will take an estimated 18 months to repair.

The nearby village is charming and mysterious. Its green is so huge that houses on the other side feel almost lost to view. This is no 18c project, but an idiosyncratic version of the garden suburb dating from the First World War.

Bucks: 22 miles W of London, 2 miles N of M40 (exit 2); Meeting House lies S of Jordans village on E side of unmarked road

Kingsbury

St Andrew

Some of the richest Victorian fittings have found their way to this remote corner of outer London.

In 1933–4 this church was moved stone by stone from a depleted inner city parish in Marylebone. It was to be the first of a series of such transfers, but remained the only one carried out. Along with All Saints, Margaret Street, it is a key monument of Tractarian religion.

Its size and pinnacled spire do not accord with the idea of a church which was hemmed into a small site in a narrow street. The interior is high, clean, light and lovingly kept. An austere contrast of stone arcades and plaster walls sets off the lavish fittings, like Street's awesome stone reredos whose lacework passes in front of the E window (which replaces a Pugin one lost in the war).

The best designers contributed: glass various and magnificent, especially Te Deum window in Art Nouveau tones (W wall), font cover of endless complexity by Pearson, iron pulpit by Street, founder's tomb high up on wall by Burges (his inlaid reading desk for St Andrew now in V&A).

All this evidence of the pious enthusiasm of a century ago becomes even

Hillesden, a perfect late Gothic church in a hamlet

more moving through its displacement, a reminder of vanished belief.

Middx/London: near the S end of Church Lane NW9 1 mile NE of Wembley Park Underground station

Knebworth

St Martin*

Edwin Lutyens

A Lutyens church of 1914–15, full of learning and imagination.

Lutyens built a good deal at Knebworth for his wife's family the Lyttons, including a major house and some cottages. This church is a wonderfully simple building informed by Lutyens' wit.

In part its mode is that of St Paul's, Covent Garden ('the finest barn in England'), brick with overhanging wooden eaves. The architect insisted on handmade bricks and best Baltic timber. Inside, two enormous Tuscan columns block the transepts. In the aisles one enters a world of tiny roundhead arcades, as if an Early Christian building had been set down inside the larger one.

Some gorgeous Lutyens fittings in limed oak, set on huge stone bases like fallen cornices from a vanished St Peter's. These are reached by chancel steps of teasing black and white chequered pattern.

Unfortunately the great columns (as well as the small ones) have been painted. Only their bases subtly merging with the

Knebworth, with Lutyens fittings including the teasing chequered stair

walls are full of dark and gritty ironstone mixed with milder white and grey. This erratic masonry looks Anglo-Saxon, and two roundheaded Norman windows show themselves vestigially in the E wall. Tudor brick clerestory, amusing brick porch and Gothick tower top in brick with quatrefoil glazing.

Inside, altar rail and font cover are best, the first deep carved with Hebrew emblems on one side, Christian on the other. The second is like a lacy cake cover. Underfoot, nice old tiles.

Middx/Surrey: 4 miles S of Heathrow Airport, not much more than a mile apart; Laleham is on B376, Littleton further E, and less than ½ mile N of this road

Langley Marish

St Mary the Virgin

One of the most interesting churches in the county. The Kederminster pew and library are unique in England.

A surprising backwater in this built-up area. The church is a wonderful mixture of flint and brick, and of forms from various dates, such as the peaked cross-gabled porch like a garden pavilion. The large churchyard is framed on both sides by almshouses in brick, with tiny Dutch gables and other charming details.

It is sad to learn that road widening after the war swept away the 16c vicarage with the churchyard and a row of old cottages opposite. The road still

wooden floor suggest the contrast of texture Lutyens wanted. A W portico was planned, and remained unbuilt until 1963. Then limited funds demanded something simpler, which was supplied by A. E. Richardson, who also designed the open pavilion sheltering the bells.

* Technically a chapel of ease to the smaller, older *St Mary's*, St Martin's functions as the main church of Knebworth.

Herts: on B197 just S of Stevenage; church lies on E side of road S of village centre

Laleham

All Saints

Littleton

St Mary Magdalene

Two surprising survivors in reservoir-land W of London.

Laleham sits at an old bend in the road, which presses against its quirky 17c brick tower with oversized quoins at the corners and a miniature Venetian window halfway up. Inside, a massive Norman arcade in chalky stone. Arches are mellow brick or stone, or a mixture of the two. The S aisle has been lopped off at some point.

The window by Wilhelmina Geddes at W end is reason enough for a visit. It

shows three anarchic saints in intense reds, violets and greens. The drawing is exceedingly strange, a little like Stanley Spencer or Wyndham Lewis. St Cecilia on the right is the oddest – a pouting juvenile delinquent.

Littleton doesn't exist any more, having disappeared under a reservoir early in the century. *St Mary Magdalene* is now wedged between Shepperton film studios and the reservoir bank. Chancel

At Little Stanmore, the duke's tomb shows him adored by two wives

appears to go nowhere, and the blanks have been filled with standard suburbia.

Inside, it feels like two naves. A variety of columns, pillars and galleries. In the 17c, most of the arcade was taken out and replaced with paired Tuscan columns in oak. Strange emblems are carved on wall panels at the ends. A barrel roof in right-hand nave becomes a shiny blue sky over chancel. The lion in the large arms of 1625 sports enormous bristles on his nose.

The Kederminster pew is a narrow slot at the back of the S chapel full of good 18c memorials and blocked by a wonderfully pseudo screen. From this family pew the altar doesn't begin to be visible, only the pulpit. It is a fabulous prison, hidden by dense grilles and inscribed all over with sayings, painted eyes and lozenges like eyes turned sideways.

Beyond it is the small cube-room (but big after the cramped pew) which Sir John had constructed from a former porch c1630. It was designed to hold his library, but there is not a book in sight. Over three hundred of them hide in painted cupboards teeming with cartouches, saints and grotesques. On the backs of doors are painted open books and a large portrait of the donor and his wife. The chimneypiece makes a fanatical display of family history on a bulging gold shield with a radiating set of heraldic coats. All the books are theological except the *Pharmacopolium*, a grisly recital of remedies in a 17c hand.

Paul Nash the artist has a peculiar tomb in the churchyard. A squat Egyptian falcon is turned towards the slab.

Bucks/Berks: now continuous with Slough; church W of Langley centre near M4 (exit 5), just N of Langley Road in St Mary's Road

Little Stanmore

St Laurence Whitchurch

One of the most ostentatious bits of 18c display in England. In small compass it sets out to equal the great Baroque churches of Rome.

Now it forms an enclave in the suburbs, but in Pope's time, when he satirized its ambitious patron, it lay on the fringe of a vast estate. The exterior is plain brick with rendered window frames and a crumbling flint tower surviving from the medieval church.

Inside, a startling embodiment of religion as theatre. Walls are completely covered in illusionistic painting – statues in niches, heavy architectural details, clouds of angels in the sky, culminating in wooden draperies and a burst of painted light at the E. Here lots of Grinling Gibbons woodwork rises towards, not the altar, but the exquisite organ (also carved by Gibbons) at which Handel composed *Esther*. For music was deified here, as the great poem about taste, Pope's *Epistle to Burlington*, suggests.

The church is staggering, but the adjoining mausoleum is more amazing still. It is reached by glass doors to the L, which lead to a large vestibule. From this grey room one glimpses, at the top of a stair and through a rich grille, an absolute feast of illusion.

At this point, painted architecture really comes into its own. Columns, niches and screens end in an imaginary dome with an oculus. Against the back wall rises a huge marble confection like a Russian stove, with the duke in a wig and toga worshipped by two Virtues – his wives in this life. Aside from the three figures and a thin tissue of coloured marbles on the front, this great bulk is mainly cardboard. Along the side wall are lodged, with Piranesian aplomb, a couple of later marble caskets much too big for the space. The whole effect is that rich and thoughtless Brobdingnag which so irritated the Lilliputian poet, Pope.

Middx/London: on N side of Whitchurch Lane, Edgware, just E of Canons Park station (Jubilee Line)

Littleton, a strange survivor on the outskirts of London which has lost its village

London

LONDON IS RICH in churches from the late 17c to the present. The Great Fire of 1666 left only a few older examples standing in the City. After the burst of Wren's rebuilding (fifty-one parish churches mainly complete by 1686), numbers of London churches reflect the proportions in the country as a whole: 18c churches come in tens, Victorian in hundreds.

Nowhere but in London can the full wealth of the explosion of Victorian church building be seen. In the abbreviated entry for the old GLC area which follows, 19c structures dominate. The rationale for this perfunctory treatment of London is given in the Introduction.

Vagaries of the wind in September 1666 saved *St Helen Bishopsgate*. It is a rich compost of the centuries: double nave, one conventual, the other parochial, many monuments, Mannerist S door, and charming wooden belfry. Its location in a pinched yard at the end of a snicket is evocative of the dense pattern of the old city. Recent reflooring by Quinlan Terry has destroyed much of its charm.

St Katharine Cree nearby is a rare example of 17c Gothic, with a Corinthian arcade, ribbed ceiling and giant E rose of bright 17c glass. Wren's *St Mary Aldermary* makes an interesting comparison. Here he was obliged by a donor to ape the Gothic he replaced, with charming and irrational results.

Of Wren's City churches, less than half survive. This case is a microcosm of the pressures which reduce the life expectancy of urban structures (as against those of country or town). Road widening and railways were responsible for 19c losses. Bombing raids in 1940–45 damaged many others. In fact the result of those raids is that Wren's City churches offer the greatest concentration of late 1940s and early 1950s design in the whole country. Many of the Wren restorations will eventually be valued mainly as expressions of post-war sensibility.

Among complete Wren interiors *St Mary Abchurch* stands out. It is a lateral (not longitudinal) space covered by a beautiful shallow dome with notable Protestant frescoes and rich wooden fittings. Wren's spires usually came distinctly later than the buildings to which they are attached. They are often exuberant Baroque conceptions. *Christ Church Newgate Street*, *St Vedast Foster Lane* and (a pair) *St James Garlickhythe/ St Michael Paternoster Royal* are outstanding.

Hawksmoor's six City churches of 1712–31 constitute the summit of his achievement and one of the high points of European architecture. *Christ Church Spitalfields* is the most heroic of this heroic tribe, with its huge porch like a large Venetian window (an afterthought, the sketches and juncture of mouldings show), looking out (no longer) on the bustle of a great market. If only the interior could have been frozen in its former half-restored state, like the ruin of a Roman bath.

Another Hawksmoor church, *St Anne Limehouse*, offers the most interesting distortion of Gothic forms passed through a classical prism. At roughly the same time Thomas Archer was building two churches full of Baroque mental gymnastics, *St Paul Deptford* and *St John Smith Square* (now a concert hall).

An exquisite product from the end of the century, George Dance the Younger's *All Hallows London Wall* is now a library. The most lavish bit of Greek Revival is *New St Pancras Woburn Place*, off Euston Road, by the Inwoods, 1819–22.

After this begins the long reign of revived Gothic: Butterfield is represented by *All Saints Margaret Street*, the first complete fulfilment of Anglo-Catholic ideals and still the place where they survive most entire. Its incense-filled interior is extraordinarily suggestive of a whole cast of mind.

G. E. Street's version of Gothic sometimes approaches Gaudí in its

Hawksmoor's Christ Church Spitalfields, the grandest English Baroque

animation, as at *St James Thorndyke Street*, 1859–61. J. L. Pearson is more rational and stately in one of the grandest of all Victorian churches, *St Augustine Kilburn*, 1870–78. All these Victorian edifices are built of brick: a kind of ultimate perfection in this realm are the red brick designs of James Brooks in East London from the 1860s. *St Chad Haggerston* is most nearly what it was.

Eccentric Victorian revival is exemplified by S. S. Teulon whose greatest London church *St Stephen Rosslyn Hill* of 1869–73 has long endured a disgraceful state of decay, by E. B. Lamb in *St Martin Gospel Oak*, 1864–6, and by Chester Cheston Jr and E. L. Blackburne in their aggressively low church *St Mark Dalston*, 1860–77. The connection between unorthodox Gothic and a low church persuasion is one of the quaintest twists of 19c revival.

Bodley isn't seen at his best in London: *St Mary of Eton* (Hackney) and *Holy Trinity Prince Consort Road* (Kensington) are probably most successful. Other late Gothic Revival highlights include gorgeous fittings in *St Cuthbert Philbeach Gardens*, one of the few Anglican churches to boast relics of its patron saint, and a series of organicist Arts and Crafts designs by J. D. Sedding and Henry Wilson – *St Peter Ealing*, *Holy Trinity Sloane Street* and *Holy Redeemer Exmouth Market*. An ultra-lavish interior by Ninian Comper is found at *St Cyprian Clarence Gate*.

The most amusing historical pastiche, which sends up the whole idea, was practised by Norman Shaw at *St Michael Bedford Park* (1879–82); also by Lutyens at *St Jude Hampstead Garden Suburb* where Byzantine, Egyptian, Dutch and farmyard vernacular join forces.

For connoisseurs of even later gasps of revived styles the works of E. C. Shearman, Edward Maufe, Sir Charles Nicholson and H. S. Goodhart Rendel can be recommended.

One of the saddest recent losses is Belcher and Joass's *Holy Trinity Kingsway* of 1910–12, whose preserved façade now fronts a speculative office development. It was a unique example of Edwardian Michelangelism. The earliest good modernist church in London was *St Saviour Middle Park Avenue Eltham* of 1933 by Cachemaille Day. Among later designs, two in Peckham stand out, *St Mary St Mary's Road* by Robert Potter, 1961–2, and *St John Meeting House Lane* by David Bush, 1965–6.

Churchwardens' pews and other original fittings at Wren's St Mary Abchurch

17c Mannerist doorframe at St Helen Bishopsgate (left) and 17c Gothic vault at St Katharine Cree (above)

Old Warden's pebbly exterior contains an astonishing jumble of woodwork from many sources

Luton

St Mary, St Andrew

There must be a lesson in Luton. It has a marvellous medieval church and an important one from the 1930s by Sir Giles Gilbert Scott, and its centre is one of the most appalling in Britain.

The surroundings of *St Mary's*, the old parish church, are truly horrible, though not in the least crowded or congested. In fact there is too much of the wrong kind of emptiness. Giant roads swirl past giant post-war buildings of no discernible character, but maybe these bleak surroundings make the chequered creature which is St Mary's all the more marvellous. This chequer-work in flint and stone extremely vivid, on fat W tower and many extensions and

protrusions. Good church offices and hall of 1960s to the E.

Inside, wide, ramifying spaces and three remarkable bits of stonework. First, the famous octagonal baptistery unique in England, insistently white in hue and heavy in its details. Next, the Wenlock screen in N chancel, an important instance of late Gothic, which puts together emptiness below and rich webbing above in a disconcerting way.

Last, and most intricate, the Barnard chantry, sprinkled with bears and spikenard jars, a rebus for the name. It consists of three miniature vaults over a little recess dropped a few feet below the floor of the chancel. This mysterious effect is due to Victorian restorers who wanted a ritual ascent from nave to chancel and so raised the level.

Sir Giles Gilbert Scott's *St Andrew* of 1931–2 is Gothic boiled to an essence. Like one of his power stations, which the tower resembles, it is built of dark brick. The residual pointed arches seem an anomaly. Powerful over-expressed buttress-vanes down the side. No windows in the aisles, only roundheaded lancets at clerestory level.

Round arches dominate inside, big in nave, small in aisles. Dark rendering is relieved only by brick window frames and wooden fittings which, though of high quality, slide much further back into historicism than the overall design.

Beds: 29 miles N of London on M1: St Mary is in Church Street, SE of railway station; St Andrew in Blenheim Crescent, NW of centre (W of Bedford Road)

Marston Moretaine

St Mary the Virgin

One of the most interesting in the county, for its strange configuration and its Doom painting.

From the N the various parts do not quite add up to a church. A large square tower sits separate to the left, and it looks as if the stranded nave has come loose from it or will snake round and join it in some way now hidden from view. This nave is very high and looks domestic. Dark ironstone in the chancel, which appears again as banding in the heavily buttressed tower. Stone textures throughout are wonderfully mixed and unpredictable. It enhances the effect to find a missing pinnacle on the porch.

Inside, the Doom indistinct in Pevsner's time is now vivid after careful cleaning. It shows a sandy waste of graves. Colours are minimal – ochre, black, and the white of unpainted plaster looking as if they had tried to reproduce a woodcut in paint. The result matches the bleak country the church sits in,* where the dishevelment comes from brickworks rather than resurrections.

An assortment of mellow fittings – an angel roof, an aisle screen and, behind it, an alabaster tomb so squeezed in that passing is difficult. The ceiling over the effigies is corrugated with bulgy diamonds.

* Reputed to be the model for Bunyan's Slough of Despond

Beds: 6 miles SW of Bedford S of A421; church to S of road

Much Hadham. Heads in the doorframe by the 20c sculptor Henry Moore

Much Hadham

St Andrew

This church is off to one side of the longest, most beautiful village street in Hertfordshire. The building is lavishly furnished and well cared for (gleaming floor tiles, the smell of oil on wood). Its most startling feature might be missed – paired corbels of king and queen's heads by Henry Moore on the W tower doorframe. Their faces are sea-smoothed pebbles; jewels on their crowns and pupils of their eyes are made by primitive pokings. They are not closely matched in size. It is a small touch but makes one wish that more churches went on being enriched by the work of real artists, integral like this and not just movable fittings.

Inside, the best details are high overhead: more carving, a late Gothic series of kings, bishops and ladies spinning as corbels for the roof posts. The costumes and postures are dramatic; bring binoculars. Another bit of sculpture in the churchyard by that final glory of the Arts and Crafts movement, Henry Wilson.

Herts: about 4 miles NE of Ware on B1004; church lies E of High Street near its N end

Northill

St Mary Virgin

A building of masculine forthrightness with two panels of extraordinary 17c glass.

The exterior is mainly ironstone of a rich mud-brown. Inside, the high dark arcades have a more purplish cast. The great windows by the noted glazier John Oliver are secular in theme and centred on florid heraldry – arms of the Grocers' Company (patron of the living) with its spice-laden camel on one side, those of Margaret Slaney, a donor, with large angel supporters on the other. The colours are aggressive – orange, yellow and blue.

These worldly subjects once reigned in the E wall above the altar, but this was too much for the Victorians, who moved them to their present location in the aisle. There they are mounted on frames a foot or so in front of Perpendicular windows, which one sees dimly through them.

Also from the restoration of 1862, Woodyer's vestry on the N side. It has a row of spy-hole windows beneath a deeply carved inscription like a cornice, and further on, an intricate rose window. This is Woodyer at his most extreme.

Beds: about 3 miles SW of Sandy (and A1), W of B658, on unnumbered road

Old Warden

St Leonard

An absolute den of eccentric woodwork, which would defeat a cataloguer.

It is a tiny building crammed with mostly Continental carving, collected by the local landowner in the mid 19c. Pews face in different directions, according to no particular logic, and a long S gallery looms overhead, reached by a curving Rococo stair. On the pew top along the aisle run two ripply snakes which stretch for twelve feet altogether. What thoughts were they meant to inspire? Even on the altar rail a crust of flower-sprouts like barnacles or sea-spawn. The roof is astonishing, full of wave forms and much hanging cresting.

In the midst of all this some old glass is lost, and a Scheemakers monument of a City trader in dignified Roman dress looks a bit nonplussed. Pevsner resented the woodwork for upstaging this stately figure, the collector's ancestor.

Beside the chancel arch an amazing piece of Victorian Baroque, a white figure of Faith in a pink marble niche.

Nearby are found many picturesque thatched cottages, and far off to the E a Victorian extravaganza looms, the house with a giant tower built by Clutton for Joseph Shuttleworth.

Beds: about 3 miles directly W of Biggleswade on unnumbered road

Northill. Rich coloured stone both inside and out and notable 17c glass

St Paul's Walden

All Saints

Here is a humble late Gothic building which has been transformed by the whimsy of an 18c squire, who saw nothing incongruous in inserting a Baroque chancel of manic exuberance and leaving everything else as it was. The viewer is left gasping at a riot of curves and frills, of putti and flaming urns, like an evening of fireworks which has congealed in wood, plaster and stucco.

The structural idea is simple but powerful: a tripartite screen at W, and tripartite reredos at E end of chancel, made of similar elements in eccentrically different order with an effect like perspectivist stage scenery. Now they are

painted chalk-white and tangy green and the surprising effect is to make the spirits fly. In 1946 the clear E window was filled with a crucified figure in a purple robe who comes straight out of science fiction.

It is fascinating to walk through the chancel S door into a Perp chapel with panelled wooden roof and pointed arcade. One sees now exactly what the outburst in 1727 covered up. Incidentally, a bragging inscription by the beautifier in charming script is found on the E side of chancel screen. A modern church hall like a concrete bunker is well hidden to the N. For another 18c folly nearby, *see* Ayot St Lawrence.

Herts: about 3 miles W of Stevenage, just W of B651 (turn at Strathmore Arms public house)

St Paul's Walden, where a Baroque screen is wonderfully incongruous in a small medieval building

Stoke Poges

St Giles

A quaint flint and brick building, whose churchyard is the one in Gray's *Elegy* and contains his grave, unmarked.

This is an example of a recognizable Home Counties type – humble originally, with mixed accretions over centuries, and later arrangement with an eye to artistic effect.

Mainly flint, with a Tudor brick S chapel tacked on the end. Different angles coalesce along the skyline. The W gable stretches picturesquely to include the aisles. Even the sceptic will be moved by the subtly sentimental inscription Gray wrote for his mother's tomb at the E end.

His own monument, designed by the architect James Wyatt, lies outside the churchyard and away from the poet's grave. It is a magnificent and daunting work of architecture, a casket hoisted high by a pedestal and blotting out the light. What a travesty of the sentiments expressed in the poem: which is all right, of course, because by now Gray has made the backwater famous, which was his convoluted hope in the first place.

Thus it is also appropriate that the interior is a place of conscious quaintness, with its chalk arcades, unexpected corners, tidy hatchments and pleasantly sentimental windows of various date.

Bucks: W of London between Gerrards Cross (5 miles N) and Slough (2 miles S); church just S and W of B146, 1 mile S of present centre

Twyford

Assumption

From many centuries hints of a delightful relaxation here, everything a little bit odd and non-standard. The Norman S door has a row of flatly carved bearded heads instead of the usual beasts or birds on its beak-mould fringe. On the outer uprights beyond the columns are wonderful fat suns, great friendly carbuncles with points raying out from them.

Inside, uneven stone floors, wide arcades and twisted old benches. Against E end of S aisle, almost filling it, a hilariously pompous tomb. It has blocked up a window but there are plenty left over, of every period, happily cohabiting.

Parish newsletters were comfortably spread on a table tomb in the S aisle with a large brass embedded in it (hidden under leaflets). Lodged against it a very ruined effigy. Many other pleasant features including a good wooden roof with uncomplicated tracery in the spandrels. 'This is none other than the House of the Lord' it said over the entrance in early 19c script, and one had to agree.

Bucks: 5 miles SW of Buckingham; church at N end of village

Watford

Holy Rood (RC)

J. F. Bentley

Built by a donor and an architect who were both passionate converts to Roman Catholicism, it contains one of the most gorgeous of all Victorian interiors. Bentley, also architect of Westminster Cathedral, spent twelve years embellishing this building on which no expense was spared.

Recent cleaning has brought back the delicacy of rich diapering over walls and ceilings. It is hoped that crude repainting (c1950) of the magnificent rood can also be undone. Screens abound – the rood screen the largest, with beautiful fretting on the cross and figures jutting up from it. Through these screens one gets teasing glimpses of rich patterns, like the

Twyford, where a pompous tomb blocks a window in the relaxed interior

gold Pentecostal flames on blood-red vaults in the founder's N chantry, branching pomegranates just outside it and foliate complexities on a green ground above the chancel.

Intricate metal fittings: chancel and chapel screens with pierced inscriptions and a variety of lavish light fixtures. Lettering in Gothic script runs the whole length of the church, crosses the screen high up and then travels down the

opposite wall unbroken, reciting Latin hymns from Passion week.

The windows – all but one to Bentley's design – are among the most refined and pleasing of their period, rich yet severe in quasi-grisaille mode. They seem to derive from Dürer or from Schöngauer, like hand-tinted engravings. The baptistery under the tower is a wonderful space, with a complex vault spreading from a central pillar.

Externally much less interesting, partly because its E end now abuts a busy ring road, partly because massing seems over-complicated and the play of flint walls against lavish Bath stone dressings is confusing. Tower at NW is a noble element.

The Anglican parish church of Watford is dim by comparison, but pleasantly aligned to the High Street (E of Holy Rood) which contains a miniature Midland Bank by Lutyens with a teapot-lid dome.

Herts: SW of M1–M25 junction, on W side of ring road A411 parallel to High Street

West Wycombe

St Lawrence

One of the strangest 18c rebuildings in England, based on Nicholas Revett's *The Antiquities of Athens*, for Sir Francis Dashwood, traveller, dilettante and reputed Satanist.

West Wycombe. A learned interior based on the Temple of the Sun at Palmyra

Willen, the most perfect surviving work by Robert Hooke, scientist and friend of Wren

The church sits high on a striking hill, inside an Iron Age fort and next to a gigantic unroofed family mausoleum. St Lawrence's tower is topped by a giant gold ball of wood covered in fabric and lead which contains seats for six to ten people. Dashwood and his cronies staged drinking bouts here. More serious rites took place at Medmenham Abbey nearby where the temple was entered through a vagina-shaped opening. Stories about Dashwood abound. He collaborated with Benjamin Franklin on a shortened Prayer Book.

Outside, the church is a plain box in flint with brick trim and a Dutch roof. Inside, a grandiose classical vision in the double cube space of the nave. Sixteen enormous mock-porphyry columns line

Woolmer Green, a Gill-like carving of the patron saint over the porch door

the walls, an arrangement based on the Temple of the Sun at Palmyra in Syria.

The old chancel to the E seems poky and dark. Exquisite and eccentric 18c fittings are a bit lost in the vastness. The mahogany pulpit on its pedestal resembles a sedan chair. Equally odd is the font: a spindly pole with a painted snake climbing up towards the miniature bowl from which four doves drink.

Dashwood's house, full of the fruits of his Grand Tours, and his garden scattered with temples are open to the public. The church is seldom visitable; service times and Sunday afternoons are safest.

Bucks: 2½ miles W of High Wycombe centre, on hill N of A40

Willen

St Mary Magdalene

Robert Hooke

A refined example of a late 17c classical church. It is the only complete work of Robert Hooke – scientist, inventor, friend of Wren and enemy of Newton – to survive.

It was built for a headmaster of Westminster School and until recently enjoyed a lovely isolated position with a ceremonial lime-tree alley to the W. Now Milton Keynes threatens it with suburbanization which cheapens its gate posts by repeating them ad infinitum.

The church is brick with stone dressings, narrow and proportionately tall. It is entered through a beautiful concave doorframe under a tower capped with pinnacles. Little rooms to either side were formerly a library and a vestry. The doors from this space into the nave have lovely openwork panels letting in light.

Inside, decorous plasterwork with open books in the frieze, and twirly altar rails. Only recently has dark Victorian glass been replaced with plain. The font is an elegant three-part affair – black marble, white marble and a crown of carved wood which dwindles into stacked vases and spills down eight little garlands.

The rounded apse, which fits so well, was added in 1867.

Bucks: about 1½ miles directly S of Newport Pagnell, just N of the M1 (exit 14) in NE Milton Keynes: follow signs to Willen village

Wing

All Saints

In most respects a modest building, it bears two traces of grander ambitions – an Anglo-Saxon apse with crypt underneath and an early Renaissance tomb of surpassing quality.

The apse is octagonal, decorated externally with an irrational system of arcades surmounted by gables containing blocked windows. A hypothetical structural system is pictured, as is familiar in Anglo-Saxon building, with stringy appliqués of stone ridging on the building's surface. Underneath this apse, a barrel-vaulted crypt about five feet high with ambulatory. This is locked and only viewable through two grilles in window openings at the sides.

Internally, the apse has been smothered in plaster and later decoration. A wide and simple chancel arch, a massive arcade and a few paired openings are the only signs of a magnificent Saxon building probably enlarged by the widow of a West Saxon king.

Incongruously, this building which learns so haltingly from Rome in its structural features contains some of the most unparochial Renaissance work in England, Sir Robert Dormer's tomb of 1552. A casket or altar sits under a canopy; on the casket elongated oxheads and garlands, on column bases finicky trophies. The whole effect is of refinement verging on the feminine, which seems very French. By comparison pompous later monuments in the chancel are irritatingly coarse.

Bucks: 3 miles SW of Leighton Buzzard on A418; High Street is a turning N and church lies W of it

Wing. The Dormer tomb of 1552, extremely precocious for its date in England

Woolmer Green

St Michael

R. Weir Schulz

A modest example of late Arts and Crafts by Robert Weir Schulz.

The little building is fashioned of slightly gloomy coloured brick with darker ones mixed in, and has a handmade tile roof. Stone dressings have turned green, and from N, partly hidden by untrimmed yews, it looks like a woodland chapel. Sparing ornament outside, just a Gill-like carving of the patron saint over the dark wood of door. (The little painted Michael-figure on the font-lid is also notable.*)

Then inside, warm materials – brick, wood and tile, but no plaster, though chancel is whitewashed. Low canted ceiling and some exquisite fittings, including an airy pulpit and an extremely open screen with lattices of grape and rose hanging down from the top. This pseudo-rustic work contrasts sharply with Weir Schulz's luxurious Scottish chapel in Westminster Cathedral.

* By the local woodcarver Harry MacDonald, who had a studio beside the Great North Road

Herts: 1 mile S of Knebworth on B197, church on E side of road

Wymington

St Lawrence

The most delightful church in Bedfordshire, in rich if rustic Decorated.

It has over-sized battlements and an E end which feels as if it has been stretched sideways, then finished off with squat turrets at both ends. The knobbly spire sits well down inside its square tower. This is covered in patternwork like the efforts of some heroic seamstress. Good flowing tracery in E window, iron- and grey-stone banding in porch.

Inside, a forest of columns. The lovely lowness of arcade makes the space seem more complex. The fat font is adorned with multiple Decorated edging. A piscina in the chancel has a pretty rose carved in its floor. Doom painting, old benches, and other charming things.

Beds: on A6 just over the border from Rushden in Northamptonshire; church higher than road and E of it

East Anglia & Lincolnshire

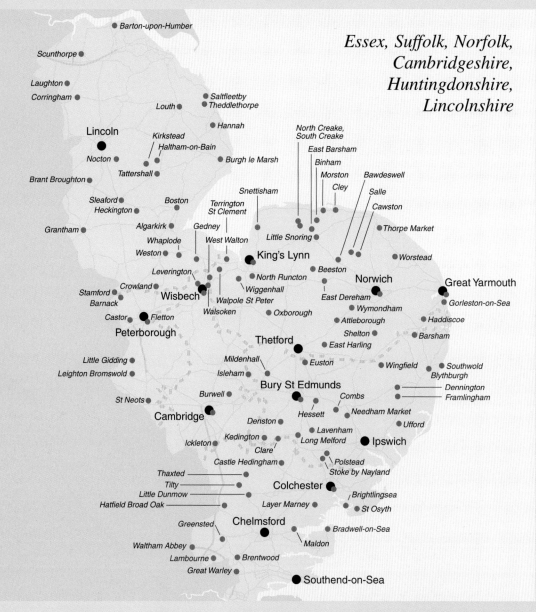

*Essex, Suffolk, Norfolk,
Cambridgeshire,
Huntingdonshire,
Lincolnshire*

LINCOLNSHIRE ISN'T REALLY part of East Anglia. In the past the Fens would have been a great divider, not a good way across. Boston and King's Lynn, which seem such a natural pair, formerly engaged in quite different trades.

The space between them is some of the strangest in Britain. Called Holland, it seems another country or no country at all. Like the American desert this place breeds optical illusions and disturbances of the time-sense. The area between King's Lynn and Sleaford is the richest church territory in the whole country and a strangely unyielding landscape at the same time.

Norfolk has remained the same because it isn't on the way anywhere. Formerly one of the most populous counties, it is now one of the emptiest and most peaceful. Its 659 old parish churches are rivalled only by Suffolk's 500-odd.

Suffolk villages are generally more engaging, Suffolk churches larger and richer. This is Gainsborough and Constable country, contented silvery green under breathtaking skies. It must be the favourite county of many church visitors.

Essex is surprising, an underrated county. It is a complicated mystery how it has kept its innocence so close to London. The north-western quadrant is particularly fine. Cambridge and Huntingdon on the other hand (except round Little Gidding) is dull country with poor churches. There are splendid towns, of course, and in the old Soke of Peterborough, where the good stone missing in most of the area reappears, some fine churches again.

Algarkirk*

St Peter & St Paul

One of the best in the county: an elaborate cruciform church which has actually been improved by Victorian restoration.

This was carried out by R. C. Carpenter in 1850–54. To him are perhaps due the four great Decorated windows which extend wonderfully near to the floor (tracery on S at least said to follow the original). These are filled with excellent Victorian glass by Hardman (S transept S window), and Clayton & Bell (everywhere else).

There is an exciting sense of many parts and views all present at once. Algarkirk is like a cathedral shrunk to manageable size. The arcade, for example, is pleasantly dwarfed by the huge head corbels over it. In fact, proportions throughout are a delight. Two eccentricities in the plan keep everything from seeming too regular: the S transept is not centred on the tower arch; there's an excess to the E, ingeniously filled near the crossing by the organ. And the chancel is wider than the nave, so that its walls angle in towards the tower to make the connection.

The S transept also has an aisle on the W, a rich feature not repeated in N or E where you might expect. There's a gorgeous Decorated piscina here, too, apparently original, and some delightful Victorian painting on chancel walls and ceilings.

* g pronounced as j

Lincs: 6 miles S of Boston, just E of A16

Algarkirk, like a cathedral of reduced dimensions

Saxon portal in the tower at Barnack, full of misunderstood elements

Attleborough

St Mary

One of the most interesting churches of Norfolk, unclassifiable and of lovable awkwardness.

A great Norman tower is immured in later fabric and looks an unwilling prisoner – it is much chunkier in proportion than anything which has come after. A ragbag of interesting Decorated and Perpendicular tracery in these accreted parts: it is hard to decide which part of the church you are looking at.

Passing through the rich N porch, you step down onto a wonderfully variegated floor. The Perpendicular arcade seems gawky because so high in relation to other features. On the E wall, a fragmentary mural has been uncovered; it looks like Eastern kings and wise men gathered to admire a large shrouded corpse.

Below it stands the most amazing fitting of all, a screen across the whole width with frilly coving and much original paint. It includes the arms of all the dioceses of England and Wales, some of which seem rather far-fetched material with which to adorn a remote Norfolk church.

In the strange-shaped S transept good post-Pre-Raphaelite glass. In the great W window lovely old figures and fragments, but they are very far away.

Norfolk: 14 miles SW of Norwich S of A11; church on NE side of town

Barnack

St John Baptist

Like Castor nearby, Barnack church is one of the glories of its district.

The story begins with a wonderful Anglo-Saxon tower, capped by an Early English spire with corner spirelets. The tower is knobbled with fascinating bits of carving, including interlace in window openings and a beast-prow on the W. Inside the large sombre porch, we are surprised to find a high vault like a medieval kitchen.

Under the tower are bizarre 'capitals' like enlarged spaghetti, further signs of the anti-structural tendency of Saxon decoration. The font is a remarkable Early English piece, raised on a little arcade and dotted with folksy rosettes. The piscina is slightly later with three-dimensional illusions in its pseudo-vault.

The churchyard contains (next to chancel on N) one of the most curious of all Victorian memorials. It shows a palm tree with clustered fruits and rumpled fronds fallen across the casket. Presumably Cadet Booth (d. 1868) was felled in some remote tropical spot.

Barnack is one of the best villages in its region. The site of the famous Barnack quarries lies to the SW in bumpy ground known as 'Hills and Holes'.

Hunts/Cambs: 3 miles SE of Stamford on B1443; church lies S of road

Barsham. Its round tower and thatched roof do not prepare you for 20c refinements within

Barsham

Holy Trinity

Near the Norfolk border between two of the best small towns in Suffolk. All three inhabit higher ground overlooking a marshy landscape made by the River Waveney.

The church possesses astonishing interest for a building of its size, including a round tower, Saxon in its lower stages, and a fancy thatched roof. The E end is unique in England and very puzzling, because one cannot believe anything so bizarre can be entirely medieval. The lattice tracery of the large window extends beyond its borders as flushwork, covering the whole wall with a continuous diamond grid. This effect, like a garden trellis or Op art, has been dated 14, 16 or 17c by different experts.

Inside, this window is filled with unusually good Kempe glass of the 1870s. Each panel contains a single small figure, culminating in an Annunciation towards the bottom, unfortunately overlapped by a later altar-piece.

The interior is one of the most characterful 20c embellishments of an old building, with a flavour folkish and elegant at once. Fittings include a Jacobean screen with coloured loft, bold folk patterns in plaster on chancel roof, and semi-grisaille windows with Italian grotesques. The whole effect is intensified by many Continental accessories. The mystery of how this miraculous interior came about is solved when we learn that a scholarly rector, Allan Coates, called in F. C. Eden after a disastrous storm in 1906.

Suffolk: between Bungay and Beccles, just N of B1062

Barton-upon-Humber

St Peter, St Mary

The interesting little town of Barton possesses two old churches wonderfully sited on mounds across from each other and E of the present centre. St Peter has important Saxon remains, notably a tower. St Mary has memorable details of various dates.

It was a sad day when *St Peter's* fell into the hands of English Heritage. They have torn up floors, ripped plaster from walls, installed a hideous new coping on the N aisle and an ugly brick wall in the churchyard. After eight years of work it still looks like a building site, defaced by signs lamely explaining why it remains inaccessible to the public (except for two hours on weekday afternoons).

The peace of the locked interior has been spoiled by the removal of seating and the installation of an intrusive 'exhibition'. Apparently archaeological pickings from the excavations were insignificant. Like some victims of drastic surgery, St Peter's will not recover unless by some miracle it is allowed to return to normal life, that is to being a place of worship with parishioners looking after it.

St Mary's retains the rich surfaces – brick and stone in a general muddle – which have been rationalized at St Peter's. Interesting tracery, particularly in S and E. There is a lovely S arcade, later and of wider intervals than the N, with four colonnettes loosely grouped around each column.

In the chancel a big wine merchant's brass and a monument of 1626 to a rector's wife, an intriguing piece of ill-digested classicism. It shows a placard on a column with a miniature column corbelled out on top of that. These strangely matched bits are glued together with strapwork.

Lincs: just across Humber Bridge from Hull; churches at E end, N of A1077

Bawdeswell

All Saints

J. Fletcher Watson

A historical fake, but a charming one – Fletcher Watson's 18c pastiche replacing a Victorian church destroyed by a crashing Mosquito light bomber in 1944.

The design is both reticent and quirky, its scale extremely modest and the overall tonality mouse grey. But materials are unusual: bleached wood and shingles in the belfry, flint pebbles laid herringbone-wise in the body, with bricks dotted scantily through and brick quoins and cornice.

Inside, recessive but effective colours, and ingenious variation on 18c forms. Windows are clear and roundheaded; pews and three-decker pulpit made of pale limed oak. The vault overhead is roughened plaster painted pale blue with light fittings concealed in flushwork stars. The shallow unwindowed apse has been painted palest pink.

The result is a restful Scandinavian-flavoured minimalism.

Norfolk: 14 miles NW of Norwich, just N of A1067 on B1145; church to W of road

Beeston

St Mary

A wonderful interior with old roof, benches, screens and floors.

Isolated in empty country with an overgrown moated site behind. Its striped Victorian slate spire announces it from afar. Nice lattice window in E and some Decorated tracery, but this building is much more interesting inside than out.

Bawdeswell replaces a church destroyed by a returning bomber in 1944

It has a very high nave and a curiously yellow roof with many figures. The font sits on a high pedestal; benches retreat from it in diagonals. All round are beautiful brick floors.

The chancel screen is missing its top edge and therefore looks Gothick. Aisle screen to N is particularly fine and

painted a subtle grey which seems the colour of the wood. Many pierced patterns in the bench backs. A strange effect is created by bright coloured (not stained or figured) glass in some window tops.

Norfolk: 6 miles NE of Swaffham in a tangle of lanes; church 1 mile SW of village on S side of road

Binham

Priory of St Mary & The Holy Cross

Impressive remains of a Benedictine priory on the edge of a village deep in farming country.

Monastic quarters here are very blurred, so the great Norman crossing E of present church looks like those eroded features on the coast of Normandy which Monet painted. The present parish church is the former nave only, relieved of its aisles, which now show from the W as lacy screens with the sky behind them.

This W front is a great historical curiosity, containing the oldest bar tracery in England, if the date in Matthew Paris's 13c chronicle can be trusted. It takes a bit of imagination to reconstitute it, because the lavish window which dominates the façade collapsed and was partially bricked up in 1809. So an eight-light window has become a two-part pattern on the wall, all subsidiary tracery having fallen out. The only glazed remnant is the octafoil with leafy cusping at the apex.

The present effect is surprisingly harmonious, and pink brick enhances the tones of flint, Barnack stone, and rendering on the front. Beneath the ghost of the great window, five Early English arches are squeezed in, awkward overall but rich in their details.

After this, surprising to find powerful Norman arcades inside – or, rather, relics of them, for the arches are blocked and Perpendicular windows inserted. This mistreatment of the original fabric is curiously pleasing, though, for the space is flooded with un-Norman quantities of light. Mellow old benches and a railing of old screen at the W, on which some wistful painted saints peer through black-letter inscriptions written over them in the 16c.

Norfolk: village midway between Great Walsingham and Blakeney on B1388; Priory NW of centre on unnumbered road

The important Saxon tower of St Peter, Barton-upon-Humber

Blythburgh

Holy Trinity

A wonderful Perpendicular church with marshes to the N and one good street running to NE – quaint buildings with spaces between, which is all that's left of a formerly important port on its silted-up river.

Richly decorated exterior with pierced battlements and spectacular flushwork under the E window, including a cryptic series of large letters tortured into strange shapes.

But the great thing at Blythburgh is the breathtaking whiteness of its interior, larger than the outside has prepared us for. One of the most humane and touching angel roofs, with large figures facing both E and W, whose feathered waists all terminate in plump star-bosses. The uneven tones of this roof are fascinating – bare wood, waterstains like whitewash, old red, green and yellow colouring. In a glass case is displayed grapeshot removed from an angel's wing, apparently fired by Puritan soldiers – an epiphany of the physical colliding with the spiritual. Uneven tiles radiate from the raised font in all directions, an effect like garden pavement or an extensive lawn. I overlooked the series of bench ends with Vices and Labours of months. They sound tantalizing in verbal descriptions.

Suffolk: about 5 miles W of Southwold and coast; church is just W of A12

Boston

St Botolph

One of the most interesting towns in England with one of the largest of all parish churches. The tower, inexplicably known as the Stump, is indeed the tallest in the country, crazily tall in relation to the body beneath. Perhaps it was meant to finish it with a spire and thus, during the seventy years these plans were mulled over, the strange name arose. Or could the name refer to the sight of the tower from across the marshes? Now the uppermost of four stages is octagonal, joined to the square part by flying buttresses at the corners, whose pinnacles echo those above.

The space under the tower is amazing, as one might have expected, and it upstages the nave. The feeling of the whole interior is surprisingly comfortable, not dull or bleak as is more usual in Perpendicular churches of similar scale.

Many reminiscences of the Pilgrim emigrants to New England who left from near Boston for Holland, including a window to the poet Anne Bradstreet. Outside, a fascinating piece of 18c Gothic: the ogee finial on priest's door in S chancel.

Boston has some wonderful examples of brickwork, like the little Mannerist building by the church (at corner of Wormgate), warehouses along the river, and an amazing row in the High Street (nos 124–136) with lanky brick pilasters the height of the building. The town's precious dinginess and a layout richly woven round its river make Boston one of the most evocative places in the whole country. Because many of the best buildings are industrial, they lie under continuing threat of disfiguring re-use as offices or housing.

Lincs: 34 miles NE of Peterborough on A16; the church lies beside the river, NW of market place

Binham, a ruined priory of which the nave became the parish church

Bradwell-on-Sea

St Peter on the Wall

Notable for its forlorn situation overlooking tidal mud flats on the Blackwater estuary.

This is a simple one-celled building of impressive scale internally which was built astride the wall of a Roman shore fort. Many of the stones are Roman and look like granite paving setts. Plenty of tiles are mixed in. At E end one can see evidence of a missing apse and signs (the gable rebuilt in brick) that this building spent some time as a ruin.

Practically featureless inside. Steep modern roof and modern imitation of Romanesque painted crucifix on E wall are both effective. A recent detached vestry like a bus shelter spoils the purity of silhouette from a distance. Scrubby clumps to N and S mark the ridge of Roman wall.

Walking back across the flat farm fields, you see for the first time the modern monument of this desolate shore – a nuclear power plant on the estuary to the N like two identical chapels of enormous size.

Essex: 10 miles due E of Maldon, but route is circuitous: Bradwell village lies E of B1021; St Peter's is 1½ miles further E near sea's edge; last ¼ mile must be done on foot

Brant Broughton

St Helen

Perfection. It seems all of a piece, but is not. To begin with, beautiful Decorated work, then sensitive embellishment by a Victorian rector employing Bodley as his architect.

The approach is memorable. Not only the spire is crocketed but so are its corner pinnacles, with an effect not of richness exactly but of activity and energy. Both porches, but especially the N, are decorated with carving exuberant to the verge of riot. Even semi-decorative buttresses have writhing creatures pinching their gables at both sides.

Inside, a venerable gloom, but an absolute absence of the usual (and often lovable) clutter. The rich darkness springs from a complete set of Victorian glass, most of it made by Canon Sutton himself with Kempe's advice, at a kiln he set up in the rectory. It is plausibly medieval in the drawing, and pale yellow

Blythburgh. One of the most luminous interiors in England, under a charming angel roof

and blue in tone. The ironwork was also made locally.

It is hard to believe that the chancel is entirely Bodley's, but this is the case. It blends exceedingly well with the earlier work. The black and white marble floor strikes just the right note of richness. Sutton donated a really exquisite German painting of the Ascension and Bodley framed it in a gilded reredos.

The whole effect is so compelling that one could stand to know a great deal more about Canon Sutton and his ideas about the marriage of religion and art. A biography seems called for.

Lincs: about 8 miles E of Newark-on-Trent, N of A17; church is just W of High Street but best approached from N

Brentwood

St Thomas of Canterbury

E. C. Lee

Brentwood has a Victorian church of real individuality and a startling Vitruvian Roman Catholic cathedral of 1991.

E. C. Lee built a few interesting churches locally, and St Thomas is the largest. Externally the primitive pebble masonry forms itself into cylindrical extensions – buttresses and turrets – which make one think of Gaudí. The porch under the N tower opens like a mouth, and the W window lurks behind a gallery. Internally very tall with fine focus on the chancel and font like a fort in alabaster.

Quinlan Terry's cathedral is only a short distance E. Outside, the new part

Burgh le Marsh, where this screen is part of a feast of Jacobean woodwork

makes the strangest junctures with a Victorian Gothic remnant. Internally, it is a light and cheery place which effectively contrasts a high central hall (the altar in the middle under the cupola) with low aisles behind Florentine arcades.

Essex: 11 miles SW of Chelmsford S of A12, just NE of M25; church lies S of High Street in centre

Brightlingsea

All Saints

A wonderful tower and silhouette and lots of good flushwork.

Brightlingsea is a former port; interesting estuarine country, scruffy with surprising hillocks here and there. The church sits on one, remote from the town, a commanding but puzzling situation.

The main material is flint, but aisles and E end are rendered. Later extensions, though low, are more lavishly trimmed in flushwork. Porch arches contain much carving, but tower is the best feature. Tower buttresses have niches in every set-off and are stitched to the body by complex quoining. Rich parapets at the top.

Inside, the lack of a clerestory makes itself felt; it caved in c1814 and wasn't replaced. The whole effect is a bit bare:

niches of various sizes dot the walls and a Victorian tile dado runs round the nave.

An interesting modern window in N is predominantly blue, sprinkled with galaxies.

Essex: 8 miles SE of Colchester on B1029; church 1 mile N of town centre

Exuberant Decorated carving enriches the porch at Brant Broughton

Burgh * le Marsh

St Peter & St Paul

Large church with a proud tower and good Jacobean fittings.

The village stands on an eminence in the marsh, and the climb towards the church from NE is quite steep. Its uneven, shady churchyard is enclosed by houses, away from streets.

The tower has fancy cresting and a lead pavilion on top which shows well from a distance. There is a wonderful series of bosses along the cornice, and beneath this, panels, ogees and loose knots which at first look like remnants of deep-cut vine trails.

Inside, the Jacobean woodwork is outstanding, especially the gabled, faceted font lid with a dove on top standing on a book and holding two containers in its beak. Symbolically this needs to be a dove, but it looks just as much like an eagle. There is a magnificent pulpit dated 1623, and a screen with hollow obelisks on top.

The E window is like a coloured German engraving. I found it obscured by plastic sheeting to prevent draughts.

* Pronounced Borough

Lincs: about 4 miles W of Skegness on A158; church S of road

Burwell

St Mary the Virgin

This is one of the best churches in the county, late Gothic except for the earlier tower. Some elements are so rich and sophisticated they have been associated with **Reginald Ely**, architect of King's College Chapel, Cambridge.

The building is placed at a kink in the road so that coming from the N you have a wonderful view of it side on. A row of bosses runs all the way round the building, and the tracery at the tops of aisle windows is memorable.

But the great experience here is the panelling in the nave and especially over the chancel arch, where a small rose window is bordered by blind roses in stone, whose spokes curve as they approach the outside edge.

In the coving of all three roofs are hiding delightful carvings, a whole series of affronted beasts with heraldic shields between. They include elephants, unicorns, mermaids and antlered deer. In the chancel very rich niches, badly

Victorianized towards the bottom. At aisle ends, the worst atrocities ever perpetrated by Hugh Easton: two pieces of pseudo-Tudor glass whose base colour is a shrieking blue.

Cambs: 11 miles NE of Cambridge on B1102

Bury St Edmunds

St Mary

One of the mellowest towns in East Anglia has two large parish churches flanking the empty space where one of the richest abbeys in England formerly stood.

In 1914 *St James* was made the cathedral and has been amplified to the E by Stephen Dykes Bower. Along with Chelmsford, Bradford, Portsmouth and others it is a member of the fascinating class of cathedralized town churches.

St Mary's is an impressive, mostly Perpendicular structure. Its tower is insignificant, and the best external feature, the lavish N porch, is marooned inside the tranquil abbey precincts.

Inside, the great thing is an immensely tall arcade capped by a low clerestory. Overhead a good hammerbeam roof is dark and hard to see. The chancel roof presents a dazzling display of figured roundels surrounded by snowflake webbing. Renewed colours here aren't nice; a pasty blue dominates.

Huge aisle windows should create a Perpendicular glasshouse effect but are full of strident Victorian glass. At the W end two interesting paintings: a Sanredam-like view of the interior with box pews and galleries, and a late 19c depiction of the vicar distributing bread to a crowd of poor women.

Suffolk: midway between Cambridge and Ipswich on A45; churches are aligned with W edge of abbey precincts

Cambridge

Parish churches in Cambridge do not stand out individually but make an essential contribution to a rich townscape. They are therefore described here topographically, starting at the Fitzwilliam Museum in Trumpington Street and moving north.

Little St Mary has good flowing tracery in the E window. Small pedestal tombs nearby and pine trees overhead make a small Romantic precinct. This is one of the rare parish churches where you can buy a paper model of the building.

St Botolph, a little further on, is heavily Victorianized but worth dipping into for a curious Laudian font like a well or garden pavilion from a prodigy house. It would be at home in an emblem book. The lively marbling and colouring date from 1977. Before that it was park-bench green all over.

Cambridge Holy Sepulchre. Built by a military order in memory of the building sheltering Christ's tomb in Jerusalem

St Bene't stands crooked towards the street in a tangle of lanes, its graveyard lower than the road. The tower is Saxon, most noticeably in its upper stages. Inside, in the tower arch irregularities abound. Crouching beasts are applied at the springing, violating structural logic. Against the inner face of this venerable arch stand metal ladders and cleaning equipment.

St Mary the Great is the largest of the parish churches, with wonderful views of the colleges from its tower, which is open regularly. In the N aisle, Henry VII's embroidered coffin cover is spangled with extravagant heraldry like that strewn even more profusely in King's College Chapel opposite.

Holy Sepulchre, 'The Round Church', is the town's most famous. It began as the project of another military order like the Templars. Externally all surfaces are dead, re-faced in the 19c. Inside, more impressive, with two tiers of massive Norman piers ringing us round. Spatially the connection between round ('nave') and rectangular ('chancel') parts is fascinating, but one feels that later builders were defeated by the cylindrical part. Now plastic chairs stacked in the circular aisle make a clear sense of the space impossible. The round part is a church hall, completely unsacred; no magic is perceived or acknowledged in the geometry.

In the 1880s Roman Catholics decided they were ready for greater visibility in Cambridge. The result was *Our Lady and the English Martyrs*, a

Burwell's richly panelled walls and its roof, which contains wonderful late Gothic carving

lavish building in Hills Road at the junction with Lensfield Road, reminiscent of Scott's new Catholic cathedral in Norwich. The architects were **Dunn and Hansom** of Newcastle, and their work is an anthology of rich effects. The interior is dark and atmospheric, transepts divided from crossing by high arches in ghost-coloured stone. Under a large rose in the N is a curious wood carving of St Andrew designed by Pugin, who also did screens and stalls in Jesus College Chapel, the greatest example of earlier medieval religious architecture in Cambridge.

Cambs: 54 miles N of London on M11

Castle Hedingham

St Nicholas

One of the most interesting in the county, a rich blend of Norman and Tudor.

The later work is more immediately striking. Hedingham boasts an early brick tower and two tiers of brick battlements. Above the clerestory windows, with mouldings of carved brick, appear alternately the de Vere emblems of boar and star in terracotta.

Norman remains include doorways and an idiosyncratic wheel rose which has carved heads only on those spokes where they face more or less

upright, as if some inhibition prevented the designer from showing them upside down. A little to the SE is a unique cross shaft with knot work inscribed, not deeply carved, and rows of baubles running down the chamfered corners.

Inside, a gorgeous Norman holy water stoup E of the door and a tranquil Norman arcade. The chancel arch is pointed but Norman in its detail. Stars and boars are met again on an interesting Purbeck tomb in the chancel. A stolen Flemish carving has been replaced by an entertaining diorama with references to Scouting.

The churchyard feels like an ovoid room just N of the pleasing tangle of streets. Houses sink below its edge on the N and W sides. The castle in the village's name looms on a steep mound to the E.

Essex: 8 miles NE of Braintree on B1058

Castor

St Kyneburgha

One of the best parish churches of all, with magnificent Norman remains.

It is built of warm grey stone and sits in a large sloping churchyard with kissing gates at two of the entrances. Though very close to Peterborough, the village is in some way untouched. Wonderful Collyweston slate roofs in houses behind the church and a good High Street roughly parallel to the main road.

The church's most striking feature is a powerful central tower with two storeys of rich arcades. Inside, the capitals of tower arches are divertingly carved with battles, hunts, plants and animals.

The mellow confusion of the interior is absolute perfection. It is entered through a door carved with bulgy inscriptions. Overhead, an angel roof with large crude figures. The font is a wonderfully misshapen object, and the Perpendicular tracery in E window pleasingly unorthodox.

Other bits of carving outside should not be missed, like Christ between sun and moon over the S door, and a wayward raised inscription on a narrow doorframe now at window height on chancel wall.

Hunts/Cambs: 4 miles W of Peterborough: church in village centre

Castor's powerful Norman tower is topped by a stone spire with two sets of lucarnes

Cawston

St Agnes

Together with its neighbour Salle (q.v.), Cawston makes a pair of ambitious buildings with many rich fittings intact. They comprise one of the highlights of English church visiting.

Cawston forms a marvellously variegated group from the SE. Nice combination of rendered and flint surfaces; only the tower is ashlar. Over its W door a green man meets a dragon, a subject repeated in an astonishing piscina in the S transept.

Inside, one of the best Norfolk roofs, with many angels, including a species feathered all over standing on beam-ends. High over chancel arch there is some ruddy painting and two mysterious wooden figures to which some have attached pagan meanings.

Norfolk: about 4 miles SW of Aylsham on B1145; church S of road

Cley next the Sea. A wonderfully variegated church in an interesting coastal village

Clare

St Peter & St Paul

One of the best late Gothic wool churches, less lavish and less restored than better known ones.

It occupies a wonderful island site which should be approached from the N. The little town, famous for pargetted house fronts, keeps its distance from the church, which displays lots of brittle

Clare's late Gothic arcade of dark stone where mouldings are given rich fringes

Perpendicular windows with mellow brick eyebrows set in gentle pebbled flint.

Both porches have old doors carved with plants. Then one enters the high, light interior with a dark, flat roof over. The great motif of this space is the frilling or discreet battlementing of all the stone mouldings, a constant suggestion of activity. The piers are raised on staged bases which increase the sense of height.

There is good Tudor carving in a S chantry screen, and nearby a blockish squire's pew jacked up a whole storey to sit under the roof. More 17c carving on chancel stalls with end ornaments like the ace of spades. These sit under good heraldic glass. To the N is a window by F. C. Eden, like a German engraving.

Suffolk: 9 miles E of Haverhill on A1092 (on River Stour which forms the border with Essex); church on B1063 to N

Cley *

St Margaret

Adorned with a wealth of carving of unorthodox form, this fascinating church lies by a former harbour which does not even rise to the status of a backwater now. The port which moved further N is one of the most charming villages in Norfolk, its river choked by reeds and

bordered by dykes, its High Street twisting waywardly.

The S side of church makes a proud moth-eaten display. Tracery here shows even better in its roofless state. The main motif is tortured or malformed circles. At ends of roof ridges foliate crosses jut up like huge stone flowers. One which was replaced with a replica can be examined in its weather-chewed state inside, high on N wall. Along the parapets an openwork fringe like swaying embroidery, which reminds Pevsner of Spain.

All details seem over-size and maverick in form. Bosses inside S porch include a woman with fox and bird, like some figure from myth; a composite goddess. The guidebook demeans this to a housewife who has lost a chicken.

Inside, light is fractured excitingly by a clerestory alternating between big eye-like cinquefoils and little two-light windows. Fabulous sculpture at unexpected levels: empty niches with intricate scenes under them. These are often over-energetic combats. The best is called St George and the dragon, but is unlike any seen before; instead of the mounted saint it shows an ordinary warrior wrestling with a beast.

The bench ends are grotesque, but far ruder, like troll or voodoo carving. One poppy-head depicts the elongated skull of an elderly monster who is half tree or root. Others look like embryos or deep sea fish with bulgy eyes. There are also monkish readers with devil's claws poking out from under their robes.

The partly hidden W door exudes more unruly plastic energy, and the graveyard is full of interesting old stones.

* Rhymes with sky

Norfolk: 7 miles W of Sheringham on A149; church lies on former estuary S of present centre

Colchester

Holy Trinity, St Botolph

Those who knew Colchester some years ago will lament the devastation wreaked by new shopping precincts, but there is still much to enjoy, preferably on a Sunday morning.

In Trinity Street the Anglo-Saxon tower of *Holy Trinity* trails behind it a museum of social history, now well housed in the 14c nave. This tower has wonderfully anti-structural ornamentation, conceived by those who had seen but did not understand what a capital was. The tower of Belcher's rambunctious Edwardian Town Hall nearby seems aware of its neighbour and forms a pair with it.

Another symbiotic relation links the two *St Botolph* churches nearby, one a Norman remnant, the other a Victorian pastiche. The earlier one is the romantic ruin of a former priory, which creates heroic Romanesque forms in brick, great cylindrical piers and laced arcades. On the W front the blurred portal of ochre sandstone makes a lovely harmony with these.

Next to the ruin is the new parish church, a coarse bit of Victorian Norman in dirty grey brick, restoring worship to the ancient site after a gap of 200 years. Its wooden Romanesque-ish doors are now a charming pale green. The contrast between these two buildings is comical but truly energizing, and far better than tampering with old remains.

St Martin, West Stockwell Street, stands in a state of picturesque dereliction. Its evocative churchyard has a Soanic sarcophagus of 1816.

Essex: 18 miles SW of Ipswich SE of A12

Combs

St Mary

Remarkable for unspoiled tracery and much 15c glass.

It sits in an interesting situation, away from the town and partway up a slope.

Dennington's fine late Gothic screens have unusual railed walkways on top

Stepped buttresses make the tower look fortified, and small flints (larger in clerestory) give a mousy richness of texture.

The aisles are rendered; their Perpendicular tracery, woven at the top, is fascinating. On N side old glass has a lovely sheen. In S chancel varied Decorated tracery.

The interior impression is a fresh and pure Perpendicular. Colours in the glass are extremely pale but distinctive. Each light is broken into many small scenes busy with activity.

Suffolk: 1 mile S of Stowmarket; church is isolated to NE of village near the end of lane to Hall

Crowland

Abbey Church of Our Lady, St Bartholomew & St Guthlac

In the fens, and still standing up remarkably from afar, though only fragments of the building remain.

The village is worth exploring and contains gracious 18c planning (preposterous in this minute place), and the famous triangular bridge spanning streams now dry (with a large Man of Sorrows from the abbey gable as its lonely guardian).

Combs. Rich tracery, both high and late Gothic, and plentiful 15c glass

The Abbey, founded on an island in the marsh where the 7c hermit St Guthlac came to rest, is now mainly a ruin. Though much of the W front survives, half of it is a punctured billboard with nothing behind it. The church occupies the former N aisle only. So the impression is comically lopsided, with the heavy W tower to the left and an airy film to the right. It all leans, or appears to lean, dramatically.

Enough of the figural decoration survives to show that it was very fine. Over the missing main door is a quatrefoil with scenes from St Guthlac's life. At the bottom he arrives by boat and is greeted by a sow and piglets. The leftover space is filled by gorgeous early Gothic tendrils.

After this, the interior feels strangely unfinished or unfeatured, though there is an impressive panelled space under the tower and a good painted screen.

Lincs: 8 miles NE of Peterborough on B1040

Dennington

St Mary

One of the great discoveries among Suffolk churches. In this insignificant place is one of the most suggestive interiors in the county.

The exterior is not especially prepossessing with its bald lead roof and coarse rendered clerestory, though the N porch is embellished with three fine niches.

Inside, a visionary glimpse of medieval completeness. The screens to side chapels have tops of incredible richness, which arises from their containing walkways, railed on both sides, so the lattices are all double.

In the aisles, painted tracery on wooden spandrels, like a 19c fairground but in fact much older. There are many bench ends and high box pews too. The earlier format was relegated but not discarded. Architecturally, the culmination is the beautiful chancel with tiny colonnettes inside the large columns in the window frames: these are rationalized by attaching them to headstops at the springing. They are each supplied with a tiny and exquisite capital. An E window of interesting lattice design, and a lavish later funerary chapel to the S.

Suffolk: 12 miles N of Woodbridge on B1116/A1120

Denston, a mellow interior with much old woodwork, little changed since the 15c

Denston

St Nicholas

One of the best churches in Suffolk, little altered since the 15c founding of a college.

It is wonderfully compact and offers a tiered richness from its slightly raised position above the road. The porch has an external stoup placed mysteriously off centre.

Inside, wonderful roofs, including a rood beam and fantastic coursing hares on the wall plates. There are many more animals, blurred by the touch of hands, on the bench ends. Over the years low benches and backs have acquired a subtle torque.

Colours and light are exquisite in this church, yet nothing makes very much of a show. A knightly surcoat dangles above the S aisle where a wooden grille imitates iron. On the other side lie two figures in shrouds tied with tassels. The big E window has a grand jumble of old glass, while in the S, Martin Travers has amused himself telling the story of St Nicholas in Gothic cartoon style.

Suffolk: 10 miles SW of Bury St Edmunds, just S and E of A143

East Barsham, a small building in a hidden position

East Barsham

All Saints

Exemplary though very modest, because of little structural mysteries and some lovely remains. It lies hidden, near the road, on its own tree-shrouded mound.

Entered circuitously by a N porch, over-massive for its function, like a cliff. In fact it is the lower half of a former tower. Tantalizing remnants of blocked Decorated window over blocked S door. Like many in Norfolk this church has been getting humbler over the centuries: the old chancel and S chapel exist only as footings hidden in the grass.

Inside, window embrasures are wonderfully thick and sloping. Gorgeous 15c glass in a N window including female figure with a silvery red bodice. Sparholt tomb in S wall is one of the most amusing of its date (1640) and shows a lady rising from her house-like coffin, faintly reminiscent of Bernini's St Teresa, but surrounded by a lamb, an eagle, two crowned skulls and five encouraging angels and Virtues, one of whose scrolls says 'Arise and meet your death'. The inscription below the casket is a delightfully resilient bit of 17c prose.

At the bottom of the hill lies EAST BARSHAM MANOR, a city of mellow towers in moulded Tudor brick: its gatehouse is nearly as grand as the main house. In 1511 Henry VIII left here barefoot for the shrine at Walsingham (2 miles NE) to pray for an infant son who

later died. In 1939 Sir William Burrell considered the manor briefly as a home for his collection now in Glasgow.

Norfolk: 2 miles N of Fakenham on W side of B1105, just S of East Barsham Manor

East Dereham

St Nicholas

A comfortably variegated building in a pleasant small town.

Framlingham. One of the early Renaissance tombs of the Howards

It sits off to one end of the central market place, a squat mass with its tower displaced to the SE. Interesting carving on the S porch, especially the monsters on top of the buttresses and feathered angels over the entrance. It is a pleasant surprise to find a Romanesque portal concealed within, from which two grinning heads project comically.

Inside, a high clean effect with yellow stone against whitewash. Chapel ceilings retain old coffering and rich paint: in the S a thrilling example of late Perpendicular tracery and in large transept window an exciting bit of Victorian garishness.

The poet Cowper died in Dereham, and his memorial by Flaxman is one of the queerest anywhere. Instead of figures it shows the Bible, *The Task* and a palm branch which looks as if it is going to talk. Above it, a grotesque storiated Cowper window.

In the vast peaceful churchyard, St Withburga's well carries a rueful inscription telling how the monks of Ely stole her relics. Just outside to the S a low building with lovely pargetting – grapes, flowers, tendrils in pale Easter colours, violet, ochre and green. It looks like almshouses but belonged to a bishop who was a famous burner of heretics. Now it contains a museum, frequently closed.

Norfolk: 16 miles W of Norwich on A47 (which now bypasses town); church W of market place

East Harling

St Peter & St Paul

One of the best places to enjoy the distinctive Norwich school of stained glass.

The church has other charms – a complicated lead bonnet, a single long moulding on clerestory windows, rich screens, and heraldry of baskets and feathers on some good tombs – but the fabulous 15c E window is the real reason for a visit.

It contains sixteen small scenes full of stumpy figures with big faces and small bodies. Particularly lovely are the Nativity, Christ among the Doctors, and the Virgin in a sunburst. Donor knights kneel at the sides.

Close up, many rich colours, but from far away the effect is speckled, a kind of dappling in which no large forms or colour masses stand out.

Norfolk: about 10 miles NE of Thetford off A11 on B111; church NW of village centre

Euston, an essay in classicized Gothic – Gothic forms, classical details

Euston

St Genevieve

A small classical-Gothic church rebuilt in 1676.

It sits in the park of EUSTON HALL, where William Kent created an early picturesque garden with a temple, an arch, and a mill imitating a church.

The plan is Gothic, the details and materials classical. Chalk window frames and mouldings punctuate a rendered fabric. After this demure exterior, the interior seems more lavish, with fancy plaster decoration in the vaults and juicy carving on pulpit, screen and reredos. In S transept a giant glass picture in brown grisaille.

Suffolk: 3½ miles S of Thetford on A1088 near Norfolk border; church in grounds SE of Hall

Fletton

St Margaret, Old Fletton

In bedraggled surroundings on the edge of Peterborough, this modest church contains some remarkable Saxon carvings.

They have recently been moved inside from their former position on an E buttress and rationalized as a frieze behind the altar. The most interesting panel shows a man struggling with two dragons. There are also birds, shield-bumps and an angel with a staff. The wiry style looks more like metal work than stone, and resembles similar friezes at Breedon, Leics (q.v.).

At some point the carvings have grown wonderfully pink in a fire. How they got to Fletton remains a mystery; they probably derive from the Anglo-Saxon abbey at Peterborough and were discarded when it was rebuilt.

Nave arcades at Fletton are fantastically mixed; Norman on one side, early 14c on the other. Outside to the W, close to the tower, is a blackened Saxon cross. Part of a Roman inscription still shows through on the front, indicating a re-used stone.

Hunts/Cambs: S outskirts of Peterborough, near E end of Fletton High Street (E of A15); church lies N of road

Framlingham

St Michael

Some of the best early Renaissance tombs of England in a large Perpendicular church.

Framlingham is an attractive town more famous for its castle, which makes an amazing silhouette from a distance – a ring of towers with occasional spindly chimneys poking up.

The church is perhaps too trim and well cared for: signs of the centuries have been polished away. But the roof is gorgeous, especially the wooden vaulting over clerestory windows. And the windows themselves are interesting 20c grisailles smacking faintly of Arts and Crafts. The organ case a remarkable 17c survival.

The notable tombs are three imposing stone chests at the E end, commemorating the 3rd Duke of Norfolk, his unlucky daughter, her husband and the next duke's two wives.

Thomas Howard was a hard, ambitious man who managed to commemorate failed dynastic hopes magnificently. His own tomb is the most awesome, circled by twelve figures of Apostles wonderfully full and three-dimensional. At each corner a semidetached post is intricately tied to the chest; trapped in an inward-facing niche on each post is a little weeper.

This tomb lies S of the main altar. The other two are N. His daughter's tomb has a row of Old Testament scenes around the top, and the wives have lively cherub-head termini on engaged classical columns. Their effigies are starved and elegant. Henry Howard, Earl of Surrey and a poet, is commemorated by a garish tomb nearby which looks vulgar in such company.

Suffolk: 11 miles N of Woodbridge on B1116; church NE of village centre, towards castle

Gedney

St Mary Magdalen

Another of the string of fen churches between Spalding and King's Lynn. To its N, sea marshes which were drained over a long period, the great push coming in 17c: Gedney Drove End is a good starting place for exploring this bleak landscape. To the S, fens proper, which extend into Cambridgeshire. Just S of Gedney is a territory of lonely farms and rifle-like parallel roads where other cars appear in the distance like ships at sea, but disappear much faster.

From afar Gedney church is an amazing sight: it stands up enormous and transparent, an archetypal Perpendicular glasshouse.

Some disappointment on reaching the apparition: it is set in a hideous churchyard with harsh 19c brick wall. But the church is entered through one of the most interesting medieval wooden doors left in England, rich in ballflower, heraldry and carved inscription. Inset in its wicket, and almost as worn and grey as the wood, is a small ivory plaque of the Crucifixion.

Inside, astonishing light, and an effect of tall grandeur. A 14c Jesse window in N aisle in rather unattractive colours (yellow and green predominating). Like many churches in this region Gedney

Gorleston-on-Sea, the only church designed by Eric Gill, built in harsh red brick

retains a stone floor, and the spongy ground makes it pleasingly uneven.

At HOLBEACH nearby, even grander Dec, and a free-standing tomb in dark mustard-coloured stone, which shows a knight lying on a helm in the form of a head.

Lincs: Gedney about 12 miles E of Spalding, just S of A17

Gorleston-on-Sea

St Peter the Apostle (RC)

Eric Gill

A fascinating sally into architecture by Eric Gill, which combines rich fantasy with cheap materials and construction.

Built in 1938–9 of harsh red brick, mass-produced tile, painted and varnished wood, its plan is centralized, a great innovation at the time, and the style simplified Roman with a Gothic flavour. Its uncomplicated, flat-footed appearance is deceptive: it is a building which hides its cleverness and feels like something thrown up quickly at a summer camp.

The formal leitmotif is a Gothic arch springing from the ground. This appears in the arcades and also in larger tower arches which stretch over narrow aisles too, looking fibrous at the intersections. Large windows in tower and transepts are this same caricature of a Gothic shape, split in three to resemble thermal windows, clashed against a simple gable above.

Colours are red, green and yellow throughout, mild on the exterior, intense within. The hanging rood with surrounding scenes looks like a carnival cutout. This is obviously the Gill graphic style, though the painting was only designed and not executed by him. The effect is not exactly Tyrolean or African but very lively. Above the S porch, glazed since Gill's time, a big relief shallowly carved across the brick, disrupted by the intervening mortar. It shows a saint waving a gridiron. The simple pine roof and pine rails and fittings within are convincing embodiments of homely craft.

Norfolk: just S of Great Yarmouth; church is S of centre on E side of B1370 (continuation of High Street)

Grantham

St Wulfram

One of the grandest parish churches in England.

Its setting is very pleasing, in its own backwaterish enclave. A little triangle of space in front increases the sensation of height. Formerly, buildings came much nearer; old drawings show a double file of low houses reaching almost to the door.

The W front seems huge, with the tower, which is one of the marvels of English Gothic, flanked by large, distinct

Great Warley. The most lavish monument in England to Art Nouveau forms and ideas

Gedney, a magnificent Perpendicular glasshouse in the Fens

aisles. The tower's corner pinnacles seem little towers in themselves.

Inside, the immediate impression is breathtaking, and attributable in part to G. G. Scott's restoration in the 1860s. His are the rich wooden roofs, the warm oak screen, and the sensation of a single vast space. The tower piers are mammoth and the rich font has an amazingly tall cover by Walter Tapper of 1899. There is a good assortment of Victorian glass, and then some of the last twenty years. Above the S porch is a chained library (open in summer) of Elizabethan date.

The view from SE is wonderfully complex, and the windows on this side an anthology of inventive tracery. On the E end internal divisions are marked by sizeable turrets. Unfortunately the Early English N porch (opposite the school Isaac Newton attended) was rather hacked about by Scott.

Lincs: 25 miles S of Lincoln on A607; church lies N of market place and E of High Street

Great Warley

St Mary the Virgin

C. H. Townsend

Perhaps the most complete manifestation of the Art Nouveau in England, a small building designed by C. H. Townsend and furnished by W. Reynolds-Stephens.

From outside it doesn't look like much, just another gloomy example of Home Counties picturesque, though trellised limes and circles of rose trees hint at the ritualized organicism of the Arts and Crafts. There are also lovely grape finials on the churchyard gates.

Inside, a ghostly and unhealthy luxury based on natural forms. Silver rose trees arch overhead down the length of the nave, embossed on the vault in aluminium leaf. The apse is a mist of silver and rose, produced by enamelled grapes against a background of aluminium leaf. Christ on the reredos wears a crinkly robe of metal foil and looks radioactive.

All this is viewed through a screen which is one of the high points of

English decorative art. It takes the form of a thicket of brass rose trees, with flowers and fruits in mother-of-pearl and red glass, and angels breaking at intervals through the leaves. To the right a mellow variation in walnut and pewter protects the S chapel. Pulpit, lectern and organ case offer more of the same: slinky forms in somewhat morbid substances and colours. The font is interesting but verges on Edwardian Baroque. The original windows were destroyed in the war, and all the replacements except the W rose seem unworthy.

Essex: 2½ miles S of Brentwood on B186; church on W side of road

Great Yarmouth

St Nicholas

A very large town church badly bombed, now well and freshly reconstituted by Stephen Dykes Bower.

Despite damage, Yarmouth still retains something of the look of King's Lynn, with much grimy 17–18c brick in forms of Dutch derivation, swamped by cranes, corrugated metal and various industrial textures. The marshy flats to the W are wonderfully atmospheric, and then you come to a zone of allotment shacks as you near Yarmouth.

Against all expectation, *St Nicholas* (which contests with Holy Trinity, Hull, the title of England's largest parish church), though much renewed and very awkward as a composition (if it even is one), provides continuous diversion as you circle it: diversion of form not texture. Particularly good is the ungainly W aspect where aisles dwarf the nave squeezed between them.

Inside, a terrific but nicely broken vastness (by contrast, Hull makes a unified impression). Dykes Bower rebuilt the arcades and won no thanks from Pevsner, who wanted something in a truly modern idiom. But the architect has got a fresh effect without jarring novelties of form. Sometimes, especially in the organ case, a note of frivolity is struck, but such lapses only show how serious the new lightness otherwise is. Bold, variegated ceilings in E parts, which only seem kinky when you stare too hard at them. Brian Thomas's windows are also lively reinterpretations within Gothic parameters. They look not quite focused and also (coming closer) like comic books in their bold line and crude colour.

Greensted, the 'oldest wooden church in the world', recently redated two centuries later

St George, of 1714–16, south of market place, with its elegant open cupola and an amusing set of bulges between tower and nave, is unharmed outside but was partially gutted when made into a theatre in 1974.

An interesting work of **J. P. Seddon**'s, *St James*, Queen's Road (S of centre), of 1870–78, was practically disused in 1990 and has now become a Health and Resource Centre.

Norfolk: 20 miles E of Norwich on A47; church just N of old centre, on E side of A12

Hannah. Unspoiled 18c classicism complete with box pews and original altar rail

Greensted

St Andrew

Famous as the oldest wooden church in the world, this little building has been formidably prettified. Perhaps one should view it as a relic enshrined.

The relic is two rows of ancient, black tree-halves forming the nave walls and dated c845.* On the N side is a famous 'niche' which looks suspiciously like a natural bole in the wood.

Earlier additions include a weatherboard and shingle tower and a 16c brick chancel. But with the Victorians the real antiquity of the place began to be buried under sophisticated charms, including dormers, a S porch and a Gothic E end.

Inside, it is pure Victorian but very cosy, enveloping you in sensations of wood. There is a good Art Nouveau memorial in various metals, covered in Guimard-style lettering. The Victorian font has now been replaced with an ingenious wooden one by Hugh Casson, 1987. The W end of this church is exactly like a National Trust shop stuffed with herbs, tea towels and trinkets.

Nearby (4 miles SE) another wonder in wood, the three-stage 15c tower at St Laurence, BLACKMORE. Nice textures in the lowest, half-timbered stage and a vast high space under it, with crossing timbers everywhere and a grand smell. Here later improvements are more tasteful: some jettied dormers and mellow rendering.

* More recent tests (1995) have suggested a late 11c date.

Essex: Greensted is 12 miles W of Chelmsford, 1 mile SW of Chipping Ongar, W of A113

Haddiscoe

St Mary

A round tower enriched with later parapets, and good early sculpture.

The church sits on its own miniature cliff, its profile enchanting from a distance. It appears impossibly white, bleached – a ghost. A late Gothic chequered crown shimmers on the stolid Anglo-Saxon tower-base. All four sides have peaked Saxon openings.

On the N side a clerestory of quatrefoils has that common regional feature, bricks alternating with flint over the windows. Here it is like eyes with eyebrows. Over the Norman S doorframe sits a relief of St Peter in an archaic pose, which looks foreign and pre-Norman. There's marvellous laced ironwork on the door beneath, probably Norman.

Inside, the arcade is startlingly blockish, with pretty niches in one of the piers. A window of 1931 by Martin Travers memorializes a lady artist via a flowering tree weeping over the Virgin and Child. With its grisaille background it feels Chinese.

Norfolk: 9 miles SW of Great Yarmouth on A143

Haltham-on-Bain

St Benedict (CCT)

An unspoiled building with an E window of flowing tracery which seems about to burst out of its frame.

There were crocuses in the path, so that one had to walk on spent snowdrops to either side of it. The small building is made of greenstone in over-sized blocks patched up with bricks at the E end. The tiny wooden belfry makes the whole building appear to be crouching low.

Over the S door a Norman tympanum on a thin disc of stone with assorted ornamental motifs rising slightly to the left, like a Milky Way spread across the space. Inside, brick floors, several wall texts and a squire's pew with Renaissance details.

Lincs: 4 miles S of Horncastle, just W of A153

Haltham-on-Bain. A detail of the squire's pew in this unspoilt little building

Haddiscoe with enriched round tower on its own miniature cliff

Hannah

St Andrew

A dear place of utmost simplicity, built 1753.

Its little churchyard is ringed by plane trees. A Venetian window over the altar has no internal frames. The altar rail bulges out in a condensed curve, and pews retreat in a similar curve to make way for it. All the box pews are a light chocolate colour (not uniform) which falls very restfully on the white walls and brick floors. Enchanting font – just a box built into corner of westernmost pew, with marble bowl inset, and a turned lid with a large knob.

Lincs: 4 miles S of Mablethorpe on A1111; church on W side of road

Hatfield Broad Oak

St Mary

An immense Perpendicular church in a beautiful village.

The churchyard is so large and cut off from the houses that this building feels forlorn in spite of its size. Formerly, an extensive monastic establishment filled some of this empty space.

The texture is varied, all pebbles with stone dressings which are particularly rich on the numerous stair turrets. The interior very lofty with clear glass and some interesting headstops.

Later woodwork makes a surprisingly harmonious effect – twirly altar rails, early 18c panelling, good Evangelist emblems

mounted near the front. Also doored pews, old screens and a Gothick roof. The whole impression is barny and comfortable inside the commodious proportions. Good 17 and 18c tombs, especially two crying putti by a flaming urn. The extension to the S was built c1708 as the library and contains three hundred 15–17c volumes.

Lanes around Hatfield are good places to sample the tranquil breadth of Essex, its wide skies, its plentiful wildflowers.

Essex: about 6 miles SE of Bishop's Stortford on B183; church N of road

Heckington

St Andrew

This large village has the most richly decorated church in the whole county, of great individuality in both outline and detail.

From afar the tower has a bizarre appearance, as of jostling pinnacles round the spire's base. In fact the confusion is caused by gallery-like connectors between pinnacles and spire.

At Heckington there are many examples of such elaboration: all the buttresses have niches and framing figures. The S porch is inscribed with three-dimensional swirls which, not for the last time here, make one think of 19c decadence. The great E window is one of those examples of flowing tracery where curves diverge and rejoin according to more than a single logic.

The most astonishing displays at Heckington occur inside, in the Easter

Ickleton. Reused Roman columns – or so it is said – under rich Norman murals discovered in 1979

sepulchre, piscina, a set of sedilia and the founder's tomb.* The overall conceit of the sepulchre seems Crashaw-like in its whimsicality. There is a carved surface stretching from the floor to a height of about six feet, which presents itself as the section of a Gothic building with nave and aisles. In the apex the risen Christ, at the base four sleeping soldiers, and in the 'aisles' the Maries at the tomb. The heart of the composition is an empty cavity, which held the corpse. On Good Friday the Host would be displayed here, the kind of literalism we find in Baroque poetry. All the spare spaces are filled with leaves of William Morris luxuriance or dotted with little mermaids and pipers. The double piscina opposite is based on the weirdest curves, and the sedilia includes some very engaging scenes like a woman feeding a bird or stroking a cat. Under its canopies are complex vaults.

By one of those happy twists which sometimes occur, Heckington has come by late Victorian and Edwardian glass of matching richness, with lots of purple – the lushest, a Supper at Emmaus with a starry sky, in the chancel.

The font is a wonderful piece of the same date as the other carving, eaten away by its niches, and bubbling with leafage. Here again the ruling principle is the one which drove Gaudí, an organicism which breaks down the integrity of forms and will before long result in their death.

* The founder's royal connections help explain the lavishness of this great Decorated church: Richard de Pottesgrave was chaplain and confessor to Edward II and Edward III.

Lincs: 4 miles E of Sleaford, S of A17

Hessett

St Ethelbert

A delight, not large, but graced with excellent detail.

It is prefaced by a seemly tower with a delicate crown, then a rich S porch with elongated niches. The battlements are fretted, pierced and niched, and on the N side sit atop a lengthy carved inscription commemorating donors. In the E window swirling tracery at the top.

The high white interior is demure and fastidious too, with nice medleys of old glass which are not easily intelligible.

Nearby at BEYTON is a round Norman tower in mustard stone, windowed later.

Suffolk: 5 miles SE of Bury St Edmunds, 1½ miles S of A45; church on E side of village street

Ickleton

St Mary Magdalene

This is one of the county's best churches, with memorable Norman murals.

An arson attempt in 1979 led to the discovery of wonderful wall paintings which show busy throngs and martyrdoms under Passion scenes. One of these is a complicated Betrayal of Christ that looks like a battle. The colours are the same rust, white and ochre found in the Sussex cycles. They harmonize marvellously with the chequered arches (Roman tile and Barnack stone, pale red and white) which were uncovered at the same time. These arches sit on beautiful cushion capitals. The columns are reputed to be Roman.

The clerestories are pleasantly diverse, roundels vs. squat arched openings. The large, narrow tower opening looks vaguely Saxon. Many old bench ends, a good painted screen and a rough font. In the W window is a post-Pre-Raphaelite window of intense ritualized power.

Cambs: 10 miles S of Cambridge, framed by major roads from which it is not directly accessible; 1 mile W of A1301 at Hinxton, 1 mile NW of B1383 at Great Chesterford

Isleham

St Andrew

Isleham lies in remote fenland SE of Ely. The first impression, made by a harsh Victorian tower, is not attractive, but there are many old textures brought together here – an 18c door, a good roof and a mellow floor in red and white tile. The panelling above the arcade is probably medieval, though its hard edges make you wonder if it could be Victorian.

A number of good brasses, especially on a table tomb in the chancel – with two wives, one in an elaborate dress. The hideous over-painting of Elizabethan tombs in the transept is an object lesson in mistaken restoration.

Strangest feature of all is the 17c altar rail: every other baluster is cut in half and the two ends sharpened to unnerving effect, an example of deconstruction before its time.

Cambs: about 10 miles SE of Ely on B1104; church to E of road in centre of village

Gaudy knight on a table tomb at Isleham

Kedington

St Peter & St Paul

A treasure trove for the antiquarian, this interior has become an eccentric storehouse.

Wonderful external déshabillé – unrestored brick, flint and render. The lowering of the nave roof has created a building which goes on and on, laterally. Some lovely Decorated tracery as one passes down the long S flank towards the porch.

The interior takes one's breath away by its profusion. No empty space – a cottage organ jostles a splendid set of Renaissance tombs. Unearthly light comes from above via surprising skylights knocked in a lowering timber roof by the Victorians.

Nave pillars have been slyly altered by painted flutings put on in the 18c. Another piece of manhandling has converted faded medieval screens to a squire's pew, and then to a vestry.

The wealth of monuments is mind-boggling, like a crowd of ghosts coming between you and the light. Perhaps the oddest fillip is a Saxon cross head further E. But at Kedington nothing looks more incongruous than anything else, and all the centuries co-exist in faintly comic harmony.

Suffolk: 3 miles NE of Haverhill, S of A143; church on N edge of village and N side of road

King's Lynn

St Nicholas (CCT)

One of the most interesting towns in England contains one of the country's most extraordinary churches, which is still only a chapel within an older parish.

St Nicholas should be approached from *St Margaret*, its jealous older sister. St Margaret, at the S end of old Lynn, lies on one side of the Saturday Market in a

Kedington, where the cottage organ jostles the Renaissance tombs

richly compacted churchyard. Heartlessly vast, the church contains dark wooden screens which slope with the cant of chancel pillars. Here too, the famous brass of a peacock feast (an event which actually took place, in 1349), so large it is patched together of many panels. The peacock is hard to pick out, tucked under the arm of a woman approaching the table from the left.

The sequence of streets between the two churches is one of the best in England. It winds mysteriously and reveals the premises of industry just behind a refined layer of merchants' houses and public buildings. Sad to say, Lynn is now obliterating many signs of this commercial past.

Beyond the Tuesday Market lies *St Nicholas* in a crowded churchyard, its older tower depressed in a little well. The S porch is decorated with rich excess, like produce from overseas piled up or not yet unpacked. To fit a door in the W end, the great W window is rudely interrupted at the bottom.

Inside, immense amounts of light through Perpendicular windows of tracery so angular it looks almost jagged. Lovely bits of dark wood and a tragic photograph

Unorthodox tomb by Robert Adam, based on a Roman altar, in St Nicholas, King's Lynn

of bench ends with local ships and their kippered catches which are now lost in the V&A. If returned here, they could help tell the story of the merchants of Lynn, visible also in a gorgeous mayoral standard and many tombs.

Robert Adam's memorial to Benjamin Keene of 1757 is one of the most original in England. It consists of a marble cube with a cylindrical urn on top – fluted, footed, and decorated with lions' heads and garlands. On the base a goddess superintends events in a harbour like an idealized Lynn. The whole composition suggests a dignified but defunct Roman altar.

Norfolk: 42 miles W of Norwich on A47; church just beyond NE corner of Tuesday Market which is at N end of old core

Kirkstead

St Leonard

A fortunate survival, it is a perfect Early English space of modest size, all that remains (besides a cliff of stone in a nearby field) of a great abbey. It was probably a lay chapel outside the precincts.

A highish stone box in a forlorn position across a few fields, it was given a simple weatherboard gable and roof in the early 20c. There's a vesica window and harmonious decoration on the W front, but the marvel here is a richly ribbed internal space.

The means are simple and the results transcendental: three equal bays, two lancets in each. The chancel is singled out and given extra ribs. The effect of this is enormous: it feels as if there are more windows there. The windows penetrate up into the vault. Everything hinges on how they are set off by their own bits of space, and on their exact relation to the curve overhead. The system culminates in the E wall, our only head-on view of ceiling resolved into wall, via three windows of graded size.

The simple wooden screen is thought to be one of the oldest in the country, probably 13c. Likewise the severe knightly effigy, which wears armour current around 1200.

Lincs: 14 miles SE of Lincoln down an unmarked turning S from B1191, just W of Woodhall Spa

Lambourne

St Mary & All Saints

A delightful church which combines Norman remains with amusing Georgianizations.

It lies at the end of a lane with a farm pond nearby. Surrounded by a white

Kirkstead. The only remnant of a large abbey, standing by itself in the fields

fence, it has been given a weatherboarded tower and lead spire, but from its rendered flank a Norman portal in a soapy stone like ceramic peeks out.

Inside, 18c eccentricity abounds. Windows are Gothick casements, and there's a stained wooden gallery. But the most remarkable feature is the plasterwork: a segmental chancel arch with giant rosettes, key patterns on the undersides of cross beams, and bolder still, a four-way leaf sprout hiding the 15c kingpost where it meets the roof.

In about 1955 the old Corinthian reredos was taken out suffering from dry rot. Eight years later it was replaced with five plaster reliefs by T. B. Huxley-Jones. At the sides, recognizable scenes, but in the centre a rococo swirl full of animals, a truly inspired response to the 18c surroundings.

Essex: within M25 ring, about 6 miles NW of Romford, S of A113

Laughton
All Saints

Corringham
St Laurence

Two modest buildings tastefully embellished by Bodley in 1894–6 and 1882–4, respectively.

In the interiors his ingenuity really comes out. At *Laughton* the original constituents include Norman arcades with good capitals and an interesting triple stop against the wall on the N. One of Bodley's cleverest touches is to match a medieval tomb chest in the last S bay with the founder's effigy in the last N one. We assume he moved the medieval monument into this exquisite position. Perhaps he didn't need to move it far.

Bodley's stone and painted reredos in the chancel is magnificent and fills the E wall. It is wonderfully lit from the side.

But in a way his most uncanny contrivance is the miniature chapel in the narrow S aisle. Here there's a small pillar-piscina, and Bodley has caused a little gabled aberration in the aisle roof just over the altar, about half a bay's worth. All the painted roofs, four of them, are different and very fine.

At *Corringham* the roofs are again outstanding – in the nave a faded rose colour. Early Kempe glass in the E, with the odd chartreuse which is the trademark of that stage. Powerful

Lavenham. One of the greatest of Perpendicular wool churches in a beautiful village

Norman leaves on the arcade. Good churchwardens' pews and stone lychgate by Bodley.

Lincs: Laughton 10 miles SW of Scunthorpe, W of A159; Corringham 4 miles further S, just N of A631

Lavenham
St Peter & St Paul

In a large and picturesque village, one of the grandest of all Perpendicular parish churches.

Lots of medieval houses line the High Street as it winds and climbs towards the church on the W edge. Its tower looks very grand across the fields to W, coming from Long Melford. It is made of flint with subtle setbacks in its buttresses.

This church has some of the richest parapets ever, especially on the porch where leaf forms are cut free and then enclosed by rigid borders. This union of restraint and excess seems very *fin de siècle*.

Inside, rich texturing on nave walls in stone of gloomy ochrish colour, which harmonizes well with dark plaster and darker Victorian roof. It makes a richer overall effect than Long Melford nearby. Like Melford, Lavenham bears the scars of Victorian tidying, especially in its floors and garish windows.

The chantry in NE corner is among the lushest of all 16c woodwork: from afar a prickly forest whose complex forms ceaselessly writhe and grow. Other wooden screens of less extravagant design nearby.

Suffolk: 6 miles NE of Sudbury on A1141; church at SW edge

Layer Marney

St Mary

A fabulously secluded spot. To reach this small 16c brick church of chapel dimensions you circle round the remnants of a more ambitious manor of the same date.

The church is built of the mellowest brick with faint blue diapering. Traces of rendering on S wall, and two S porches; the miniature one to SE is now cemented shut.

Inside, a barrel vault and wall painting of a giant St Christopher. The N aisle screen is wonderfully plain, of wood and iron; in its gates, wood painted to resemble iron. Lavish marble and terracotta tomb between chancel and aisle.

But an even more surprising use of terracotta is found in LAYER MARNEY TOWER, as the manor is called. Only the gatehouse was built and the side we see would have faced an interior court. Shell forms around top edges enact a wonderful parody of battlements. Terracotta of pale yellow, cream and burnt white contrasts with richer tones below. Window frames are terracotta too, and the thin towers are eaten away by them most preposterously.

Essex: 7 miles SW of Colchester off B1022 to SE

Leighton Bromswold

St Mary

Little Gidding

St John Evangelist

A charmed group connected by obscure lanes; two small churches precious for their associations with early 17c piety.

The poet George Herbert made it his special project to reinstate *Leighton Bromswold* church, which he found ruinous when ordained deacon in 1626. It is now approached down a wide avenue from W, with a feeling of spacious order like Deerfield in Massachusetts. In fact the medieval village lay to E, past the Jacobean manor house.

The church has a tower dating from the 17c repairs, of abstract Gothic topped by obelisks. Its door panels shrink in perspective like a theatre scene. The nave is a mixture of Early English and 17c Gothic, but the dominant impression is made by Herbert's woodwork, which fills the space. It is not overwhelming, but mild and rational: identical pulpit and reading desk with pendant knobs, which appear again (right side up) on benches, all of a sobriety which eventually seems mystical. The 13c piscina with intersecting arches reads like a Herbert poem: angles and curves forming a kind of mental lace.

In N transept two ruined effigies of prostrate gentry, of which one can buy postcards like X-ray prints.

Nicholas Ferrar was a more extreme character than George Herbert. He studied abroad and came back to found a devotional community. He and his mother bought *Little Gidding* and collected a group which followed a regimen that sounds almost as much like William Morris as Continental monasticism. Embroidery was a sanctified activity here.

The present church is magically small, with plain brick body and elaborate stone front. This front is like a metaphysical poem, displaying a punctured spirelet and tiny obelisks at the corners. Though it matches our idea of rigorous, extravagant 17c religion, this façade is dated 1714.

The interior looks perfect at first, all wood, with collegiate seating along the sides, but apparently much of it post-dates Ferrar's time. The most amazing fittings, large brass panels with inscriptions and a brass font with a fantastical crown for a lid, are survivors from 1626. They might be Arts and Crafts.

When Herbert died he left the manuscript of *The Temple* in Nicholas Ferrar's hands. Puritan attacks on the settlement came in the 1640s, and the community ceased to exist a decade later. A revival began to be mooted in the early 20c; one of Eliot's *Four Quartets* makes Dantesque reference to this church. The present community took up residence in 1977.

Little Gidding, built for a small devotional community by a friend of the poet George Herbert

Little Snoring. The round tower is a reminder of an earlier Saxon building which later acquired a French chateau roof

Not far away, at CONINGTON, lived Ferrar's friend Robert Cotton the antiquary. Wonderful monument with his bust in the church there.

Hunts/Cambs: Leighton Bromswold: 10 miles W of Huntingdon, 1 mile N of A604; Little Gidding: about 5½ miles N of Leighton Bromswold

Leverington

St Leonard

This elegant church has the most refined of spires which doesn't seem flimsy because four small turrets at its base articulate it. A good churchyard, old trees. Arcades with piers of diamond section; strange and effective wooden tie-beams on effusive leaf corbels – a rare instance of Victorian consolidation of shaky fabric as true embellishment.

Wonderful Jesse window at E end of N aisle, cleverly restored. It consists of an amazing number of small figures (sixty-one altogether), each forming a separate division of the design. More 15c glass in chapel S of chancel (the organ blocks

access from nave), a Pietà and two pairs of knightly donors. This chapel has its own slender arcade and a floor of old quarry tiles.

Cambs: about 1 mile NW of Wisbech, N of B1169

Little Dunmow

St Mary

A thrilling place, perhaps more exciting for being such a weird fragment. This smallish space under a simple wooden roof is one of the pinnacles of English church visiting.

What remains is only the Lady Chapel of a large priory with the arcade towards the vanished chancel now filled in by later plaster. First one sees the Victorian N wall and its absurd towerlet, and is misled, but circling round to the S, finds rich tracery and textures.

Inside, the revelations come. The S wall is one of the most gorgeous ever, lined with shallow panelling which has animals in the spandrels, including a person with a pet. The arcade is chaste

Little Dunmow. An exquisite Decorated fragment of a vanished priory

Transitional as against this luscious Decorated. Surprisingly effective is the dark grey paint of the later plaster infill, setting off two marvellous alabaster effigies in their shallow niche.

At Holy Cross, FELSTEAD (2 miles SE) is found one of the highlights of Mannerist sculpture in England, the Riche monument, plausibly attributed to Epiphanius Evesham, and dating from c1620.

It's a work of un-English refinement in detail, but not a totally co-ordinated composition overall. It is jammed into a corner and made lopsided by a gilded Fame at one end and a kneeling effigy like an afterthought at the other.

The canopy with its four pediments is supported by two bronze and two marble columns. Slate scenes below in fake marble surrounds, but much alabaster above, including gorgeous allegorical reliefs, and heraldry where antlers tangle like sea growths. The effigy is a disappointment – hard, soulless, swallowed by luxurious clothing. Apparently Riche, a leading politician under Henry VIII, was a self-serving brute and not the fittest subject for such an ambiguously beautiful work of art.

Essex: Little Dunmow 2 miles E of Great Dunmow, S of A120; church at S edge of straggly village

Little Snoring

St Andrew

Perched on a little mound and divided by a stream from its tiny straggly village. Its round tower, oddly detached from the church, has been given a picturesque conical roof like a French barn in a painting by Boucher. This is an early 19c embellishment, but the tower beneath is a precious relic of an Anglo-Saxon building, and its speckled masonry incorporating courses in variously coloured ironstone is like a rustic geology lesson.

On the tower, marks left by the steeply pitched roof of a vanished nave. The S doorway, shrouded by a perfunctory wooden porch, is a charming Romanesque piece, unrestored by modern hands but at some earlier point crushed into Gothic shape. This mistreatment has given it a mysterious Moorish look and prompted speculation about returning Crusaders.

Inside, quite humble, a pretty angle-piscina like a little farm lean-to for washing one's hands in (S side of chancel). A wooden board records sorties over German cities in 1944–5 from the nearby airfield, now disused like many in this area. These are evocative places where one finds chicken farms in old hangars, and runways reused as part of the local road system.

Just two miles N is the delightful village of GREAT SNORING; its old rectory a gorgeous piece of early 16c brick and terracotta work, now comfortably garbled.

Norfolk: 1½ miles NE of Fakenham, about a mile up a signed left turning off A148

Long Melford

Holy Trinity

One of the largest and most lavish of Perp village churches.

The tower is controversial: it is a Bodley design of 1903 in West Country style, which replaced a slightly dwarfish 18c effort in brick. Nave battlements in flushwork are so wide they appear to overlap the windows. With their missing pinnacles they would have been even richer. All round the parapets runs a fantastic series of 15c donor inscriptions, perhaps the most remarkable feature of this remarkable church.

Beyond the chancel to E stretches a large Lady Chapel which is almost a separate building. Its three parallel pitched roofs are not reflected inside. There the chapel proper is enclosed by an ambulatory or gallery circling the whole way round. Over this runs a fine wooden roof.

In the main body of the church, entered separately, there is rich stone clothing and panelling above the arcade. Lady Chapel roofs are visible through the great E window.

Along the N side is ranged a fabulous collection of 15c glass, mostly kneeling donors in pale blue, wine red and purple. Among them are a number of Cloptons; the queerest internal space is the little Clopton chantry to NE with miniature vaulted vestibule. Its roof is painted and inscribed with a monkish poem. Further inscriptions formerly spilled onto the walls past the carved Vine of Life frieze. Indeed the whole space is dense with carved enrichment, and in the E window is the unforgettable vision of Christ nailed to a nightmarishly big lily plant, a pagan or perhaps Jungian symbolism.

Long Melford is indeed long, a string-settlement with a gorgeous green, which the church sits at the top of, protected by the 16c hospital. Two great houses stand at either end of the village.

Suffolk: 3 miles N of Sudbury on A134 which now bypasses village; church at N end, W of road

Long Melford. Lavish Perpendicular church with much good 15c glass

Louth

St James

Louth is the best town in some of the best landscape in the county. The church has a marvellous tower and spire and a Victorianized interior.

Corner pinnacles are detached and joined to the spire by lacy buttresses. The tower forms a beacon from many of the delightful surrounding streets.

With a great deal of trouble the early 19c roof, formerly dark, has recently been stripped and is now a strange blond colour. (It is pine not oak.) Its angels are also light in colour – pink, blue and grey: perhaps someone's idea of adherence to the heavenly hierarchy. Of the various fittings the metal lectern is outstanding.

Lincs: 17 miles S of Grimsby just off A16

Maldon

All Saints

A fascinating former port with precipitous descents to the quays.

All Saints boasts a triangular tower, an ingenious device for coping with a pinched street plan; under it a very curious space. The adjoining nave is a friendly jumble, with florid 14c niches in S wall and a gaunt 18c screen across the chancel.

Maldon also processes a unique late 17c re-use of a ruinous church. When Dr Thomas Plume, a local divine, donated his library to the town, homey brick quarters were built for it on the foundations of the derelict nave of *St Peter's* church. So this institution, still flourishing, sits in a graveyard behind a medieval tower, like secular learning just working free of its theological past.

On the less industrial of two approaches to the harbour, with its restored examples of the local sailing barges which used to ply these coasts, you pass *St Mary* whose early Norman wall incorporates lots of Roman bricks.

Essex: 10 miles E of Chelmsford on A414

Mildenhall

St Mary

One of the largest, richest Suffolk churches, in a small town with good old buildings now acquiring a suburbanized feel.

The church puts its boldest feature towards the High Street – an E end with a large window of mind-boggling

Louth. A large town church with a spectacular Victorian roof of bright unstained pine

strangeness, framed by buttresses eaten away by niches in their bases. The window's seven lights of irregular widths explode at the top into forms like two giant oak leaves and an almond. Around this last, and around the whole group, are starry borders of small quatrefoils.

The interior is entered through a lavish N porch with rich carving over an old door. A vast space which is pleasantly gloomy because plaster hasn't been whitewashed for a long time. Enormous space under the tower, beautiful high nave roof with frilled and adorned beams, and angels with the largest wings imaginable.

The best feature is the N aisle roof, unlike any other. It assumes simple lean-to form but of strange proportions, with enormous strainers which display some of the best late medieval carving in England. Here over-size figures jut out, and underneath, in spandrels, secular hunts and mythical combats go forward, not looking much like the Scriptural subjects which Pevsner lists. In fact it is all so unruly and unsacred it seems a reversion to Romanesque wildness in the last stage of Gothic.

Nineteenth-century glass makes a wonderful effect in E window, like an opera where you understand the words.

135

It carries a grey tinge like printer's ink which smudges the colours.

Around the humble churchyard a kind of anti-close, with low almshouses and a gloomy white 17c building at SW corner. An ivy-covered ruin apparently incorporates the old charnel house.

Suffolk: 13 miles NW of Bury St Edmunds on A110; church lies to SW of this road

Morston

All Saints

Near one of the best stretches of North Norfolk coast, a delightful situation best approached by the lonely lane to the S.

Unrestored, with a clerestory of large quatrefoils which let in lovely light. It is humble and pleasing throughout. Small Jacobean monument with black tablet surrounded by white fruit and morbid emblems is inordinately attractive. When Pevsner transcribed its inscription, he added new archaisms to the spelling. The font sits on a magnificent Maltese-cross

Morston's Jacobean monument with morbid emblems including gravedigger's tools

platform, and outside the door is a Gothick double tomb in dove-grey stone whose table-top one would have to climb upon to read the message. It is dated 1762.

Norfolk: about 6 miles E of Wells-next-the-Sea on S side of A149

South Creake, a wide interior with much pale medieval colouring

Needham Market

St John Baptist

One of the most remarkable wooden roofs in England floats above a bleak interior.

The church is crowded against the High Street of this pleasant small town at an interesting angle. Its plot was so small a passageway had to be hollowed in the fabric at the E end for processions to pass. The only sign of the wonders within is the rendered and timber-framed clerestory. On the Victorian porch sits a miserable clock turret.

Inside, the roof is like a skeleton suspended above you. It begins high up with hammerbeams and, after that, goes up and up in great vertical members trussed and braced in wonderfully lucid ways. Light let in near the top has more force because bare lower walls are relatively unwindowed. The angels on the hammerbeams, and other timbers here and there, were renewed in Victorian times.

Suffolk: 8 miles NW of Ipswich on B1113; church on N side of High Street in centre

Nocton

All Saints

Sir George Gilbert Scott

A surprisingly lavish Victorian church with rich furnishings, but not a high work of art.

Much spatial ingenuity was applied to the tower, at the expense of the rest. It has an octagonal stair bulge pressed into it, with its door in a wall buttress which widens to accommodate it. Under the tower a pompous 17c monument has been banished.

Nocton's enrichment continually falls into sentimentality. Many capitals have full-blown roses drooping sorrowfully, or birdies pecking grapes. Lots of alabaster scenery round the chancel including pierced pinnacles. Plentiful incised pictures on walls in rose and tan. The brass candlesticks and altar rail are good, in that they are bristly and complex.

Nocton is a test case for one's feelings about the Victorians. In order to like it, one must become a bit thick-skinned. The literary equivalent seems Kingsley not Dickens, enthusiasm unhampered by critical intelligence.

Lincs: about 8 miles SE of Lincoln, 1 mile E of B1188

North Creake

St Mary the Virgin

South Creake

Our Lady St Mary

Two beautiful interiors where medieval colouring survives.

North Creake's square tower sits up against the road near its iron gates. There has never been a S aisle, which makes that wall with its clerestory seem very tall inside and out.

The interior is wonderfully clean under a marvellous angel roof in soft original colouring. High windows throw generous light on many of the carved figures. A Victorian screen makes a complex fringe for the chancel, where there are gorgeous Decorated sedilia.

At *South Creake* absence of fixed seating makes the space seem very wide. Old tile floors, vase pulpit and screen in faint colours. Behind it stretches the long chancel. Mellow bits of old glass are sprinkled through the N windows, while angels in the roof have been garishly repainted.

Norfolk: 7 miles NW of Fakenham on B1355; first is E of road, second W of it and 1 mile nearer Fakenham

North Runcton

All Saints

Henry Bell

Henry Bell is an architect whose work must be known first hand; its great distinction doesn't come through in photographs. This little church, like the more famous CUSTOMS HOUSE in King's Lynn, or like a baby's hand, is an exquisitely formed miniature: a grand idea whose realization happens to be small.

North Runcton is virtually a suburb of Lynn and not very attractive, until you reach the generous green which slopes away from the church like relaxed arrangements in colonial Virginia. Old churchyard with impressive yews crowding the W tower. Through various chances Bell's building, though built all at once in 1703–13, resembles the usual accretive type of church which has evolved over centuries, because at later date some of the rendering has been removed from the walls, revealing reused stones from the old church and brick in the chancel, giving a pleasantly humble and variegated effect overall.

North Runcton. Idiosyncratic local Baroque by Henry Bell

Inside, the miniature spaces are finely orchestrated – first a dark vestibule under the tower with tiny vestries under either side; then we burst through into the nave – a light cube of space with a hipped vault, almost a dome, springing from four richly carved Ionic columns which stand well clear and make a square within the square. They are connected by frilly plaster ribs like tripe or coral, picked out in white against the teal blue ceiling, the dome of heaven. The refinement of all the ornamental detail, including four cartouche memorials demurely placed in the corners, lifts this simple geometry into the realm of the ideal. The space becomes that rare thing: a vision of heaven in the 18c, clearly articulated but transcendent too.

The three-part rhythm of the building is completed by another darker and narrower space – the chancel behind a columned screen, equipped with rich Bell woodwork brought from a church in Lynn.

Norfolk: 2 miles S of King's Lynn, just S of A47

Norwich

St Peter Mancroft

More medieval parish churches here than any other English town, and some of the finest early Dissenting chapels.

The streets of the old core are positively cluttered with thirty-two old churches, mostly modest in scale and invariably locked.

St Peter Mancroft is the best by far and easy to visit. It sits slightly raised at the end of the market place with its impressive tiers of Perp windows and frilly tower, which is open at the base.

Inside, marvellous roof, font canopy and organ gallery in wood, mayoral staffs in painted metal, and a treasury of pictures in 15c glass.

Across the river to N are the *Octagon Chapel* of 1754–6 and the charming *Old Meeting House* of 1693 in brick whose way of secluding itself speaks volumes.

St Catherine, Aylsham Road, Mile Cross in a N suburb of 1935 (by **A. D. R. Caröe** and **A. P. Robinson**) is an impressive, virtually non-historicist essay in two colours of brick. Inside, heavy Tudoresque woodwork seems incongruous in the simple tunnel space.

Norfolk: 44 miles N of Ipswich on A140; St Peter Mancroft at S end of market place near 1930s City Hall

Oxborough

St John Evangelist

A church partially ruined in the 20c which contains marvellous 16c tombs in terracotta.

Its great tower crashed down in 1948 destroying the nave roof. Only two fragments are intact and these are entered separately: the former chancel has become the parish church, and the Bedingfeld Chapel is administered by English Heritage. Otherwise this large church is an unroofed garden-like space whose walls with Perpendicular tracery are airy screens.

A model in the chapel gives the proportions before the collapse. The Bedingfeld tombs are among the most fantastic bits of Renaissance ornament in England, moulded in soft material of gentlest pink. There are two: one incorporates a door or passage, and the other communicates by a window-like opening with the chancel. Overhead a good roof.

Adjacent is OXBURGH HALL, one of the greatest marvels of 15c brickwork.

Oxborough. Renaissance ornament in terracotta on a Bedingfeld tomb

Pugin did the Catholic church of *Our Lady and St Margaret* to the W (next to Hall gatehouse). It contains many rich Continental furnishings.

Norfolk: about 6 miles SW of Swaffham Market, 3 miles NE of A134; church just beyond Hall to E

Polstead

St Mary

Remarkable for Norman arcades in a mixture of stone and brick.

It sits on a hill's flank overlooking fields, divided from the houses by a tranquil village pond. The proportions are squat and ground-hugging. Original tracery remains on the side you enter from.

Inside, a surprising arcade of Roman or at least non-English flavour. Its round arches are brick but piers are stone, of a design too ambitious for the skills of the carvers. Most unusual are small roundhead openings outlined in brick and now blocked, positioned directly above the much larger arches, making a violent disproportion of the matched motifs.

On the 13c font with rebuilt brick legs rests a pleasing fibreglass lid of 1964, its handle an angular dove, a British gesture, typically hedged, towards the non-representational.

Suffolk: 9 miles N of Colchester, 1 mile N of Stoke by Nayland: church W of village centre

St Neots

St Mary the Virgin

A large church in an attractive town, which has a magnificent late Gothic tower, richly decorated. The *Reformed Church* to the N emulates this tower in brick, with even rowdier tiers of pinnacles.

The contrast of brown cobbles with white battlements and dressings at *St Mary's* is very pleasing. Its churchyard is enormous, reached through a quiet passage from the High Street.

Inside, very tall arcades and a dark old roof. Nice molten font like a big block of nougat. The most striking fitting is a series of large Victorian windows by Hardman. They show episodes from Christ's life like German Romantic illustrations, with spidery figures and smoky colours.

Salle. One of the largest and most richly equipped of all late Gothic churches

In the chancel lurks an astonishing bit of gilded metalwork like a burst of Spanish extravagance or a crushed tower. It is the tomb of Mrs. G. W. Rowley, designed in 1893 by F. A. Walters. Her effigy is almost completely lost to view in this gorgeous prison.

Hunts/Cambs: 12 miles NE of Bedford, E of A1; church lies S of High Street

St Osyth

St Peter & St Paul

One of the most curious churches of the county with miracles of varied masonry and early brick arcades.

From the W it looks like a city, so clumped and various are its forms. The brick tower seems to spread and spread, like an ample woman sitting down. Aisles are independent gables, with strange linking bridges. Later S aisle is consistently brick, but E end a riot of materials – chequered grey and mustard stone mixed with Roman tiles and a few

flints. Again gables peer over other ones or slide off into flatness.

N aisle has the richest textures of all: more chequering, brick eyelids over flattish Tudor windows, and brick patching around the roofline.

Inside, the wide brick arches are a harsh unweathered orange. In the transepts a surprising cross-arcade with clustered stone piers, somewhat defaced. The communion rail takes a curious horseshoe form. Present stonework is mostly Victorian, but the animal corral idea is evidently earlier.

Unfortunate plans are afoot to close off tower and chancel arches, shrinking the central space. The S transept will be re-allocated as a 'church room'. If these plans go ahead a crass defacement of history will occur.

On the font St Osyth appears as a severed head. She was assaulted by the Danes at her monastery nearby. Presently this is a wonderfully mixed set of buildings, playing variations on the materials of the church. Its gatehouse is one of the most dazzling displays of

flushwork in England. Charming old core to the village.

Nearby at GREAT BENTLEY, an amazing despoliation has taken place. The great rambling green which forms the old centre of the village, one of the most interesting greens in England, has been supplied with rigid stone kerbs.

Essex: St Osyth is 4 miles W of Clacton-on-Sea, S of B1027; church SE of Priory

Salle

St Peter & St Paul

One of the best and largest of Norfolk churches, with a remarkable wealth of furnishings of all kinds. The more remarkable because now there are only scantiest remains of a village, so all the wonderful reminders in this building exist almost without context.

It is very regular Perpendicular: the W tower is flanked by porches with good vaults and old doors. Chancel buttresses are all capped by shield-bearing angels.

Over the W door, by which you enter, feathered angels.

Inside, you are met immediately by a towering font cover still attached to a crane protruding from the W gallery. Up there, the crooked timbers of the next stage of the tower are visible. The roof, though plainer than Cawston nearby, preserves much decorative old lettering.

The whole impression is mellow, clean and seemly: old floor tiles, stalls, bench ends, and best of all, refined old glass in chancel and S transept, with lovely red and soft green, depicting cardinals and bits of devil.

In the N transept windows are remarkable 19c approximations to medieval colouring, which capture the subtle washed-out tones of the old glass, especially a Tree of Jesse and the window opposite.

One of the loveliest features at Salle is difficult to see: nine great wooden bosses on the Life of Christ in the chancel. Unless you bring binoculars you must make do with the good photographs displayed there.

Norfolk: about 6 miles SW of Aylsham, ½ mile N of B1145

Saltfleetby

All Saints (CCT)

Theddlethorpe

All Saints (CCT)

Two mellow redundant churches in the deserted marsh between Louth and the sea. Like Romney Marsh in Kent, this landscape feels archaic and unmodernized. Like churches there, these are untampered with.

There is a wonderful approach to *Saltfleetby* along a lane due W. Leaning walls, bumpy roof, greenstone and faded bricks occur unpredictably. Unpretentious tracery.

A wonderful space under tower, great blocks of stone underfoot. The whole feeling is pleasantly domestic. Old wooden roofs and screens, as if dissected. In chancel, arcades are pink; in nave, grey. Wonderfully simple Victorian pine fittings.

Theddlethorpe is more ambitious, though more dishevelled in its combination of materials. More greenstone, more brick.

Theddlethorpe. Interestingly dappled stonework in an isolated marshland location

Here the most amazing effect is dappled stonework over the arcades: green, white and rusty brown like an animal's coat. There are good Renaissance motifs in the screens and rich and crusty niches over the S altar (a simpler version of this effect at Saltfleetby).

Lincs: 8 miles E of Louth, Saltfleetby just S of B1200; Theddlethorpe 1 mile W of A1031

Scunthorpe

St John, St Hugh

J. S. Crowther; Lawrence Bond

An idiosyncratic Victorian church now part of an arts centre, and an interesting building of 1939 by Lawrence Bond, which keeps its original fittings intact.

Scunthorpe, St Hugh. Mild modernism of the 1930s that looks semi-industrial

Scunthorpe bills itself disarmingly as an Industrial Garden Town. The tower of *St John* makes a fine silhouette from afar among the steel mills. It has been rescued from dereliction, and extended in black steel and glass. Amazing carved bosses along the cornices, vigorous and intricate in the extreme. These light dressings contrast effectively with the dark mud colour of the walls. New gates in idiosyncratic ironwork; the nave has become a display space for the town's collection of painting and sculpture.

St Lawrence, just off the High Street to W, is now the main parish church. A nice low tower, but otherwise extensively re-managed, with a white interior very Charles Nicholson; arches dying into piers, clear glass, etc.

Further S is *St Hugh*, in yellow brick with pebbledash trim and a dark tile roof like something in a mining town. The pared-down portico reminds one of Italian fascist architecture, while the gentle gables of roof and tower look faintly Dutch outside and industrial within.

The altar and its canopy remain untampered with. An airy elongated cage makes an impressive cover for the stone font. Original colours of the interior strike a nice balance between lightness (pale blue) and sobriety (grey, tan).

Lincs: 22 miles SW of Hull on A18; St John in NE corner; St Hugh S of centre on main N–S route (E side of road), in Old Brumby

Shelton

St Mary

A stupendous late Perpendicular building of red brick diapered with darker vitrified bricks, in a wonderfully isolated position.

Except for an older tower, it was built all at once by Sir Ralph Shelton near the end of the 15c. The incomplete beginnings of a lavish tomb arch in the chancel are presumed to be his. A high and narrow clerestory whose internal proportions feel magically right. Corbels for a timber roof survive, but it was replaced with plaster in the 18c when the original timbers were transferred to a tithe barn.

There is a clownish praying monument and much entertaining original glass including small scenes and a portrait of the donor and his wife.

The wide empty spaces of Saltfleetby, an isolated church in the marsh

One of the most gorgeous royal arms in any English church, of William III's time, is mounted high on the W wall.

Norfolk: 13 miles S of Norwich, 2 miles E of A140

Sleaford

St Denys

One of the county's most characterful churches.

The W front looks friendly from afar, sitting at the end of the market place, with its fat tower framed by fancy later aisles. The effect is less consistent and more invigorating than at Grantham. This tower is powerful Norman and Early English, and the rest is the most excited Decorated, like an old grandsire in a Hawthorne story dragged along by his frivolous daughters.

The later work is in fact of superb quality, though very irregular and oddly meshed with the old. There are railings, pavilions, frilly upside-down spandrels, and gorgeous towerlets which held chantry bells. The N aisle doorway which juts into a magnificent window is a little ecstasy of ripeness. Luxuriant window tracery abounds at Sleaford, especially in N transept.

The interior is a collection of interesting spaces. The screen bellies forward wonderfully in the middle of its course to make a kind of balcony. On either side, Elizabethan tombs placed like perspective wings or flaps lead one into the chancel. The reredos with painted portraits of Christ and twelve disciples in fresh Nazarene style dates from 1953.

There is much interesting Victorian glass, but the real surprise is an airy S window with angels and oranges by William Morris & Co., 1900.

Lincs: 14 miles NE of Grantham on A15; A153 skirts church's S flank

Snettisham

St Mary

Magnificent Decorated W end and spire, chancel missing.

It sits apart from the village among pines, and presents a splendid face to the road. Two towerlets frame a large window with tracery like water weeds, wavering organic curves which tangle with each other in their ascent. The towerlets merge wonderfully with the gable and buttresses. More merging in the gallery or porch under the window. The piers which create its unequal bays are beautifully complex. More good tracery elsewhere, especially in clerestory and panelling of tower.

Inside, an obscuring gloom is produced by some poor Victorian glass and the pines outside the windows. But the arcade is high and noble. The chancel fell in long ago, so the space comes to an abrupt end under the tower.

Norfolk: 12 miles NE of King's Lynn, E of A149; church lies well E of village core

Thaxted. A large airy interior that retains mementoes of early 20c radicalism

Southwold

St Edmund

This fifteen-mile stretch of the Suffolk coast contains one of the proudest displays of church building in England. Between Walberswick and Lowestoft come five large churches and the remnant of another. The best of them, at Blythburgh, is treated in a separate entry.

Of KESSINGLAND only the striking tower remains, eked out with 17c rebuilding. Two more, at WALBERSWICK and COVEHITHE, are grotesque or Romantic relics of former greatness. Now the tower and part of the S aisle are the only functioning elements at Walberswick. The rest is an evocative, ivy-covered ruin. At Covehithe (St Andrew, 5 miles N of Southwold) the shrinking occurred in a more bizarre manner. The villagers applied for permission to unroof and reconstruct their church, and the result is a little thatched hut cowering in an empty shell the size of an aeroplane hangar. Bits of tracery, pier mouldings and corbel heads suggest how magnificent the former vastness was. The head of an old bearded king is incongruously re-located in the brick gable of the present porch. Inside, it is 17c religion at its most starkly minimal.

Southwold survives intact, grand in a slightly chilly way. Its silhouette is striking, and its S porch a wonderful bit of display, with profuse chequering

and panelling. On the tower an interesting flushwork inscription. Much clear glass, good stalls, screen and painted roof in chancel.

In the S churchyard an astonishing concoction in tile, brick, and various coloured stones. It looks like the resting place of an Anglo-Saxon king, but is the monument erected to one William Bardwell in 1853.

LOWESTOFT church (St Margaret) stands apart from the town core, aloof and high up to the NW. It too is of grand proportions with a magnificent E window of staggered Perp tracery. There is a high angel roof, good Whallish glass and a spectacular Comper font cover. In the N aisle a folkish curiosity: scenes in painted glass by Robert Allen, the self-taught artist who worked in the local china factory putting little shepherdesses on teapots.

Suffolk: Southwold is 19 miles S of Lowestoft on A1095

Stoke by Nayland

St Mary the Virgin

One of the most lavish in its district, silvery green Constable country.

Stoke village with its array of old half-timbering has a high situation, and the church tower shows wonderfully from afar. There are

vigorous setbacks towards the top and pinnacles like knobs. It is surprising to find so much brick mixed with the flint especially in middle stages, but the effect is varied and rosy rather than red.

This tower trails a long Perpendicular body, which is entered through a gorgeous pale grey door, with many delicate figures forming a Tree of Jesse. The carving inside isn't so fine, on font and tiny capitals for example. Wonderful sensations of light and height.

In S chancel a fantastic monument of 1615, on which the deceased woman's headdress presents a veritable landscape of curls.

Suffolk: 8 miles N of Colchester on B1068; church to W of this road

Tattershall

Holy Trinity

A large Perpendicular church in ashlar dwarfed by the brick castle adjacent.

The two of them form amazing silhouettes, seen from the flatness round about. The church is ambitiously big, but surprisingly bare, not the result of poverty but a cast of mind.

You enter through an old door with a functioning wicket. The internal height is incredible, and all disappointment at dead external surfaces is forgotten.

There are some large brasses in a cage or corral in the aisleless N transept and good wooden roofs. The chancel forms another world, shut off behind its stone screen. In here the great thing is old glass of cartoon pungency in the E window. Various scenes are jumbled: Acts of Mercy, Sacraments, assembled sunbursts, angels enclosed in frames like fetterlocks or drooping purses.

Terrington St Clement. Impressive marshland church with remarkable font cover

Probably purses, because chimneys in the Castle are repeatedly carved with a loaded purse encircled by bay leaves. This was the badge of Ralph Cromwell, Henry VI's Treasurer. The castle pre-dates the church and has some of the most breathtaking brick vaults in existence, especially in the cellar and in window bays of the top floor. Its moat has been restored, and a good model of the complex in its prime is displayed in the gatehouse.

Lincs: 9 miles S of Horncastle on A153

Terrington St Clement

St Clement

Cowfields lie to S and E of this impressive Marshland church, the first one W of King's Lynn, set in an unattractive village.

The S elevation is best, with pleasing variety of material, Tudor brick in chancel clerestory, rough brown carstone on transept end, which boasts a fabulous pyramid of closely spaced Perp windows, 3, 2 and 1. Unfortunately, the organ blocking N transept spoils what would be a splendid view through and out the other side. Two rows of panelled battlements, and sophisticated panelling on the porch.

Inside, a heavy W screen of 1788 is picturesquely effective. Inner frames of clerestory windows beautifully rich. The best fitting is a wooden font cover, which is a tall steeple of Jacobean motifs. Hinged doors open to reveal Flemish-type landscapes, not expertly painted, but the overlaps – as doors are brought together again and the miniature flower-bossed vault disappears inside – are bewitching. The whole assemblage of columns and pinnacles is gaily coloured.

In a similar vein are two enormous Creed-boards of 1635 which fill the transept walls with exuberant festoons and masks mixed into the texts.

Norfolk: 5 miles W of King's Lynn, N of A17

Thaxted

St John Baptist, St Mary & St Laurence

One of the largest churches in the county, well placed in a very attractive small town.

The sloping approach past the Guildhall and up a cobbled lane is one of the most memorable in England. At the

Stamford

One of the most beautiful towns in England, built almost entirely of pale local stone. An important commercial junction in the Middle Ages, it has been in gentle decline since, most house-fronts 17–18c. Best approach is from the S, on B1081, the former Great North Road. The E bypass threatened in 1990, which would have severed the town from the grounds of Burghley House and destroyed the approach described below, was not built.

The town slopes down to the river and up again on the other side. High Street St Martin's used to be in Northamptonshire. *St Martin*, crowded against E side of road, contains the best Baroque monument of Stamford – a multi-figure composition in serious, grey-tinged marble with standing allegories and a reclining couple theatrically lit by a concealed window.

Much medieval glass entertainingly displayed in 18c borders. In chancel an anthology of heads; in S aisle some large-boned scenes including a wonderful wine-coloured Samson. The churchyard extension, across a lane to E, contains the slab of Daniel Lambert, 1809 (the only slate one), with a preposterous inscription. He is famous for weighing 52 stone 11 pounds, and was visiting Stamford for the races when he died. Ever since, a set of his clothes has been on public view here.

St Mary juts into the street as you climb the other bank. It seems poised on its toes and ready to spring.

Stamford. A theatrical Baroque tomb in St Martin's

The strange kink in the Great North Road at this point has not been satisfactorily explained. Even more than All Saints' this powerful tower is too big for the piled boxes of Perpendicular nave huddled behind.

Cobbled square to S and E is one of the best spaces in Stamford, which seems to grow smaller as you move further into it.

Inside the church, a peculiar castellated arcade and mellow, re-made screens shut you off from N chapel, which contains much of interest, especially a rich 15c roof. Also Art Nouveau glass which improves on inspection and good medieval tombs. Sedding's painted ceiling patterns in the chancel are very pleasing.

All Saints has the prime position in Stamford, at another deviation in the main road. Along its S and E sides runs a head-high Early English blind arcade which never feels monotonous. Under its impressive tower, entered via a miniature-castle porch, are an amusing rustic warning to bell-ringers and carved figures plugging their ears.

Behind All Saints rises Barn Hill, one of Stamford's best streets where Stukeley the antiquary lived at no. 9, since decorated with woodworker's patterns in stone, as if Chippendale had built it. A *Methodist chapel* of 1803 is hidden near the upper end of Barn Hill to E.

Following Broad Street to E, and then Star Lane and St George's Street to S (past another early chapel), one arrives at St George's Square – a wonderfully secluded bit of old Stamford. *St George*'s strongly battered tower is turned sideways so that it looks Arts and Crafts. Inside, good monuments and a curious 18c assemblage of over 200 mottos of Garter knights in stained glass.

Lincs: 10 miles NW of Peterborough, just E of A1

Tilty, a lovable small building with gorgeous tracery in the E window

top you find more of Thaxted, which feels like a different place.

Externally a building of comically mixed texture, with plenty of writhing bosses and complex tracery in chancel aisles. The N side has been less restored. The slender stone spire is unusual in Essex.

Passing under a chapel in the N porch dedicated to the rebellious 14c priest John Ball, a favourite of William Morris, you come into a startlingly white and empty interior. Lovely panelling in clerestory window frames. Adam and Eve glass in S aisle, and a great iron corona under the crossing designed by Randall Wells.

He was the architect retained by Conrad Noel, Vicar of Thaxted, 1910–42. Noel was a Christian Socialist equally devoted to architectural purity, liturgical renewal and left-wing ferment. He stirred controversy by displaying the red flag of the International in the church. His wife led a revival of folk dancing in the district. A sad and moving remnant leans against the aisle wall, a banner inscribed with lines from Blake's 'Jerusalem', which shows field labourers against the background of a city. There are also wildflower garlands in papier-mâché, used as light fittings or crowns over statues. This is a building which still retains traces of a dream that faith could be refashioned in a more human image.

Essex: 7 miles SE of Saffron Walden on B184

Thorpe Market

St Margaret

A delicious bit of gimcrackery. It lies remote from the settlement (a market in 13c, but now resembling a diminutive 18c estate village). The venerable medieval location has been graced with a seedy theatrical prop of 1796, a simple rendered box with spindly pinnacles at the corners and two small porches also with pinnacles (perhaps 19c improvements).

Inside, two rickety Gothick screens at opposite ends, inset with weakly coloured glass mainly heraldic. Windows glazed with garish red, blue and purple, which makes the visitor think of Gothic novels or Keats's 'warm gules'. So powerful is the pervasive atmosphere that the 14c font will probably be mistaken for Gothick too.

Nearby, another interesting 18c church at GUNTON (4 miles SW in grounds of GUNTON HALL), a small Tuscan temple with a lovely porch, by Robert Adam, 1769, like a garden ornament.

Norfolk: Thorpe Market church is 5 miles S of Cromer, off A149 less than 1 mile SE of village, on road to Gunton railway station

Tilty

St Mary the Virgin

One of the marvellous small churches of Essex, an enchanting blend of Decorated richness and the 18c. It began as the chapel-outside-the-walls of a now vanished abbey.

Its position is remote and delicious. It looks wonderful from afar, crowned by its delicate cupola. The 18c W parts are painted a beguiling mustard colour, and the shape of the older chancel is intriguing, with an oddly hipped roof and glorious E window. Unfortunately the tracery has needed renewing externally, but it remains a design to study, tracing and retracing it.

Tilty has received many recent folkish embellishments including a

painted chancel beam, font cover and pulpit canopy. They are delightful in themselves, and valuable as signs of continuing appreciation of this wonderful place.

Essex: about 4 miles NW of Great Dunmow, ½ mile W of B184

Ufford

St Mary

Famous for its towering wooden font cover, regarded by some as the most beautiful in the country, and a haven of rich fittings and textures.

It lies in an attractive cul-de-sac with a lovely Margery Fish-style garden to the left. A nice simple tower ends the vista, and there is outstanding flushwork on the S porch, better than some more grandiose examples because less restored. Especially interesting is the 'slipped quatrefoil' motif,

Ufford's towering font cover under a fine roof among other lucky survivals

Walpole St Peter, one of the most satisfying late Gothic churches in the country

which shows one circle sunk to rest inside a larger one, the extra space filled by two mouchettes, with a perspective effect like looking down a tube.

Inside, an older arcade on one side and two storeys of Perpendicular windows on the other. The font cover is complex and slender, and seems to gather its breath for a further climb, then bulge out a bit and keep going. There is much colour left on it and flattened vaulting like spiderwebs. It is finished by a pelican on top.

The roof also retains beautiful colouring and old decoration on the beams. In the chancel, angels and tracery decorate the fringe along the wall.

There is pale old glass and a very good early Comper window, more delicately shaded than his later work. At the W end a classical monument in black and white marble with bull's heads, urns and little else. This refined and enigmatic work somehow resembles a shop-counter.

Suffolk: 3 miles NE of Woodbridge, ½ mile E of B1438

Walpole St Peter

St Peter

One of the most satisfying churches in England, Perpendicular when the style had not progressed very far towards its final cold consistency.

Walpole is one of the group of Marshland churches founded on revenue from sheep and called forth by a landscape whose charm is its bleakness. The territory around the church is strangely suburban, but the churchyard is large, with the building placed lopsidedly in the NE corner. Inside the low wall, all is harmony.

It is a grand example of a well-windowed nave where you see in and out the other side, like those X-rays of one-celled animals. All the walls are battlemented with delicately panelled cresting. It is strange to note that spaces between aisle windows are rendered (brick showing through here and there), but at the E end rich expanses of stone softened by a red lichen which gives it an indescribable individuality.

To accommodate an ancient right of way, a passage under the chancel was contrived. It is a wonderful if now gratuitous space, barely high enough to stand upright in, but wide enough for tethering rings on the sides, with writhing animals on the bosses. Out the other side a great copper beech shades the S aisle and the even more elaborately carved S porch.

The interior seems vast and infinitely gentle. Much 17c wood of a mousy colour, a large screen and a font cover which is a Tower of Babel in itself, mixing Gothic and Renaissance most giddily. The stone of the arcades has so much yellow in it that it feels more like the colour of wood than the greyer wooden screen.

Behind each chancel stall, theatrical illusions of vaults traced on foreshortened surfaces. On the stalls, armrests which are among the glories of late Gothic carving. The Three Kings as a Janus-head construction, a camel with a sunburst of hair round its hump, a crowned head crowded by a wolf, are among the subjects. A 20c carver has been at work making replicas which usefully clarify the worn originals.

In the S aisle are less sophisticated bench ends, including a marvellous lion collared with a crown whose mane passes under the collar and is then teased out like a lady's hair. In the churchyard illusionistic headstones of Rococo style but early Victorian date: one showing an oval tablet hung up by carved ribbon with carved reeds growing up to obscure it below, another with a fat obelisk carved in shallow relief on the tapered plate.

Norfolk: 2 miles S of A17, between King's Lynn and Wisbech; follow brown tourist signs

Walsoken

All Saints

Though Walsoken is now joined to Wisbech, its churchyard still seems a secluded, special preserve. In an area rich in fine churches this is one of the mellowest and most interesting.

The Early English tower and spire make an impression of real refinement, especially the third stage with a subtly outlined blind arcade. Surprisingly, the exterior of nave and aisles is whitewashed, and you can see that the battlements are brick under this covering.

There are charming folkish touches inside, like the faded angels on the roof

and the great wooden Solomon above the tower arch with painted extensions either side: a mother and the soldier threatening to slash her baby. At the other end of the nave, a large David. Further quaint and clumsy renditions of such subjects painted on large boards.

The arcade is Norman, of an exuberant toothiness. To the S chapel a beautiful two-tiered screen. There are good Tudor bench ends and a Seven Sacraments font with many saints.

Norfolk: on NE edge of Wisbech; church lies SW of junction of Wisbech bypass (A47) and old road NE of town centre

Waltham Abbey

Holy Cross & St Lawrence

A major work of Norman architecture wonderfully embellished by one of the great Victorians.

The problem of how to terminate large abbeys dismembered at the Dissolution has often been attempted and even more often been left to solve itself. William Burges's solution at Waltham is one of the best.

The homey 16c tower, chequered at its base, is a wonderful sight, staring down the street as you approach from the W. Within it is a lively 14c doorway which has many birds and animals, including an owl, hidden in the foliage.

This does not prepare you for the awesome scale of the interior with its ample Norman arcades, whose contented proportions are echoed in Burges's E end. Here the gigantism of his carved detail seems exactly right. There's a leaf and animal fringe to the reredos which includes two of Aesop's fables. Overhead looms a flat painted ceiling based on the one at Peterborough, with easy to read portraits of months, heavenly signs, and times of life.

Best of all are the stained glass windows by Burne-Jones before his association with Morris, executed by Powell: a wheel rose above three lancets. The central Tree of Jesse is sublime – rich in colour, medieval in the drawing.

In the detached S chapel gorgeous double tracery and a pale Doom painting on the facing wall. In N aisle one of the best late 17c tombs in England shows a relief of a ship labelled *Industria* surrounded by very three-dimensional trophies.

Essex: just outside the Greater London boundary and beyond the M25 across the River Lea from Hertfordshire, on A112

Weston

St Mary

In fen country which is very strange: more like Iowa or the moon than England. As there are few through roads here, they tend to be busy. So territory which is quite deserted can also seem heavily travelled. Weston is on the road between Spalding and King's Lynn, which links one of the best series of churches in the whole country. But it isn't a pretty district. Buildings tend to be harsh and unassimilated in a landscape whose contours are almost nonexistent.

The church seems crowded against the road, though the churchyard is ample. Sturdy lancets on chancel end give a clue to the forthrightness of effects inside.

There, one is immediately struck by the rich grey of unscoured stone, and by the controlled exuberance of the carving. Even fillets and mouldings on the arcade seem to partake of an excitement most obvious in the strong, curling leaves of the capitals. Everything is more soberly or literally meant than in later Gothic. It seems a sincere rather than sophisticated phase, in which the pointed shape of the chancel arch, for example, is not a

Walsoken. Solomon between a distraught mother and soldier threatening her child, under an angel roof

convention but a discovery, at which the maker still marvels.

The beautiful font is of the same vintage, and quite architectural – octagonal with diminutive columns at the angles, graced with simple capitals. In between, the most gorgeous but restrained foliage, usually a single frond, but once (on S) a double one. These furls never fill their allotted spans too full, leaving them just half empty, and seeming almost musical. So some observers want to make these plain leaves stand for the Tree of Life, wakened into growth by the water of faith.

Lincs: 3 miles E of Spalding just S of A151 which now bypasses Weston; church on N side of village street

West Walton

St Mary

At the W edge of Norfolk on the fringes of the fens.

One of the best buildings of its date in England, in spite of a W front which threatened collapse at some point and was repaired with clumsy buttressing. Even this interference just gives earlier purity of design a cloud to shine through.

The moment represented by West Walton is Early English. The best details, like the S porch and nave arcade, are like filling powerful lungs with fresh air. It is a moment of happy confidence tinged by childishness, which presents leaves and tendrils larger than life, magnifying God's work for our more easy understanding. But right beside this enlarged comprehension we find certain elements crushed or crammed, usually at the edges of a compositional group. The inspired lucidity of this vision comes almost more poignantly through soot on the stone. Long may this treasure remain unrestored.

As at Binham (q.v.), Perp windows make earlier details easier to read, and one of the greatest human joys in Norfolk, West Walton's angel roof, also dates from that later time. There are twenty-three of them (one missing), each with a face thoughtful in its own way.

The detached tower fifty yards to the S is the most famous feature of the church; it looks overbearing in photos, but in fact has the large-boned grace of everything in this wonderful place.

Norfolk: 3 miles directly N of Wisbech

West Walton. Large-boned early Gothic, with later windows to bring more light

Whaplode

St Mary

One of the most pleasing in England. The tranquil churchyard is a funnel widening towards the church, whose E end is met first. Then you navigate around the chunky semi-detached Early English tower, passing an illogical but harmonious set of parts, including an assortment of window tracery some of which has the rough look of 17c replacement. In fact there is an idiosyncratic drawing by Gimson, reproduced in Lethaby's beautiful book *Ernest Gimson and His Work*, of wooden tracery replacing stone, labelled 'Whaplode church'.*

The interior has the feel of spaces lovingly treated by SPAB† repairers. An unusually wide nave flooded with light, the three W bays switching to Early English (from heavy Norman) with leafy capitals less florid than Weston. At this end there is a step up onto a wide platform like a concourse on which the 17c font sits. This font is a student's exercise in architectural ornament, very amateur, and rests on small barley sugar columns.

Also at this end, in the S aisle, an enchanting compound like a Montacute

garden pavilion, closely ringed by a high iron railing. Under the canopy two effigies.

The church is full of interest, with lovely roof, good S porch, great W door and window (still huge though partly blocked), and gorgeous stone throughout, of a slightly rosy cast.

* Local memory has it that the wooden tracery in the N transept window 'was given by a friend of William Morris'.

† SPAB: Society for the Protection of Ancient Buildings: called by William Morris 'anti-Scrape' and founded by him, Philip Webb and others in 1877 in immediate opposition to Gilbert Scott's plans for revamping Tewkesbury Abbey. The Society attacked the style of Victorian restoration which revised buildings to make them more consistent examples of whatever style predominated. Buildings repaired according to SPAB principles include Inglesham, Wilts; Sutton Courtenay, Berks; Hough-on-the-Hill, Lincs; Eglwys Brewis and Eglwys Cummin in South Wales.

Lincs: 6 miles E of Spalding; church a few hundred yards S of A151

Wiggenhall

St Mary Magdalene

Mellow, richly textured building in strange fenland country.

The Wiggenhalls are straggling settlements in a peculiar region where roads make awkward patterns and you are continually crossing channels with banked-up sides.

St Mary Magdalene presents a beautifully mottled s side to the road, of brick with the render coming off, of carstone and much else in the tower, with some gorgeous Perpendicular tracery and a plainer chancel.

Long may its churchyard remain scruffy and its interior with little saints and bishops in the N windows retain its slightly bare and desolate feel.

Not far up the Great Ouse to the N lies WIGGENHALL ST GERMANS, an even more mouldery building with decayed brick tracery in its porch, a lovely Rococo cartouche brutally implanted in one of its walls, and a delightfully patchy interior. Bench ends here have many creatures and figures clinging to their tops.

Very sculptural royal arms at Wisbech

One of the Wiggenhall churches, *St Mary*, has been recently renovated by the CCT. It sports a new roof and a thick coat of cream paint. But the brick tower, the bench ends and a 17c font cover like a miniature building remain delightful.

Norfolk: 10 miles SW of King's Lynn, 2½ miles W of A10; St Mary Magdalene at N end, on W bank of Great Ouse

Wingfield

St Andrew

A lavish Decorated and Perpendicular church in evocative isolation next to the decorous 18c quarters of Wingfield College.

The headstops on the s aisle are a telling revelation of medieval attitudes. Each face is different and extremely characterful, the overall impression chaotic or rich according to your taste. All aisle windows have four leaves in tracery at the top, making a kind of flower. Clerestory windows become richer and twice as numerous in the chancel.

Inside, a wonderfully clean, airy and well-cared for but somewhat sterile space. In the s chapel are tombs of the Dukes of Suffolk, whose residence at Wingfield explains the magnificence of the church. Over the second Duke hangs a grand panelled arch with many knots, wings and blank shields. It is now a chaste cream colour, far better than originally when covered in bragging heraldry.

Suffolk: about 6 miles NE of Eye, and less than a mile NW of B1118

Wingfield, perforated by plentiful windows of both High and late Gothic

Wisbech

St Peter & St Paul

A large rambling late Gothic church charmingly placed in the centre of one of the county's best towns.

Wisbech is a decayed port which winds along the canalized River Nene. These frontages, known as North and South Brinks, are lined with merchants' houses, mostly 18c. After floods in the 20c fences at the edge were replaced with brick walls.

The church sits beneath road level as if sinking. The top of its squat, detached tower is jagged and fretted, and its upper stages are peppered with heraldic decoration. The sprawling group of nave and aisles gives the impression of more than one building. Unfortunately it is kept locked except on weekday mornings.

Cambs: 14 miles SW of King's Lynn on A47 (which now bypasses town)

Worstead

St Mary the Virgin

A large and regular Decorated building with special claim to the title of wool church.

Worstead is a pleasant shrunken place which gave its name to a kind of cloth. The former market place lies comfortably idle E of the church.

Its tower is impressive from afar, with flushwork at top and bottom. The interior is vast, clean and somewhat featureless, like a Dutch church, with good uneven brick floors and screens with interesting 19c painting in the coving. There are box pews, practically no stained glass, and some 18c Virtues on the tower screen, copied by a nearby rector's wife from Sir Joshua Reynolds.

Norfolk: 3 miles SE of North Walsham, 1 mile S of A149

Wymondham *

Abbey Church of St Mary & St Thomas of Canterbury

One of the glories of Norfolk, the remains of a large abbey church in a very attractive small town.

The churchyard is enormous and full of beautiful old pine trees. The building which remains has towers at both ends – rivalrous projects originally, parochial and monastic. The E one, with octagonal

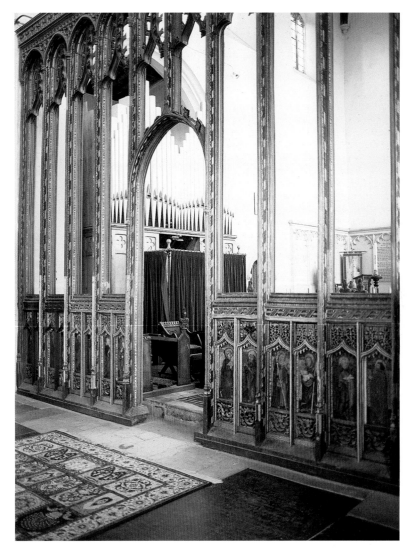

One of a number of medieval screens at Worstead

top, is semi-ruined and more beautiful, readily penetrated by the eye and by flocks of birds which eddy round it at dusk. To the E lie the ruins of the choir.

The flushwork clerestory is spectacular, as is the patterning on the tower, enhanced by rose-hued lichen. Finials on S windows look positively Rococo in their floridity.

Inside, a spectacular Norman arcade with huge square chamfered piers and perplexing variety in decorative trimmings. Roofs here are very wonderful, both in N aisle and nave; fancy florets at crossing points are a peculiar motif.

A spectacular Comper reredos embellishes the E end and a high rood beam instead of a screen. Practically the whole wall is filled by fifteen large figures in niches with much gilt and surrounding fretwork. It's a great improvement on the truncated effect one often finds in broken-off pieces of abbeys.

To the right, spectacular sedilia which look like a three-bay Renaissance tomb, or three stoves. They are a riot of irrational classical motifs in moulded terracotta.

In N aisle some fascinating scenes in naive pictorial glass, early 19c, like Robert Allen's at Lowestoft.

* Pronounced Win-dum

Norfolk: 8 miles SW of Norwich on A11; church at W end of town

Midlands

Derbyshire,
Nottinghamshire,
Leicestershire,
Rutland,
Northamptonshire,
Warwickshire

Blyth

Worksop

Tideswell
Buxton
Eyam
Chesterfield
Youlgreave
Ault Hucknall
Teversal
Matlock
Wirksworth
Holme by Newark
Newark
Ashbourne
Norbury
Strelley
Nottingham
Morley
Derby
Dale Abbey
Bottesford
Bunny
Repton
Melbourne
Breedon on the Hill
Staunton Harold
Exton
Teigh
Tickencote
Whissendine
Great Casterton
Gaddesby
Leicester
Oakham
Empingham
Brooke
Ketton
King's Norton
Tixover
Stoke Golding
Hallaton
Apethorpe
Great Packington
Stoke Dry
Fotheringhay
Astley
Lyddington
Warmington
Birmingham
Rothwell
Lowick
Coventry
Berkswell
Crick
Raunds
Lapworth
Brixworth
Higham Ferrers
Ullenhall
Warwick
Wellingborough
Wootton Wawen
Lower Shuckburgh
Earls Barton
Stratford-upon-Avon
Northampton
Burton Dassett
Brailes
Middleton Cheney

THIS IS DIVERSE TERRITORY. At the top, the high moorland of the Peak District in Derbyshire, valued for landscape not buildings, though the special power of a town like Wirksworth comes from its slightly forbidding circumstances.

At the other end of the region is the favoured country of northern Northants. Here and in adjacent Rutland we are back in the great limestone belt which sponsors some of the most beautiful towns in England, above all Stamford in Lincolnshire. As Pevsner says, it belongs in Northamptonshire.

Rutland is one of the most satisfying corners of England, as if its small dimensions had meant it could be more carefully formed, more considered. Churches here reach a consistently high level but are not startling.

Rutland's larger neighbour suffers a bit from the comparison. Leicestershire at its best, in the south, seems a continuation of Rutland. Nottingham is another of those counties surprisingly bare of interesting churches, and Warwickshire is a curious amalgam. In the space between Birmingham and Coventry are sprinkled diverse remarkable churches. This county has found very workable compromises between country and town.

Apethorpe

St Leonard

Amazing accoutrements in the modest church of a good village.

The W tower is a somewhat bland 17c replacement. Inside, a lovely faded Last Supper in stained glass above the altar. This dates from 1732 and seems unusually apt, like a bit of sacred dumb-show.

Then, a vision – seen through openings to the right, a huge catafalque appears, like a Renaissance round temple with pierced lantern and marble drapery. It is the Mildmay tomb of 1621, carrying Virtues at the corners and effigies inside, and it engorges the space of its chapel. High up, the walls are panelled in Fontainebleau-type cartilage, including lions' legs thrust out horizontally to pin down drapery.

There is old glass with many small scenes in one of the windows and interesting smaller monuments.

In the nave, Whallish windows dated 1916 and 1918.

Northants: 5 miles N of Oundle on unnumbered road

Ashbourne

St Oswald

Ashbourne church is a gorgeous sight in its valley meadow, especially when seen from the S (from A515). It has a perfect

Apethorpe's theatrical Mildmay tomb

position at the W end of Church Street, one of the best streets in England.

The church embodies a kind of ideal, with its fine Early English chancel, great central spire and ample churchyard. Entered through S transept, where the size is immediately impressive. The setting sun fires Kempe glass in the great W window (a Tree of Jesse) to

Ashbourne. Local maidens in Christopher Whall's window of 1905

incandescence. One of the best windows of its date – by Christopher Whall, 1905 – lies to your left as you enter. It is full of pretty girls and decadent plant life. The maidens it commemorates are portrayed again in a painting posted on the NW crossing pillar.

Another painting, of tombs in Ashbourne church, by Collingwood (Ruskin's pupil and a famous student of Saxon sculpture) hangs in the Boothby Chapel, with its fine effigies and marvellous double brass of 1538. A later monument steals the show here: it presents the five-year-old Penelope Boothby in marble, asleep, her pose slightly crooked. Queen Charlotte cried when she saw it. The sculptor, Thomas Banks, is better known for cooler, more Homeric work.

Derbys: 13 miles NW of Derby on A52

Astley

St Mary

The curious relic of a large collegiate church mostly knocked down at the Dissolution, Astley seems frozen in time. But this aura of a mouldering ruin is misleading. It is not abandoned but gently and unobtrusively cared for.

The air of desolation is enhanced by the castle just behind, which is collapsing into its moat and so overgrown that its lines are indecipherable. The desolation is increased by patchy old rendering on the nave walls, and by the patchiness of tower and chancel tacked on c1609; and increased further by the church's position beyond the pale, past the houses, so it feels as if one is venturing into a thicket or onto waste ground.

A few beautiful details survive from the 14c, like the leaves spreading upward from the window tops onto the cornice; or the furls remounted on the tower face.

Inside, a vast barny space with a blocked Perpendicular window filling the whole E wall. This blockage sums up the story of Astley. Its walls are defaced with lots of 17c black-letter inscriptions. Its fine alabaster effigies are herded together and fenced off near the entrance. Its painted stalls moulder on further along, somewhat disfigured. All in all, it is a grand exhibition of time's misuses, which has, so far, escaped the tidying zeal of the present.

Warwicks: about 7 miles N of Coventry on B4102; church lies N of this road

Ault Hucknall

St John Baptist

Carving of two different periods, rudest Norman and most refined Renaissance, embellishes this small church.

The older bits are embedded in the W wall, which is a treasure trove of antiquity. There's a Saxon window-top with herringbone ridges and loose bits of pattern. Then a barbaric tympanum over a barbaric lintel. Both of these show encounters between men and animals, one ambiguous, the other violent.

Inside, a very scrambled chancel arch with beakhead and figural voussoirs which some have managed to read as a history of the world, very rough of course. There is also a re-set Saxon arch to the E.

In the S chapel a marvellous tomb not much like anything else. This dates from 1627 and includes a row of elegant female Virtues two feet high. Tragically two of the heads have disappeared since the photo in Pevsner, and a third is stored elsewhere for safekeeping. Apparently the damage was done by workmen cleaning the window above, which contains good old glass. In the floor beneath, the philosopher Hobbes is buried.

A fascinating window of 1892 in S aisle – just primary colours and violet, in a simplified archaic style like an illuminated manuscript. In the other aisle pearly glass of 1932 with late Symbolist Virtues, not unlike the Rope sisters'

Ault Hucknall. Norman carving of primitive struggle in two tiers

work in Suffolk (especially Blaxhall). Butterfield's font is worth a look, and his simple wooden pews are a delight.

Derbys: 7 miles SE of Chesterfield, S of A617, just N of Hardwick Hall

Berkswell

St John Baptist

A building with real surprises, one of the most interesting in the county.

Though near Coventry, its village is a sylvan enclave, and the sheltered churchyard an enclave within that. The E end of red sandstone, which you see first, is an impressive Norman

composition with half pillars attached to the corners making a classical effect. Lots of rude corbels next, which are anything but classical.

You enter under the Tudor vestry like a little half-timbered building perched in the air. Then through a door like old leather, and you find yourself in an interior which slopes down to the S and up to the E.

The best surprise here is the crypt, entered through one of the pew doors. It contains two marvellous 12c spaces: an octagon with a complex vault, followed by a two-bay rectangle. Now you will understand the odd widening of chancel buttresses outside: they are growing to accommodate the crypt windows.

Up above ground are screens with grapes and berries trailing on and on along them, many hatchments, and an exquisite but rather spooky memorial of 1818 by Westmacott with cloying damsels, a moth corrupting a flower, and sickles felling lush roses.

Warwicks/W Midlands: 5 miles W of Coventry on unnumbered road 1 mile E of A452

Birmingham

St Agatha, Stratford Road, Sparkbrook

W. H. Bidlake

One of the best late Gothic Revival buildings, by W. H. Bidlake, a local man who had studied with Bodley.

Its tower is high and straight, a beacon from far off. It is made of dark red brick which breaks into stone richness at the top, and finally terminates in pierced pinnacles and parapets. It sits on a busy road among garages and semi-derelict housing. You have to walk round behind to get a sense of its wonderful scale and its relation to the original neighbourhood of humble terrace houses, not many of which survive.

Its flanks are endless and contain much brittle ultra-Perp tracery. The great E window is filled with eccentric snowflake forms profusely cusped.

Inside, war bombing and a fire in 1957 cleared away much of the original apparatus of High Church ritual, leaving pale brick arcades and walls of nervous angularity in great unbroken stretches. Because of its location, difficult of access, but worth persisting.

An earlier work of Bidlake's is *St Oswald*, St Oswald's Road, Small Heath, ten minutes away to the NE.

Although it became the cathedral of Birmingham in 1905, perhaps

Ault Hucknall in a tranquil location near Hardwick Hall

Berkswell. Norman and Tudor in a sylvan enclave near Coventry

Thomas Archer's only major church outside London can be mentioned here. *St Philip's* is set diagonally in a green at the centre of the city and is one of the great embodiments of English Baroque. It contains a series of huge Burne-Jones windows, painted with a broad brush in a simplified palette. The collision of those spindly angels with Archer's giant orders is indeed bizarre.

Warwicks/W Midlands: 118 miles NW of London on M1; St Agatha lies near junction with Mole Street, SE of city centre

Blyth

Priory Church of St Mary & St Martin

The later re-fashioning of a great Norman priory.

When it became a parish church, Blyth was supplied with a frilly W tower and a vigorous Doom painting on the blocked arch of the crossing. This has cartoon-like force, and consists of

outlines without a great deal of colour; in spite of this mural the truncation of the building is cruelly felt.

The nave arcade which remains is glorious, like one of the great French abbeys. It is built of a soft grey stone, and the vertical system, of three stories, is conceived with awesome rationality. In the nave, a later vault, but in the N aisle, low original vaults survive, and a slight depression of the curve only makes them feel more powerful.

Notts: about 6 miles NE of Worksop just W of A1, on B6045; church NW of main crossroads of village

Bottesford

St Mary

Rightly famous for its monuments, of which there is an overwhelming glut. The church has a proud crocketed spire and a lavish clerestory, panelled and pinnacled.

Acrobatic corbels and label stops in the arcade are very entertaining, as is the folkish late 16c font with animals' heads, balusters, thorny roses and angels in flames or clouds.

But of course the culmination at Bottesford comes in the chancel, which is virtually unusable now, with alabaster four-posters blocking the way. These make a fine effect in photographs, but on the spot you can't really tell if the separate pieces are good any more. Certainly the spiritual aims of the building are buried under family pride in this sector. One helm shows a peacock emerging from a lidded container like a jack-in-the-box. Vigorously carved Rutland peacocks also appear on 19c bench ends. In fact, the greatest height of virtuosity is reached in the wooden royal arms which intrudes in the chancel arch to proclaim VR – another gorgeous blockage in a place well used to such things.

Leics: 7 miles W of Grantham on A52; church a short distance N of road

Brailes

St George

A large church with a commanding tower, known as the Cathedral of the Feldon (the Feldon being the open country S of the Avon, as opposed to the woodland N of it, the Arden). If you follow the road to Chipping Campden you find that Brailes is on the edge of an escarpment with wide views of the Stour valley to the W.

The most impressive external decoration is an openwork parapet like a huge piece of ribbon; under it lies a corbel course with heads crowded so densely it is like a dentil. At the E end of the nave a fancy sanctus bellcote. The N side is much plainer than the S, and hardly meant to be seen.

Unfortunately, the high interior has been scraped. There we find a font like a textbook of tracery and the most ruined effigy ever, on a nice 15c base. The sedilia are of unusual form, with arms (partly renewed). In the N aisle a large matchstick model of the building includes such details as the little lead figure of 1900 on the lychgate.

An early *Catholic chapel* made from a malt barn c1726 can be reached by a convenient path to the SE, which goes down and across a stream. The chapel is hidden in a shambling manor farm. You climb an external stair and find yourself in a low room with simple 18c panelling and plain, coloured glass. There's a dark painting of the Crucifixion which looks Spanish and very exotic, as the Catholic faith must sometimes have felt in this space. The first English Catholic bishop after the Reformation was born on the farm. One of his descendants, also a Catholic priest, is buried in the nearby churchyard with a tolerant plaque. The comfortable path between the two buildings may not be so misleading after all.

Warwicks: about 14 miles SE of Stratford on B4035; church on N side of road in Lower Brailes

Breedon on the Hill

St Mary & St Hardulph

Stands alone, a beacon on the top of its hill, made steeper by lime quarrying at the base. Like a number of other early

Breedon on the Hill contains a marvellous collection of 9c sculpture

churches it lies within the bounds of a prehistoric citadel. The present village climbs part way up the S side of the table-shaped eminence.

Breedon church contains one of the best collections of Dark Age sculpture in Europe, but from any distance the building looks pure Perpendicular, with those inspiring views straight through, which are characteristic of well-windowed late Gothic. When you get nearer, signs of greater antiquity. After all, there was a monastery here from the 7c.

Internal textures are very pleasing, especially the mottled clerestory and a barbaric squire's pew of 1627. Early 9c sculpture is dotted through the building without much rhyme or reason. Formerly it must have been external decoration. In fact some of it has come indoors quite recently. Among the bits are long pieces of horizontal frieze with spindly animals who seem to wear comical grins. The technique is extraordinary: it looks like cloisonné whose enamel has fallen out.

There are enigmatic panels too – a Byzantine virgin under an arch (in a tomb?) and, most wonderful of all, two figures holding leafy staffs or swinging censers, bursting with tumultuous energy. Unfortunately the biggest and possibly the best carving cannot be seen because presently built into the wall of the ringing chamber. It shows a blessing angel wearing robes like storm clouds.

Other tantalizing fragments – wine jars and feet, a lion pawing a plant. Some interesting bits of Saxon crosses, which look strangely prosaic beside all this other carving of strongly Eastern flavour.

Leics: 6 miles NE of Ashby-de-la-Zouch on A453

Bottesford, an overwhelming set of mainly Renaissance monuments

Brooke. Pleasing variety of stone textures in a small church on the village green

Brixworth

All Saints

Brixworth has been called the most impressive 7c building north of the Alps. Not surprisingly it has been one of the most carefully studied of English churches.

The scale is remarkable for the date; it is by far the biggest early Saxon building known. Its form is basilican, and the present external walls were formerly arcades giving onto partial aisles and other smaller enclosures. The columns of the arcade are simply 8-foot chunks of wall, connected by round Roman arches.

Remains of a Roman villa have been found nearby, and Roman tiles (these not from nearby) are much in evidence both inside and out. The most moving sight of all is the tapestry of various stones and these Roman bricks mixed pell-mell in the large round tower attached to the great square tower, and in the walls at the W end generally. Ruddy stones scattered

through this part were evidently taken from a building which had burned. On the N, ruddy stones occurring together indicate a fire on the spot.

Visually the most wonderful product of current research is a coloured diagram of the geological census carried out on the walls. Each kind of stone is coded with a colour of its own, and the fabric is recorded stone by stone. Thirty mineral varieties have been identified, most of them not local. So this building, huge for its time, was made of materials collected from many sites and transported many miles. The Roman city of Towcester and the Jewry wall at Leicester probably contributed.

Brixworth now feels more like an exhibit or puzzle than a building. The bookstall in the church is like a visit to a scholarly conference. The process of learned tampering began with a 19c vicar who rebuilt the rounded apse and removed haphazard Gothic intrusions in the walls. Most of the medieval rendering

had disappeared by 1865* and by now many conventional signs of age such as lichen and mellow textures are missing.

Right inside the S door is a remarkable Saxon eagle, hidden there in Norman times. Now this carved stone sits in a kind of reliquary cabinet: a glass panel in the doorframe lets us see the survivor, spotlit.

* Some remained, to be excised in the re-pointing of 1977.

Northants: 7 miles N of Northampton now bypassed by A508; church W of road at N end of village

Brooke

St Peter

A small building of great charm in an isolated setting.

The drive S from Oakham is very pleasant. The church sits at the centre of a wonderful green in the middle of this

Buxton. Arts and Crafts with roofs of stone slates that blend with the walls beneath

dispersed village. A bit of new building in debased picturesque vein tries to blend in but does not.

The mixed form and piebald texture of the church is amazing – smooth ashlar, bumpy ironstone, rubble in the tower. Inside, a Norman arcade is followed by an airy Renaissance chancel. Here some nice pierced woodwork and a discreetly tinted tomb of 1619, very retardataire.

The font is Norman with many little colonnettes.

Rutland: 2 miles S of Oakham on unnumbered road

Bunny

St Mary

The efforts of Sir Thomas Parkyns, the Wrestling Baronet, have made the church and village among the most curious spots in England. His style might be described as Vanbrugh with trimmings. He died in 1741, so his architectural ideas were very antiquated by that time.

The church pre-dates this prodigy, but his spirit infects it. Fancy parapets – pierced in chancel, panelled elsewhere. The porch of humpy tunnel shape is most beguiling. Inside, there is one pillar in S arcade with fabulous vegetable carving like magnified sprouting seeds. It looks Art Nouveau. The vast boxy chancel has an 18c window, but otherwise good Decorated fittings.

The wrestler's monument is one of the oddest in England. Its interminable inscription boasts of the subject's mathematical, architectural and hydraulic learning. The piece was designed by him and executed by his chaplain in a barn, so the story goes. It is divided into two equal parts: in one, Sir Thomas stands ready to take on all comers, a fighting pose, nearly life-size; in the other, two tiny figures, Time and the baronet. He has lost the match, and death is the penalty. The disparity between the two halves is ludicrous.

Returning, you see over the wall, across the main road, his preposterous

Mannerist porch at Bunny, near Nottingham, the Wrestling Baronet's church

design for the Hall, like a folly or unfinished triumphal arch in brick with stone trim. Nearer, the modest school – now almshouses – sports a crippling orgy of heraldic ornament.

Notts: 7 miles S of Nottingham on A60; church in Church Street W of road

Burton Dassett

All Saints

One of the most delightful in the county, and a great advertisement for conservative restoration.

Formerly a place of some importance, until recently Burton Dassett was a remote backwater consisting of a few farms among a landscape of bumpy mounds like leftovers from prehistoric mining. Its seclusion has now been damaged by the extension of the M40.

When J. Cossins did his painstaking restoration in 1890 he found seven different floor levels and a variety of textures beneath rotting boards. So it has become a real landscape underfoot, and a kind of hill climb to the chancel which lies far above the nave. The chancel is big and empty, and the whole so irregular that the space seems to grow and change. From under the tower a great expanse stretches E, and touring the building you feel you've been in many different places.

On the capitals in the arcade, animals like Scandinavian Christmas ornaments follow each other around the mouldings; some of them walk upside down.

Outside, lichen covers the E end (fifty years ago it was discovered that some of the walls are mud, not stone), and the churchyard has many half-buried tombstones.

Warwicks: about 8 miles NW of Banbury, 1 mile E of A41

Buxton

St Mary the Virgin, Dale Road

Currey and Thompson

A late Arts and Crafts building of impressive power. Currey and Thompson, the architects, did a number of churches in the county.

The style is rustic Early English. A single roof of stone slates runs continuously over nave and aisles, changing pitch slightly at the division. It ends low and near the ground; even buttress-tops are slated, and over dormers a slinky curve which makes them resemble eyes. At the crossing a modest timber belfry. Roof and walls are the same rich tawny colour.

Inside, more aggressively rustic, especially in hefty arcades and low aisle windows which seem hewn from cliffs. The screen is a particularly fine bit of woodwork, rich with flowers and leaves of Art Nouveau cast: it was designed by the architects. There are other fittings by the Northern Art Workers' Guild.

Derbys: 12 miles E of Macclesfield on A53; church SE of centre

Chesterfield

Our Lady & All Saints

Famous for its grotesquely twisted spire, the town's insignia, this is a large church with interesting spatial effects to the E.

The spire of lead over wood has warped and makes a comical effect from many directions. Its leaning and spiralling away from true are quite complex. The church is large, plain and heavily renewed but sits in a very attractive position somewhat hidden away at the top of the town.

Inside, screens good and various, with a couple of Comper- or Eden-type reredoses hiding within. All this follows after a tall arcade of gloomy hue, and seems another realm, a zone of numerous rich spaces and confusing barriers. The most interesting is the southernmost chapel with the Foljambe tombs – a wonderful ensemble including enigmatic allegories in classical frames, and a kneeling knight entirely covered by his armour so not a single feature of his face or body is visible.

The great W window shows the Life of Joshua. It is entirely out of the common run of Victorian windows, its drama as confident as Rubens.

Derbys: 11 miles S of Sheffield on A61; church at centre

Coventry

*St Oswald, Jardine Crescent, Tile Hill;
St John the Divine, Robin Hood Road,
Willenhall*

Basil Spence

Two churches built in late 1950s in new housing estates to similar design by Basil Spence.* They are rudimentary and still bare, but convey a strong period flavour.

Their lack of adornment contrasts with the new cathedral, which Spence designed on a more lavish budget. His parish churches are rendered boxes with gently peaked roofs and glazed W ends. There is minimal fenestration on the sides, where small extruded window frames become a sparing decoration.

At *Tile Hill* a bronze Christ with large hands hangs on the E wall, and at *Willenhall* on the W, a cross of steel I-beams in a hideous bright green, which I was assured is the original colour. The openwork bell tower here, connected by a pleasant walkway, is also adorned with metal panels in this colour.

Burton Dassett. Seven different floor levels provide many spatial surprises in this interior

Dale Abbey, a former infirmary chapel, now built into a farmhouse

Inside, Willenhall feels well-loved, with beautiful Spence fittings which are occasionally chaste to the verge of invisibility, especially the slender candlesticks and the font on a fluted column. Here the walls are coarse-textured concrete and the floors linoleum tile, with a 'runner' of red ones making a path through a dark grey ground.

These buildings and their immediate surroundings are moving reminders of the hopes and visions alive in the country just after the war. They speak of a simpler, more open society. Though touchingly optimistic, they are, alas, flimsily built.

* A third Spence church, *St Chad*, in Hillmorton Road, Wood End, NE of centre and S of M6

Warwicks/W Midlands: 18 miles E of Birmingham; Tile Hill is W of town centre, and W of A45; Willenhall is SE of centre, N of A45–A46 junction

Crick

St Margaret of Antioch

At Crick different colours and types of stone make for a diverting and alert effect.

Approached from the N, this place can still feel like a backwater, but to the W various new developments are closing the space between a once-sleepy village and the M1.

Outside, from the high lumpy churchyard with its fir trees, three colours are visible – a red tower, a brown aisle of very small stones, and a golden chancel, in which window tracery is again red. Some of these tracery forms are like pulled taffy, and on the E end one window sports an oval like a gaping mouth.

Inside, too, there's a pleasant feeling of many parts taking their separate courses. The S wall leans out

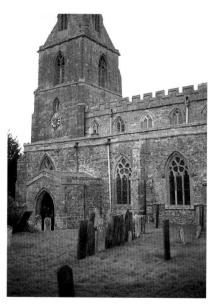

Crick, notable for varied stone colours and eccentric tracery in aisle windows

dramatically and again colours are mixed – mouldings in yellow, carvings in red, and the walls painted cream, for once a harmonious choice.

Especially in the chancel stonework, a great deal to look at. There is also a beautiful organ up in a small 18c gallery, and a bizarre Norman font resting on Mayan figures, its bowl covered in large stone mumps, its lid a pierced wooden steeple.

Northants: about 6 miles E of Rugby on A428 (just E of M1, junction 18); church to N

Dale Abbey

All Saints

One of the smallest, quaintest churches in England, built into a farmhouse.

The whole place has a real cul-de-sac feeling. In one of the village gardens skimpy remains of the abbey jut up. The church probably pre-dates the abbey, and later became its infirmary chapel. From outside, its medley of stone, brick and half timber makes it look like a pretty work of the Chester architect John Douglas.

Inside, a very twisted, cramped effect with pews fitted in every which way like animal pens, and a pulpit which lurches vigorously sideways. The font is interesting, and there is a lovely perished painting of the Visitation which is usefully recorded in Professor Tristram's copy hanging opposite.

Derbys: 7 miles NE of centre of Derby, ½ mile SE of A6096; church at SE end of village street

Earls Barton

All Saints

The Anglo-Saxon tower is justly famous. In some parts more richly three-dimensional than most Saxon work – especially in the upper stage with its bulgy columns – it is also adorned with flimsy, wood-inspired lattice patterns.

A fascinating W doorway reveals the perverse or unwitting use of architectural motifs so familiar in pre-Norman buildings. Original windows of various kinds are dotted here and there on the tower, and then at the seam with nave you find the enigmatic carving of an angel-archer. After this, some rich Norman remnants – the S door with much beakhead and leaning columns, and blind arcades inside the chancel.

But the most charming interior details are found on the screen, and date from the 20c. From afar its coving seems diapered with stars, white on blue. But coming nearer, you realize it is a meticulous catalogue of hundreds of varieties of butterfly and moth, graded from small to large as you move upward. On the base of the screen are eight paintings of saints as sturdy peasants, by Henry Bird, 1935. They form an inspired if subversive sermon.

Northants: 7 miles E of Northampton, between A45 and A4500; church lies above and N of village centre, its tower overlooking a Norman motte and bailey

Empingham

St Peter

A harmonious and pleasing church in a good village.

The churchyard stands above the sloping street, which gives extra force to the impressive tower and spire crowded against the road. Some remarkable Perpendicular tracery in N transept, from which I couldn't tear myself away. I never figured out why this became one of those moments uncannily filled with meaning.

Even so, Empingham is better inside than out. An ample nave with wide aisles and transepts, the S unfortunately blocked off (wall paintings remain here).

In the chancel, Early English traces which are all the more appealing for a certain awkwardness. Lancets do not match their sloping reveals (more regular outside) and the columns of the piscina-sedilia lean dramatically.

Rutland: midway between Stamford and Oakham, just N of A606

Exton

St Peter & St Paul

Remarkable monuments, especially three spanning the years 1580–1686.

A good situation in parkland and an interesting castellated tower, but the rest looks Victorian.

Inside, lots of banners and helms mounted above the arcade. There's a 14c tomb in the chancel with traceried buttresses on the base. Then one of the best of all Elizabethan monuments, in S transept, with a shrouded baby offered

up like a sacrifice on a little ledge between two exquisite grown-ups of dwarf-dimensions.

In the nave a black and white marble tomb with a female figure like a languid vestal virgin. Then, in N transept, the showiest of all, whose big architectural surround with obelisks for columns is like a false perspective. Grinling Gibbons was probably responsible for the reliefs with small figures in antiquarian dress; these portray four wives, each with a herd of children.

Just beyond church to NE are poignant ruins of the Jacobean Old Hall.

Rutland: between Oakham and Stamford 1½ miles N of A606, in grounds of Exton Hall

Eyam

St Lawrence

An important Saxon cross survives in this lovely village, the site of interesting plague-memories from the 17c.

Deep in the Peak District, it is one of those villages which crouches below the level of a tranquil old churchyard, as if held peacefully at bay. In truth, the church is a somewhat insignificant building, though its wall paintings are memorable. These comprise fragmentary remains of a set of blazons for the Twelve Tribes of Israel, represented giant-size between the clerestory windows. The conjunction is so incongruous, between 16c heraldry and Palestinian antiquity, that it is hard to penetrate the designer's intentions.

Earls Barton, with lively Saxon tower and entertaining 20c screen

Curious Norman font like the upper half of a barrel, and behind it a small window where every imaginable colour collides, like a harlequin suit.

The Eyam cross is the most interesting object here: a shaft with giant beast-infested spiral, and a head nearly intact, with Evangelists and angels. In cold weather it glitters with moss and frost, like a kind of living velvet.

Memories of William Mompesson, the heroic vicar who sealed off the plague-ridden village and went on ministering to his flock, are still alive here though nowadays they are fostered somewhat artfully to lure the tourists.

Derbys: 12 miles NW of Chesterfield, ½ mile N of A623, W of B6521

Fotheringhay

St Mary & All Saints

An astonishing fragment whose grandeur is explained by royal connections.

It has a wonderful position in a watery fen landscape, and sticks up abruptly like a huge ornament on a table. Like Lowick's, its tower ends in a fanciful octagon, with two heraldic beasts on the N turrets. More heraldry on the gilded weathervane – a falcon in a fetterlock, an insignia which recurs all over the Plantagenet tombs inside.

From some angles this big Perpendicular glasshouse with slender flying buttresses looks teetery like a billboard. Before long you realize why – you are looking at less than half a

Fotheringhay, a lavish late Gothic fragment with royal connections

church. The chancel was torn down in 1573; the cloister and other college buildings which lay to the S have vanished. The castle nearby, where Mary Queen of Scots was kept prisoner, is only a forlorn mound. Two great medieval inns survive in the High Street, but the visitor to Fotheringhay is mainly dreaming of what has gone.

Against the E wall of the present church is an incongruous Gothick reredos. Otherwise the space is notably bare, except for an oak pulpit with vaulted canopy like an architectural miniature of the richest kind. Some of the Fotheringhay choir stalls which used to fill the space survive at HEMINGTON and TANSOR nearby.

Perhaps the emptiness lets the light-saturated stone shine out more clearly. There is an amazing continuity of wall with roof, for the engaged columns lining the sides run up the whole height and on into the beams without a break. The other great architectural effect is a magnificent fan vault under the tower.

Northants: 3 miles N of Oundle, halfway to Wansford

Gaddesby

St Luke

One of the best churches of the county but not really harmonious.

The Decorated carving is wonderful but skewed and the first impression is of an awkward piebald creature. Like others in the district, it is built of two kinds of stone – for the body, yellow, much eroded sandstone, for trimmings, harder grey limestone. Tower and especially spire look Victorian, too sharp-edged.

Decoration of the S aisle is astounding and asymmetrical in more than one way. All this richness is carried halfway down the aisle and then runs out. On the W end, which is the finest display, there's a lopsided corner pinnacle carrying niches over a window like a huge spinning eye, which is linked in turn to a door beneath by swerving mouldings which obey no rule.

You enter through an 18c porch, placed off centre on a good Early English doorway. Inside, wonderfully unrestored – mellow brick floors and simple octagonal arcades on high old bases which have not been interfered with. Old pews, walled on the aisle side.

In fact everything is good here – clerestory, font, wall tombs, piscina. And then in the chancel we meet an intruder – a military monument with a horse falling under a marble rider. There's a Baroque sense of the moment, of a sudden twist in reality, expertly conveyed and entirely out of place.

Leics: about 9 miles NE of Leicester, just N of B674

Great Casterton

St Peter & St Paul

Simple but refined Early English work makes this a very satisfying church.

It lies in a main road village, with its E end angled pleasingly against the street. The bare purity is broken by a few fine touches, like elegant tomb recesses inside and out. One in S aisle contains a good priest effigy. Much clear glass, a pulpit in bright orange wood, and the font a large cube scored with diamond ridges.

The porch is wonderfully hulky, and the new SW vestry appalling.

Very near (1 mile NE) lies LITTLE CASTERTON, whose All Saints is a simpler version of the same thing. Its situation is charming: you follow the curve of a wall and then come upon the church among its trees. Wonderfully plain window openings and a nice contrast of rendering with stone. There's a lovely Norman tympanum inside with a Tree of Life between stars, presently obscured by junk stashed around it. Christopher Whall's E window is not one of his best, but there is also a charming Art Nouveau memorial in which cherubs materialize from the mist.

Rutland: Great Casterton is 1½ miles NW of Stamford on B1081 (formerly Great North Road); church on W side of road

Great Packington

St James

Joseph Bonomi

Unique in England if not in Europe, this fanatically pure bit of neo-classicism is perhaps the kind of experiment which should be tried only once.

It has a perfect setting in the grounds of Packington Hall. There is nothing anywhere near it in an expanse of flat parkland, though in summer it might be partly masked by trees. Designed in 1789–90 by Joseph Bonomi it is a work of the grimmest consistency, which has

Idiosyncratic High Gothic carving fills the space unevenly on the aisle end at Gaddesby

been compared to the obsessional projects of the French dreamer C. N. Ledoux. The forms are massive and regular: a cube surmounted by windowless cubic towerlets at the corners, and pierced by large thermal windows high up.

The materials are surprising, bright pink brick for the body and brownstone (i.e. reddish sandstone) for the towers. Surely stone would have been the architect's preferred choice for the whole design.

Inside, more astonishing and oppressive consistency still. The space is a single vault with vestibules hollowed out in the piers at the corners. The

weight of the vault is expressed and over-expressed by the only decorative detail in the interior – four bulgy Doric columns without bases which sit under such big chunks of entablature they are like slave-labourers with pads on their heads. All these surfaces except the columns consist of plaster cleverly painted to look like Cyclopean masonry of varying hues. The columns are pinkish, the walls and ceiling greenish.

Very few accoutrements clutter this space, but they do clutter it – a too-small marble reredos, scuffed benches and a ridiculous Elizabethan tomb. Even the organ Handel played looks pretty dim in this monumentally bleak place.

Underneath is the family mausoleum with a ramp cut down to it for easy approach of the hearse.

Warwicks: between Birmingham and Coventry in grounds of Packington Hall, a turning N from A45, 1½ miles W of M42

Hallaton

St Michael

A pleasing village or small town in a beautiful corner of Leicestershire has a church of considerable and variegated interest.

Meeting of streets E of the church is picturesque. An Early English tower stands forth, but the best detail is Decorated carving on N aisle, especially a turret-niche like a gorgeous carbuncle

Packington. Bonomi's severe classicism in the grounds of a country house

on the E corner. Against the wall next to it, an aggressive Rococo monument emulates its form.

A surprise inside the porch: built into the wall above the stone bench we find a vivid Norman tympanum. Michael fights the dragon from behind a shield and holds three little souls in a fold of his robe.

Down a few steps into the nave. Two bold capitals rather vague about leaf structure. Many authentic details in the stonework and a barbaric font.

Leics: 16 miles SE of Leicester, S of A47; church at SW edge of village

Higham Ferrers

St Mary

One of the most impressive churches in the county.

It is still surrounded by the institutions founded in the 15c by Archbishop Chichele, who was born here. Together the buildings make something like a cathedral close, displaced from the pleasant market triangle into a seclusion of its own.

The W approach is lopsided but ceremonious. Before the church comes a rich little building with lacy parapets: it was built as a grammar school, though it looks like a chantry chapel. Some way off, at the edge of the green, is the striped Bede House, where twelve old men lived in a dormitory with their lady keeper, while in front of us stands the church with its exceedingly graceful spire, tied down by openwork buttresses.

Over the double doors is a lot of 13c carving, neatly laid out in a series of roundels. This makes one realize how rare such co-ordinated programmes are on English churches, whereas in France they are commonplace. Unfortunately the scenes have been damaged just enough to become semi-intelligible patterns instead of individual dramas. The doorframes make a rich, crinkly effect underneath.

Windows in the chancel are pulled out at the top like taffy into elongated ogees, a familiar Northamptonshire foible.

After the imposing exterior, the large nave seems a bit bare. It looks as if someone like Charles Nicholson has

been at work on it, producing over-clean effects like the floor of cream tiles. But there are some tasteful painted ceilings further E and a remarkable canopy over the rough font which must form part of the same restoration.

The ironstone arcades are of beautiful and generous proportions, and there is a pleasing assortment of old screens. Many good misericords and a particularly notable brass. It lies within a rust-coloured arch and includes smaller figures around the effigy.

Northants: on A6 just N of Rushden, with which it is continuous

Holme by Newark

St Giles

One of the most intriguing churches in the county, remote and idiosyncratic; one would say *sui generis*, except that there are parallels – Thorpe Salvin in the West Riding, for example.

Holme is strangely marooned, even more inaccessible in the marsh than

Holme by Newark. Isolated, dishevelled and magical

Lapworth. It leans over the road, awkward and fascinating

formerly, now that the river is not a highway but a barrier. Children from the village went to school by ferry as late as the 1930s.

The shape of the church is awkward and fascinating. It appears to consist of two naves loosely spliced, and a peculiar porch – bumpy, bulky, crenellated – growing out from the side. The tower, too, is a piece of real character, and like the other parts not quite assimilated. It has an Early English broach spire with gargoyles at the tops of the broaches and lucarnes very near the tip. The porch wears a proud heraldic band of a different colour across its forehead, and there is a fabulous rose boss just to the R, one of the most teasing bits of carving on any English church. Sad to say the roofs are newly tiled in harsh orange, but the outline of the whole from afar remains stunning.

After this, an interior just as mellow and dishevelled as the exterior. The walls have been scraped and then white-washed. The result is like an F. C. Eden restoration without his preciousness, one of the most interesting and authentic interiors in the country.

There is a gorgeous piscina in the SE corner – a real work of architecture, old benches and screens with some folksy painting, good glass in the SE, and an effigy with its feet on a large barrel.

Notts: 4 miles N of Newark, up against the River Trent; reachable only from S and E, by turning off A1133 (church lies 1 mile W)

Ketton

St Mary the Virgin

One of the most perfect situations of any church in England.

The street twists past the church and crosses a stream. This narrowing or focusing makes a passageway of stone, barns and walls on one side and the high raised churchyard on the other. An Early English tower and spire form the crowning part of this view. Some hard edges from Victorian restorations, but beautiful details, like figures in niches at top of spire broaches. The chancel looks Victorian.

Inside, the space is very high, and tower arches are extremely fine. A canted chancel with Comper windows and a roof by Sir Charles Nicholson. Even if they are Victorian, the three lancets with vesica above look just right viewed from the nave.

King's Norton. Gimcrack Gothic outside, well preserved classical within

On the W front a three-part Norman doorway. Here lots of pale 18c tombstones have been formed rather heartlessly into a fence.

Rutland: about 4 miles SW of Stamford on A6121; church lies E of this road towards Collyweston

King's Norton

St John Baptist

John Wing

Demure 18c Gothic Revival with complete wooden interior fittings which are not Gothic.

Built by John Wing the Younger 1760–61 in a remote-seeming bit of the county. The spindly pinnacles make a fine display from a little way off. The church is raised on a mound and introduced by fine iron gates and an incongruous balustraded stair. This gives it a teetery or giddy appearance from the W.

The interior surprisingly unadorned, except for a great profusion of dark

Norwegian oak. Pulpit and reading desk thrust forward like the prow of a ship in centre of nave. Rails have angular piercing, the only non-classical detail.

The font is amazing, like a marriage of Rococo and Perpendicular. Apparently it dates from 1850, when lightning sent the spire crashing down on the old one. Maybe the plain wooden roof high above dates from the same time. Surely the 18c would have wanted a plaster vault to finish off.

Lots of bull's eyes in window glass, with surprising explosions of colour in the tracery tops.

Leics: about 8 miles SE of Leicester, 2 miles S of A47

Lapworth

St Mary the Virgin

An unspoiled church surprisingly near Birmingham.

It leans over the road in an intriguing complex grouping. Stretching furthest is an arched chantry chapel with a passage under.

Inside, the clerestory and roof are the most magnificent features with interesting corbels and stops at various levels. Perhaps the greatest pleasure here are the early 20c fittings of high quality, including a war memorial window like early Kandinsky, with romantic landscape inside patterned borders. The young subject of this window is shown called to war from study, and finally, wounded on the battlefield. It was designed by R. J. Stubbs, Master of Birmingham School of Art, in 1922.

Better known is Eric Gill's relief showing a mother and child. It is one of his best works, deliciously small and instinct with life in every feature. There's also a reredos of vaguely Pre-Raphaelite flavour by Earp via Leonardo. The church goes on being enriched by carefully thought out ornaments.

Warwicks: 6 miles S of Solihull just S of B4439

Leicester

St Mary de Castro, St Margaret

Good Norman remains and spatial complexity at *St Mary de Castro*.

This church is indeed near the castle, now domesticated to a police court. Its

silhouette of melancholy hue topped by a slender spire is impressive. The chancel is lower and older than the S aisle and decorated with vivid corbels, some of which look like rustic 17c replacements.

Inside, the effect is dark, irregular and mysterious. Good arcades against W wall and then a strange effect: where nave meets SW tower there is a narrow passage between them and two storeys of Norman blind arches formerly outside, now imprisoned here. Tiers of strange bulges fill up the barbaric Early English font.

Best of all, the justly famous Norman sedilia, a combination of wild zigzag arches and refined tendril capitals. Beyond them a spectacular Victorian alabaster reredos. An interesting rubbery relief fills the N transept arch. In the graveyard a dense population of slate headstones like large pages.

St Margaret's proud W tower, Perpendicular, sports a lot of good ogee arches. It now fronts a busy road. Colours of the stone mottled pink and grey. Inside, a bare, clean impression with much white plaster and clear glass; a dark roof above the Early English arcade.

St Martin, Leicester's largest and most central parish church, became the cathedral in 1927. Its E window is by Christopher Whall.

Leics: 33 miles S of Nottingham on A6

Lower Shuckburgh

St John Baptist

John Croft

Among eccentric Victorian churches, this work of John Croft's stands out as one of the most curious.

It is a building of real, if gross, plastic imagination. Take the vivid bench ends, nightmarish but friendly. They are like a twisted (and phallic) dream of the tropics, vegetation which never was, except in the mind of man.

The combination of flavours here is quite unaccountable. From afar it seems a lively Gothic, with tracery like paper cut-outs and pebble mosaic like a gingerbread toy. Inside, echoes of the Alhambra in toothy brick arches. Are they really brick? Some are, and some aren't, but very well faked.

The patron was just back from the Crimea, so perhaps that and not Spain is the inspiration for the oriental coffering in chancel and baptistry vault. This building makes one curious to see more of Croft's work. Unfortunately his church at Cold Hanworth, Lincs was declared redundant in 1980, and converted to a private dwelling.

The vigorously rumpled country round Shuckburgh is particularly attractive.

Warwicks: 6 miles W of Daventry on A425; church lies N of road

Lowick

St Peter

One of the most remarkable in the county, now isolated above its village full of mellow old houses.

From afar its tower appears jolly and secular, the octagonal top like a small pavilion, with metal flags on every pinnacle turning in the wind.

In the N aisle is the most attractive old glass in Northamptonshire – four windows with four largish figures each, many perched on the vine-stalks from a Tree of Jesse. The colours are wonderfully obscure – green and dirty yellow on a dusky red ground.

The tombs of Lowick make an entertaining medley. The best is a large table tomb of 1420 with an alabaster knight and his lady holding hands. Her elaborate headdress defies description. Over their heads hang (or jut up, as they are lying down) intricate canopies. There is an odd complication here: the tops of these canopies facing the nave, surfaces

Lower Shuckburgh. Eccentric Victorian Gothic outside, a mixture of flavours within

which have no analogue in architectural actuality, are covered with miniature tracery in low relief.

Nearby are some of the silliest 18c tombs ever. On one of them the children are parked at right angles like buses. Decorated sedilia have been colonized by a Jacobean aedicule monument with a peacock crest as its central pinnacle.

Northants: about 12 miles E of Kettering, just W of A6116

Lyddington

St Andrew

A gorgeous ironstone village, and near its end the telling group of church and former palace of the Bishops of Lincoln.

The village is the straggle or string-type, of rich gold colour. The church wonderfully textured, deep mustard with a little grey. Its stumpy spire looks sunk within its parapets. Tracery more interesting on S, masonry on N. From the E it forms a good splayed composition with the palace (of which the internal spaces are very suggestive, as medieval proportions often survive).

Virtually no external ornament on the church, and an interior of fairly heartless Perpendicular. Traces remain of painting over and around the chancel arch. A king on the left is best preserved. Communion rails of 1635 surround the altar on four sides.

Rutland: 2 miles S of Uppingham, 1 mile E of A6003

Melbourne

St Michael & St Mary

One of the noblest and most perfect of all Norman interiors.

The external aspect is deceptive. It has been cloaked in late Perpendicular/17c aisles and given a tidy top edge. A tower of modest scale continues the programme of misinformation. Three Norman doorways survive but so ruined that remaining authentic detail is almost entirely worn away except on S.

Inside, a different story – magnificent Norman spaces of heroic scale, dark in spite of later windows. Above the massive arcades, a tripartite galleried clerestory, and within the central tower, several arcaded storeys. The E arches are plentifully supplied with carved capitals whose details disappear in the gloom.

Melbourne's ambitious Norman arcade, one of the best of its date

One of the most impressive features is a vaulted W bay, forming a shallow narthex. Originally the church boasted two W towers, now reduced to boring stumps.

There is an interesting devil on left tower pier and some discreet Victorian glass, but the space feels generally denuded. Mellow immediate surroundings have been cobbled into something like the stable court of a country house.

Derbys: 8 miles S of Derby on B587; church on SE edge of town near Hall

Middleton Cheney

All Saints

One of the best collections of early William Morris glass anywhere, mounted in a harmonious envelope.

The nave is high and has a delightful painted roof whose folkish colours were apparently not supplied by Morris. Under the roof above the chancel arch, a small window with descending Dove by Philip Webb.

The various Morris windows are of extremely different characters, and do

Norbury's large and beautiful chancel: silvery light and alabaster effigies

not form a unified scheme. The E one is pale and irradiates its space, looking almost like an over-exposed photograph. It contains paired saints carefully drawn, the Twelve Tribes and, near the top, the Elders round the Lamb – a strange spatial conception by Burne-Jones.

Perhaps the most stunning of all is the Three Israelites in the Fiery Furnace, high up in the W tower space. The flames which envelop them are the colour of ripe grain, and resemble water or hair in their movement. Above are six evanescent angels holding symbol-discs for the days of Creation. They are flanked by harpists. The drawing throughout is as fresh as if done this morning.

In the chancel windows a number of small scenes, mostly by Burne-Jones. In N aisle two vigorous figures by Rossetti (or perhaps Morris) and Burne-Jones, of later date.

The remarkable but ruined tomb of one of the donors lies outside in the churchyard. It looks like a faceted house or ark leaning low over the casket within, almost crushing it. The finials

from its complicated roof have been smashed by the weather, and fragments lie round about.

Northants: about 3 miles E of Banbury on A422; church lies N of road

Morley

St Matthew

With monuments among the most interesting in any small parish church, Morley also preserves a good deal of medieval glass from Dale Abbey.

The church has an elegant spire, low Tudor aisles and a good Early English doorway.

Inside, a powerful Norman arcade and later chancel, but attention inevitably centres on the rich detritus of tombs. This covers a wide historical range and includes a quaint 17c memorial wedged diagonally in the SE corner, with a couple holding hands and infants sleeping, to the accompaniment of lots of skulls and snakes.

Nearby a lovely cusped recess with a wonderful brass on the surface beneath, a knight and three ladies, many leaf furls round his head.

The N chapel has the greatest wealth of glass and tombs and many old tiles in its floor. In the windows, a monkish saint's life and the history of the True Cross. It is always interesting to see well-preserved medieval glass close up, but the drawing in this plentiful haul is weak. E window with the Virgin seems better composed. Good 19c imitations further W.

There are many alabaster slabs with effigies incised and a wonderful 17c tomb with five urns and melted draperies slung from acanthus fronds. Its animation is unnerving.

Nearby a terrific oblong squint in chancel pier, with cusps in the top of the opening. On the same pillar is a furly-topped piscina of real character.

Derbys: about 4 miles NE of Derby, just E of A608; church buried in trees N of unnumbered road

Newark

St Mary Magdalene

A satisfying town church with gorgeous tower and spire (Early English turning into Decorated) and vast later interior.

Its situation in the town is very fine – immured in streets, without a large churchyard, yet asserting itself grandly at the end of Kirkgate. Both tower and spire stand thrillingly free from a distance. Panelling and arcading on the top two stages is eccentric but splendid. Original figures of various sizes survive in niches. There is much enjoyable carving on the exterior, fancy panelled battlements and a fine three-part E end.

Inside, the Perpendicular arcade is extremely high and slim; faces look out from leaves on the capitals beneath a flat, coloured roof far overhead.

At the E end a pulpitum with a good frieze of bosses and a low spreading undercroft. To N one of the biggest brasses in England; to S, a strange concoction: glass of extremely different periods (c1300 and early 15c) assembled in one window. This arrangement makes it difficult to appreciate (or even really look at) either period, though a panel by panel description is provided.

Notts: 14 miles NW of Grantham on A1

Norbury

St Mary & St Barlok

A lovely setting, a beguilingly eccentric plan and a gorgeous Decorated chancel.

The church is hidden from the road by trees. Its yard is like a clearing in the forest, with slate markers, big yews and the sound of many birds. Built of red sandstone; its proportions are unexpected. The tower seems to have sunk down and become immured in the aisle, while the chancel has grown into something quite large, with wonderful ruffled tracery. This has flower bosses at the intersections like Checkley, Staffs, only more so. There is a priest's door like Checkley's, but more elaborate.

Inside, a silvery airiness in chancel, and some pale glass, especially old bearded faces. Alabaster effigies take up much of the floor space. There are good shield-bearers on these tomb bases, and both knights wear mailed fists as emblems atop their helms.

Two Saxon cross shafts look forlorn, cemented into the nave floor. An intriguing figure on one, who appears to blow a horn and wield a club, is shown doing something else entirely in a drawing in the church guide. George Eliot's father is supposed to have made the altar table, and his parents are buried in the churchyard.

Derbys: 5 miles SW of Ashbourne on B5033; church set well back N of road

Nottingham

St Mary, High Pavement

The grandest Perpendicular church in the county, well placed so that it dominates the old street which creeps around its S rampart.

St Mary's is an archetype of the stately, well-proportioned pile, raying out from its great central tower. This complicated subordination in a complex whole is worth savouring. Much exterior detail is, as usual in such cases, renewed, but this does not spoil the overall effect.

Inside the porch is one of the greatest curiosities of the church, heavy bronze doors by Henry Wilson, 1904 – among his most pompous and secular works. They show scenes from the Virgin's life, but it might as easily be some romance. Over it a molten tympanum with large figures and an inscription standing up in small pierced letters above the lintel.

Inside, an appealing sooty colour to the dark stone. It is a true Perpendicular glasshouse. The W window, for example, fills the entire end of the nave down to a certain level. Exceedingly good and entertaining glass in S transept S window: Biblical, garish, much green and purple. This is by Heaton, Butler & Bayne, and dated 1867.

Many good animals as labels and stops in the arcade, but this is a church strangely devoid of interesting fittings.

Notts: 15 miles E of Derby on A52; church S and E of current centre

Oakham

All Saints

A large church well situated in the smallest of all county towns.

The approach down a snicket from SE is marvellous, and the tower and spire, all turreted and holding three old figures on W front, stand out boldly. Under them a fine variety of Perpendicular levels and extensions range themselves. Many small friezes, especially on the other side.

After these harmonies, the interior disappoints, looking scrubbed. Interesting nave capitals, all different, and wide arcaded transepts. The font cover a very fine bit of late Victoriana.

The high late Gothic interior at Newark, with its rich screen

167

Lively carved detail on Stoke Golding's font

Huge yews to N in cleared churchyard. Complicated market spaces to the E. This makes a pleasant core, and there is surprisingly little of Oakham beyond it.

Rutland: 11 miles W of Stamford on A606; church NW of market place

Raunds

St Peter

Raunds has one of the county's best towers and very entertaining wall paintings.

The church is set atop the village, so one gets good steep views of the eccentric Early English decoration of the tower's W face, which includes gorgeous pierced and even windowed quatrefoils. There is a wonderful example of a common Early English motif: many-moulded arches overlaid around inner and outer door frames. In these arrangements the outer arch is usually steeper, and the overlay creates a harmonious confusion which evidently pleased early Gothic designers, for they practised something much nearer to Baroque perspectivism than we allow. On the N side many little musicians are squeezed into the spandrels.

Much interesting tracery in N aisle, but the highlight of the interior is the painting over the N arcade. Three bold scenes. From left to right: a devil piercing a languid lady, from whom sins come out in bursts. This is Pride, mother of all the vices. Then St Christopher; then three yellow skeletons and three robed folk with rabbits

underneath in rose, pale green and chalk white. This is the Three Quick and the Three Dead, merrymakers surprised by a reminder of their end. In scale and vigour these images stand out among English wall paintings.

Northants: 4 miles NE of Higham Ferrers just E of A605; church near N end, E of High Street

Repton

St Wystan

The Saxon crypt at Repton is the most serene and beautiful composition in all pre-Conquest architecture.

To the archaeologist this is a building of the highest interest. Luckily it has not been sterilized by dissection, and its ancient elements are lovely as well as rare. The oldest parts do not show at first. There is an elegant spire and a mellow S porch (where we meet the first Saxon carving – a bit of cross-base with a man pruning).

Inside, the 14c arcade is so excessively sharp it could be mistaken for 17c, as could the tall, flat ceilinged, slightly bare chancel.

To appreciate this end you might start outside, where abnormally large stones stand out, and stepped courses at the base lend a classical air. The most wonderful experience comes in

The Saxon crypt at Repton, remarkable for its sophisticated geometry

following the short curved subterranean passages with their Cyclopean paving until one arrives at the columned and vaulted cross-shaped space under the E end. It embodies a simple and perfect geometric conceit. Each column is carved with a rope spiral. Following each vault rib to the wall you come to a pilaster united to its fellows by a string moulding at cornice level. Three arms of the cross end in three windows; the W bay ends in a niche, as if the altar is reversed and the building has doubled back on itself.

Back above ground there is long and short work over the chancel arch, and a short wooden nave to the W is conjectured. A Viking army wintered at Repton in 873. Excavation has disclosed many Viking burials in the present vicarage garden, an Anglo-Saxon cemetery E of the church and some interesting reliefs now in Derby museum. Good coloured drawings of these now hang in church. To the E the buildings of Repton School incorporate mellow remains of the priory.

Derbys: 4 miles NE of Burton-on-Trent on B5008; church N of road

Rothwell

Holy Trinity

The nave arcade is an apotheosis of ironstone, one of the glories of English stonework.

This pleasant market town has one of Thomas Tresham's buildings at its core, a two-storey MARKET HOUSE of 1578 covered in inscriptions, heraldry (ninety-five county families) and clover leaves (*trefoil* for Tresham). Just as remarkable for violations of classical system as for exquisite observances of it, it remained roofless until 1895, and now has two imitators within sight, a Conservative Club and a Methodist church.

Holy Trinity is well approached from the market place, along a narrow passage which makes the tower seem dumpy and the body endlessly long. The effect is increased because we cannot get back far enough to gauge its dimensions.

As a result, we are unprepared for the sensation of slender height internally. Arcades and wall over chancel arch are a marvellous gold colour, with beautiful clustered piers of earliest Gothic date. Apparently the work was done soon after the church came into the possession of Cirencester Abbey.

Staunton Harold. 17c Gothic survival in an 18c picturesque landscape

The font is a wonderfully gimcrack construction like a badly built wedding cake. Perhaps its authentic 13c parts were rearranged at a later date, say 17c or 18c. Under S aisle a vaulted bone crypt, where over 1500 remains were found, including vast piles of human skulls.

Northants: 3½ miles NW of Kettering on A6; church SW of market place

Staunton Harold

Holy Trinity

One of the most perfect survivals in England of richly decked out 17c Gothic.

It sits facing a grand country house like an ornament from the gardens which has come indecorously near. Just behind it are the tame slopes and artificial lake of an 18c picturesque landscape. Together these elements make an idealized palimpsest of the centuries from which real habitations of real villagers have been removed.

The frontispiece over the entrance on the W tower includes lavish heraldry and makes an effect like a triumphal arch. At this particular tail end, Gothic becomes almost self-parody, with huge knobbly pinnacles and openwork parapets.

The interior is more amazing still. The chancel is separated off by a gorgeous iron screen loaded with heraldry, made by Robert Bakewell, famous for garden pavilions and the screen in Derby Cathedral.

Jacobean woodwork fills the space, including panelling on pillars, a font lid which squares the circle, a great nodding pediment on the organ gallery, one of the highpoints of strapwork, and a special wealth of appliances in the chancel. Most unaccountable is the survival of various velvet frontals and hangings embroidered in metal thread. Or perhaps more staggering still the boarded ceiling painted to resemble the heavens, and showing the separation of the waters from the firmament.

Leics: 3 miles S of Melbourne, Derbys, in grounds of Hall (National Trust)

Stoke Dry

St Andrew

A charming miniature with good details, like a late porch and some Norman figured columns inside, largely untouched.

In a particularly tranquil part of a tranquil county. The road twists and slopes precipitately at this point.

The tower is comically miniature, the porch delightfully so, like a dwarf castle.

Very interesting tracery in the two E windows.

Inside many traces of painting remain – a sin or martyrdom in S chapel and the Tribes of Judah in the clerestory. The screen has lovely coving arching forward, and on either side of it are Romanesque columns brocaded with carving. The whole effect is mellow and undisturbed.

Rutland: 6 miles N of Corby, Northants, and 2 miles S of Uppingham W of A6003

Stoke Golding

St Margaret

One of the most beautiful churches in this or any county. Not that it is grand or consistent, far from it, rather a wonderful *piece* of a building.

Part of the secret is that Stoke's late 13c and early 14c fabric has been conservatively, that is to say very little, renewed. Tracery in the S aisle wonderful, alternating between three trefoils and something more broken. The system is detectable yet the stonework so little altered it looks quite irregular. Above the windows, an airy parapet of quatrefoils.

Inside, the arcade is breathtaking. It divides the lovely aisle space from the nave to the N. There are only four columns but the mouldings are rich and the capitals diverse. Wonderful traces of plaster or wash remain on the mouldings. Gorgeous old plaster with fragments of medieval wall paintings on the S wall, which leans out at the top. A floor of dull old tiles, black, red and cream. Charming small carpets scattered here and there.

The font is unusually interesting, with saints and tracery in low relief. The tower is not magnificent but adorned in a pleasantly quirky way. All in all, it is one of those miracles which springs up in a village which is otherwise nothing special.

Leics: 4 miles NE of Nuneaton

Teigh. Fanciful 18c Gothick with the pulpit perched over the way in

Stratford-upon-Avon

Holy Trinity

In spite of the crush of pilgrims, the centre of Stratford remains a pleasant, small-scale market town. The church occupies a peaceful place apart, by the river, in an enormous churchyard.

Its exterior textures, of grey rubble with yellow stone dressings, much restored, are not attractive, but the scale of the interior is impressive.

Shakespeare is buried in the chancel (the stone obscured by an enlarged rubbing taken from it and propped upright on it). Set in the wall above, a monument dating from seven years after his death with a plump and unintelligent-looking bust of the poet in a niche. Just behind his

head, an altar bursts into flame in the Victorian stained glass. These windows, having been over-scrubbed, now look more like the 16c glass they imitate.

There is more good glass by Kempe in S aisle but the best fitting of all is a huge Gothic organ case by Bodley suspended high overhead on the chancel arch.

Warwicks: 22 miles S of Birmingham on A34

Strelley

All Saints

Surprising to find anything so mellow and complete so near to Nottingham. Road systems have increased its untoward isolation. Lovely colours – salmon stone with tan tower and dressings. Necessary vandal-proofing somewhat mars the richly textured exterior.

Inside, a very pointy chamfered arcade and an extremely beautiful screen of wood which is dark but not shiny. It looks like a thicket, or thorn trees interlaced.

The other great feature is the medieval tombs, especially the N one (John de Strelley, 1501) with a large apron or background of carving, including a central figure like Abraham sheltering little souls in his bosom. The male effigy rests on a strangled Saracen head with bells on its cap and its tongue sticking out. Underfoot, a lion with a gorgeous mane. Even nearer, against the soles of the dead man's feet, are two tiny figures weeping and telling their beads.

Notts: 5 miles NW of centre of Nottingham, between M1 and A6002; church adjacent to Strelley Hall

Teigh

Holy Trinity

Charming 18c Gothick on a miniature scale.

A Chippendale frieze goes all round the nave, cut in the silvery grey stone the church is built of. After an ovoid vestibule, a delicious interior with pulpit and altar at different ends, and, in between, a little world of wooden enclosures. Overhead in the plaster rib-vault, blue like a summer sky, is the date of completion, 1789, at the furthest possible remove from Revolution.

The pulpit is the crown of an amazing ensemble. It joins with reading desks on either side in a tiered, aspiring system. It is perched on their shoulders and teeters there precariously. Unwitting, we have walked under it coming in. One of the readers' seats must fold back to let the priest ascend to his high perch. Behind are painted trees and sky, the most artificial effect imaginable.

Teigh has two remarkable fonts – one of old wood, a flower on a metal stem, the wood polished to tortoiseshell gloss. The other more recent, like an Aztec totem, suitably quirky for Teigh.

Rutland: 8 miles SE of Melton Mowbray, 3 miles N of A606

Teversal

St Catherine

Interesting Norman remains, an untouched interior and a fine location.

Country to the N is fascinating, somewhat despoiled by mining yet isolated and of such rolling contour it creates a kind of seclusion. The S door is jumbled but very lively Norman work, with roundels of seasons, animals, warring angels. At the sides instead of columns, capitals stacked three deep and not all facing upwards.

Inside, rich spatial effects include a beautiful Transitional arcade and the narrowest N aisle anywhere. There is just room for a bench along the wall under the 17c domestic windows inserted there. Opposite, a squire's pew with scrolly columns. Other box pews scattered higgledy-piggledy. In one, incised tomb chests are allowed to take up much of the space. A good monument in chancel with an important-looking couple presented bust length. Numerous hatchments and a W gallery complete the impacted, overlaid impression.

Near the church, many impressive stone buildings suggest a supply of rich farmers at some stage in its history.

Notts: 4 miles W of Mansfield, N of B6014; church on N edge of village

Tickencote

St Peter

One of the strangest churches in England, where magnificent Norman work is overlaid with imitation-Norman of 1792 by an architect of real imagination, **S. P. Cockerell**.

Some writers lament that Cockerell interfered with surviving old work, but his contribution ranks with Sara Losh's

Teversal in its large churchyard

Strelley. One of the medieval tombs with interesting heraldic creatures underfoot

at Wreay, Cumberland. It is not a replica but a fantasia on Norman themes, infused with idiosyncratic life.

Roughly speaking, there is more Cockerell outside and more authentic Norman within. He added a tower in the middle of the S side which looks like part of an Italianate villa. Frond motifs derived from the old chancel arch come out looking like tropical vegetation. And his re-working of blind arcades along the chancel walls is full of geometrical boldness, like Cubism before its time. The E end, shrouded in yews, with its rich tiers of round arches, remains nearer to its original state.

Inside, the chancel preserves the Norman spirit at full strength. The arch is outstanding and consists of six fat rolls of carving, its overall shape boldly distorted by compressive force. Further in, a tent of heavy ribs with three animal faces looking down from the central boss makes us think we have ventured into a cave inhabited by untamed beast-presences.

The E window of 1929 by A. K. Nicholson, finicky and refined, seems a strange intruder. Though the font is a good Norman piece, it too feels mild in the presence of so much powerful barbarity.

Rutland: 2½ miles NW of Stamford on B1081, just W of A1 (but accessible from southbound only)

Tickencote. Cockerell's imaginative 18c fantasia on the Norman style

weathered criss-cross moulding above eye level.

Inside, very tranquil, with oldest traces on W wall. The tower arch looks Saxon, with uncontrolled capitals which have worms wriggling every which way instead of organized tendrils. Off centre above is a small 12c opening. Under the tower a lovely window with leafy background.

The font is rough, the arcade rude Early English, and in the chancel a gross, unlearned Jacobean tomb.

All the churchyard trees have drifted to the E side of this little walled precinct in the fields.

Rutland: 7 miles E of Uppingham just S of A47; church lies beyond village to SW near River Welland (⅓ mile walk)

Ullenhall

St Mary

J. P. Seddon

One of the rare works by J. P. Seddon, friend of the Pre-Raphaelites. Modest in scale as they usually are, but of an unaccustomed simplicity. A few freakish features outside, like the series of swoops beneath the little columns applied to the apse, making an upside-down arcade which is almost prickly, like a creature's carapace.

The interior is a space of radiant purity, whose main focus is the stencilled wagon roof (half-wagons in aisles). In this building Seddon's fascination with round endings is well fulfilled. The roof in graded vegetable colours makes a bowl over the apse, and the matching mosaic beneath fills a circle. Side chapels jut out in angular contrast. There is another offshoot at the door with a rose window over, and this is balanced by the font with mixed foliage and fish trapped in a net.

A light and flowery metal railing runs all round the churchyard, and five large cedars make an apse at the unapsed end.

Warwicks: 10 miles NW of Stratford (4 miles E of Redditch), on B4480; church on unnumbered turning W of this road

Warmington

St Mary

Perhaps the best Early English church in Northamptonshire.

Though not particularly large, it reveals a satisfying elaboration in many of its details. The tower and spire are

Tideswell

St John the Baptist

'The Cathedral of the Peak', because it is an unusually ambitious building for its rugged location.

Very entertaining skyline with corner turrets on the tower which are virtually towers in themselves. The church is pleasingly and insidiously placed. It seems to rub its back against a curve of houses on one side and to stand free towards a widening of the street on the other.

Interesting weeping tracery in the aisle and flowing design in N transept windows. Inside, a noble arcade with fillet enrichment and rounded mouldings on arches, all very sleek. The roof is impressive, and there is lavish Victorian woodwork, especially stall ends with many versions of figures leaning over flames or urns.

In the chancel large brasses with borders intact. The E window breaks into complicated lattice at the top and contains a good Tree of Jesse by Heaton, Butler & Bayne. The large W window, Perpendicular, with glass by Hardman, is also interesting.

Derbys: 9 miles NE of Buxton on B6049; church on N side of road

Tixover

St Luke

A humble building in wonderful isolation with interesting Norman remains.

It sits among rolling fields far away from the village. The exterior is plain, except for the early arcaded tower with a

Warmington. Fine Early English interior with original wooden vault

notably rich, with a trilobe doorway in the W and lavish dogtooth. Lucarnes (spire windows) boast especially bulky ornament. Inside the S porch are some tranquil blind arcades, and between the columns of door frames, gorgeous fragments of leaves. As at Raunds nearby, a surfeit of fine mouldings occurs in the overlay of the outer on the inner opening.

Inside, the arcade is very clean. Above it, a lovely system of support for the vault; corbels becoming stone-strings which end in leaf fillips. In the event the vault was built in wood not stone, and this 13c carpentry largely survives.

The aisle windows are very harmonious: triple lancets under single arches. There is a clever 20c painted pulpit and well-drawn Victorian glass in the E window.

Northants: 3 miles NE of Oundle, just S of A605

Warwick

St Mary

Warwick is the best town in the county, and its church is one of the most interesting in England.

St Mary's tower is visible from far away and Gothic in outline. The building sits at the top of a hill among pleasant old streets. Only as one comes nearer does one see that it is not Gothic, but a strange approximation. The tower's sides are peppered with classical niches and its fabulous parapets are Jacobean in character. The nave has balustrades and urns along the top and a relaxed parody of Gothic tracery in its huge windows, with simplified tulip shapes at the top.

You enter under the tower which straddles the road, making for some good views looking through. The interior is one of the most transparent and lucid of spaces, and feels more like a 17c French abbey than anything in England. Here the great piers of curvilinear design seem Baroque on the way to Rococo.

Beyond the glorious nave of palest grey stone are found some of the best late Gothic spaces in the country. These E parts survived the fire of 1694, which necessitated the rebuilding by Sir William Wilson that we have been examining so far.

In the chancel, instead of vaults, lacy free-springing ribs not filled in. In fact, the real springing is higher than this illusory lower set. Right in the middle of the space is a double alabaster tomb with thirty-six figures round the base – 'weepers' once, now mainly an exhibition of 14c costumes.

The church's most famous feature, the Beauchamp Chapel to the right, was built in the mid 15c and is inconceivably rich. At its E end, a single wonderful window filling the upper wall: figures in the glass, all with huge hands and faces, include two ravishing judge-types in pale green and rose. Around the edges of this feast of images are more, for the window is encircled by a double row of stone figures delicately painted. Beneath this lie the best late medieval tombs outside Westminster Abbey and tawny stalls with muzzled bears and twisting ragged staves, emblems found often on the tombs.

There is also a Romanesque crypt and an exquisite fan-vaulted chapel. The churchyard is a breeding ground of pleasant melancholy.

Warwicks: 9 miles SW of Coventry on A429

Wellingborough

St Mary, Knox Road

J. Ninian Comper

Comper's biggest church and his most magnificent, built 1908–30.

It sits in a large scruffy churchyard which feels like unused allotments. Among wide streets of ordinary terrace houses its scale is breathtaking. Comper used deep gold ironstone with tan dressings. The style is late, late Perpendicular with plentiful glass and inventive tracery. From the E there is a lively stepped effect rising to the high N chapel, which almost detaches itself from the body. Inside, the passage between chancel and chapel is one of the most entertaining places to stand.

The interior is staggering. Immensely high ironstone columns of concave-facet type with fanciful Renaissance capitals. The E vista is engorged by a gigantic gold God in glory, from which shooting rays fan out over the Rood. The ceiling is a dazzling fan-vault with dripping pendants.

It is as if Comper broke off in mid-career, because only sample vaults have been painted blue and gold, leaving most bays a stark white. If this work were completed the overall richness would be overwhelming.

Tall iron screens surround chancel and chapels, of carefully thought-out historical variety (15–17c). The view through various layers (a rich baldacchino the final impediment) to the coloured glass beyond is ravishing, like seeing through to the truth at last. Here Comper's usually anaemic stained glass comes into its own, as the finishing touch in a concerted effect.

Every visitor will have a favourite detail: mine are the painted putti on the lower panels of the screen.

Northants: 10 miles E of Northampton; church almost at town's E edge, backing onto B573, Elsdon Road

Tixover. Humble building among fields with a Norman tower

Whissendine. One of Rutland's grandest, with entertaining diversity in the arcade

Whissendine

St Andrew

A good introduction to Rutland, a little grand and fairly unorthodox.

The tower is marvellous, early Decorated just beginning to find its way to exuberance. A feature Pevsner doesn't like is a point in its favour: it squeezes in an extra blank arch on S and W for the stair at the corner, lopsided but individual. Peculiar peepholes in the parapet.

Inside, arcades very irregular and entertaining. The N leans and has leaves and faces. Under the roof are amazing wooden kings in large niches, with grimacing corbels below, which also seem made of wood. The effect is inconceivably lively.

Interesting castellated tracery in aisles and a Kempified, or at least Victorian, chancel. Unlike most towns in Rutland, this one is not specially attractive.

Rutland: 7 miles SE of Melton Mowbray, 1 mile NE of A606

Wirksworth

St Mary

This church inhabits one of the most atmospheric small towns in England, formerly an industrial estate (quarrying and lead mining). In George Eliot's time it was apparently grimmer and dourer: it figures as Snowfield in *Adam Bede*.

The church's situation is fascinating: it lies in its own sizeable yard completely hidden from the main road behind a wall of houses. The ground slopes away in two directions, so that buildings ringing this egg-shaped green (which include the handsome rectory and a Gothic grammar school, donated by a boastful local son buried in the church) seem to drop below its edge.

The interior is remarkable for a rich collection of Norman carving, which has been built helter-skelter into later walls so that it takes detective work to locate. These gems are scattered through the transepts mainly, especially in N and S walls (NE and SW corners above all)

where one finds vine ornaments crowding demonic faces, sturdy little warrior figures, perhaps even a Derbyshire lead miner. The very best find of all is a barbaric tomb lid dug up in 1820 but now displayed like a picture on the nave wall. It is one of the most memorable images of its period (c800), cramped, lopsided (being the leftmost two-thirds of an originally symmetrical layout), and teeming with stumpy figures and beasts engaged in inexplicable ritual acts. To say that it represents specific episodes of Christ's life and Passion is quite misleading. In spirit it seems as far from such familiar subjects as any Aztec piece.

Just over the hill to the W of Wirksworth is Peak country and BRASSINGTON, best of the lead villages. Just to the N is CROMFORD, the charming locale of Arkwright's early industrial innovations (his mill now a museum).

Derbys: on B5023 4 miles S of Matlock; church E of market place

Wootton Wawen

St Peter

Most parish churches conform to certain spatial conventions. Wootton Wawen does not, and seems curiouser and curiouser the more you delve.

Of a pleasant bleached stone, with odd bursts of power in unexpected places. The nave, for example, is much higher and grander than the other parts, and the porch is grabbed and held by two big triangular buttresses.

Inside, fresh inconsistencies. Walls are plastered but the clerestory is bare stone. Our path is blocked by the intrusive tower arch, which – no sign of this from N – is Anglo-Saxon. The ancient space under it has been made into a chancel, lit by a marvellous modern window with a blessing figure like an owl (by Margaret Traherne, 1958).

So you go around the tower, and there you are with more nave and chancel and many monuments. In the E two wonderful and diverse windows – one rich Perpendicular, the other willowy Decorated, and rustic screens and benches. It is another world.

Approached from the N this memorable church looms up surreally. It sits at a strange bend in the road, which could only be explained by some feature now missing. There is a fair amount of traffic but nonetheless a feeling of isolation and unsolved mystery.

Warwicks: about 6 miles NW of Stratford-upon-Avon on A3400 (formerly A34); church lies N of road

Worksop

Priory Church of Our Lady & St Cuthbert

Remains of a large late Norman priory, completed E of the nave by Laurence King in the 1970s.

The effect of the W front is bare though pleasing, with plain flanking towers and minimal Norman portals.

Inside, the arcade is eccentrically decorated with spaced-out dogtooth and sparse leaf forms on capitals. This effect very satisfying. The next storey is most confusing – a Baroque phase of the Norman style, Pevsner calls it.

There are practically no fittings except a wooden Christ the King (c1960?) and a new organ as the main decorative emphasis under a John Hayward window in the E. The modern E end is a marked success. Light floods down at the

crossing from a large skylight. Narrow new windows behind fit happily with the earlier work. From outside, the forms are full of incisions, severe though not harsh, like a theory of Gothic rather than unthinking practice.

To the S lies the sober early Gothic Lady Chapel, an even better and more consistent composition outside than in.

Notts: 19 miles SE of Sheffield on A57; Priory lies E of centre, at E end of High Street

Youlgreave

All Saints

One of the best churches in the Peak District with a proud tower and early William Morris glass.

The village is wonderfully placed – to the E contorted valleys, to the W a high, bare plateau, including the prehistoric circle at Arbor Low.

Good churchyard gates with acorn finials frame the building at both ends. The impression is ambitious, with plenty of pinnacles on the tower and battlements everywhere else.

Inside, though thoroughly restored by Norman Shaw, the fabric retains many original traces, such as pleasantly disparate arcades, the S fatter, the N more richly carved. Fifteenth-century roofs survive largely intact with grotesque bosses.

In the E window is found the Burne-Jones and Morris glass – Evangelists and angels with fruit hidden among dark leaves at top and sides. The colours are

Wirksworth. Barbaric Norman carving is built into many of the interior walls

surprisingly gloomy. The chancel is somewhat congested by an alabaster tomb chest which carries a miniature knight with long hair. To the left is a ruined effigy which raises its heart with both hands.

The most beautiful tomb does not look like one – an alabaster reredos in N aisle, formerly part of the Gilbert monument. It is a horizontal composition with the Virgin and Child flanked by members of the family at a distance.

Youlgreave's font is awkwardly placed but fascinating. The large Norman bowl has an integral holy water stoup jutting from its side. Sparse but robust carving includes a reptile, in which some have detected a salamander, biting the base of the stoup.

Derbys: 3 miles directly S of Bakewell, 2 miles W of A6

Jacobean tomb at Wootton Wawen with exuberant strapwork

Welsh Borders

Leek ●

Whitchurch ●
Stoke-on-Trent ●
Cheadle ●
Denstone ●
Adderley ●
Checkley ●

Oswestry ●
Slindon ●
Eccleshall ●
Tutbury ●
Stretton ●
Llanyblodwel ●
Peplow ●
Stafford ●
Hoar Cross ●
Burton on Trent ●
Forton ●
Ingestre ●
Gnosall ●
Barton-under-Needwood ●
Melverley ●
Mavesyn Ridware ●
Shrewsbury ●
Blymhill ●
Clifton Campville ●
Tong ●
Minsterley ●
Hopwas ●
Wolverhampton ●
Tamworth ●
Longnor ●
Leebotwood ●

Lydbury North ●

Ludlow ●
Chaddesley Corbett ●
Dodford ●
Richards Castle ●
Burford ●
Great Witley ●
Shobdon ●

Worcester ●
Eardisley ●
Great Malvern ●
Monnington on Wye ●
Brinsop ●
Croome d'Abitot ●
Pershore ●
Eaton Bishop ●
Besford ●
Hereford ●
Elmley Castle ●
Kilpeck ●
St Margarets ●
Hoarwithy ●
Abbey Dore ●
Brockhampton-by-Ross ●
Clodock ●
Rowlstone ●
Garway ●

*Herefordshire, Shropshire,
Worcestershire, Staffordshire*

HILLS ARE ALWAYS IN VIEW in the western half of this territory. There is more embowered seclusion here than anywhere else in England. Many of these churches, built of red sandstone, lie in green surroundings.

The landscape and the building types partake of Wales to a degree; there are plentiful examples of chapel-like simplicity. In unspoiled country one meets strange survivors, like the amazing painted wooden memorials of Besford and Burford. Unexpectedly, this region also has more than its share of late Victorian and Arts and Crafts, perhaps sign of the late developing enthusiasm for these counties.

A somewhat unlikely one, Staffordshire, is unusually rewarding for the church visitor. Shropshire on the other hand, a county without a cathedral, is a little thin, but Ludlow and Shrewsbury are pleasanter than many cathedral towns.

Hereford has a special place among English counties. Like Northumberland it remains under-populated and protected from change. Following the local school of Romanesque carvers from one small church to another is among the great treats of English church visiting.

Abbey Dore

St Mary

Large fragment of a Cistercian abbey with beautiful early Gothic E end and some curious 17c fittings.

The first impression is awkward, because a tower and bulky buttresses were added c1632 to surviving E parts of a derelict building. It had decayed since the Dissolution and was then sheltering cattle.

A local squire rescued it and commissioned the lively Jacobean screen with pinnacles and bold heraldry whose heroic scale lives up to the dimensions of the church. The same carpenter, called an architector, built the grand wooden roof with grotesque corbels and grape pendants. Somewhat later the W walls were covered with bold paintings of Father Time, David the harpist, and admonitory texts in cartouches.

The glory of the church is the forest of columns in the ambulatory, with some of the best vegetable carving in England, various as a real forest. Pevsner compares the clustering richness of the piers to Wells Cathedral. Even squeezed arches make beautiful rhythms here.

An unexpected delight is a collection of large stone bosses leaning against walls and piers, including monks kneeling before saints, abbots, and the Virgin. These are much more enjoyable than if properly lodged far overhead.

An interesting 17c window in E makes a strong clear effect from far away.

The churchyard is large and atmospheric, with remnants of the Norman nave and on the N side a door with zoomorphic hinges, said to commemorate a 13c campaign against local wolves.

Hereford: about 11 miles SW of Hereford on B4347 in the Golden Valley

Adderley

St Peter

One of those places very evocative of Georgian ways.

A small building of three different dates which feels homogenously 18c, it stands on a rise at a bend in the road, not part of a village. The stone mounting block remains beside the little circular drive, near a market cross turned into a sundial. At the base of a large pine tree stands a railed grave enclosure.

All the windows are filled with Perpendicular tracery of iron, and the

Abbey Dore. A great 17c wooden screen and roof adorn an Early English chancel

interior is very plain. The Norman font like a giant cushion capital has plant designs incised. Its later inscription suggests that children are the fruit of sin ('Here the first man wickedly enjoys the apple with his wife').

The most interesting part of the church lies behind an oafish partition of 1956 which blocks the nave off from the E parts. These are under separate jurisdiction (CCT) and require a separate key. In a strange way this arrangement perpetuates the feud between two leading local families which had them fighting over special seats near the altar.

One of these private pews is a piece of 17c Gothic with a frilly Jacobean screen, later heraldic glass and the feel of a historical romance. Opposite is a nice little neo-classical monument of a suppliant maiden, sited above a stove flue.

Shrops: 4 miles N of Market Drayton on A529; church on W side of road

Barton-under-Needwood

St James

Built all at once by John Taylor, a local donor of humble origins who had it erected on the site of his parents' cottage, so the story goes. The church was consecrated in 1533 which makes it the very last gasp of Gothic.

Though it is not a building of great finesse, its consistency is pleasing. Approaching from the E, you are met by a wonderful silhouette – ranges of toothed battlements, bulky pinnacles and a low tower which doesn't overwhelm.

Soothing combination of colours inside. A plain, tawny arcade is matched by plaster higher up and a very black old roof above.

The chancel windows are fascinating atrocities. Upper parts of the centre light are original. Apparently the rest are mid-19c attempts to reproduce the destroyed Tudor glass. Each panel contains an

Besford. A timber-framed building with more wooden wonders within

Apostle dressed in harsh purple, green or blue, with faces like cartoons. Their crudity grows on you.

Just to the SE, a classical former vicarage of the early 19c, which looks like the sleek houses Oliver Hill built in the 1930s.

Staffs: 6 miles SW of Burton on B5016; church W of road in centre

Besford

St Peter

The only timber-framed church in the county, which contains more wooden surprises.

It does not look promising, with its Victorian chancel and bellcote. But on closer inspection you find wonderful old wood in the porch and in the tracery of the W window.

Inside, miraculous survivals, including parts of the rood screen with delicate friezes, and two astonishing tombs. In the chancel lies the alabaster effigy of an adolescent Renaissance fop. It is framed by wooden panelling covered with heraldry and inscriptions. Around the prone figure runs a delicate wooden railing or cresting. All is so mellow and unrestored that the different materials are wonderfully interfused. Nearby a helmet and tattered banner are posted up.

In the nave an even rarer monument, like a richly painted cupboard. Four

doors open to reveal a ruined triptych centred on the deceased at prayer in a sharp green doublet. He is surrounded by weeping putti and Mannerist emblems of mortality. Below, a cadaver (him) in its shroud. Above, and in the same room as him, a picture of the Last Judgement in an ebony frame. It seems a very Elizabethan conceit to present the supernatural as a painting inside the

painting. Because his face has been scraped away, we could not guess that this figure who looks like a diplomat or a gentleman soldier died in childhood.

Worcs: 3 miles W of Pershore in a tangle of lanes N of A4104, not well signposted

Blymhill

St Mary

G. E. Street

One of the most delightful and eccentric of Street's works.

It is small, and early (1856–9). Part of its charm is that it begins with a medieval core; it is a parasite which devours its host. The tower is Perpendicular, and medieval masonry remains on the S side – the most interesting aspect, but not the usual direction of approach.

Street's windows are incredibly various, and there is a writhing gargoyle on the S, inside whose body the drain-spout turns a corner. Also outside is marvellous primitive carving by Street himself, which is contained in the interstices of plate tracery around a W window. It shows the Adoration of the Magi divided in two by the intervening glass.

Inside, the arcades are comically different – three bays vs. four. Benches, ironwork and chancel paving are simple and vigorous. Font, pulpit and chancel

Blymhill, whose medieval core is overshadowed by inventive 19c additions

178

screen are also by Street, but seem mechanical. Incidentally, the dormers on one side only, in tune with the prevailing whimsicality, are not by Street. His school next to the church is now a recreation centre.

At BREWOOD nearby (to the SE) Street added a remarkable S aisle with cross gables, which forecasts Lethaby or Prior.

Staffs: about 8 miles E of Telford, 1 mile N of A5; church S of main street

Brinsop, a favourite of the Wordsworths with notable Romanesque sculpture

Brinsop

St George

One of the enchanted places of England. There is no village to speak of, and the humble church lies up a farm track.

It contains a harmonious muddle of ingredients, including some of the best Hereford Romanesque sculpture, especially a big St George with one bird on his shoulder and another on his raised bridle. His heavy cape sticks out behind, and lions lurk under his ridgy skirts.

The church, deep in daffodils, was a favourite of the Wordsworths, who visited in-laws nearby. Dorothy Wordsworth window by Comper, who also did a reredos which harmonizes comfortably with the old things. These include gorgeous bits of glass, among them a seated Christ and St George with small gold lions in the border.

When we came out, a herd of heifers were crowded round our car licking it like a lump of salt.

Hereford: about 5 miles NW of Hereford, take unnumbered road N of A480; church at end of lane E of this road

Brockhampton-by-Ross

All Saints

W. R. Lethaby

One of the most extraordinary buildings in England, the only church designed by W. R. Lethaby, a late follower of the Arts and Crafts and the author of *Architecture, Mysticism and Myth*. It finds an original relation to history, combining learning with vernacular methods and materials. The result resembles a farm complex built by Byzantine refugees from a Yeats poem.

The roof is thatch and the belfry over S porch is weatherboard capped by humble shingles. On the central tower, patterning in the stone which looks like fancy thatching. Tracery throughout is rude but whimsical, sometimes like wickerwork, sometimes deranged Elizabethan strapwork. Creepers climb the bell tower picturesquely.

Inside, it resembles an upturned boat, the ceiling a roughly pointed arch descending almost to the floor. The strong arch-series is broken by mysterious irruptions of light from tower windows at the crossing.

A vigorous star-window shines in the E, other glass by Christopher Whall, heroic vine-clad font by Lethaby. Textures throughout are ceaselessly diverting: for example the delicate chisel marks on small cylinder-posts in deep reveals of double quatrefoil windows.

It is perhaps the most militantly handmade building in the world, and Lethaby's seed has continued to sprout in an astonishing way. Not long ago a set of embroidered prayerbook covers appeared on the altar, left by an anonymous donor. They represent 100 different flowers of the local fields and came with a notebook claiming that insects and animals have proved the truest lovers of the wild vegetable art of the countryside. It asked that a sanctuary be made for them in the churchyard and this was done.

Hereford: 7 miles NE of Ross-on-Wye, 1 mile W of B4224

Burford

St Mary

Aston Webb

A small rural church lavishly recast and fitted out by Aston Webb in 1889.

It abuts a famous garden near the Worcestershire border. Webb added frilly enrichment to the tower and lushest carving to chancel parapets and boss course.

Inside, it is very dark and rich with some striking fittings of gilded iron. A

Brockhampton-by-Ross. Lethaby's handmade Arts and Crafts masterpiece

row of heavy Art Nouveau lights hangs in the centre aisle, and a series of large altar lamps dangle in the chancel. Screen and chancel roof are dark reddish wood with more gold metal grilles.

A bizarre crowd of tombs in the E, including painted wooden effigies and, most remarkable of all, a huge wooden cupboard with small Apostles on the outsides of doors, which contains portraits of the three deceased within, painted by Melchior Salaboss, 1588. Long horizontal doors beneath open to reveal a figure in a shroud who was 7 feet 3 inches tall in life, we are told.

On the way out you pass a Tree of Jesse in the tower window like a gold mist.

Shrops: 8 miles SE of Ludlow; church W of Burford village, S of A456 next to Burford House

Burton on Trent

St Chad, Hunter Street

G. F. Bodley

One of Bodley's last churches is found in a northern working-class district of Burton.

Its great feature is a detached tower with much scribbly ornament in its long bell openings. Effortless variety in the N aisle traceries and vivid setbacks towards the street.

Inside, a sandstone arcade, wooden barrel roof and good screen. The fancy reredos in N chapel, much praised for its richness, is an instance of Bodley's well-informed detail become mechanical from over-use.

The brewer who paid for it died before Bodley had finished, and his heirs are said to have withheld money which would have paid for more lavish decoration of the interior.

Smells of brewing are everywhere in Burton. Its old parish church of *St Modwen* is a square, no-nonsense 18c design behind iron gates at the top end of the market place. The ground slopes quickly to the river behind. At Whitchurch (q.v.) in Shropshire there's a more elaborate version of this plan by the same builders.

Staffs: 11 miles SW of Derby on A38, which now bypasses town to W; church lies N of town centre, N of A50

Monster-ridden Romanesque font at Chaddesley Corbett, one of a group in the region

Chaddesley Corbett

St Cassian

A lovely village and a church with many features of interest but it is really the Norman font, related to the great Herefordshire examples, which justifies the trip.

This is a sensationally vigorous piece of carving and an essential text for interpreting the meaning of interlace, so important in northern Romanesque. Five

Pugin's patterns cover all internal surfaces at Cheadle

dragons fill the wide central band unpredictably. Above and below are further tangled strips. All these deeply cut, writhing patterns carry the same meaning: a vivid depiction of evil.

In the chancel, good Decorated carving – a lively assortment of niches and some largish heads.

Worcs: about 5 miles E of Kidderminster, just N of A448

Cheadle

St Giles (RC)

A. W. N. Pugin

This Roman Catholic church is probably the most satisfying work by the greatest propagandist of the Gothic Revival, Augustus Welby Northmore Pugin, whose buildings sometimes disappoint the hopes raised by his fervent writings.

Cheadle is different because Pugin had an unlimited budget (unusual among Roman Catholic congregations in the 19c) and could take his time over the design, which he perfected from 1840 to 1846.

The spire is inordinately graceful without the insubstantiality Pugin sometimes falls into. It dominates the church and the setting.

The exterior is richly dotted with sculpted figures let into niche-hollows in its sides. A very Pugin touch is the W door with large affronted lions as brass stencils, like a finicky drawing magnified many times.

Inside, every surface is painted, tiled, inscribed. Patterns of different scales abut each other, and there are no empty spaces. Most remarkable are the chancel steps which accommodate tiers of letters filling the vertical faces completely. In this place nothing is function, all is meaning. Gothic revival is revealed as a vocation not just a style.

Pugin's dream of re-medievalizing England comes truer around Cheadle than anywhere else. Adjoining the church he built a school, convent and presbytery. Almost within sight of it, ALTON CASTLE, a jagged Gothic phantasm designed for the family of the Cheadle patron, Lord Shrewsbury. The recent popularity of ALTON TOWERS nearby as a fun-park would seem to this devout architect the last indignity.

Staffs: 9 miles E of Stoke-on-Trent on A521; church is S of road (Anglican church is also called St Giles)

A profusion of rustic fittings and leaning chancel arch at Clodock

Checkley

St Mary & All Saints

One of those churches made harmonious by a large number of survivals and tasteful recent embellishments.

Oldest are the three Anglo-Saxon cross-shafts near a chest-tomb to the S, with knots and tiered figures but no animals, unless two feet issuing from a patch of knotwork are animal feet. On the font a lamb in a vat, flanked by curly-horned columns, curiously reminiscent of Sumerian themes. The rest of the font is taken up with Xs like a child's attempt to make runes.

The chancel beautiful from outside with little rosettes and faces where tracery bars cross, and a subtle curved moulding on the priest's door. Inside, much fine old glass in need of cleaning and wonderful bench ends, large, rustic and late. The motifs include affronted heads of bird-like jesters, and other heads in feathered hats known locally as red Indians. The 17c roof has big faces and knobs; Comper's S

chapel screen of 1922 is well knitted in, and the vestry screen a model of how such necessities should be managed.

Staffs: 5 miles NW of Uttoxeter on A522; church S of road

Clifton Campville

St Andrew

Very rich in fittings but strangely cool overall, perhaps the effect of all the clear light admitted by three huge windows under the tower.

The village enjoys an isolated position and the elegant needle spire shows from afar, joined to its tower by little flying buttresses. Inside, the profile of the nave columns is fascinating, incorporating a curve of Baroque complexity. Overhead a very steep roof with elaborate braces. Perhaps the best fittings are the screens of various date, including some nice punched-out decoration and rows of something like gingko leaves.

In the S chapel an alabaster tomb with very lively carvings, including a little animal frieze, seated readers and praying children.

Good recent fittings too: hanging lights in black metal and limed woodwork in a N chapel. Harsh Victorian floors are the only jarring note.

Staffs: 6 miles NE of Tamworth on unmarked road

Clodock

St Clydawg

A perfectly preserved 17c interior in a large medieval carcase near the Welsh border.

Very isolated, in sight of the Black Mountains. A Celtic saint's burial was the founding cause of this church. Entering the vast churchyard through a stile from the SW you are confronted by solid walls of gravestones so it seems that there is no way through.

After a low benighted doorway in the porch, a wide barny nave with an island of box pews down the middle. The great chancel arch lists dramatically. Within are some interesting tombs and a painted architectural surround for a N window, a flimsy, cut-rate essay in Baroque.

The large W gallery shelters the font in darkness underneath. This secluded, cleared space has beautiful stone paving. Remnants of wall texts, carved frills on the teetery three-decker pulpit and a great variety of window shapes.

Hereford: about 5½ miles W of A465, 18 miles SW of Hereford

Croome d'Abitot

St Mary Magdalene (CCT)

Robert Adam and Capability Brown

A Gothick gem of 1763 on which Capability Brown and Robert Adam collaborated.

It has a wonderful position on a crest overlooking the Malvern Hills, with Croome Court just below. It lies a few hundred yards from any road, but makes a fine and demure Perpendicular silhouette from some distance away.

The porch under the tower has iron gates, after which one is ushered under a gentle segmental vault in grey-blue and white over ultra-slender arcades in yellow.

The fittings are delicious and were even better. The tall pulpit has an openwork ogee top with icicles leading to a palm tree or feather duster in mellow mahogany. Pews enriched by Gothick panelling.

The chancel is stuffed with Baroque tombs. Notice particularly a vivid woman holding a baby, who lies across from a fatuous male lounger.

The tragedy of Croome is that the exquisite wooden font by Robert Adam was stolen in 1988. It stood in the centre at the W end and met you as you came in the door. It had a rich bowl with putto-head 'handles' and fluted shaft, splaying to three feet. Fortunately it has been recovered but it is unlikely that it can ever be trusted to its proper place again.

Worcs: 4 miles W of Pershore, overlooking Croome Court

Denstone

All Saints

G. E. Street

A small but lavish work by G. E. Street, who also built a large vicarage and school nearby, but not near enough to form a group with the church.

Outside, our expectations are overturned by the church's forms, whose angular apse is set against its round towerlet. Textures here are harsh and colours grim, though punched-out tracery is enjoyable.

Inside, a single undivided space and very complete furnishing, of which the highlights are windows by Clayton & Bell and a font carved by Thomas Earp. Especially in the apse this is some of the most entertaining glass of its period. Stories are clear, yet there is plenty of enrichment too – the Virgin's starred robe, for example.

The font consists of a massive chunk of alabaster. Four rivers of Paradise are emptied from pitchers by angels at the corners. Each of them has his hand on two rivers. As often with Street, iron light-fittings are particularly fine.

Staffs: 5 miles N of Uttoxeter on B5031; church W of road

Dodford

Holy Trinity & St Mary

Arthur Bartlett

An Arts and Crafts church of 1907–8 which is one of the most delightful surprises of Worcestershire.

It sits on a slope with pines in front, prefaced by a cloister of grey timber and mellow brick. The main structure is humble pebbledash with stone dressings. Inside and out it has been loaded with naturalistic imagery, sometimes recessive as in the tracery of the low rose window in the transept, sometimes breaking through as in the moulded squares showing local fruits implanted in nave arches. Here one feels a breath of English fields, while atop the rood beam, something more arcane. A cross of hammered metal encrusted with enamels depicts the 'twelve manner of fruit' found on the Tree of Life.

Colours throughout are subtle – a series of browns and tans – and glass is predominantly clear. Many fittings were made by the Bromsgrove Guild, a tradition which has continued. The former vicarage to the N is contemporary with the church.

Croome d'Abitot. 18c Gothick by the most imaginative of Romantic Classicists

Dodford is oddly laid out, with gabled bungalows in large plots. It began life in the 1840s as a Chartist village in which each allottee owned a little piece of land and thus acquired the vote.

Worcs: 2–3 miles NW of Bromsgrove, ½ mile N of A448; church on E side of unnumbered road

Eardisley

St Mary Magdalene

This church has the best Romanesque font in England.

It takes the form of a giant calyx, a bulb-like bloom on a thick stalk covered in deep carving. Framed top and bottom by large braid, which boxes in various chases and combats – warriors attacked by tendrils, St Peter fleeing with his book, Christ pulling a sinner out of a patch of clinging vine, and an enormous lion. It makes the battle against sin look hard, but winnable.

Another font of similar vigour and more complex design, at CASTLE FROME (13 miles NE of Hereford, just E of B4214), is sometimes attributed to the same sculptor.

Hereford: 16 miles NW of Hereford on A4111

Eaton Bishop

St Michael & All Angels

Notable for 14c stained glass which can be closely inspected.

Charmingly placed among trees. It groups very nicely from the E, with the shingled broach spire on its hefty tower. Inside, the window embrasures in tower are immensely deep.

There is a surprising angular window over the chancel arch. All the old glass is found in chancel, especially the large E window. Colours of this are truly wonderful, various greens (occurring together), yellows, brown and red. Lively single figures against deep backgrounds. Overall restful effect.

On N side the same sideways-trefoils in window tracery that are met at MADLEY (Nativity of the Virgin, about 2 miles W) where there is a large, consistent 13–14c church with an impressive apse, which contains more lovely glass, especially the 13c narrative roundels.

Hereford: 7 miles W of Hereford, about ½ mile N of B4352

Eccleshall

Holy Trinity

A grand Early English building whose scale is explained by the presence of the Bishops of Lichfield. They spent much time at their palace here until the 19c.

The little town is very charming with a strongly sloping High Street at right angles to the main road. The church lies at the top, to one side. From lower down you catch glimpses of its tower between the houses.

Restoration by Street made the whole impression more perfect and consistent. He put a pointed, aspiring chancel arch in place of a squat one, and made three lancets in the E wall. The 13c stiffleaf arcade is very fine and justifies Street's changes, which raised the whole space to the level of the best details.

In the chancel the exuberant strapwork tomb of Bishop Overton with fine vegetable ornament, heraldic figures, etc. To the N Caröe's memorial chapel of 1931, a preposterous construction of limed oak whose reredos fuses with the organ case. The display of virtuoso carving takes a classical framework and fills it with Gothic detail.

At the far edge of the churchyard some vigorous pedestal tombs. The memorial to Thomas Perry, 1870 (W of

Stirring scriptural drama on the best Romanesque font of all at Eardisley

church), encases a cross in a tight architectural garment, the Victorian equivalent of a telephone booth.

Staffs: 7 miles NW of Stafford on A519; church just N of B5026

Elmley Castle

St Mary

A charming village whose church has some eccentric features.

It lies far back in a low churchyard. Huge battlements make it look half-buried in the ground. Wonderful textures in the walls facing us, and herringbone masonry in the chancel.

Inside the porch, an earlier pig and rabbit set in the walls. The latter looks like a hippo with exaggerated ears. What a pity that the inside has been scraped, giving that agitated, indistinct impression which scraping usually produces.

The font at Elmley is very special. On its base are four lively dragons who twist in a predictable pattern. They look like embryonic worms and belong with a strange but numerous brood – those Norman fonts which depict what baptism casts out – sin in its full ugliness. These creatures are not much later than Norman, though to confuse matters a cruder heraldic bowl of Tudor date has been set on top of them. In a side chapel a fine Jacobean alabaster monument with a woman holding a baby. Both she and her male companions are dressed in ruffs and headdresses of amazing complexity. Opposite, a monument of the lounger class, refused admission to Croome church and buffeted here.

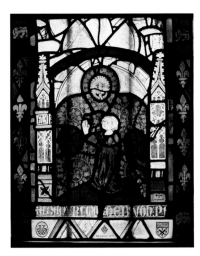

Fine 14c glass at Eaton Bishop showing a kneeling donor in deep tones

In the churchyard, two curious 17c sundials. The larger one looks like a mechanical man, the other like an African doll stuck full of pins. They both run up to twenty minutes slow except in October and November.

Worcs: 5 miles SW of Evesham, 2 miles S of A44 at foot of Bredon Hill

Forton

All Saints

A very entertaining mixture of Gothic and classical on a small scale.

The situation is lovely, in deep country; extensive prospects with old trees dotted like monuments. The church half conceals itself below the brow of a ridge and just beneath a large house.

Iron gates lead to this pleasantly bifurcated object – onto a Gothic tower with frilly top is tacked a symmetrical box full of roundheaded classical openings. Two doors, with a large ox-eye window over each, frame the composition. Keystones below the ovoid windows fuse with those above the doors below.

Inside, the most memorable detail is a gorgeous Tuscan arcade on high bases, which runs down the middle, separating a vestigially Gothic space from a new classical one.

15c glass at Great Malvern

The woodwork is mainly 20c classical pastiche, a little bit innocuous, but more pleasing than the Victorian stained glass which sullies a few of the windows.

Staffs: 14 miles W of Stafford on A519; church lies SE of road

Garway

St Michael

Garway's situation, sunk in the middle of a set of rolling hills, is one of the most satisfying of any English church.

Among the most eccentric of spatial organizations: a massive red tower stands apart to the NW. It is set diagonally to the body, and you only realize when you get nearer that it is connected to it by a low passage.

Originally this was a round Templar structure, a fact of which no sign remains internally. The chancel arch survives from that time, a rich concoction in deep brown stone, fringed like drapery or a sea cave. Within the chancel is a gorgeous Early English arcade of awkward proportions – huge piers, tiny attached pierlets – leading to a S extension.

The nave's old walls are painted pink and lean appreciably. Bench ends are like thick slabs of dark bread. Overhead six-pointed stars punctuate the roof.

Hereford: 9 miles NW of Monmouth on unnumbered road, ½ mile N of B4521

Gnosall

St Lawrence

A large and impressive church with peculiar Norman remains.

It sits atop the village in an enormous mounded churchyard. From the great central tower lean huge gargoyles which, like the prominent clerestory, suggest a later date than the most powerful evidence inside.

This is a remarkable Norman chancel arch with great bands of unplaceable decoration, deeply cut. One of these is based on furled Xs with three-dimensional dots in the leftover spaces, which could almost be degenerate 17c strapwork. These details are bold, but the supporting capitals are finicky, with dense patterns of thin braid like tiny candlesticks. In the S transept are rich Norman arches framing a passage to the tower stairs.

Because the tower makes such a break in the space, the barn-like E parts at Gnosall seem a different world. The main window is an effective Victorian composition of half-length figures. The whole space radiates a relaxed comfort that may arise in some measure from a lot of newish carpet, which at first seems inappropriate.

Staffs: 7 miles W of Stafford on A518

Oversized battlements and herringbone masonry at Elmley Castle

Great Malvern

Malvern Priory

A large priory with the largest collection of 15c glass in the country.

The building appears to be a consistent and somewhat heartless example of late Gothic, overbearing but with pleasing variety of tone, especially in tangerine-coloured stone dotted through the tower. It is built into a steep hill, and this makes for interesting complexities of approach: at first you cannot see how to reach the W front.

Inside, a hefty Norman arcade combined with late Gothic height, under flat wooden ceilings instead of vaults. The windows are worth long perusal: the size of the E one is awesome, but it is too far away to appreciate details except around donors in the lowest row. Glass in the N transept is nearer and has wonderful scenes like Christ among the Doctors. The focal moment is placed off centre here – the Virgin in a yellow circle of heavenly light with stubby trees beneath.

In the S aisle you can come right up to the stories, and they are marvellous. In Noah wonderful ruby stones and delightful faces and gestures throughout. One's intimacy with medieval narrators here is uncanny.

Some of the best windows are out of reach in the clerestory. For those, you will want binoculars and a useful book (L. A. Hamand, *The Ancient Windows of Great Malvern Priory*) produced by a former organist heroically obsessed by the subject.

There is a further priceless feature here, hundreds of medieval wall-tiles on the curved back-side of the altar screen, of lovely dusky hue and densely scribbled with patterns.

Worcs: 8 miles SW of Worcester on A449; church lies just E of road, but hidden from it, in town centre

Great Witley

St Michael

Not great architecture but an overwhelming experience.

The carcase has been attributed to Gibbs and is charming, if derivative. It is a classical box with plentiful urns and a little open cupola.

But the interior is an astonishing, un-English riot of white and gold plaster, ceiling paintings and pictures in glass. It

Garway's deep brown Norman chancel arch, fringed like a sea cave

is not what it seems; when the Duke of Chandos' chapel at Canons Park, Middlesex, was broken up in 1747, the local landowner bought it and re-created it here. The plasterwork could not be moved, so he took casts and reproduced it in papier-mâché. Thus it is even more light and fictitious than it looks.

The paintings by Bellucci are objects of real quality and enchantingly integrated with the many subtle shifts in the wooden vault. But the pictorial windows, ten of them, are perhaps the highlight of the space, especially two glimpsed imperfectly above, through the balcony.

In the 1850s many fittings were added, including a font with kneeling angels, pulpit, pews, etc. They don't quite fit, but form a fascinating Victorian approximation to high Baroque and rococo. At the same time the exterior was faced with stone (it had been brick before), and the large house which almost touches the church was enlarged to royal palace dimensions.

After various vicissitudes, the house caught fire in 1937, and is now a ruin, administered by English Heritage. You walk through from one hollow portico to another, experiencing an X-ray of the Edwardian country house. At a great distance, a dry fountain and stranded pavilions stare back at you like the ghosts of Versailles.

Worcs: about 10 miles NW of Worcester, W of A443 in grounds of Witley Court (1–2 miles SE of village centre)

Hoar Cross

Holy Angels

G. F. Bodley

Rightly regarded as one of the high points of the Gothic Revival in England.

Perfected by Bodley over many years, sparing no expense. The nave was lengthened and the screen heightened after completion simply to improve their proportions. Chapels and narthex were added later. Bodley's partner Garner should be mentioned, for Bodley's later work, after their separation, often shows a certain deadness, even in such major projects as CLUMBER CHAPEL, Notts.

Anyway, Hoar Cross is perfection. It commemorates Mrs Emily Meynell-Ingram's husband who died following a hunting accident. Delightfully isolated and near no settlement, this church is one of the most self-absorbed expressions of Anglo-Catholic piety.

It is surrounded by an extremely low sandstone wall, like a line drawn round the idea. This is breached by a lumpy lychgate, whose form contrasts with the elaboration of the church. Two elements dominate: the tower, all angular and made entirely of buttress and bell-openings, long and rectangular. And the chancel, with incredible richness in its tracery, formed of Decorated frills contained in a Perpendicular rectangle. Again encasing mouldings suggest many layers. The nave by contrast effaces itself behind the aisles, each of whose buttresses is adorned with two tiny gargoyles. On the more private ritual S (actually W) side,* saints' statues harbour likenesses of Bodley, Mrs Meynell's brother and others.

Coming into the interior is not a church visit, but an operatic storming of the senses. At first it seems impossibly dark. Even when the eyes adjust, the contrast remains between mysterious gloom in the accessible nave and dazzling radiance in the closed-off chancel, behind its lacework screen. A feast of stimuli reside there – suffice it to mention the organ case like something from the *Très Riches Heures* and bosses like flowers which punctuate every arch-reveal from floor to ceiling. Far-off glimpses of even more privileged spaces, chapels with their forlorn effigies.

The stained glass by Burlisson and Grylls is superior to that by Kempe, especially the W window, based on wine, pale green and approximations to gold. The Stations of the Cross were carved by two old woodworkers in Antwerp. Each is a shallow diorama with folding doors.

* Churches are conventionally described as if their chancels were in the liturgically correct eastern orientation, whether they are or not, so one gets ritual E, actual S, at Hoar Cross.

Staffs: 7 miles W of Burton-on-Trent, W of A515, at edge of Hall grounds

Great Witley, a Baroque chapel reproduced in papier-mâché

Hoarwithy

St Catherine

Revised by J. P. Seddon

A fantastic dream of Italy in a tiny village beside the River Wye. J. P. Seddon, who had links with the Pre-Raphaelites, was engaged in 1875 by a wealthy rector to improve a bleak brick box of 1843. He made it a Byzantine extravaganza of great richness and refinement.

The mode of approach is novel: up steep steps between ilexes, under a campanile, and along a surprising cloister on the S flank, with constant vistas ahead and to the side, then a W porch with charming beasts in the tympanum, which opens into a narthex.

The theatrical approach is justified by the visionary interior, which culminates in a maze of Byzantine arches and grey marble columns. In the apse real mosaic, of the Pantocrator. Much neo-Romanesque carving of high quality, windows by Seddon and a pupil (large on one side, but tiny and high above the cloister on the other), and mosaic floors throughout.

This devoted project took nearly thirty years to complete.

Hereford: 7 miles NW of Ross-on-Wye, 2 miles E of A49

Hopwas

St Chad

John Douglas

A small brick and half-timbered conceit of 1879–81 by John Douglas.

The exterior is eccentric. Even bell louvres are shingled so they look like sub-roofs. A little peaked stair turret is attached to the larger mass of the tower, which is capped by a rustic spike.

The interior, by contrast, is blissfully simple and focused on two wide brick arches at the E end. Outside, craggy pink brick; inside, tan. Windows are small with faintly pastel glass which makes the space dark. A gorgeous roof looms overhead. In main braces, many pieces fit together to approximate a single curve; it is intricacy about to revert to simplicity.

Douglas designed stalls, pews and sanctuary rail. Among other fittings some are blatantly not his.

Staffs: 2 miles W of Tamworth on A51; church N of road, higher up

Ingestre

St Mary the Virgin

Christopher Wren

A Wren church preserved virtually intact in the depths of the country.

It lies in a cul-de-sac along with a lavish Jacobean house and an even more lavish mock-Jacobean stable.

The exterior is a bit dour and box-like, with a tower proportionately big for the body, which carries the only sculptural frills on its W front.

The internal effect very pure and strong: dark screen, pulpit and panelling are played against chalk-white columns in clumps of four, and a spectacular plaster ceiling. Here are large flowers, garlands and vigorous ribbons.

There is an inappropriate Burne-Jones window with gross angels, and two

Hoar Cross, the most aesthetically luxurious of all Gothic Revival churches

interesting tombs: a young woman who died in Naples is shown with wonderfully delicate slippered feet, stretched out on a couch, while in the second, busts of a child and young woman sit on top of a casket, looking away from each other. She has lushly ringleted hair.

Staffs: 5 miles E of Stafford, W of A51

Kilpeck

St Mary & St David

An extremely modest building but one of the high points of English architectural sculpture.

Not many English churches approach the vast carving programmes of French Romanesque. For curious reasons, tiny Kilpeck comes nearer than many grander buildings. One cause is its remote

location, to this day a source of joy to the visitor. The other is the hardness of the local stone, which has coloured the whole countryside a dusky red.

The church at Kilpeck sits against the tree-covered mound of the (mostly) vanished Norman castle. It is surrounded by barely detectable bumps of the medieval village, which has disappeared. To see these outlines clearly you need an aeroplane or a snowfall.

The building has been well cared for and may feel a little tidied up. But one must be grateful for the discretion: there are no signs or stalls here, only the riveting spectacle of the S doorway, with a giant Tree of Life in the overdoor panel. It is a tree consisting of one leaf, and some snaky dependencies. Most curious are the doorposts, one containing Viking warriors in long padded coats, lost among vines, the other intricate and never-ending beasts.

Ingestre, a Wren church in the country, the only one outside London

Around the eaves many amusing corbels, some original beasts, most re-carved. On the W wall two curious dragon prows as if this is a boat not a church, or at least a wooden building somewhere in Norway. One cannot suppress the feeling that a more ancient pagan imagination is struggling to break through.

Appropriately, the most remote corner of the nave, the NE, enshrines heroic bits of Anglo-Saxon masonry – long and short work, which is to say large roughly dressed stones laid alternately upright and sideways to form the corner.

Inside, Kilpeck is quite perfect but less powerful. More figures on posts of chancel arch, both cruder and tamer than S door. This time it is saints and priests not warriors, in a blocky style like the famous capitals in Hereford Cathedral.

Hereford: 8 miles SW of Hereford, 1 mile up a signed left turning off A465; church is 100 yds NW of village centre

The finest Romanesque carving in England on the south doorway at Kilpeck

Leebotwood

St Mary

Longnor

St Mary

Two rustic gems in which the 18 or early 19c inhabits medieval fabrics.

Leebotwood is bleakly simple outside with a mean cross-wise tower. Inside, it is a carpenter's fantasia of props and braces and gloss paint in various colours. The door leading in is operated by a pulley system, and there is an attempt at classical pilasters against the walls. A little garish glass in E, but mostly clear with charming iron tracery. Even heavy varnish on pews and three-tone floor tiles are pleasing here. On N wall some interesting fragments of medieval wall paintings. Light filters in from the W gallery most beguilingly.

Longnor is delightful from the E, with its window tracery simplified in later centuries to make a quasi-17 or -18c effect. The belfry of wood and lead is charming. Inside, it is hard to believe that the early Gothic window frames are real, so strong is the imposed later feeling, but checking again outside will reassure you. Here the size of the W gallery complicates the space unmedievally.

Shrops: 9 and 8 miles S of Shrewsbury respectively, on A49; Leebotwood W of village and road; Longnor E of road in village

Leek

All Saints, Compton

Norman Shaw

One of the best Arts and Crafts churches. The architect was Norman Shaw, and the building seems to rise slumbrously from the ground, as if just breaking the surface. Most of the windows except huge ones at both ends are like half-closed eyes. The whole forms a low mound capped by a massive central tower.

Inside, the presence of this tower is subliminally felt in the wider W arch turning to strainer arches in the aisles. Purple stone dressings contrast wonderfully with white plaster walls. From a clear W window light floods the wide nave; the flowing tracery of this window is one of the highpoints of the filtering of Gothic through Ruskinian organicist sensibility.

At both E and W ends, walls are lavishly painted, like an Arts and Crafts emblem-book – trees of life, heavenly cities, peacocks and pomegranates. Horsley's panels on the chancel ceiling are particularly fine. Lethaby designed reredos, pulpit and font: pulpit with organic openwork, font a primitive lump of polished black granite. The church also possesses five gorgeous contemporary altar frontals.

The old parish church of *St Edward the Confessor* in the centre of town is worth visiting for its churchyard with two Anglo-Saxon cross stumps, one of which changes imperceptibly from fat cylinder to melted square shaft. There are two tombs by Street, one with a vandalized iron fence.

Inside, this church is remarkable for preserving its W gallery. The effect of this structure swooping down to bisect the space may be uncomfortable but is an unforgettable echo from the 18c.

Staffs: 9 miles NE of Stoke-on-Trent on A53; All Saints lies on E side of A520 about ⅓ mile S of town centre, at the corner of Southbank Street

Llanyblodwel

St Michael Archangel

A high flight of Victorian whimsy, carried out on an underlying medieval fabric by an artistic rector.

The Revd John Parker was a gifted watercolourist who is said to have sketched at least part of every Welsh church. His alterations at Llanyblodwel span the years of his tenure here (1845–60) and make a joyfully cacophonous impression.

The approach is deceptive, for the Perpendicular E wall is the least Victorianized part of the church. But rounding the corner you come on odd dormers, buttresses made up with brick, and the strange convex spire – his proudest stroke, which gave him great difficulty, but in the end possessed, to his eye, 'a certain scientific and geometrical grandeur'.

The grotesquely narrow S porch contains a wonderful concentration of flavours: wavy wooden roof with bright bosses, tall Norman arch and bleached door dated 1714.

Inside, a forest of jittery detail culminating in a Tudoresque roof with dangling pendants and lots of criss-cross bracing. The W balcony is one of the summits of gimcrackery, lively and

unhistorical. Another gallery at right angles, which holds the organ, is visible through the arcade.

Almost every available surface has been covered with some kind of stencilling. The deep Siena colouring on the aisle arches is especially surprising. All these patterns were later covered with wash and only revealed again in 1960.

The hare on a fragmentary tombstone in the porch may represent a connection with PENNANT MELANGELL further up the Tanat to W, one of the loveliest churches in Wales. St Melangel was patroness of hares.

Shrops: 7 miles SW of Oswestry just off B4396; church at W edge near River Tanat

Ludlow

St Laurence

A grand late Gothic church in a charming old town, interestingly immured in urban fabric on the S; open to a view beyond the hill Ludlow sits on, to the N.

The tower is immensely tall, like a craning neck, an effect increased by the large blank space between bell openings and tower windows. These light the space under the tower very dramatically. This is the culmination of a very high nave with slender piers.

Glass at Ludlow is unusually interesting, especially some elderly men in dwarf architectural enclosures in N

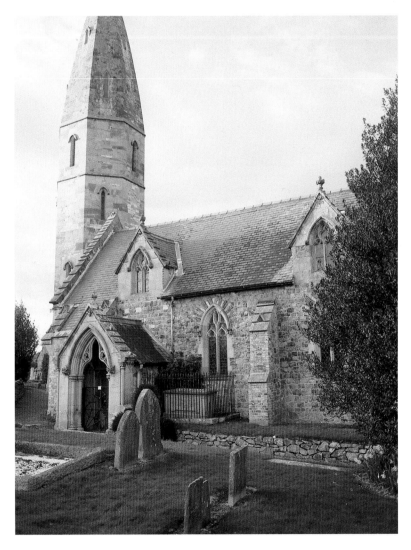

Llanyblodwel, with a host of odd improvements by a Victorian vicar

Ludlow, the Victorian reredos made up of medieval fragments

chapel, and scenes with stumpy trees nearby. The plentiful glass in chancel looks more like a 17c idea of the medieval than the Middle Ages themselves: many figures with grossly large jewelled borders on their cloaks; E window with plausible medieval drawing and implausibly harsh colours including lots of violet. Good remnants of screens, Renaissance tombs and a famous set of misericords, plentiful but crude.

Ludlow Castle Chapel is an important piece of Norman design with an unusual circular nave.

Shrops: 24 miles N of Hereford on A49 (which now bypasses town)

Lydbury North

St Michael

Exceptionally interesting for the way Arts and Crafts restoration has harmonized work of various earlier periods through its discreet interventions.

In beautiful country near the Welsh border. The first impression of amazingly varied textures and types – a square 13c tower, a pink rendered nave with exquisite imitation late Gothic window frames, and a wooden porch. The effect is rich but quasi-domestic.

Past a heavy door into the unaisled nave with sloping walls. Most of the chancel arch is filled by a long text in black letter, an upper extension of the screen.

Over the S transept is a large room, reinstated by Micklethwaite early last century. The corresponding N transept is quite different, an unfeatured barn-like space with a marvellous stone floor. This

Lydbury North, the complex roof viewed from under the screen, which carries an enormous inscription

transept is now a Roman Catholic chapel, one of very few such in an Anglican church.

Light fittings are exquisite, like vine tendrils. Some fine wood surfaces in nave, knobbed Jacobean pews, complex roof, and subtly vernacularized tower door à la Lutyens.

This is one of Shropshire's most pleasing churches, in which Micklethwaite's work is so well blended that we cannot be sure exactly how much of the credit is his.

Shrops: 15 miles NW of Ludlow on B4385; church on N side of road

Mavesyn Ridware

St Nicholas

A fascinating conglomerate of actual Gothic joined to schoolroom Gothick in brick, which contains a unique instance of the ancestral obsession.

A large brick rectangle with a flattish hipped roof has been married to the stone tower and aisle surviving from an earlier church. Windows in the new part are large and airy; they just barely remember to have pointed Gothic tops.

The interior is more surprising still. It has been denuded of its plaster except in the polygonal apse extension, a quaint little space painted baby blue. Amazingly enough, here scraping works: it shows that many old stones were re-used lower down, uncovers brick cut to concave mouldings in the window sills, and provides a transit to the venerable arcade surviving on the N boundary of the rectangle.

Beyond this is a perplexing space which is reached by going down a few steps. You now find yourself in a cellar or pantry-like place surrounded by a fence of alabaster portraits in 16c clothes. Something is wrong: these are all mock tombs, and the long incised texts under reliefs of battles keep breaking out of black letter into Roman and then reverting. The whole propounds an invented genealogy, with its kernel of truth under heavy layers of obfuscation. This riddle can't be easily cracked and remains a unique expression of early Romanticism.

Staffs: 12 miles SE of Stafford, S of B5014

Melverley

St Peter

A small 15c timber-framed building on the Welsh border.

It hangs over a small river which you drive along coming from the S. Black fills more space than white in its half-timbering. Internal space is almost square because the gallery has been subtracted to make a vestibule, where there are old quarry tiles underfoot and a crooked stair rises to the crooked gallery.

The main space is cut almost in two by a heavy openwork screen like something one might find in a barn. Denser framing under the W belfry and around the gallery.

Formerly lots of timber, wattle and daub structures were found in these regions. Melverley, in which pegs not nails are used throughout, is now the lone survivor substantially unaltered.

Shrops: 12 miles W of Shrewsbury, 1 mile N of B4393; church at end of lane to W

Minsterley

Holy Trinity

A miniature essay in country Baroque of late 17c date.

The brick exterior is charming. Onto the W front is crammed every conceivable motif including skulls and bones. It is topped by a wooden belfry which looks Edwardian in its combination of weatherboard and bulging balusters.

A great drop in temperature is felt on the sides with their sloping buttresses reminiscent of Arts and Crafts.

After such exuberance outside, the interior comes as a disappointment – full of Victorian pews and silly pastel glass. But there is a wonderful low screen and a partially blocked W gallery. Up here in plastic bags hang six of Minsterley's seven maidens' garlands. These enchanting constructions were made for the funerals of young girls and were formerly suspended over their pews as memorials. They are like little garden pavilions of wood shavings and stiff paper, dotted with paper flowers and hung with paper gloves. The seventh one can be inspected in a glass case.

Shrops: 10 miles SW of Shrewsbury on A488; church just W of this road on B4387 to Westbury

Minsterley. Rustic Baroque in brick, covered in assorted motifs

Monnington on Wye

St Mary

A rare example of 17c Gothic perfectly intact.

Near the river, and approached by a clovery grass walk. There is a good

lychgate and then the simple exterior with few windows, all roundheaded inscribed in square frames. Only the tower is older.

Rudimentary whitewashed interior with shallowest curve to ceiling and hanging oil lamps. Lots of spindly barley sugar columns in screen, altar rail and pulpit. The very three-dimensional royal arms on the wall formerly sat on the screen and engorged the angular chancel arch.

A coarse bust starts forth from the wall memorial of a man who scorned the quiet life hereabouts and died defending Venice from the Turks.

Hereford: 10 miles W of Hereford, ½ mile S of A438; church next to and E of Monnington Court

Peplow

Epiphany

Norman Shaw

This simple vernacular structure in brick and half timber by Norman Shaw lies deep in the country. There is no village near, only a farm and the great house.

Brick infill between the dark timbers, slender belfry and roof sweeping down over the vestry. Inside, the screen is the great feature; it thickens under the canted ceiling to allow a narrow passage. It also teasingly interrupts our view of

Melverley. A rare survivor of the local building tradition in wood and plaster

the E window. Chancel walls have been covered later with grandiose and gloomy murals of 1903, real period pieces.

Brick and timber infill between bands of windows has been carried inside too, and makes a strong tiered outline on the W wall.

Near the Herefordshire border Shaw built a church of more ambition at RICHARDS CASTLE (All Saints, Batchcott). Subtly battered; organic silhouette in harsh masonry of bilious colour. Unintended bareness inside, with strong orange tile floor and ghoulish painted reredos of the period.

Shrops: Peplow is 13 miles SE of Whitchurch, ½ mile E of A442 (turning unmarked) at edge of Hall grounds

Pershore

Abbey Church of the Holy Cross

The surviving parts of a large abbey contain some of the best Early English work in the country.

Hidden off to one side in an attractive small town, only the E parts of the old church remain and not all of those. Apse and Lady Chapel were torn down at the Dissolution to be partially replaced in 1846 by Gilbert Scott, who opened the lower arches at the E end and left the upper ones brutishly blocked.

Pershore has the odd charm of a fragment (the transept now functions as a vestibule), together with the grandeur of a perfect chancel, largely intact. Here the stone roof carries marvellous leafy bosses and the curving arcade is extremely tranquil. Two very literal windows of 1870 tell the story of the Abbey – particularly good are purple-robed monks scurrying through red flames which envelop the rood. Signs of these disastrous fires still persist on S transept walls inside and out: the stones are stained pink.

Inside the marvellous tower space, Gilbert Scott has inserted an ingenious cat's-cradle ringing platform.

To the L on entering the church is a benefactions board excluding bastards and other undesirables.

Worcs: 9 miles SE of Worcester on A44; church lies W of road in large grounds

Richards Castle

St Bartholomew (CCT)

A rich medley of parts, long disused and hence held motionless in time.

The church sits on a peculiar sloping site with a vast outlook. To the W lie indistinct remains of the important pre-Conquest castle.

Its detached 13c tower looks like a dovecote. It is patched at the top and has great ragged bell-openings.

Entering the church by a low porch you come into a tall interior. The roof is half panelled and half exposed, the timbers a pleasant light grey. Whitewash remains on nave piers and the whole dusty effect of this interior, with numbered box pews and plentiful hanging hatchments, is very powerful. English Heritage is now renewing roofs and tracery, and one must pray they resist the urge to tidy this huge, dishevelled space.

There's old glass in some window tops and an amazing star pattern in N tracery. Sadly, flowing tracery in E will probably be fresh stone before long.

Norman Shaw's *All Saints*, just over the Shropshire border, replaced this church in 1893 (see Peplow above).

Hereford: 4 miles SW of Ludlow, ¼ mile W of B4361 and village centre; church S and W of road

Monnington on Wye. 17c Gothic miraculously intact

Rowlstone

St Peter

Much good Romanesque carving on this simple church deep in the country.

The churchyard is overshadowed by a big ancient oak. Dark red tympanum above the S door shows Christ in a mandorla gripped by four flying angels whose feet stick out.

Inside, the chancel arch is decorated with rows of birds and a more abstract pattern of paired wings. By a strange inadvertence, two little figures have been carved upside down. Further E two folkish candle-holders depict metal cocks or doves lined up in rows like toy soldiers. On the walls are slate tablets discreetly coloured. The whole bare interior breathes a wonderful simplicity, with rudimentary pews, bowl font and square tower.

Hereford: 1½ miles W of Pontrilas and A465

St Margarets

St Margaret

Famous for its carved rood loft to which you can ascend by exceedingly steep stairs.

Another of Herefordshire's simple isolated churches, with a little boarded belfry roofed in stone slates.

St Margarets, where the wooden rood loft is an exceptional survival

Inside, beautiful details on the back of the door and painted texts here and there like scattered thoughts of an idle brain. The screen with all its wooden leafage is harshly bleached; it hides the E end and chancel arch. Through it you can see a Bromsgrove Guild window in which the River of Life glitters.

Hereford: about 3½ miles N of Abbey Dore on unnumbered roads

Shobdon

St John Evangelist

This is the most extravagantly Gothick church in England. Richard Bateman, who pulled down a Gothic building and substituted this amusing fake in 1752–6, was a friend of Horace Walpole, whose Strawberry Hill converted Bateman 'from a Chinese to a Goth'.

The results aren't far from chinoiserie, though, and this is the most frivolous, secular interior imaginable. Nearly everything is made of wood and painted in delicate ice-cream colours, white, ochre, pale blue. Bench ends are pierced by quatrefoils and trefoils; the bishop's throne sports a rose window in its back.

Because they are mostly appliqué, forms are free to defy structural logic, and hanging ogee arches recur, notably in the lacy fringe of the chancel. Pope's line about a parson 'who never mentions hell to ears polite' pops into your head; a funeral here is nearly unimaginable. By comparison Bavarian Rococo looks grown-up.

In a matching gesture, even more profoundly revealing of 18c attitudes, Bateman saved two Romanesque doorways and the chancel arch from the old church, re-erecting them on an eminence to the N as eyecatchers and viewing frames. So two distant realities have changed places: the church becomes a boudoir or bower; its former decoration, still expounding solemn truths, is converted into a garden ornament.

Peplow. Norman Shaw building in the local vernacular, timber with brick infill

The sculpture has suffered badly from the prank, and one of the tympana is much more readable as a 19c plaster cast at the V&A than it is in Herefordshire. But figured columns supporting the arches leading nowhere remain obscurely vivid and provoke comfortable 18c reflections on the vanity of human wishes.

Hereford: 14 miles SW of Ludlow on B4362; church is up a lane N of this road at E end of village (in grounds of Shobdon Court, now demolished)

Slindon

St Chad

Basil Champneys

An exquisite miniature of 1894. It has a feminine delicacy we would call rococo if it were not clearly Gothic. It shows how that style was being adapted to specialized expressive purposes by this time.

Its central tower is proportionately huge and squat, the window and gable mouldings very original, fading or continuing unexpectedly past their normal limits.

Inside, a lovely little queen-post roof, and then an intricate stone vault in the tiny chancel. Many Champneys fittings, including font, stalls, lights: but the interior not at all lavishly furnished. Particularly nice ironwork on the mast atop the tower.

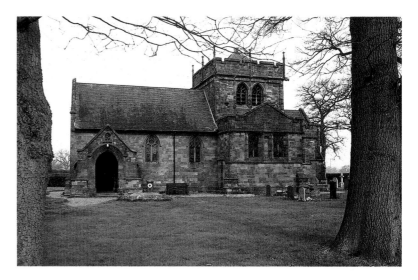

Slindon. A very free late 19c variation on Gothic by Basil Champneys

St Chad's sits very near the road and under current conditions feels vulnerable.

Staffs: 2 miles N of Eccleshall, on E side of A519

Stretton

St Mary

Micklethwaite and Clarke

A rich late Victorian church on the point of tipping over into Art Nouveau, with wonderful glass.

Shobdon. The freest of all 18c variations on Gothic by a local landowner

Stretton is a suburb of Burton, an evocatively barren one. The church sits in a vast churchyard recently denuded of old trees. Its massive tower makes a powerful impact, appearing melted from afar, but sharp-edged close up.

A rich interior, especially woodwork of rosy hue in screens and font cover. The stained glass is some of the most intriguing of the century. Sir William Richmond is said to be responsible for all of it, but it falls into two distinct groups. The chancel is earlier, with a colour wheel of angels in E, a great dragon and birds in N. Most sensational are two later windows in S chapel. The drawing and proportions of these are archaic, quasi-Byzantine. One shows Pentecost as a mystery play on a wooden platform high above a city, glimpsed as through a telescope.

Staffs: 2 miles N of Burton on A38; church W of road

Tamworth

St Editha

A late Gothic/Decorated town church on a grand scale with good Victorian and later glass.

Tamworth must have been a very pleasant town before its recent uncontrolled growth to the E. Near the church there are still pockets of peace in the graveyard with large trees on one side, while on the other a new shopping precinct presses in.

The tower with its huge pinnacles is still the crown of the town. You enter through it and pass a grandiose Baroque monument by Arnold Quellin and C. G. Cibber. The space between red sandstone arcades impressive, the roof (recently restored) good, remnants of an 18c iron screen further on.

Some pleasing surprises among the glass: in the wide Perpendicular window at end of N chapel is Morris glass of 1874, designed by Burne-Jones. The panels contain single figures and the colours are subtle from afar, an effect almost of grisaille made by faint green and rose tones with plenty of white.

Clerestory tracery is interesting but hard to see. Towards the E are three windows which look like Ford Madox Brown, in an arresting palette with lots of rich yellow.

The best surprise is three windows on Old Testament themes in the S aisle. Below figures like Daniel, Esther and David are a single scene from each of their lives. These yield a powerful whiff of the Victorian romance with Palestine. They date from 1859–86. Henry Holiday was the designer.

A last surprise as one leaves, the large abstract fireburst in the big tower window. This is a design by Alan Younger guided by G. G. Pace who, as church architect for some years, was responsible for other less obvious improvements.

Staffs: about 15 miles NE of central Birmingham on A453

Tong

St Bartholomew & St Mary

This is one of the most atmospheric churches in England, formerly collegiate, with some glorious survivals among its tombs and fittings.

It makes a jolly effect from afar because its octagonal central tower is hoisted on broach-like slopes and then capped by a squat spire. The golden brown exterior seems varied, though there is not much ornament one can point to. In the NE corner a surprising figure in a niche, c1950, of stark white stone.

Through old doors and under dark roofs with carved tendrils like snakes. The vegetable friezes on the screens are among the most delightful in any parish church – many different species of leaf and interwoven stem. A wonderful series of heraldic birds juts up along the back of the chancel screen.

Tong's tombs are rightly famous. A wealth of good alabaster effigies are

Shrewsbury

Topographically, Shrewsbury is one of the most exciting towns in England, with good medieval, 18c and 1930s churches.

The old core sits within a loop of the River Severn and rises steeply to an eminence on which a few of the old churches are perched. Narrow paths and flights of steps which thread the spaces around *St Alkmund* and *St Julian* make this part into a kind of English hill town. These two churches are intriguingly crowded together. Both were revised in the 18c leaving their medieval towers intact. St Alkmund is an amusing assemblage of rectangular solids with Gothick detailing. Inside, a flat ceiling and an enormous painted window of 1795 with the Virgin like a Romantic heroine (after a painting by Guido Reni).

St Mary, Shrewsbury's best medieval church, is unaccountably redundant, and like other town churches in CCT care, difficult of access. Notices abound, but nothing to say whether or when it is open. The local tourist office and the CCT in London gave inaccurate information about opening hours, and on two occasions I spent long periods admiring its rich red and purple exterior which jumbles various styles vigorously. But I never got in to see the great arcades and the notable stained glass of two different periods.

Between St Mary and St Chad lies *Old St Chad*, a partly recuperated ruin in a tranquil open space along which runs Belmont, the great 18c street of Shrewsbury.

St Chad at the edge of the old town by **George Steuart** (1790–92) is a powerful combination of ovoid, cylindrical and rectangular forms in stone of rich yellow hue. Inside, some large empty spaces and an intense Rubens window by David Evans.

Just across the English Bridge to the E with a tranquil backwater along its N side is the *Abbey*. Its great W window shows well from the bridge. In the 19c it was brought back from semi-ruin, and old masonry in moth-eaten pink and grey contrasts effectively with the harsher red of Pearson's restoration. Inside, a powerful Norman space, squeezed arches in N aisle particularly notable.

In a N suburb, one of the best English churches of the 1930s survives in mutilated form. *Holy Spirit*, Roseway, Harlescott, 1936 by **Herbert North** was sold in 1963 because it had grown too small, and became a private club. Originally grey brick with green tile roof in a kind of moderne Gothic. Floor patterns survive inside, as well as delicate Voysey-like flowers and leaves on ceiling arches now closed off in a loft.

Shrops: 21 miles N of Ludlow on A49

crammed in like packing cases: note especially crests on the helmets the

Romanesque birds and upside-down figures on the chancel arch at Rowlstone

knights' heads lie on. A forest of columns under one set of effigies encloses another.

In the Golden Chapel to S, traces of gold on a quirky fan vault, with pendants of different lengths. For once late Gothic richness seems flexible and alive. Here there is a vivid figure reading and writing in an oriel and some lovely smudged floor tiles.

Despite a motorway nearby, the church on its mound seems to exist in a time of its own. The little village gives plenty of signs of a dignified past, fallen into disuse but not much overlaid.

Shrops: 7 miles E of Telford just N of M54 (junction 3)

Tong, a detail from the most engaging forest of tombs in England

Tutbury

Priory Church of St Mary the Virgin

In a commanding position below Tutbury Castle, this is the most impressive Norman church in the county.

It was built as a Benedictine priory, of which the monastic parts to the E were demolished at the Dissolution. The magnificent W front is centred on one great portal: five deep rings of beakhead, with a further fringe each side, and interesting blurred capitals. Uniquely, one of the arches is carved in alabaster. Above it are lots of noughts and crosses.

The S door is more ruined and mysterious. Its tympanum with the remains of a boar hunt – not in its original position – is the most interesting bit of narrative on the building.

Inside, a powerful Norman arcade, embellished with an unfortunate Victorian apse. An old mushroom font with ears has been cast into a corner, and a Victorian imitation by Street takes its place. Attractive late Gothic lancets have been inserted into the Norman triforium. On the W wall a very entertaining beast frieze.

Staffs: 5 miles NW of Burton on A50; church W of road at N edge of town

Whitchurch

St Alkmund

A pleasing Wrenish building of 1712–13 in local sandstone.

It dominates the little town, standing above it at the end of the long High Street. A consistent classical conception with a few exuberant touches, like the semi-circular S porch and the patron's arms on the tower.

Inside, a good stair vestibule and a Tuscan arcade which would have seemed less stark before 1972 when decayed galleries were removed.

Not everyone will agree that the E window is a fine example of pictorial glass. In this swirling Ascension, bodies fill the entire space – rich work which is not late 18c, as I assumed, but High Victorian. Even the greatest enthusiast of that period may have had too much of colours blocking the light before he has worked through all the aisle windows.

Slenderest remnants of a medieval church on the site – two tombs (one hidden by the organ) which got Victorian Gothic canopies in 1874, a dispiriting show of reverence.

Shrops: 20 miles N of Shrewsbury on A49; church at N end of town

Wolverhampton

St Peter

A large and imposing town church, mainly Perpendicular.

Outside the S door is the mid 9c Wolverhampton cross. From afar it looks like a column suffering from comically exaggerated entasis. It is very black and hard to decipher, but at the right distance you see roundels separated by decorative bands, then a subliminal lattice and, depending from it, V-shaped feelers of decoration which trail off into the uncarved base. It is an inventive scheme without parallel elsewhere.

St Peter's chancel is long and prominent, made that way in the 1860s by Ewan Christian to balance the 16c tower. Old photos reveal that the E end is all Victorian. Here they were right, because the 17c chancel was undeniably mean. Inside, however, we deduce the addition was planned for external effect, because from within it feels much too long.

The nave is an awesome space, towering up to the gloom of a good roof. In the N aisle interesting Whallish windows of local provenance. On the

196

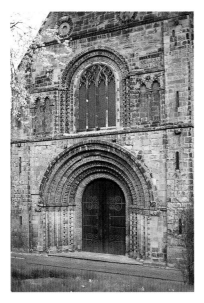

One arch of Tutbury's impressive Norman front is carved in alabaster

Perpendicular stone pulpit a wonderful lion guards the stair.

Behind one of the mellow screens in the S transept is a compelling monument to an admiral by Le Sueur, with a mannered lifesize portrait flanked by sprawling babies, a bronze trio of enigmatic force.

St John, built 1758–76, has lost much of its seemly 18c setting except some fragments to the E. A suburban brick church of the 1930s by **Lavender and Twentyman**, *St Martin*, Dixon Street, Ettingshall, is out of the ordinary in its cliff-like simplicity.

The most interesting church in outer Wolverhampton is **Bernard Miller**'s rebuilding at *St Michael & All Angels*, Church Road, Tettenhall after a devastating fire in 1950.

His design seems to grow out of the surviving tower and the idea of the Gothic original – but a decomposed Gothic, deliberately fractured. The roof, which ends in a row of rustic Tudor gables in the aisles, is a virtuoso performance. The arcade is reduced to huge caps on squat columns which render leaf forms in Art Nouveau curves. Copper lights are the most prominent fitting, and the E window by Cooper-Abbs of Exeter, garish from afar, is well drawn when you look closely – spaceman angels with streamlined hair.

Staffs/W Midlands: 12 miles NW of the centre of Birmingham

Worcester

St Swithun (CCT)

A lovely early 18c town church which straddles various styles.

Within recent memory, Worcester was a very attractive city. Now it holds a certain sinister interest as an exhibit of the damaging effects of cars on urban space. After the road-building programme of the 1960s, traffic makes it the most frightening place of its size in England, at least among old towns. (Guildford might become the great example in the next generation.) But pockets of the real Worcester remain and are worth exploring.

Like old churches in the City of London, *St Swithun's* finds a way of producing a classical effect within the constraints of the medieval street pattern. The W approach is cramped. A vaguely Gothic tower looks out from behind other buildings, not quite on axis. Along its flank, surprising fluted pilasters. In the E it has more space, so there it makes its display, centred on a Venetian window, yet conveying a cranky, almost Elizabethan flavour.

The interior is a haven, with its warren of high pews and shallow, residually Gothic vault, now painted in attractive colours. The pulpit is staggering, with a pelican on top of gorgeous ogee cresting, and a serpent on an anchor, dangling just beneath. The whole construction seems extremely precarious. Built somewhat awkwardly into its base, as if napping there, is the mayor's chair with its sword rest over.

Unfortunately, *All Saints*, Worcester's other fine 18c church, is not opened except for services.

Worcs: 25 miles SW of Birmingham on A38; St Swithun lies E of High Street halfway along

Whitchurch, a classical town church in the local sandstone

North

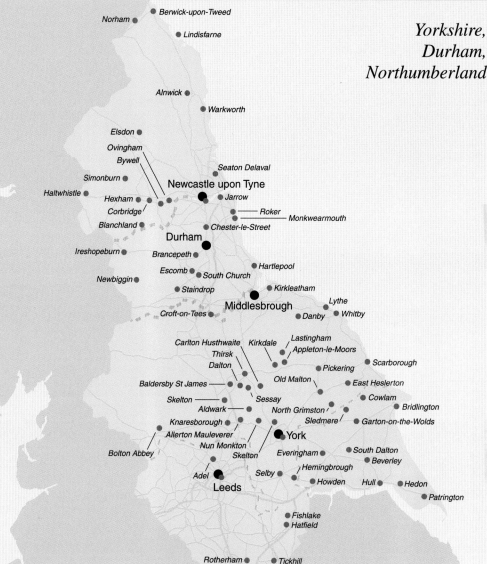

THE MOST SUBLIME hill country in England falls within this region. Moorland – subtle, aloof and inhospitable – exercises a continuing fascination for the southerner or town dweller. *Wuthering Heights* is the archetypal fantasy of human encounter with the uplands. For many, moors require a great shift of view: here the relative weights of man and nature are completely different from elsewhere in England.

Stone walls and low stone buildings form essential parts of this landscape, but significant churches seldom penetrate past its fringes. There are those like Goathland and Bransdale which I might have included just for their relation to moorland, but essentially the grandest landscape and architecture inhabit different spheres.

Of course Yorkshire is more than one county: in the south-eastern corner is flat country of compelling blandness with very great churches.

County Durham is grim. Mining country often lies under a cloud, as if some fundamental grit had worked its way into roads, houses and even trees. It is like that here. Along the coast is some of the most poignant outmoded industry in Britain. Inland we find sylvan enclaves, but cannot easily shake the sense of oppression. It is a place which cries out for its Orwell or its Agee.

Objectively, Northumberland is not great country for churches, but the routes between them are the most perfect in England. Manageable hilliness, few buildings, none of them ugly: modern ills are excluded here.

Adel

St John Baptist

One of the most perfect small Norman churches in England, on the outskirts of Leeds.

The little gabled box is richly supplied with carved detail. On both sides a three-dimensional fringe under the eaves, ending in head-corbels of men and animals. The S porch is of different colour and texture because it was treated with limewash at some point to protect it from weather and pollution, treatment which has hastened its decline. Old pictures show its toothed borders and capitals in much clearer focus than their present blurred state. Compacted in the gable are a number of rectangular carved panels, like a picture gallery, all forming a message which is being washed away.

Inside, a small dark cave, an effect produced by discreet Victorian reinstatement of Norman slit windows. Here the carving is concentrated at the chancel arch, and there is no problem of weathering. Thirty-seven faces follow the arch on the outer side. The capitals are the most original details of all. Facing each other across the opening are two scenes of intense activity, with creatures flying through the air and beasts nosing about, all with wide spaces between. Like much Romanesque imagining it is not really circumstantial depiction but spiritual synopsis or vision.

The 12c S doorhandle shows a beast head swallowing a little human one, and Eric Gill's font cover depicts the Sacraments.

W Yorks: 5½ miles N of centre of Leeds, E of Otley Road (A660) in Church Lane

Aldwark

St Stephen

E. B. Lamb

Six churches by the Victorian rogue architect E. B. Lamb make the region N and W of York the best place in England to study his work. Except for Thirkleby they are intimate buildings, and all the better for that.

Aldwark is the most amazing and shows Lamb, just this once, a forerunner of E. S. Prior in his obsession with textures. It is built of bricks employed like stone – set diagonally in the midst of pebbles and fieldstone, and framed by ashlar dressings which point up the craziness of the rest.

Adel, a well preserved Norman gem

Allerton Mauleverer. Looking west in this strange Vanbrughian hybrid

Internally simpler, but wonderfully unaltered. Over the altar is placed a snowflake rose-window, to each side a smaller baby rose, producing an indescribably unorthodox effect. In the transepts, low bay windows as in a comfy Victorian villa.

None of the other Lamb churches is quite as rugged and creatural, but St Mary, BAGBY (3 miles SE of Thirsk), the simplest, comes nearest. It feels like a central plan onto which an extension, the nave, has been tacked. When you venture into that part, you feel remote and superfluous. Over the central space, roofs rise steeply to a lantern, from paired eyehole windows poked out through mustard-brown stone.

All Saints, THIRKLEBY (4 miles SE of Thirsk), the largest, suggests that Lamb works better on less lavish budgets, saddled with less conventional expectations. His best spaces are low in more than one sense – squat, hugging the ground, and intended for ritual-free worship. Thirkleby follows a longitudinal plan and is most interesting in its excrescences, a baptistry under the tower and a S chapel roofed like a chapter house.

St Andrew, BLUBBERHOUSES (12 miles SE of Skipton), the smallest, in a wild location; very muscular though minute. St Oswald, SOWERBY (a S extension of Thirsk); a major renovation by Lamb. St Paul, HEALEY (14 miles NW of Ripon), another exercise in exaggerated centrality.

N Yorks: Aldwark is 14 miles NW of York, 5 miles W of A19

Allerton Mauleverer

St Martin (CCT)

A fascinating oddity, rebuilt in Vanbrughian style around 1745 and then left unaltered because the local squires, being Catholic, took no interest in it.

Though John Vardy is most likely as its author, the building, and especially its masculine W front with three severe, colliding pediments, is influenced by London Baroque. Aisle windows are a cross between Gothic and classical, and the tower an early instance of Norman revival.

Inside, stylistic bifurcation becomes acute: pointed arcades, but heavy round arches when you step into the aisles. The hammerbeam roof seems to wish it were a segmental vault. All in all, a powerful but inconsistent spatial imagination has been at work.

In E window, entertaining pictorial glass including two views of the church. In the transept are the famous wooden effigies, now strapped down like mental patients.

W Yorks/N Yorks: 5 miles E of Knaresborough, ½ mile E of A1, ½ mile N of A59

Berwick-upon-Tweed. A rare (and dour) church from Cromwell's time

Alnwick

St Michael

A rarity in Northumberland, lavish late Gothic with good fittings.

Alnwick is a pleasant small town whose main street splits to enclose a complicated core containing unexpected courtyards. The church lies isolated at the N end, near the castle with its preposterous skyline of half-lifesize figures on the ramparts.

To N and W of St Michael the ground drops off abruptly. Proportions of the building very satisfying, wide, low and generous.

Inside, the unusual width seems powerfully relaxed, especially in the chancel. Here richly carved ruffles on the columns. The famous Hotspur capital contains crescents, fetterlocks and vines.

In the N arcade, intriguing panels are hollowed on facets of the columns. There are two canopied effigies, a wooden chest with tiered monsters and two mysterious stone figures, antiseptically displayed, a king and a saint stuck with arrows.

Northumb: 18 miles N of Morpeth on A1 which now bypasses town to E

Appleton-le-Moors

Christ Church

The village is a classic example of a one-street settlement, which feels eighteenth century in its clarity, but is in fact medieval.

A surprise to find an elaborate early work of **J. L. Pearson** in this isolated spot. Its steep stone spire is visible from far out on the moors. A rose window fills the entrance gable, under it an unexpected lean-to porch, apsed at both ends.

Inside, multicoloured stonework in four different shades, all natural and local, we are told, except for the maroon of Clayton and Bell's sgraffito scenes covering the apse and the pulpit. Pevsner finds the arcade supports overcomplicated; columns are hedged with four smaller ones at the corners and four small capitals jostle the larger one stuck within. Under the wooden roof runs a peculiar cornice like interlaced heating pipes.

The richest feature lies in the NE corner, a chapel reached through pierced openings that was meant to hold the donor's tomb, judging by the nautical

Alnwick. Long and low late Gothic at the edge of a large churchyard

themes. He was a shipowner who made a fortune in guano and built the villa (latterly a hotel) across the road. Even outside, this chapel abounds in quirky details. The frame of its little rose window rises to form a pointed arch and the drain spout next to it is kept in place by a stone moulding which bulges out to hem it in.

N Yorks: 2 miles N of A170 between Kirkbymoorside and Pickering, on minor road. The turning (2 miles E of Kirkbymoorside) is marked but difficult to notice. Church lies at N end of village on R.

Baldersby St James

St James

William Butterfield

A large Butterfield church in a Butterfield village.

Introduced by a powerful double lychgate roofed like the church in harsh red tile. In fact the whole exterior is grim, the interior much better.

Walls and arcades striped pink and white; roofs amusingly different in nave and chancel. Aisle windows segregate the sexes, as was the actual practice in some High Church congregations in Butterfield's time. Here women saints are on the N and men on the S.

The best fittings are a huge wooden clock, depicted as a wafer-thin building high on the wall above the arcade, a peaked font cover, and an ironwork corona in the chancel. The alabaster reredos must be Butterfield as well. He also designed vicarage, school, and many surrounding cottages.

The house just W of the church is a prime instance of Butterfield's irregular vernacular, with stairs displayed externally, windows pushing into roofs toward dormer-status and lively piebald mixing of materials.

N Yorks: about 5 miles NE of Ripon, to E of A61 (1½ miles SE of Baldersby village)

Berwick-upon-Tweed

Holy Trinity

One of the most exciting towns in England has a curious Cromwellian church which lies just within the Elizabethan ramparts and across from the early 18c barracks.

Exceedingly few churches were built in this period; rarity is part of this building's

Baldersby St James. Butterfield designed every detail of the interior and most of the nearby buildings

appeal. The outside is better than the inside; side elevations are positively peppered with triple windows – half with roundheaded central lights, like elongated parodies of Venetian windows.

The end, with its corner turrets, is engagingly awkward, like an upside-down table. The grey stone interior is soberer, with files of Tuscan columns and a huge lateral arch from which the N transept/vestry leads off.

Behind the altar a reredos by Lutyens like Arts and Crafts gone classical and, in the W, a gallery like Jacobean gone tame. Victorian coloured glass creates appalling confusion in this interior and you look in vain for the military tombs which centuries spent guarding the Scottish border should have left behind.

Berwick is bracingly grim, and its star-like set of 16c bastions makes it one of the

few places in Europe where that particular human folly can be studied so well.

Northumb: on E coast just S of Scottish border; A1 now bypasses town

Beverley

St Mary; The Minster (St John Evangelist & St Martin)

The two great churches of Beverley, at opposite ends of the town, make a satisfying contrast. St Mary's is mellow Perpendicular, soft and comfortable in outline. The Minster is larger and colder, of harsh but fascinating intricacy. It ranges from Early English (in the E) to Perpendicular (in the W).

Beverley is a modest-sized place with a lovely 18c market cross and one of the

Beverley Minster. On cathedral scale, with the most gorgeous of all High Gothic tombs

best old pubs in England, near St Mary's and formerly owned by the church. Its old wooden horse emblem has been replaced by a fibreglass copy.

St Mary's is wonderful from every side, its crumbly stonework a lovely pale colour. The silhouette reminds one of Henry Wilson at his best: a compensating bulge like entasis prevents any sensation of gauntness or excessive height in the central tower. Openwork turrets which frame the W front are of different sizes, as are two solid ones at the far end. Flying buttresses make a fine pierced effect. Varied cresting along the skyline, and complex fringes around the main doors.

Inside, painted ceilings are a notable feature, especially the series of sword-waving kings in the chancel. The colours are of course renewed, but original ones may be seen in priest's rooms over St Michael's Chapel, which has a beautiful vault and flowing tracery. The font is a lovely slice of grey marble.

The Minster at S end of town is announced by two W towers of jagged thinness. The entire W front is a study in

flatness, panelled all over, and lower down giving great occupation to Victorian sculptors. In the gable here and in S door, Hawksmoor may have had a hand. We know he was consulted, 1716–20.

Very high, grand interior. Much grotesque carving at eye level on aisle walls. The musicians here are legendary and have been explained by the Musicians' Guild being headquartered in Beverley. They are a severe test of one's tolerance of caricature and distortion.

The chancel is one of the world's great riots of Purbeck marble shafting. Its builders revelled in dead ends and abrupt terminations. Here on N is the famous Percy tomb, one of the richest bits of Decorated carving in England. The profusion of jutting and dangling heads will again test one's appetite for excess. Fourteenth-century wooden sedilia opposite, and Victorian screen adjacent, take their cue from the tomb. The screen is like dry flames searing anguished leaves.

The 16c stalls and misericords are famous but very few of the latter are

shown and it is too dark to see them. The 18c font cover is more accessible and a marvel of Baroque furls.

E Yorks: 8 miles NW of Hull on A164; St Mary near N end of central spine, Minster at S end

Blanchland

Abbey (St Mary Virgin)

A marvellously isolated place, named after the white monks, remnants of whose abbey went to make up the present church and village.

Tower, transept and choir survive from the medieval building, largely re-windowed in the 18c and re-roofed in the 19c. The result is an uncanny L-shaped space which you have no sooner entered than you must change direction. The high tower arch is magnificent, but otherwise the building has been agreeably de-characterized and domesticated by reconstruction. Interesting tomb slabs in the floor.

The village, which can be entered through the monkish gateway, disposes itself around an L-shaped piazza. Though houses follow the lines of the monastic complex, they are 18c in detail, except for bits of Gothic ribbing and leafage set ornamentally into their façades.

Best view of village from a bridge over the stream to S, along whose banks enchanting walks. This stream is the boundary with County Durham, and just the other side lies a modest Victorian curiosity, St James, HUNSTANWORTH, rebuilt by **S. S. Teulon** in 1862–3. Teulon also provided a vicarage, school and cottages.

Northumb: 10 miles S of Hexham on B6306

Bolton Abbey

Priory Church of St Mary

This priory fragment, memorable for its setting, provoked a rhapsody from Ruskin and inspired Romantic paintings.

The Wharfe runs dreamily behind the ruined chancel.* Over it, trees nod atop a miniature cliff. It feels like nature coaxed towards art, or country crossed with a landscape garden.

Within the base of a tower left incomplete at the Dissolution is the earlier W front, of stone originally pink or reddened by fire. Noble lancets tower over those squeezed-up motifs common in compositions of the period. A smaller, more pinched version of such a portal around the corner at the end of N aisle.

Inside, a stirring row of double lancets in deep embrasures. Good Norman blind arcades and tomb recesses in the ruins, where sheep no longer stray.

* A spokesman for the Priory calls the Wharfe a 'swift and turbulent river, sometimes dangerous and always unpredictable'. Ruskin depicts it 'stealing … eddying … and gliding calm and deep'.

W Yorks/N Yorks: 6 miles E of Skipton on B6160; church below road to E

Brancepeth

St Brandon

Seventeenth-century porch and woodwork made this one of the richest churches in the county before a devastating fire in 1998.

John Cosin, later Bishop of Durham, was rector here from 1626 to 1640. He embellished the largish medieval church with fittings that were a surprising blend of retrograde Jacobean and very early Gothic Revival. Both styles tend to elaboration and insubstantiality. They harmonized extremely well.

The N porch is a wonderful bit of Renaissance stonework thickly pilastered. It formerly had three pointed entrances. Inside the church, a forest of dark woodwork (completely consumed in the fire) and a great deal of welcome light pouring in from the Perp clerestory. The pulpit was the most astonishing piece:

Blanchland. L-shaped fragment of an abbey of which the village contains more echoes

countless scrolls, knobs and lacy pinnacles stacked precariously. Near it stood rich pews with rusticated bases and lots of tiny gables waist high. Behind it was an even more fanciful construction, the chancel screen, partly inspired by the stone reredos in Durham Cathedral, but also looking like a series of stall canopies without the stalls. All in all, this was the most exciting instance of an early historicist mentality. There were also a lavish font cover and assorted frilly tablets on the walls.

Restoration has uncovered interesting fragments of medieval wall painting. In the new windows intricate leading frames clear glass.

Brancepeth lies in a little leafy and salubrious pocket of what is not generally a pretty part of the county. Next door to the church is a grandiose vision of a castle, a huge ruin perfected by rebuilding in the 19c.

Durham: 4 miles SW of Durham, just E of A690

Bridlington

Priory Church

A large priory church in a seaside town.

Bridlington is a place of mixed character; the charming old town sits apart from the friendly, seedy seafront with its donkey rides and Victorian hotels. Likewise the church is quite a mixed bag externally. Its proudest feature from afar is Victorian, the SW tower bristling with protuberant

Bolton Abbey, an abbey fragment in a memorable landscape

pinnacles. Peeking out from under Sir G. G. Scott's restoration of the W front are intriguing ruined doorways and a great Perp window which, close inspection will show, inhabits two different planes.

The N side has the earliest traces, including lancets in original frames, a gorgeous porch (only the inside original, in silver grey stone) and entertaining fleurons on the buttresses.

Inside, at first it makes a noble and consistent impression, but the two elevations are very different: complex early Gothic tracery on the L and a late galleried effect on the R. The E end is visibly and mysteriously canted.

In the N aisle, wonderful fragments of the Romanesque cloister. On a three-bay section leafage follows the arches. Inside the openings of a two-bay section is deep zigzag, resulting in a lively fractured look.

In the S aisle, a bizarre black marble slab, 12c, carved with menacing animals. Its meaning is obscure.

E Yorks: 18 miles SE of Scarborough on A165; Priory is about 1 mile NW of present centre, on E edge of the Old Town

Bywell. St Peter is one of two churches in this tranquil place

Bywell

St Andrew (CCT)
St Peter

Bywell, so sylvan in its lovely position beside the Tyne that the village hardly seems to be there, has two venerable churches in sight of each other.

St Andrew's Saxon tower has rich openings at the top. Its N wall has been covered in old tombstones and there is an interesting niche over the transept door.

The Victorian windows are entertaining in this part, as is the low brass altar rail. Multiple transepts in such a small building make for complex spaces. Interesting Saxon stone in the chancel.

St Peter, by the river, has a lovely Early English end whose lancets fill the space. This chancel gives the small interior a kind of impressiveness. The N aisle, a simple box with squareheaded windows, is strangely attractive, and the churchyard is delightful.

Northumb: 14 miles W of Newcastle, S of B6309 on N bank of Tyne

Carlton Husthwaite

St Mary

This little ironstone building with highlights in limestone, sitting at the top of a sloping green shaded by a large horse chestnut, contains a complete ensemble of 17c furnishings.

Square window frames have would-be ogee-headed lights inscribed in them. The E window goes further in cramming two mind-sets together. Here Gothic trefoils are subsumed by a classic arch with a little keystone. Inside, the original fittings are intact under a flat ceiling divided by dark beams supported on simple brackets. The pulpit, not the altar, is the focus of the space. It is dated 1678 and imitates the frilliness of Gothic canopies in a new and unfamiliar formal vocabulary. Behind the preacher's head the words 'Feed my Lambes' seem poignant in a farming community. The N wall, against which the pulpit stands, is windowless, for no visible reason except to increase concentration. The old pews are

Carlton Husthwaite. A calm 17c building on a village green with memorable trees

decorated with a forest of knobs, rudimentary products of the lathe, and the altar rail passes very near the altar, making a narrow pen across the E end.

N Yorks: 1 mile E of A19 midway between Thirsk and Easingwold; church in centre of village on N side of road

Chester-le-Street

St Mary & St Cuthbert

A church built in the centre of a Roman fort which contains several curiosities: the best preserved anchorite's cell in the country and a bizarre row of fourteen effigies comprising a mostly bogus family history.

The site is venerable: here Cuthbert's body spent more than a century before it was finally moved to Durham, but the church now lies among parking lots at the back of the High Street. Its W front is made attractively lopsided by rooms added to the Anker House when it became almshouses after the Dissolution. The tower rises above the W door and turns from square to octagonal to meet the spire.

A dark and atmospheric interior, with arcades which lean outward. In the chancel, good woodwork and curious historicist paintings. But the most astonishing feature is the Lumley tombs, some of them plundered from distant graveyards and the majority Elizabethan fakes. The westernmost effigy has his head in a tunnel. Many have had to lose their feet to fit in. This freight train of ancestors doubles up at both ends.

The Anker House became a museum in 1987 and contains an interesting collection of Roman and Saxon fragments. The really telling feature of this narrow dwelling is the squint which gave the anchorite his or her only view of the outside world. It shows a tiny sliver of reality – the altar in S chapel, and not much else.

Durham: 6 miles N of Durham on A167; church lies E of High Street in the centre

Corbridge

St Andrew

A very special small town whose church contains Saxon and early Gothic traces of considerable interest.

The churchyard connects the main public spaces of this intricate settlement. In one corner is the fortified vicarage, a

A re-erected Roman arch leads into the Saxon tower at Corbridge

miniature tower-house built of Roman masonry in the 14c and one of the best preserved in the county. It now functions as the tourist office.

Saxon remains are most evident on the W side of the church tower, Early English ones in the chancel, especially the trilobe priest's door. This is a building more interesting within. The space under the tower is the Saxon porch, and the opening into the nave is a re-erected Roman arch.

At the other end, chancel lancets have rugged cusping at the tops, a satisfying complication. A lean-to aisle on N transept, not matched on the S, gives a pleasant sense of the building breaking its bounds and opening out.

Northumb: 3½ miles E of Hexham just S of A69

Cowlam

St Mary

Very close together in the Yorkshire Wolds, four exceptional pieces of Romanesque carving survive in village fonts.

There is no longer a village at Cowlam, only a large farm in whose

East Heslerton. One of a series of Street churches in the Yorkshire Wolds

yard the church sits, rebuilt in 1852 when the population had already disappeared. It is a charming miniature building equipped with its own little iron fence and jostled behind by Nissen huts. Inside it retains homely wooden fittings.

The font sits in the corner under a window, its surface filled with large figures. Mary and Christ, regal in crowns and elaborate clothes, receive a gift from one of the Kings. The next King waits too far behind to take part. Beyond this an enthroned ruler guarded by a man with a dagger, Adam and Eve with the serpent in the tree, a pair of wrestlers and one of those bishops who often turn up in these settings.

Within a couple of miles of Cowlam, and reachable by a path through dry valleys, is the site of *Cottam* from which the font now at Langtoft originally comes. Cottam is an important deserted village site. The font, only moved to LANGTOFT (5 miles further E on B1249, S of B1253) c1950, repeats some of Cowlam's subjects in cruder, more ravaged form: Adam and Eve with large figleafs like doilies, an abbreviated dragon who swallows a saint, Andrew being crucified, another dragon.

The final font, the most primitive and confusing, is at KIRKBURN (10 miles S of Langtoft, SW of Driffield on A614, village and church N of road). Here two tiers of carving don't seem to have much

thematic connection. Above are Christ performing a baptism by pushing someone's head into a tube, Peter running to catch hold of keys almost as big as he is, another bishop with a flowering staff and lots of hangers-on. Below, diverse animals including a cat with a mouse.

The format of all these works adds greatly to the mystery. We are always chasing the subjects over the edge of our field of vision and in the tumult something escapes us.

E Yorks: Cowlam church lies halfway between Malton and Bridlington ½ mile S of B1253 in farmyard of Church Farm

Croft-on-Tees

St Peter

For devotees of mellowness and rich stone textures, this is one of the best parish churches in England.

Yet it isn't at all grand. The tower, of an alien grey, has sunk itself in the fabric and does not seek to rise above it. Next to it, a S porch spreads itself gracefully. Like the rest, it is a mixture of yellow and red stone. The decorative culmination comes in the E, where the corners are marked by rich ruined niches.

Inside, a preposterous private pew like several theatre boxes blocks the nave. It is raised on high stilts and has a twisting

ceremonial stair on which three people could easily pass abreast. Wedged half underneath it, a gargantuan tomb in black, white and grey marble, with lion heads at the corners. This has its own railed precinct, within which is kept one of the most refined of all Saxon fragments.

The highlight of the interior, though not the most conspicuous feature, is rowdy carving in the chancel which Pevsner despises. Fact and fiction, large and small, monstrosity and normality are jumbled together here. Every fibre of the greyish stone is instinct with life, enough to make one adopt Ruskin's dream-vision of medieval workmen.

Bryon sat in the pompous pew, and we can imagine Lewis Carroll lingering over the carved beasts; his father was rector here and is buried in the churchyard which runs down to the river.

N Yorks: 3 miles S of Darlington on A167; church on W bank, N of road

Dalton

St John Evangelist

William Butterfield

One of three village churches by Butterfield within short distances of each other S of Thirsk.

Dalton, built in 1868, is the least promising externally but very rewarding within. It stands out baldly but insignificantly along the road, low and mouse-grey. Interest is concentrated at the ends – on the E a buttress pushes up between lancet windows, forcing a lobed vesica into the space above; on the W a large window carved into the centre of the little towerlet takes one's breath away by its freakish boldness.

Inside, the richness of brick mixed with stone is unexpected and becomes more mottled and irregular the further up you go. The chancel screen looks like something from a medieval hall with odd punctures and half timber effects. The Dutch gable shape of the roof, not signalled externally, also feels more domestic than ecclesiastical. Toward the apex it becomes a thicket of scissor beams.

Reredos and altar are too rich and dark to be easily deciphered, lit by Morris glass with rich blue backgrounds. In fact every window in the church contains Morris glass, much of pleasing simplicity, single figures against white surrounds in the aisles for instance. Further fittings like a bass chandelier in the chancel and a small but powerful font like an upended capital complete this perfect Victorian interior.

2 miles W in TOPCLIFFE church is found Burne-Jones' earliest stained glass in a S chancel window of three big lights. The colours are so lurid and the surrounding decorative borders (not by Burne-Jones) are so powerful that his characteristic figures and plants are largely swamped.

N Yorks: 2 miles E of A168 between Thirsk and Ripon; church at E end of village N of road

William Morris glass of pleasing simplicity in the aisle at richly furnished Dalton

Danby

St Hilda

The church is isolated in a moorland dale far from the village, which postdates it, having appeared only with the railway. The dead outnumber the living in Danby Dale: on surrounding slopes infrequent farms, but immediately around the church a dense thicket of tombstones among vase-like yews.

The church is large and appropriately rustic, a stone box Gothick at the edges, to whose side is attached a more venerable Perpendicular tower in simple country style. A bulky stone stair climbs the outside of the building to the gallery.

Inside we find a surprisingly elegant Gothic arcade of tall yellowy brown pillars, a re-medievalizing by Temple Moore of 1903. The chancel is conventional Victorian Gothic, some say by Butterfield. All the large nave windows but one are filled with clear glass, giving glimpses of the hills. On one sill is a book with biographies of local boys and men dead in the Great War. Danby is the setting for John Atkinson's *Forty Years in a Moorland Parish* of 1891, which describes a way of life rich in habit and haunted by superstition.

N Yorks: about 15 miles due W of Whitby, in obscure location halfway down Danby Dale, 3 miles S of Castleton

East Heslerton

St Andrew (CCT)

G. E. Street

The six small churches G. E. Street built in this part of the East Riding form one of the most interesting Victorian projects in the country. The patron was Sir Tatton Sykes, who instead of opting for magnificence wanted every village to be supplied. The churches constitute an alphabet of ecclesiastical forms. The ideal way to see them would be in two or three batches, returning to one's favourites for purposes of comparison.

East Heslerton is small and rudimentary, but bursting with different motifs and showing his ingenuity at full stretch. In fact it is a question whether all the interesting parts really make one whole.

The tower sports a series of angles and interruptions before culminating in the spire. The most entertaining is four largish statues set diagonally near the top. They were originally carved for Bristol Cathedral, a much bigger building. The lean-to W porch seems an unchurchy feature. It is supported by two large polished columns. Inside, the initial impression is not exciting: no aisles, no evident spatial complexity. Unfortunately the organ fills the tower space, blocking three of the best windows. The view back, to the file of lancets over the W door, is perhaps the best. Two wonderful iron screens, complicated in chancel, simple in baptistry.

Across the road is Street's brick vicarage, a bed and breakfast within recent memory. Immediately W of the church an ambitious garden surrounds a bungalow.

Street's other churches are at HOWSHAM, THIXENDALE, FIMBER, KIRBY GRINDALYTHE, WEST LUTTON, HELPERTHORPE and WANSFORD.

Fimber is the smallest, announced by a lively lychgate and tower. Aisleless interior, with a metal screen as good behind as on its more glittery front.

Thixendale is the most remote. Just W of the village the road runs along the bottom of a twisting dry valley. Further variations here on screen and lychgate, quasi-architectural forms which particularly engage this architect. Street's vicarage next door now sports PVC windowframes, and his school is equipped with Velux rooflights, but its roofs remain entertaining from the W.

E Yorks/N Yorks: East Heslerton is 9 miles E of Malton on A64, village S of road

Elsdon, a rugged church in an isolated Northumbrian village

Escomb, one of the most intact and atmospheric of Saxon churches

Elsdon

St Cuthbert

A charming rustic building in a wonderfully isolated position.

Although there's little of it, Elsdon village still feels like a real centre, with its wide green and surprising castle mound. The fortified priest's house to the N is one of the best examples of the type.

Elsdon's bellcote is a less monumental composition than the one at nearby Ford, but sports an entertaining set of 17c finials. Inside, characterful arcades run so near the walls that passages not aisles are left. Amazingly in so small a building, transepts are aisled too. Good humble windows and a set of sedilia like small ovens.

The churchyard is full of interesting stones including a large pedimented memorial built into the S wall. Like certain places in Scotland, Elsdon seems to keep the flame of civilization alive and the surrounding moors at bay.

Northumb: about 12 miles SW of Rothbury on B6341; church N of road

Escomb

St John Evangelist

One of the best preserved, most atmospheric Saxon buildings in England.

Like most of the others, it is a modest structure. Like theirs, its present setting is problematic. It sits asymmetrically in an ovoid churchyard, surrounded by a circle of grey council houses. But this contrast between shabby newness and stern antiquity casts a powerful spell.

A rustic porch was added to the S and an outshot to the W, matching the chancel, was removed, leaving a two-celled building tall and thin like a German Expressionist film set. The old stone is magically black, many pieces bearing chiselled diamond broaching left by Roman masons. High up is ensconced a sundial held within the grip of a beast, in stone of an utterly different colour.

Two tiny Saxon windows remain in each side wall, while on the S a peppering of larger 17 and 18c openings admit welcome light to the interior and make the heavy fabric transparent. Beyond the high, eared chancel arch is a

beautiful little carving of a cross between sun and moon.

Durham: just NW of Bishop Auckland in a cul-de-sac running N of B6282 towards the River Wear

Everingham

St Mary & St Everilda (RC)

One of the most astonishing early Catholic churches in England, built in the 1830s by the local lord.

There is nothing English about it. Craftsmen and probably architect too were Italian. Perhaps it has been improved by demolition of the bell tower and the passageway linking it to the house. At least it has been made more independent: it appears a practically windowless solid, the patchy rendering relieved only by caryatids stranded high on two symmetrical W vestibules.

Blankness outside, richness within. Large Corinthian columns of yellow scagliola line the aisles under a lavishly coffered tunnel vault. Between the columns, Apostles in niches. Over these are placed good reliefs of Christ's life, culminating in the Passion high on the curve of the apse. Here the light, elsewhere stingily meted out, floods generously in.

One believes in the founder's fervour, yet sees it issue only in cool magnificence, yellow, gold, grey and white.

Sadly now redundant, with an uncooperative owner who discourages visits.

E Yorks: 5 miles W of Market Weighton; church S of village in grounds of Everingham Park

Fishlake

St Cuthbert

Exceptional Norman carving in one of the most pleasing small churches in the county.

Fishlake is wonderfully unrestored and mouldery. At the time of the first edition of this book someone was growing pale and straggly house plants in the lamp holders along the arcade. The feeling in this building is indescribably pleasant, and the tiny village seems insulated in its fenny fastness from the present age.

The S door is quite fabulous, with broad arches and plump rolls of carving. Animals, pairs of figures and, towards the springing, angels fighting dragons who look like 18c women wielding hayrakes.

The arcade is simple, but much variety in window tracery behind it. One of the most vigorous of all medieval tombs in the chancel, with much Gothic lettering, Passion signs and grapevine borders. Near the door, a cutout (1908) of the Lord's Prayer like a Victorian advert.

On the tower the mitred figure carrying a crowned head in his hand is Cuthbert with King Oswald's head. The two of them are preserved as relics in just these proportions at Durham Cathedral. Before he came to rest there, Cuthbert's corpse was carried around ahead of the advancing Danes, and Fishlake was the southernmost point in its travels.

W Yorks/S Yorks: 7 miles NE of Doncaster, directly N of Hatfield

Garton-on-the-Wolds

St Michael

One of the most elaborate of all Victorian decorative schemes survives complete in this out of the way spot.

The church sits above the village looking onto a vast landscape. It is a powerful Norman building whose tower resembles a Northern fortified house. Pearson rebuilt the chancel, and then Street was brought in to equip and decorate the space, creating a dazzling cover for all the simple surfaces Pearson and the early Middle Ages had left. Street designed a bristling screen and other furniture, and Clayton and Bell covered the high narrow space in tapestry-like narratives which are unusually easy to read. As learned Victorians were wont to do, they show Biblical scenes like the meeting of Joseph and his brothers in Egypt taking place in Gothic interiors. Among other highlights are Mary as Queen of Heaven on the south chancel wall and an Art Nouveau ocean near the entrance.

The multicoloured roof is matched by strong mosaic patterns on the floor. Under the tower a set of original cartoons for the labours of the months is exhibited, which hung a century and more in the local school.

E Yorks: 2 miles W of Driffield on A166; church S of road

Haltwhistle

Holy Cross

Unusually complete Early English survivals and fine early Morris glass.

Holy Cross has no tower, and so is hard to find among the houses. In fact

Romanesque south doorway at Fishlake

the churchyard is relatively large and nicely hemmed in. Though stone textures are good and repeated lancets in the chancel satisfying, the exterior is more modest and nondescript than the interior, where one is struck by an impressive consistency and purity.

Aisle windows have been renewed and pleasing Kempe patterns applied to the chancel roof. These in aisle too, until a vicar in the 1940s whited them out. But otherwise all is tranquil early Gothic with wide splay windows, stepped sedilia and handsome arcades.

The Morris glass fills the E lancets with a Crucifixion on a white background and exquisite small scenes. When I admired this, the vicar observed that the Pre-Raphaelites 'weren't Christian', a thought-provoking view.

Against the W wall is a venerable lump of stone on a Roman column. The font bristles with barbaric thistles, fleurs-de-lys and suchlike, of the 17c.

Northumb: 22 miles E of Carlisle on A69; church lies in centre, S of Main Street, reliably open 4 hours per week

Hartlepool

St Hilda

One of the most exciting churches in the county, for its scale and fineness, and its situation.

After an extensive industrial wasteland you come onto a little peninsula which is the old core of Hartlepool and now seems entirely covered in modest terrace houses. The sea is visible in several directions, and these humble streets precipitate you abruptly towards it.

St Hilda sits in a vast barren rectangle of graveyard. At some point its tower received elephantine buttresses, unpierced, mountainous. Certain details shine through – a gorgeous Early English clerestory above all – but there is something fortress-like and forbidding about the exterior.

Inside, wonderful colours and textures in the grand arcade which is dappled in different stones, with beautiful mouldings in the aisles.

There's a lovely 18c font cover, but essentially it's the unitary effect of all that well-ordered space, completed by a chancel mainly Victorian.

In WEST HARTLEPOOL one of **E. B. Lamb**'s largest churches, Christ Church, Church Square (1850), formerly standing derelict on its island site, has become the

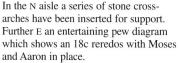

town museum. The clotted E end is the best aspect. Internally, rich only in the shallow apse, but there are many interesting intersections between the building and its new use, around the café in the N transept for instance.

Durham/Clev: about 12 miles N of Middlesbrough on E coast; St Hilda near the tip of the peninsula – follow signs to Headland

Hatfield

St Lawrence

Best from outside: vast and of lovely proportions under its grand central tower.

Inside, the tower arches are magnificent and out of scale with anything else nearby.

In the N aisle a series of stone cross-arches have been inserted for support. Further E an entertaining pew diagram which shows an 18c reredos with Moses and Aaron in place.

Much tasteful clear glass and black light fittings, and in the W a lively Victorian window on the theme of children in the Old Testament. An elaborate Millennium window in N includes a picture of an early WC. In S transept a very curious cartilaginous monument, real folk art.

In the end, you'll probably go back outdoors to contemplate this transept jutting out under the tower, a very satisfying consonance.

W Yorks/S Yorks: 7 miles NE of Doncaster on A18; church N of road

Hedon

St Augustine

Another of the grand churches of the East Riding.

An overpowering late Gothic central tower sits astride a very ambitious Early English transepted church. Although the church is large, the tower suggests something grander still. Perhaps the rest of the building seems a little rough beside its perfection.

There is beautiful early ornament in the N side particularly, which faces a pleasant green, as if this had at some point been a monastic complex on the edge of town.

In the S transept is a peculiar doorway with sparse beaks clasping a moulding, so that the frame looks like a loosely laced-up shoe.

The font at Hedon is the loveliest example of an East Riding type, which takes a complex geometrical solid and eats away at some parts while encrusting others with bubbling leafage. Here the bowl form is dissected and elaborated. Each of the panels is filled differently, according to no discernible logic; a ragged cross is perhaps the most diverting.

E Yorks: 5 miles W of Hull on A1033; church near NW edge of town

Hemingbrough

St Mary the Virgin

Famous for its grotesquely elongated spire, which looks like a dangerous thorn or piercing mechanism from afar.

This is a very ambitious church in attractive white stone. The transepts are the grandest and most interesting feature, and were presumably the last element built. In the S, the huge window which fills the wall breaks the cornice of the almost flat roof. The near-collision of two boundaries – the gentle slope of the window and the imperceptible peak of the roof – is extremely satisfying.

Inside, a bit empty, with some notable wooden survivals. The oldest is a single Romanesque misericord, a clean and timeless design. Some Renaissance bench ends have been mounted behind glass in S chapel. Lastly, a forlorn but interesting piece of Elizabethan screen leans against the wall.

E Yorks/N Yorks: about 5 miles SE of Selby on A63; village S of road, church on village's W edge

Hemingbrough, with its ambitious late Gothic proportions and astonishing stone spire

Hexham

Abbey (St Andrew)

One of the largest churches in the county – containing wonderful relics of early Christianity – which has suffered some chilling Victorianizations.

Wilfrid's chair sits in the middle of the chancel. It is a lump of stone polished dark grey by the touch of hands. It dates from the 7c and was probably a bishop's throne. A large fragment linked with Acca, Wilfrid's successor, by Collingwood* stands in S transept, a tall Saxon cross with grape patterns of almost Art Nouveau sophistication. Here also a large Roman tombstone showing a mounted standard-bearer riding over an abject local warrior.

The transepts are marvellous Early English. Down almost the whole length of S transept comes a wide night stair, the most impressive and eccentric architectural feature of the building.

Under the present nave a 7c crypt with two ancient entrance passages, whose stairs are heroic Roman blocks and whose walls are freely larded with Roman cornices and ornament in no special order.

In N chancel a strange 15c chantry decorated with savage carving including a free-standing figure with a club. The effigy is remarkable but not viewable except on request. Nearby, many Saxon fragments. Though the nave was added (in 1907–8) by a good architect, Temple Moore, it seems rather bleak. The medieval nave had been abandoned shortly after the Dissolution.

* W. G. Collingwood, disciple and biographer of Ruskin who later became an authority on the Northern crosses. He made meticulous drawings of practically every one which remain valuable aids to interpretation.

Northumb: 20 miles W of Newcastle on A69, which bypasses town to N

Hexham, noble Early English proportions of the N transept

Howden

St Peter & St Paul

One of the most astonishing parish churches in England; its scale takes one's breath away. The fact that Howden is half ruined only seems to increase its power.

Ruin spreads from the church to its surroundings. There is a lovely but desolate little square to the W. Its charming hotel was up for sale at the time of the first edition. This tiny market town is one of the most atmospheric in England. Like Bruges at the turn of the century, it seems a place around which legends might be spun.

The church's most striking feature is an awesome tower with bell stage over endless windows. The derelict E end is lavish to the point of decadence. Up to the arched top of the empty E window a series of open niches climbs in steps. At the peak a belfry like another image frame. It would be at home in Venice.

The octagonal chapter house is an equally luxuriant piece of design. All these parts are now in English Heritage care, but fortunately tidying hasn't gone too far. Still, this place could easily be spoiled by a repairer's zeal.

After the magical exterior, some letdown in the huge, dank interior. Modern roofs kill the space to a degree, but there is also the unpleasant way the arcade comes within inches of clerestory windows. In the little gaol for tombs to the SE is a foppish double effigy of 14c date. It would be easier to accept as 19c medievalizing fantasy.

E Yorks: 10 miles SE of Selby on A63

Remnants of the monastery at Jarrow associated with Bede

Hull

Holy Trinity

Magnificent mainly Perpendicular town church which may be the largest in England.

Its wonderful silhouette rises from a vast stone platform. Here the mass is powerful enough to dominate a considerable blank surrounding space. Transepts and chancels are, surprisingly, brick – probably the earliest such use of the material in the country.

The central tower is a masterful piece of design, remarkably unheavy. It seems pure articulation with little mass. Bell openings merge imperceptibly with an open parapet. Corner buttresses express the corner without decorative emphasis.

The W elevation should have prepared one for a glasshouse effect inside, for there are three wall-filling windows. It seems a rational space. The amount of light continues to surprise and please. There are some Op art patterns on chancel ceilings and a couple of lurid, almost Art Nouveau windows in S aisle and S transept. These turn out to be designs by Walter Crane and are among the most richly coloured works of their period. There is also a Whall window further E.

Monuments here are more curious than beautiful. An organist is commemorated by an organ in relief, and the man who brought a good water supply to Hull by a crude diorama of Moses striking the rock.

E Yorks: on N bank of Humber near its mouth, 37 miles SE of York; church is just N of A63, E of present centre

Jarrow

St Paul

Bede spent most of his life in a monastery here, a place presently so

Gibbs' powerful Baroque mausoleum upstages the classical church at Kirkleatham

desolate it doesn't even qualify as industrial wasteland.

At first it seems a site from which life has fled, but inside this building there has been a miraculous resurrection. Much of the Saxon original does not survive: there were two churches and the W one became ruinous and was demolished in 1782. So at first one is met by bogus elements: a well-meaning conversion of the graveyard to a little park and the Victorian nave which prefaces the Norman tower space and Saxon chancel. Even there you are in the land of relics, and must sift the genuine from the fantastic. 'Bede's chair', for example, is centuries too new for him to have sat in, but we have a picture of him studiously writing which it reinforces.

Modern works commemorate the great past – a Piper window like a child's drawing and a lifesize Bede carved from a twisted stump. But there are tiny Saxon windows, one filled with some of the oldest stained glass in Europe. An even better coloured window, with a figure in a blue robe, is shown, together with cross fragments and paintings and models of the monastery as it was, in the large new museum and visitor centre a few hundred yards N of the church.

In the nave, heaps of carved fragments formerly embedded in walls of N porch. They include wonderful interlace and curious balusters which may have formed part of a screen. Now they are all presented 'as in a mason's yard', one of the strangest displays ever. But whatever one's quibbles, the spirit now abroad in St Paul's among its elderly stewards is of infectious enthusiasm and good humour.

Outside, remains of the Norman monastery. A stilted Saxon portal or two remain. One of the strangest sights in the world is the vista of pylons framed in these arches. To the E lies the Jarrow Slake, an eerie tidal mudflat.

Durham/T&W: about 6 miles E of Newcastle on A19, near S entrance to Tyne Tunnel and less than ½ mile E

Kirkdale

St Gregory

Secluded position in a miniature valley whose stream is crossed by a ford. The church looks like a rustic chapel because of later additions in local vernacular, consisting of a small tower and a large porch, but it contains traces of great antiquity.

Its pre-Conquest masonry is best seen in the W wall with its huge Saxon quoins (outside) and its narrow entrance arch (inside). In the porch is set a famous sundial no longer reached by the sun, which names the carver, the priest, the rebuilder, the local earl and the king in its Old English inscription. Still embedded in the walls are stones from even earlier versions of the building; disinterred from the fabric and displayed in the N aisle are two beautiful half erased tombstones, eighth and ninth centuries, one a subtle pattern of laced circles, the other a spidery cross. The interior, though a compost of assorted centuries, makes a harmonious impression, arising in part from the easy way the airy arcade of 1200 extends the space. The rambling graveyard to the S contains quirky memorial words for Herbert Read, the art critic, whose autobiography mentions visits to this church. Nearby to E lies a cave where important bones of many extinct animals were found in 1821.

N Yorks: N of A170 in a net of lanes 1 mile W of Kirkbymoorside

Kirkleatham

St Cuthbert

A strange concoction – an octagonal mausoleum upstages the plain 18c box on which it forms a NE excrescence.

In fact the historical sequence is odd – the mausoleum was added to a medieval church by James Gibbs, 1740, and not long after, the main building was updated.

The mausoleum is octagonal with heavily rusticated base and conical roof. A rich stone coat of arms which formerly graced the cornice sits on the ground nearby. The design somehow suggests a ruin in the first place. The octagon's interior is disappointingly mild; Pevsner thinks it was simplified by 19c restorers. Three effigies in asymmetrical niches under a shallow vault. The most interesting leans on a bulgy column hemmed in by piles of books.

Nearby to the SW is a much richer church interior of the period, in the *Almshouse Chapel* re-edified by the same Cholmley Turner who built the mausoleum when his son died on the Grand Tour. This chapel is small, but as magnificently decked out as the parish church is bare, with carving, plaster work and iron balcony of the most exquisite quality.

Ireshopeburn

Weardale

Newbiggin

Teesdale
Methodist Chapels

These are the oldest chapels in the Dales and speak of a culture which is nearly gone.

The valleys are separated by the austere vastness of the moors. Teesdale is softer than Weardale, whose northern heights have a desecrated look. John Wesley preached regularly to the lead miners of these parts for the last forty-five years of his life.

The chapel at *Ireshopeburn* has been revised more over the years and now wears a look of mid-Victorian pomp. It is an impressive galleried space focused on the raised pulpit, a real extravaganza of 19c carpentry. This grand piece of furniture is now too commanding for the shrunken congregation and is rarely used. Various tones of yellow, brown and peach make a restful harmony of this interior. The attached preacher's house is now a local museum.

At *Newbiggin*, the Sunday School adjoins – an eminently practical arrangement which relinquishes any architectural pretension at a stroke. It is not the pulpit but a free-standing stove which supplies the main focus at Newbiggin. Yellow glass colours the daylight. As in many chapels, the room is turned sideways to the entrance. Tiers of benches rise as in a schoolroom, and at their back a row of glass cases expounds the building's history. These are a charming sign of coming museum status.

Newbiggin is a delightful and unpretentious place. It straggles along the old road which lies a few hundred yards above its modern successor, a displacement which explains the village's preservation. A good building-by-building guide has been produced locally.

Durham: Ireshopeburn about 12 miles SE of Alston on A689 (N side of road E of village centre); Newbiggin 20 miles SE of Alston on A6277 (considerably above road)

Wesleyan chapel at Newbiggin

Though it is one of the finest small Baroque spaces in the country, the chapel's authorship remains a mystery. It forms the centrepiece of a complex which housed ten old men, ten old women, ten boys and ten girls. Each of these groups is represented on the exterior by a vivid statue in painted lead.

All these residues of 18c grand folks' projects exist within a stone's throw of the giant ICI plant to the NW which is more like a city or a whole landscape than a plant, a vast and ramifying nightmare come to life from science fiction.

N Yorks/Clev: 7 miles E of Middlesbrough just N of A174, but only reachable from A1042

Knaresborough

St John

An impressive church in one of the most picturesquely sited of English towns.

Knaresborough perches above the Nidd and has been strangely bisected by the railway. The large churchyard is a platform suspended above the river; St John's a regular building dominated by its square central tower.

Inside, high, plain-chamfered arcade and some good Victorian glass, Morris in W, and at other end of the aisle, lurid Palestinian scenes.

In the Slingsby Chapel are two prone effigies stiff with nervous intensity. Hidden in a corner, in a niche like a closet, a standing figure by the Jacobean sculptor Epiphanius Evesham. He seems militantly languid, or languidly militant, and could be the author of a book on melancholy.

W Yorks/N Yorks: just beyond Harrogate to the E, on A59; church on W edge of town, S of High Street

Lastingham

St Mary

A village in a dell on the edge of the moors whose church contains a remarkable Norman crypt.

St Cedd founded a monastery here in 654 which was overrun by Danish invaders a couple of centuries later. The present building began in an ambitious campaign of 1078–85, at which point the site was again abandoned.

The churchyard is raised above the road and partly tended by sheep. Sadly, it recently lost a ring of ancient (and healthy) yews. Externally the building is modest; its surprises lie within. The Norman apse and arcades survive, now roofed with beautifully clear groined vaults from Pearson's restoration of 1879.

Originally the crypt was entered sideways down a dogleg stair. Now we go straight down from the centre of the nave and find ourselves in a low, classically proportioned space consisting of nave, aisles and chancel. The three bays of the little nave are supported by stumpy columns on stepped bases crowned with simple but varied capitals, from which the heavy square ribs of the vaults sprout. The crypt at Lastingham is a place both rugged and tranquil, from which all the oppression of going underground is banished by a fine sense of measure and proportion. Many carved stones – bits of crosses, tombs and window or door frames – survive from the dark centuries between the seventh and the eleventh, and are well displayed in the dim light of the crypt.

N Yorks: 1½ miles N of Appleton-le-Moors or 2 miles E of Hutton-le-Hole, which is 3 miles N of A170 on unnumbered but B-grade road across the moors to Castleton, the turning 1 mile E of Kirkbymoorside

Laughton-en-le-Morthen

All Saints & John the Baptist

A building of impressive scale with a remarkable spire linked to its slender

Kirkdale. Remnants of a Saxon minster in a secluded spot

tower by buttresses which fly out, link to the body, and then separate again.

The village name preserves the memory of a small pre-Saxon kingdom, Morthing, or field of slaughter. The church shows well from afar because it sits on an eminence which also contained the castle, now ruined to the S.

Entertaining tracery, especially where chancel meets S aisle. There two windows adjoin, one of cusped, prickly Perp, the other with hanging forms and a spear bisecting fat lobe shapes.

On the N, a Saxon door: here iron-streaked red stone intrudes and the old anti-structural approach is met – verticals and capitals laid onto the surface, like drawing not structure.

The interior has been horribly scraped. There are lavish stops in the arcade, consisting of angels in flowing gowns, about two feet high. The Victorian glass mostly ugly, except for a bold picture in the S chancel.

W Yorks/S Yorks: 7 miles SE of Rotherham, 1 mile N of B6060; church on W edge

Leeds

St Peter, Kirkgate
St John, New Briggate (CCT)
St Wilfrid, Halton

One of the most interesting Northern cities contains several very original churches.

The parish church is cut off from the centre of (mainly Victorian) Leeds by railway viaducts. This marooning of Leeds' most venerable monument in a grimy industrial backwater is strangely moving. *St Peter's* is not quite what it looks, but an early 19c reconstruction of the old Gothic church by **R. D. Chantrell**.

Inside, the effect of his work is outrageous and powerful. You enter through a high tower space and then are pressed down on by lowering galleries, amazing contraptions of mellowest wood with rich unfunctional canopies along their fronts. It is an irrational but effective device for making the utilitarian gallery contribute to Gothic gloom. Chantrell achieves a theatrical approximation to antiquity which moves us more than later, more knowledgeable revivals. In fact the only authentic medieval fabric to be seen here are a few pinnacles collected and re-set as a monument for the antiquary Ralph Thoresby.

The great sight of this interior is an Anglo-Saxon cross, found as re-used

Lastingham. Stone vaults from Pearson's restoration, stairs down to the Norman crypt

stones in the old tower as Chantrell was taking it apart. He recognized the carvings and spirited them off, developing odd Masonic theories about them and erecting them in his garden. After many vicissitudes they came back and are now set up under the S transept arch. Pictorially the Leeds cross is one of the most engaging Anglo-Saxon artefacts. Its most peculiar scene shows Wayland the Smith in his flying machine, which appears to be made of snakes and a valkyrie. The Museum of Leeds has published a helpful booklet full of drawings reconstructing this puzzling monument according to different tastes and theories.

The next church to look at is *St John*, five minutes' walk to the N, with the

richest early 17c interior in the whole country. It was built by a local wool merchant in 1631–4. In the 1860s when there was talk of tearing it down, Norman Shaw happened to see it and devoted himself to saving it over local opposition, an experience thought to have influenced his later design for St Michael's, Bedford Park.

St John has a fairly non-committal late Gothic exterior. Inside, it is an absolute orgy of woodwork and plaster. The plan is peculiar in the extreme, two naves of almost equal status and no aisles. The chancel screen has the most complex balusters ever seen, a frieze of hearts, grapes and flowers, and on top, royal arms smothered by surrounding strapwork. From the beam overhead hang spandrels of equally lacy knot-work.

The bench ends are covered in knobs and papery volutes. On either side of the pulpit, which resembles a little Tower of Babel, are eagles with necks gone long and pliable like geese.

The first vicar of St John was a notorious Puritan, a fact that gives one pause in trying to interpret this space which is like a gigantic piece of Elizabethan jewellery.

With the full guide published by the CCT you can pick out embellishments added to the ensemble by Shaw and Temple Moore.

For the next stop we jump 300 years into the suburbs, where we find an eccentric church of the 1930s by **Randall Wells**, who built only one other and is better known as Lethaby's and Prior's clerk of works on the two best Arts and Crafts churches (see Brockhampton and Roker).

St Wilfrid is a spiky Greek cross, with a central tower very barn-like, and brick-sized stonework of thatchy colour. All in all, odd and discordant forms with a vernacular flavour. Inside, folded vaults, lots of light, nice woodwork, and an Eric Gill sculpture.

W Yorks: 38 miles N of Sheffield on M1; Halton 3 miles E of centre, N of A63/Selby Road (St Wilfrid off Halton Hill)

Lindisfarne [Holy Island]

St Mary

One of the most evocative places in England, the scene of Aidan's monastery and Cuthbert's hermitage.

No 7c buildings survive. The priory ruin is Norman, and the parish church is Early English. Yet it is the best place to imagine what earliest English Christianity was like. Twice a day the island is cut off by the tide; the long ride across duny expanses towards the sea is fraught with excitement. Ideally, one would spend a day exploring the rocky north coast and then come to the ruin, of pinky orange stone, with Lutyens' amazing castle on its mound across an inlet.

St Mary's shoulders the ruin. It is a simple but powerful building with lancets between buttresses in the E and a heavily buttressed belfry in the W. Blocks of stone forming the chancel seem unusually large. This is palpable inside as well. The arcade is striped pink and white, an effect more muted on the front.

In the chancel is a carpet modelled on the famous carpet page of the 7c Lindisfarne Gospel, one of the highest peaks of early medieval art.

Northumb: 12 miles SE of Berwick-on-Tweed, E of A1; church near S shore of island

Lythe

St Oswald

One of the most dramatic settings of any parish church, in a huge churchyard sloping down a hillside toward the sea.

Many traces of an older building, especially the N wall, but essentially this is a design of 1910 by Walter Tapper. The result is an outstanding example of the mock-accretive mode, that is of a building which looks as if it evolved slowly over centuries. The powerful square tower with its squat stone spire peppered with lucarnes looks Early English, as do the airy arcades in yellow stone, well contrasted with white walls. Workmanship throughout of a high standard: ordinary vernacular materials are treated with special reverence. Floors are a satisfying combination of oak under pews and stone in aisles. The screen is very seemly in limed oak with a charming irregular balcony sticking from the organ loft behind, supported or rather finished off by its own hanging fan vault.

The S chapel, lavishly vaulted in golden stone, is entirely Tapper's invention, while in the chancel early Gothic piscina and niches are reset. Under the W gallery a huge collection of pre-Norman fragments is displayed including many bits of hogback tombs and a wrestling pair with a dragonish beast beneath.

N Yorks: 3 miles NW of Whitby on A174; church is ½ mile E of village on N side of road overlooking the sea

Monkwearmouth

St Peter

Paired with Jarrow. These were two branches of one monastery, founded by an intriguing character, Benedict Biscop, who collected books, paintings and architectural ideas on his trips to Rome, which later adorned and informed the institutions he started here.

Like Jarrow, Monkwearmouth lies now in an industrial landscape, which is in process of becoming a former industrial landscape. The shipyards, once among the most productive in the world, are now largely inactive. Here too the frail Saxon tower is framed by enormous cranes.* It preserves some of the most elaborate external sculpture of the period, in the form of ruined friezes and figures. Under the later tunnel vault of

Lindisfarne. Modest Early English church near the priory ruin on Holy Island

Lythe. Walter Tapper's noble rebuilding of an earlier church in a kind of Gothic vernacular

the porch are paired serpentine beasts, faintly inscribed on the doorposts.

Inside, mainly Victorian, with many good recent windows by L. C. Evetts. In a display case are wonderful fragments of a Saxon throne. The arms survive: each contains a trapped lion, one of whom turns his head away in a vivid gesture.

* The last cranes have since disappeared.

Durham/T&W: part of Sunderland, 12 miles SE of Newcastle on A183; church on N bank of Wear near its mouth

Newcastle upon Tyne

All Saints
Church of the Divine Unity

The large medieval parish church of *St Nicholas* became the cathedral in 1882. *St Andrew*, Newgate, is the most interesting medieval building which remains a parish church.

But Newcastle's most distinctive religious building is *All Saints*, a late 18c

replacement for an older church. Though presently deconsecrated and open to the public as an arts centre, it is one of the most successful Baroque churches in England. Hemmed in by hideous recent building to the N, All Saints is still wonderful to come on from the S. It towers overhead at the top of many steps, crowned by a tower and spire which combine cylinders and concave triangular solids most divertingly. Tower, porch and vestibule project from the great elliptical body.

Inside, disorienting. After the vestibule, whose font cover emulates the tower, you enter the church sideways. The apse has been entirely stripped of ritual fittings, but the wealth of pews and galleries remain, all in Honduran mahogany of chestnut hue.

Near the Civic Centre, an engaging piece of 1950s municipal bravado, is the *Church of the Divine Unity*, a Unitarian building from a rare moment for churches, 1939–40. Outside, an understated modernism, with subtle mouldings on windows of the plain brick tower and an ingenious porch-courtyard.

Inside, no images, but geometrical liveliness in the laying out of space which recalls Frank Lloyd Wright's temple for the Unitarians in Oak Park, Illinois.

Northumb/T&W: about 9 miles inland from mouth of Tyne/North Sea. All Saints is on Dog Bank, E of Tyne Bridge (N approach); Church of Divine Unity is in Ellison Place, S of former polytechnic

Norham

St Cuthbert

Some of the best Norman work in the county, especially the blind arcades on outside wall of the chancel.

Norham is a pleasantly spread out village on the Scottish border. Its castle, famous from Turner's paintings, is a tower-house of pink stone set high up.

This same stone gives the church's fine S arcade some of its character. Internal textures very wonderful, and there is a Piranesian column of variegated Saxon carving – an 18c conceit but confected recently, as these stones have all been

Monkwearmouth. Another Anglo-Saxon monastic remnant

discovered since the first edition of Pevsner. Norham's 17c royal arms are the biggest, blackest and most three-dimensional in any English church.

The tower is obviously rebuilt, but perhaps its pleasing sideways proportions are copied from the Norman original. The graveyard is full of deep-carved old, mostly rustic, tombstones.

Northumb: 9 miles SW of Berwick-on-Tweed on B6470

North Grimston

St Nicholas

Four nearby village churches in the Yorkshire Wolds contain four exceptional Norman fonts.

The most intriguing feature of this landscape is a special kind of steep, narrow dry valley. Many deserted villages attest to depopulation in the Wolds, which may partly account for the high survival of prehistoric remains and this dense concentration of fonts, two from deserted villages.

St Nicholas' church is reached through one gate and then another, with a yew alley between. So the long low building bursts upon you like a vision of tranquility sitting in its well mowed lawn. Medieval and seventeenth century features are mixed up together here; a pair of large rectangular windows stand out in the mellow aisle wall.

Inside, a simple and comfortable space with a flattened Norman chancel arch. The font is placed off centre and shows a complete Last Supper wrapped around two thirds of its girth. Some of the disciples hold books and all show their legs under the table, which is tilted upward so that we can see the food and appliances laid out on it. The repetitive nature of the scene lets us keep hold of the thread as we follow it round the corner. In the rest of the space a bishop, a patch of lively decorative filler and a Deposition with Christ like an impaled butterfly. See Cowlam for three further fonts.

E Yorks/N Yorks: 4 miles SE of Malton on B1248; church on N side of road in centre of village

A Romanesque Last Supper winds around the font at North Grimston, in the Yorkshire Wolds

Nun Monkton

St Mary

A very special place with gorgeous Transitional remains in its church.

Nun Monkton lies at the end of a lane going nowhere, because here the Nidd and the Ouse converge. At the centre of the village a pond, lots of cows, and a ring of brick houses which recede from the huge green where the maypole survives.

In front of the church (the nave of a Benedictine nunnery), an enormous weeping beech partly veils the wonderful doorway. It is rich with ballflower, teeth, and capitals like jelled or partly frozen leaves.

William Morris windows in the E are the freshest and most uplifting ever. Against a springy swirl of rose and bay leaves, a few figures and scenes. Down the sides of the undivided space run beautiful and very odd wall arcades which become, against all expectation, thicker and richer in gaps between windows.

Turning back, we are met by the bad sisters of the Morris windows, all red, yellow and black; effective, but malevolent like sorcery.

On the W front is a fine carved Mary, stiff like the ones at Chartres, and opposite her a pair of feet, probably Gabriel's.

W Yorks/N Yorks: about 10 miles NW of York on lane which runs NE from A59

Old Malton

St Mary

This is an impressive fragment of a Gilbertine priory. Gilbertines were the only monastic order begun in England. Their peculiarity was the inclusion of both sexes, who were kept strictly separate.

As usual, the building has been truncated in various ways during the 17 and 18c. It was shorn of both aisles, the E bays of nave, chancel, central and NW towers, and perhaps worst and least obvious of all, its clerestory.

This makes the internal proportions awkward, but the remainder is still magnificent, especially from the W. High quality masonry in beautiful pale grey stone. Some wonderful early Gothic details, especially the punched-out quatrefoils over the bell openings. A large Perpendicular window was inserted in the centre of the façade and then at some later time half blocked up.

Inside, lovely details, especially in SW, but a general effect of squashing, through lowering of roof and pulling in of E end. Chancel fittings by Temple Moore. Over-sized animal misericords are entertaining.

To the S, a high wall and large house incorporating much cannibalized stone from the priory.

N Yorks: 21 miles NE of York on A64; Old Malton a mile to NE of Malton

Ovingham

St Mary the Virgin

A church which grows on you, whose charm is founded on the understated purity of early Gothic.

Like Bywell a few miles W it has a rich Saxon tower and some carved stones, but the great delight is the chancel and the way it meets the S transept. Outside, it's a dignified march of lancets.

Inside, in spite of distracting Victorian roof and hanging lights (scheduled for removal), wonderful spaces, with lean-to W aisles on transepts, and special devices where these meet the nave and the outside wall.

Two interesting recent works – a tiny lancet by Leonard Evetts just inside the chancel with roses and prism effect, and over the S porch, a Madonna and Child by Daniel Oates of very white stone in a kind of hulk style.

In the churchyard is buried Thomas Bewick, the engraver of British birds and mammals and a native of these parts.

Northumb: 12 miles W of Newcastle on N bank of Tyne

Patrington

St Patrick

Patrington is one of the very best English churches, large, all of a piece, approaching perfection. Description may

make it sound cold, but it is not. It possesses a secret of harmony which looks easy, but is proved hard by its rarity.

This is a building of amazing scale. No length of time is long enough to savour every detail; some must be singled out: the central tower and spire, of gradual slope but telling idiosyncrasy: the spire base has a close-fitting, faceted ring of arches which veils the lowest stage of the slope. This idea was borrowed by Bodley at Clumber chapel. It softens a transition by enrichment.

The end elevations of transepts are exceptionally beautiful, because aisles are treated as different from, yet part of, the main body. The whole is three and one at once.

Tracery throughout various without wildness. Ashlar of a pleasant mousy colour.

Inside, arcades of clustered shafts set on the diagonal. Tower piers enormous and the space under well handled. Richest foliage bands at capital level. Colours of the stone faintly tan, faintly

Norham. A long low building of pink local stone, in which the Norman chancel is outstanding

silver, but basically grey – the building shimmers. In S transept the Lady Chapel fills an angled-out bay with a miniature vault over and a lovely pendant boss with Mary on the front side.

The font bubbles with various leafage and tracery. A striking absence of monuments in this church but a lovely Easter sepulchre in compensation. The large rectangular space the building sits in produces a purposeful isolation. In the attractive little village, an unusual widening of the High Street is somehow consonant with the spirit of the church.

E Yorks: 16 miles SE of Hull on A1033; church S of road

Pickering

St Peter and St Paul
St Joseph (RC)

The market place of this little town runs downhill from the churchyard hidden between houses and reached by steep snickets. The churchyard forms thus a kind of secret world on top, except that it functions as a convenient through-passage from one part of town to another.

The setting of St Peter & St Paul is more important than any single detail, though the tower has a nice wavy parapet, the S porch is capacious and the jutting of chapels and transept into the

green space makes nice variety. Inside, the spaces above the nave arcades are almost completely covered with late medieval wall paintings. The immediate effect is very exciting. Every scene teems with figures. Martyrs in Pickering do not die alone but surrounded by crowds of spectators. Different scales are mixed and stories switch sides when they run out of space where they are. Over everything a general spirit of tumult presides. It forms a relatively quiet moment when St Edmund is fired at by four symmetrically arranged archers. At other times Christ's robe may droop down into Herod's banquet where diners inspect John the Baptist's severed head. One of the ladies leaning back thrusts her tall headdress into the Coronation of the Virgin above. In the grisly narrative of St Catherine swords and wings are always overshooting the dividers between scenes which someone carefully drew before it all began.

When the paintings were first uncovered in 1852 the vicar of the time got them whited out again on the ground that they were distracting. One can see what he meant – though all the colors are muted vegetable dyes more like yarns for a hanging than painter's pigments, the approach is shamelessly sensational and uncontemplative, like a modern comic book in more ways than one.

On the other side of the beck lies *St Joseph* by **Leonard Stokes** which contains an intricately carved font by Eric Gill, another narrator whom some critics have found sensational, unwholesome, un-spiritual.

N Yorks: 17 miles W of Scarborough on A170. St Peter and St Paul E of marketplace in centre; St Joseph a few hundred yards W of market place

Roker

St Andrew, Talbot Road

E. S. Prior

One of the most exciting churches in England, historically and aesthetically. It was designed by E. S. Prior and built by Randall Wells in 1906–7.

It surpasses Prior's Dorset churches and ranks with Lethaby's Brockhampton as an expression of the Arts and Crafts spirit. The vocabulary is still Gothic, very freely interpreted. Ideas of tower, nave, window tracery and pointed arch are taken and melted down or transfigured to serve

Ovingham's Saxon tower is one of many in the area

idiosyncratic expression. The material is an elephant-grey stone quarried locally, and the coursing, full of variety, repays study. Outside, the tower is strongly bowed, and handmade glass bulges outward in the nave windows, which thus resemble living membranes.*

Inside, we find surprising floods of light and a single unobstructed space. The great arches of the roof come almost to the floor, giving the building the character of an upturned boat, appropriate to its coastal position in what was then a shipbuilding area. Tracery, especially in chancel, is based on stilted arches, like a bony skeleton or the Saxon antecedents nearby, at Jarrow and Monkwearmouth.

Roker is famous for its furnishings, some of which seem rich to the point of fussiness in the rugged setting Prior provides. This is certainly the case with Gimson's inlaid lectern, Payne's pictorial glass, and the murals painted by Eric Gill's brother MacDonald in 1927, though these last were Prior's design.

More successful are Gimson's altar cross, in iron which looks like steel; and the font, like a great chafing dish, carved by Wells. Burne-Jones contributed a tapestry and window design, and there are large Morris carpets. The church hall of 1920 isn't Prior, but blends well. From Monkwearmouth beach you see the tower above the trees.

* This bulge is not a design feature, but caused by rusting frames.

Durham/T&W: part of Sunderland, just N of Monkwearmouth, one street in from coast road; open weekday mornings

Rotherham

All Saints

A grand Perpendicular church whose position seems semi-miraculous.

Although the town has developed in a rather unattractive way, this red sandstone pile maintains its pre-eminence at the centre, a culminating ornament. Pevsner calls it the perfect *Stadtkrone*, which was Bruno Taut's* name for an architectural summing-up at the heart of a city.

First of all, the terrain co-operates – there is a central eminence from which the surroundings then slope gently away. Trees in the churchyard form a protective ring, lifting the church above the town.

And then the design itself is subtly single-minded. Everything leads by slow

Patrington, one of the loveliest High Gothic buildings

degrees to the central spire. The transept roof makes a gentle slope under the more insistent thrust of the tower, placing its one big window under the double bell opening. This single effect is flanked by the multiplied transparency of the clerestory. Bulk is never allowed to accumulate long without being pierced or dissolved. All in all, it is one of the most telling and well-calculated Gestalts among English churches of less than heroic scale.

* Early 20c German Expressionist architect

W Yorks/S Yorks: 5 miles NE of Sheffield

Scarborough

St Martin
St Mary

A seaside town made exciting by dramatic terrain, which breaks up the built stretches. Its old parish church is wonderfully sited below the castle, above the sea. Since Scarborough now feels mainly Victorian, it makes sense to start with *St Martin*, an early church by **G. F. Bodley**, which contains marvellous early painting and glass by William Morris and his friends. This is one of their most elaborate schemes, perfectly intact and more accessible than others, like the one in Brighton for example.

The building is modest but solid, a self-effacing medium for displaying its wealth of decoration. The exterior is united by a strong saddleback tower; inside, the plain stone nave sets off the richly coloured chancel. There are too many Morris windows to enumerate them all (a task well done by the church guide) but the E ones are outstanding – the Crucifixion unexpectedly entangled in the Parable of the Vineyard, an obscure allegory of the divine sacrifice.

Also marvellous are the St Martin panels now in the SW vestry, and hence harder to see. The Vineyard is Rossetti; St Martin, Ford Madox Brown. In both we find a passionate involvement in the drama not very usual in Victorian glass.

Perhaps the most famous fitting is the pulpit covered in painted panels now under glass. Don't miss the lilies turning to birds (martins!) on the darkest side. Much more Pre-Raphaelite painting in chancel and Evangel windows by Philip Webb.

St Mary's, the old parish church in attractive golden stone, lost its chancel through shelling from the nearby castle in the Civil War. Its most entertaining internal effect is an extra aisle on the N (lively capitals on these columns), which entailed the internalizing of the clerestory on that side. The recent E window by H. J. Stammers is a great success. It looks both rich and fresh from afar, and close up has plenty of clear emblematic and figural detail.

The churchyard carries on at several different levels. There are interesting

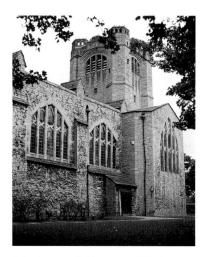

Roker, largest and richest Arts and Crafts church with typically melted features

mariner's graves, as well as Anne Brontë's, whose touching wish to die in sight of the sea was here fulfilled.

N Yorks: 44 miles NE of York on A64. St Martin about ½ mile S of railway station, just to E of A165, open 11–2 in summer; St Mary just W of castle

Seaton Delaval *

St Mary

This tiny church within the grounds of one of Vanbrugh's best houses is a wonderful conflation of Norman and early 18c.

Seaton Delaval. Humble Norman building near Vanbrugh's ruined masterpiece

The Hall is a marvellous series of jokes – appropriate to Northumberland – on fortification. It is built of black and tan masonry in fantastically jagged and stepped form, as if all has become battlement, turret and outlook – upjutting expressions of force.

By contrast the church amid trees is inconspicuous. A Victorian W porch is as big as the chancel of the original two-celled building. Only the N side has much Norman evidence in the form of blocked windows.

Inside, much more exciting. Heroic Norman chancel and sanctuary arches join their attached pilasters in unexpected ways. Overhead a delightfully incongruous coved plaster ceiling à la Wren with a ruby red panel at the centre.

Giant hatchments adorn the walls and there are good tombs on ridged bases like piles of mats, especially a woman in a furrowed cloak.

* Listed thus in Pevsner and Betjeman, but a local vicar suggests a different place name and dedication which may be more accurate: Seaton Sluice, Our Lady, Delaval.

Northumb: about 8 miles NE of Newcastle on A190; church and Hall are about a mile NE of Seaton Delaval towards Seaton Sluice; church SW of Hall

Selby

Abbey Church of Our Lord, St Mary & St Germain

A magnificent abbey church in which most periods are well represented. One should not be put off by the towers which are mainly 20c.

A fire in 1906 gave the impetus to regularize the external appearance by completing the two W towers (which had been stumps before) and making a prouder assertion of the central tower. Views will differ. Perhaps by blending too well, modern builders have degraded the old work, a complaint also voiced about Pearson's nave for Bristol Cathedral.

To appreciate Selby at its true value one should approach from the E. The stone is marvellously pale, white with a tawny undertone; the E window a gorgeous flowing design, as are the chancel clerestory lights. Lower down, interesting lattice patterns. Parapets are wonderfully graceful.

The fire destroyed many fittings, but the interior is a satisfying composition on the largest scale. The nave arcades are Norman, scored and patterned like Durham's, turning to Early English in upper ranges.

The chancel is rich Decorated with gorgeous leafage and entertaining corbels for statues. In the E window Victorian replacements have been unusually faithful to the original design, which is a satisfying Tree of Jesse. Some of the original panels are preserved in the S chapel. There is also much Ward and Hughes glass (favourites in this district), of which that in the N transept is the most interesting.

W Yorks/N Yorks: 14 miles S of York on A19

Sessay

St Cuthbert

William Butterfield

One of those larger compositions hinting at a whole organic society which many Victorian architects were hankering to create. Here the group includes the church with a separate gatehouse, the school and a bridge over the beck. The whole is early work of 1847–8 by Butterfield, full of ingenuity and variety, but without the aggression and stridency found in his mature designs.

The gatehouse roof of cedar shingles puts together five or six different slopes in a short space. This diminutive building incorporates a closed part and an open, a boiler house and the passage. Two more roofing materials appear on the church: stone slates for nave and chancel, oak shingles for the spire. Because the tones are all mellow and the shapes slide into one another, variety isn't obtrusive. Most interesting of all is continual variety in the window tracery. Little windows in the porch with iron grilles (now eating at the stone frames) are condensed essays in the use of cusps. A set of flame-like lancets in the aisle merge surreptitiously with the wall masonry. After this, the interior disappoints. Does the cream and grey paint of this well kept interior perhaps hide textures of the materials Butterfield meant for us to see?

N Yorks: Little Sessay on OS map; 7 miles SE of Thirsk, 2 miles W of A19 at bend in road just before bridge

Selby. The magnificent Norman and Early English nave of the Abbey

Simonburn

St Mungo

Formerly this parish stretched to Scotland and was the largest in England.

In a wonderful position just N of Hadrian's Wall, the village has more trees than houses.

A lovely churchyard and a cubic lychgate by R. J. Johnson. To the N lies the rectory, sometimes linked with Vanbrugh. It is a work of heroic vigour whose rusticated window frames merge with each other, forming almost a veil of mouldings.

In walls of church porch, Saxon fragments pleasantly immured. Inside, the floor slopes noticeably down into the chancel. Just before the arch is a wet spot which never dries. It marks St Mungo's Well and the stream which dictates the slope. The saint came from Glasgow Cathedral as did the early rectors.

Interesting remnants of a Jacobean tomb including a man in an Elizabethan cap and bits of his family. Some of the glass looks like early Kempe, but better, especially Gabriel in an opalescent robe. A marble carpet climbs the sanctuary steps.

Northumb: about 10 miles NW of Hexham just W of B6320

Skelton near Ripon

Christ the Consoler

William Burges

This and its near neighbour at Studley Royal are among the greatest marvels of the Gothic Revival.

Skelton, near Ripon. An extravagant memorial by Burges to a man killed by Greek brigands

William Burges built both of these rich, smallish buildings, one of which commemorates a young English aristocrat murdered by Greek brigands while visiting ancient sites. Skelton was paid for by his mother using money intended to ransom him, while Studley was commissioned by his brother.

The richness of its sculptural decoration and the amplitude of its forms (not absolutely large) make Skelton a very engaging building. Spaces are full and over-full with plump forms. In the porch gable stands Christ the shepherd; trapped in flanking niches, some of his flock. When I was there, lambs were bleating just outside the churchyard gates.

On the E gable are two little dogs performing heraldic duties; great visored helmets have landed on the pets' heads, and they look bewildered and uncomfortable.

More beasts inside, six of them on a giant corbel holding up the organ gallery, feathered and furred, with tails which turn into leaves. The organ case itself is a large wooden building overhead.

The whole space over the chancel arch is taken up with a heavy three-dimensional depiction of Christ's Transfiguration. At the other end of the nave, a wheel-rose which seems to strain against the side walls. This window is decorated outside with the four ages of man at the compass points.

Pictorial glass fills every single window with clear Easter egg colours. The church is dedicated to Christ the Consoler – and the consolation Burges offers is a multitude of stories.

W Yorks/N Yorks: 4 miles SE of Ripon in grounds of Newby Hall; entered through E gate

Skelton near York

St Giles

A miniature Early English gem on a quiet green.

The S door is narrow but exceedingly rich and lodges in the memory, especially the arch mouldings which do not quite line up with the columns below. A simple belfry and gorgeous crosses on the roofline.

Inside, pier mouldings are very sophisticated. A wonderful piscina bulges out unexpectedly with a drapery of leaves underneath. Lavers, Barraud and Westlake's good E window shows the table in the Last Supper stretching towards us as in a print of Dürer's time. It is plausible that York Minster masons were responsible for the building, erected in one go c1240.

N Yorks: 4 miles NW of York, just E of A19

Sledmere

St Mary

Temple Moore

The seat of the Sykes family who built many Victorian village churches in the Yorkshire Wolds and reclaimed this landscape for agriculture.

St Mary, of 1893–8, one of the most lavish buildings of its size, sits within the grounds of Sledmere House. Pevsner thought it lifeless, and it is true that the outside, though exquisitely carved in grey Whitby stone, is cool at best. All the more effective then, the warmth of an interior clad in red sandstone. The floor of Kilkenny marble with faint flushes of pink in the grey feels almost Venetian. In this space details are hard to pick out because plentiful late Victorian glass interrupts most of the daylight. Extremely rich fittings, especially the screen and two immense brass chandeliers.

This is a miniature cathedral with clustered piers, barrel roofed nave and stone vaulted aisles. The north aisle ends in an ecstasy of richness where, before a screen carved in deep red stone, a lamp flickers.

On the other side of the road skirting the park is a surprising piece of modern primitive carving, inheritor of the Romanesque fonts, a memorial to the Waggoners Regiment designed c1919 by Mark Sykes and filled with scenes of local life.

E Yorks: 9 miles SE of Malton on B1253; church in grounds of Sledmere House

South Church

St Andrew Auckland

A church of impressive proportions and irregular detail which contains important Saxon carvings.

Its situation is uncanny, hoisted on a little cliff like a pedestal, from which it towers over crowded council houses at its base. The tower is old and proud, the rest of the building a collection of large pieces. Peculiar rhythm of single and double windows down the long flank of the chancel. All in all, great richness and variety in the masonry and the grouping.

Inside, the arcade is impressive, and the wall above the chancel arch gorgeous. Somehow the gawky alternation outside has been regularized; the two and one are made equal.

The famous Saxon cross has bland frontal figures and an archer shooting up into inhabited tendrils. A conscientious reconstruction leaves painful blanks for missing pieces.

Durham: a SE suburb of Bishop Auckland, which is 11 miles SW of Durham; signed from A688

South Dalton

St Mary

J. L. Pearson

A lavish work by Pearson, 1858–61, where no expense was spared but the energies are somewhat strangely invested.

The unusually slender spire rises to 200 feet (taller than Patrington) and its proportions arouse disbelief. The church is aisleless but has two grand transepts. It is placed well above the road. Patterns on

Butterfield's charming vernacular at Sessay

the outside sometimes look like carpenter's fretwork or designs in plaster. The chancel cornice is the most elaborate.

Inside, nice piercings above chancel and transept arches. Wonderful glass by Clayton & Bell, including a Victorianized Doom in the E to which no

Simonburn, in a wonderful position near Hadrian's Wall

devils are admitted. A bristly font lid and lights, and pews designed by Pearson. Under the W tower a special section of child-sized ones.

Three miles E, just off A164, lies St Leonard, SCORBOROUGH, another Pearson church, earlier (1857–9), smaller, simpler. Here the only ornate bit is the E end, with a delightful extra window at the apex which lights the traceries of the roof.

Inside, this active roof is the best feature, along with a thorny metal grille which pins the organ pipes in place.

E Yorks: South Dalton is 5 miles NW of Beverley, ½ mile W of B1248

Staindrop

St Mary (formerly St Gregory)

One of the most interestingly variegated churches in the county.

The village is centred on a long irregular green to W of church. Best approached from SE, where E end sprawls comfortably, with its strange little sacristy hollowed out of what looks like a bulky buttress on the corner of aisle. The fortified tower looms above.

Collegiate buildings have disappeared to N, but upper floor of vestry has been linked to the presence of an anchorite. Windows poke through its wall into the chancel.

The first thing one notices within are some remarkable tombs – one with three effigies under whose feet are readers at little desks; rich niches run along the sides. Next to this one is a curious holdover in wood, now black: a chest-tomb with stiff effigies and kneelers round the sides.

Nave walls craggy and impressively tall. Above the castellated arcade, stretches of Saxon masonry are exposed. There are lush early Gothic sedilia in chancel and a lively Decorated wall tomb on S with tasteless carving.

Durham: 11 miles NW of Darlington on A688

Thirsk

St Mary

A small market town with a proud Perpendicular church, in a region which has few of that date.

Thirsk is built of brick, of a mealy texture, almost as if grain were mixed

South Dalton. All the fittings here, including lights and pews, were designed by Pearson

the stranded façade of Thorpe Salvin Hall, usually attributed to Robert Smythson. It is symmetrical, with turrets at both ends and chimneys treated sculpturally; the windows perhaps even more perfect as elements in the composition now that there is only sky behind them. In front, a little gatehouse with a stepped gable survives. The space around the ruin has been filled with new housing since this was written and now feels suburban.

W Yorks/S Yorks: 5 miles W of Worksop, 3 miles W of A57

Tickhill

St Mary

The largest and most lavish in its district, a consistent late Perpendicular building.

Its proud tower has a pierced top. The decorative elaboration of the rest is amazing – spindly pinnacles all round, traceried buttresses all round. On the clerestory they form vanes richly panelled the whole height of the storey.

Inside, the height and the whiteness of the stone are startling. Arches of the arcade are prolonged by finials into ogees. Tombs are collected towards the W, including a 19c mother and daughter in alabaster and a good knight's tomb with lots of heraldry. There's also an Art Nouveau lectern of 1906. A recent canopy over the font looks like something out of a Dream of Byzantium c1930, a sleek gessoed and coloured vault supported by four columns. This is by the architect G. G. Pace and dates from 1959. Maybe it was inspired by the 18c rotunda which functions as Tickhill's market cross.

W Yorks/S Yorks: 11 miles E of Rotherham on A631; church N and W of road

Warkworth

St Lawrence

Topographically of high interest: the Norman church sits at one end of the little town, the late medieval castle like an enormous jewel at the other. In between, a precipitous High Street, all squeezed into a finger of land made by a hairpin loop in the River Coquet.

For elegant geometry the castle is in a class of its own. It sits high on a sculpted mound, while the church which answers it crouches low by the river which runs

with the clay to dull its brightness. The church sits at the edge of the town, connected to the vast market place by a curving street of 18c houses.

The parapets are glorious and multiplied, so open they sometimes look insubstantial or like a mathematical puzzle. From afar the clerestory tracery presents tier on tier. From inside, all its cusps make a wonderful agitation.

High, impressive arcade and nice roof. There is a thorny Victorian altar rail and a tantalizing fragment of Morris-like glass in S chapel. Don't miss the traceried wooden door coming in, its edges rounded by age.

N Yorks: 9 miles SE of Northallerton on A19/A168; church NW of market place

Thorpe Salvin

St Peter

Small and very mixed, but one of the most charming in the county.

From E, chancel and N aisle make a beguiling group, neither one subordinate to the other. There is lovely flowing and droopy tracery in various windows, especially S and E.

Passing through the Norman door, you are met by a primitive font which shows a Baptism in two frames, miraculously ill-organized, and then the seasons – sowing, harvesting, riding out, warming oneself at a fire – before it runs out of steam and fills the last spaces any which way.

A little to the N of the church is the most beautiful of all Elizabethan ruins, along its N side. This is the most unspoiled Norman bit. The spire which completes this view dates from the 14c. Inside, the single arcade makes a refined effect.

There's an interesting effigy of a knight in elaborate armour vividly portrayed, the details over-sized. Iron altar rail with lively cocks on the gates, folkish and heraldic.

Northumb: 6 miles SE of Alnwick on A1068; church at N end, W of road

Whitby

St Mary, St Hilda

St Mary's, Whitby is one of a kind (unless Minstead, Hants is counted a junior version) which it is amazing to find living on into the present age.

The town is one of the most exciting in England for melodramatic terrain. It consists of two steep halves divided by a winding harbour which still supports a fishing fleet. Extensive views of sea and huddled houses are continual; it is full of the oddest corners.

The church is silhouetted, along with important abbey ruins, atop one of the bluffs. The Abbey is noble Early English in stone of rusty iron mixed with grey. The church adjacent is like an endlessly charming 18c joke. Chinesey stairs in wood climb its venerable sides, and huge long windows have been poked in its walls to light tortuous galleries and further stairs glimpsed within.

Before entering, a sense of agitated dynamic space. Once in, the most higgledy-piggledy effect imaginable, a delightful confusion. Try to tell anyone who has edged in under the looming gallery and watched light filter through in separate shafts about the rationality of that century!

A heavily populated, undulating graveyard stretches away in all directions. Nearby lies the derelict banqueting hall of a Jacobean house made from abbey stone, like something in Magritte.

On the hill opposite stands *St Hilda*, a minor Victorian masterpiece of 1884–5 by **R. J. Johnson** of Newcastle. It has the expressive outline (battered tower crowning a mound of masonry) more familiar in churches of two decades later, and much rich woodwork of reddish hue in a dignified, peaceful interior.

N Yorks: about 30 miles E of Middlesbrough on A171. St Mary is high on S side of harbour; St Hilda high on W side

York

Collectively, York's churches have more old glass than any other town's in England. And G. G. Pace's designs for churches incorporating or resurrecting old fragments are among the best of the 20c.

Second only to Norwich in quantity, the nineteen parish churches of York have suffered a variety of fates. St Michael Spurriergate is a restaurant, St Mary Castlegate a museum, St John Micklegate a theatre. Inevitably most of what they were built for is lost, but at least their place in the townscape is preserved, and that is one of the pleasantest features of a walk round York – coming upon its churches unexpectedly.

All Saints, North Street, is the best remaining interior, full of subtle life which inheres in tattered carpets* and dark figures of uncertain provenance, as well as in fine old roofs and glass. The space is broken into a series of long rooms, well marked off by the richly carved modern screen. Windows in the N aisle are sensational. One is based on a 15c devotional poem, 'The Pricke of Conscience'. At the E end is old glass

Medieval glass in All Saints, North Street

mixed with a little new to indescribably jolly effect. Faces in the chancel window have soulful 15c expressions. Nowhere else in York can one come so comfortably near to the old pictures and colours. On the SW corner of this church is tacked a strange 20c 'anchorage' of concrete disguised with half-timbering.

Holy Trinity, Goodramgate (CCT), is even more obscurely wedged into the town fabric. A narrow passage leads from a busy street to the torpor of its little churchyard. Its stone is patched with brick. Inside, the old floor sways dramatically passing between high walls of old pews, in which one feels almost submerged. In the E window old figures with much pale pink and deep blue.

St Martin, Coney Street, is a fascinating reconstruction by **G. G. Pace** of a bombed building. The nave and N aisle remain open to the sky and form a garden which feels like a ruined cloister in Rome. They are closed by attractive metal grilles. The S aisle has become the church. Its rich exterior resembles a bony skeleton. Just inside the door one is met by the St Martin window brought down almost to floor level where its lively 15c scenes may be closely inspected. Exuberant Baroque font cover and some interesting 20c work, including a window which shows the fire destroying the rest of the church.

Pace's *Holy Redeemer* in Boroughbridge Road, a wide thoroughfare through nondescript W outskirts, is worth a pilgrimage. Here he brought the bombed fragments to a new site. Bits of the demolished St Mary Bishophill Senior are used to form the S wall. It is inspired salvage: one of the richest of modern church interiors results, a wide, low space with aisles so narrow they are like double membranes. On one side the mottled wealth of the past, on the other, exposed concrete and painted brick forming a contemporary equivalent. The walls contain bits of Anglo-Saxon carving, and there is a fine inscribed dedication stone.

* These have since been removed.

York: 37 miles NW of Hull on A19

North West

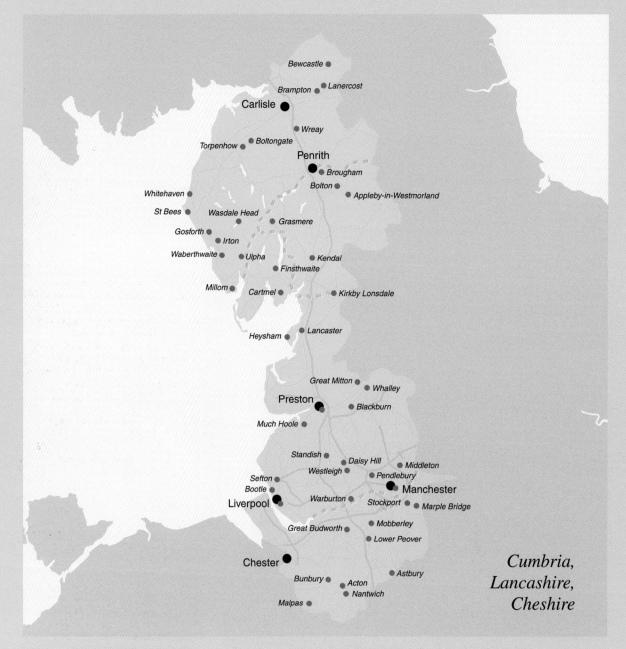

Bewcastle
Brampton · Lanercost
Carlisle ●
Wreay
Torpenhow · Boltongate
Penrith ●
Brougham
Bolton
Whitehaven · Appleby-in-Westmorland
St Bees · Wasdale Head · Grasmere
Gosforth · Irton
Waberthwaite · Ulpha · Kendal
Finsthwaite
Millom · Cartmel · Kirkby Lonsdale
Heysham · Lancaster
Great Mitton · Whalley
Preston ● · Blackburn
Much Hoole
Standish · Daisy Hill · Middleton
Westleigh · Pendlebury
Sefton · Manchester ●
Bootle · Warburton · Stockport · Marple Bridge
Liverpool ●
Great Budworth · Mobberley
Lower Peover
Chester ● · Astbury
Bunbury · Acton
Nantwich
Malpas

Cumbria,
Lancashire,
Cheshire

ALONG WITH WALES, the northern part
of this district is the best hunting ground
for small churches of timeless purity
like spring water. Of all mountain
regions, the Lake District at its best
stands out for harmonious human
presence. That is, in places like Eskdale
and Wasdale, not Windermere, though
of course around Rydal or Esthwaite
one can glimpse what it must have been
like in Wordsworth's time, before
railways and hotels.

Coming down from the northern
fastness, past the remarkable sandflats
of Grange and Morecambe, one enters
the contradictory mill country of
Lancashire, where chimneys and hills
collide. Here chapels have played
an important role in social life, and
Edgar Wood, best of Manchester

architects, built strictly for Non-
conformists. The other outstanding local
firm, Paley & Austin, produced endless
variety in both rural and urban churches.
The Cheshire architect John Douglas
worked mainly on small scales. In the
19c this region was populous enough
and far enough from London to support
imaginative local architects, an unusual
state of affairs.

Acton

St Mary

True magnificence in a tiny place.

Acton church stands out marvellously above everything as one approaches from Nantwich. There is entertaining 17c cresting on the chancel – hearts and inverted hearts in lattice, and shells alternating with scrolly peaks. The tower, too, has later trimmings. Like all the churches roundabout, Acton is built of rich red sandstone.

Inside, behind the soot-blackened font are some truly primitive Norman carvings, assembled into an enigmatic pyramid which is now a monument in its own right. An old guidebook writer saw a man in a cave (signifying Resurrection) where Pevsner sees Christ in a mandorla.

In the churchyard, to E, a famous cricketer's grave with a vivid relief of bat and wicket, and his signature inlaid in white metal.

Cheshire: 1½ miles W of Nantwich on A534

Appleby-in-Westmorland

St Lawrence

This unusually attractive town possesses a church of wonderful texture with amusing Gothick improvements.

Appleby is like a Burford of the North. Its focus is a steeply sloping High Street with wide grass verges and low 18c façades. At the bottom where the church closes the view, the road takes a

Astbury, with a tall and lavishly glazed clerestory

sudden turn before crossing the river. The result is an extensive core which feels like a single place, a novel variation on the piazza or square.

The churchyard is entered through a Gothic arcade of pink stone, perhaps modelled on the classical one at Kirkby Stephen nearby. The colours of the S elevation are gloriously rich, transmutations of the pink local stone. The clerestory leans, the soothingly wide porch presents its gap-toothed skyline, and a squat tower balances the nave.

Inside, a surprise – the ceiling is early Gothic Revival in panelled plaster. A chandelier dangles from a large central

rosette. The 16c organ is famous and said to be the oldest in the country which still works. The corporation pew has fine pierced cresting and in a N chapel is the tomb, combining learning and pomposity, of Lady Anne Clifford who repaired a number of churches and castles near Skipton and Penrith. Behind it stands an exposition of family heraldry. Nearby is the tomb of her mother, Margaret, Countess of Cumberland, whose alabaster effigy wears a metal coronet.

Westm/Cumb: 13 miles SE of Penrith on A66 (bypasses town to N)

Astbury

St Mary

A stupendous late Gothic building of very individual character.

From a distance it looks like a church with a castle behind it, because the former W tower has come loose and drifted N, while on the W front a tall tower-like projection has sprung up resembling the entrance porch of a prodigy house, except that it is impractically narrow and leaves even narrower spaces on each side for the aisles to fill with elongated windows. Overall, the proportions would be at home in German Expressionist cinema.

The building is theatrically framed to the W by a remnant of old village and an entrance arch, beside which lies the present gate. Among external details a high clerestory is noteworthy.

Appleby-in-Westmorland, a large church in pink local stone

Bolton, a building 'as if grown from the soil'

W face of cross is least clear, least wild, most interesting. Lacking its head, it now consists of three scenes which are so worn one needs help interpreting them. RUTHWELL repeats some of them and is better preserved, but perhaps it's best to make one's own guesses first. The lowest scene looks like a Greek blacksmith at his forge but is apparently St John and his eagle; the middle one, a saint with huge splayed feet, is Christ standing on two beast- or serpent-heads; at the top the man who seems to have an over-expressed shoulder joint or a miniature person dangling there is actually holding the agnus dei.

The other sides less enigmatic, the contrast with Ruthwell extreme: for there the cross is like a caged animal for which a special apsed extension of the church has been built, within which the re-assembled cross has been lowered five feet into the floor (so ceiling height can be maintained) and ringed with a classical iron railing. A pamphlet excerpted from the Revd Dinwiddie's book details the preposterous story of the Ruthwell cross's mistreatment and final enshrinement (key to church at first house on L just as one turns N into signed lane off B724).

At Bewcastle the cross is visible at all hours, as is the castle ruin in the

Inside, wonderfully mellow Perpendicular. This is one of those places littered with venerable objects not quite identifiable, like the knobbled railing in the vestry near a misplaced effigy in a bulky skirt.

Nave and S aisle roofs are astonishing, covered in carved decoration like pastry and dotted with bulky pendants like lanterns. Diverse screens with cut-out patterns, and the most eccentric altar rail in existence, a Jacobean Rorschach. The font cover is a fantastic work of architecture in its own right. Seen head on, it shrinks to a sliver, but from the side (together with the framework for raising and lowering it) forms a complex pedimented building. There is also a wooden eagle lectern with fierce feet, lovely panelling in the warm sandstone arcade and two Whallish windows by Irene Dunlop, one commemorating her son who lived for only ten hours.

Cheshire: 1½ miles SW of Congleton on A34; church lies to E

Bewcastle

St Cuthbert

A wonderful situation among the hills. One of the great pilgrimage spots for students of pre-Norman Christianity.

The Bewcastle cross is the 14-foot stump of an Anglo-Saxon preaching cross now located a few yards from the SW corner of a mainly 18c parish church, like a homely Methodist chapel in its highwalled graveyard, where many 18c stones are carved in a primitive style which looks a couple of centuries earlier.

Bewcastle with a fourteen-foot Anglo-Saxon cross stump in its churchyard

farmyard to the N, with wonderfully irregular courses and two bands of orange lichen across its nearly windowless walls.

Cumb: Bewcastle is 20 miles NE of Carlisle, 9 miles N of Lanercost on unmarked road. Should be seen in conjunction with Ruthwell just across the Scottish border in Dumfriesshire

Bolton

All Saints

A humble building utterly enchanting.

Begin at the back, where contrast is strongest between green slate roof and walls of mellow red. Finials like furniture knobs on the gables, belfry like a little house, with a buttress dividing the wall beneath.

Over the blocked N door is a treasure of primitive carving, two battling knights. On the other side a female effigy is mounted like a ship's figurehead, starting forth from the wall. The proportions of the whole could have been an inspiration to the Arts and Crafts, complacent and low as if grown from the soil.

Inside, knobbed pews and a miniature gallery, all in mustard brown. The screen like a lace doily is truly hard to see through.

Westm/Cumb: 10 miles SE of Penrith, 2 miles NW of Appleby; church on street which runs E–W

Boltongate

All Saints

An amazing building, small but powerful. Traditions of Scotland and Provence have been called on to account for its most remarkable feature, the ceiling vault.

Even from outside All Saints declares its specialness; it looks like a solid cube of stone. Heavy parapets conceal the roof, set far back inside them. Everything is composed of large ashlar blocks. An impressive peaked stair turret at NE corner of nave is the nearest thing to a tower.

Inside, the stone roof dominates, a single pointed vault running the length of the space. The best view is towards the corbelled 'gallery' in the W, which is the inner face of the parapet walk. There are few openings in this, including a

Blackburn

St Gabriel, Brownhill Drive
Holy Trinity, Mount Pleasant (CCT)
St Mark, Buncer Lane

F. X. Velarde; Edmund Sharpe

The medieval parish church was raised to cathedral status in 1926. An embellishment of 1961 has given it a great crown of thorns on the skyline, perhaps inspired by the Ely octagon.

Two early Victorian revival churches by Edmund Sharpe, and F. X. Velarde's suburban work of the 1930s are worth seeking out.

St Gabriel is Velarde's only Anglican commission from his great period. If it survived intact it would be his best work. Of heroic proportions and simplicity, which have reminded people variously of a brewery, a cinema or an early Christian structure, it is built of dark brown brick with sparing stone trim. The massive tower was shortened and the flat roofs made into pitched ones in 1971, in order to deal with rotting roof timbers and problems of settling (St Gabriel is built on reclaimed land in a contemporary housing estate along a ring road). The horrible fibreglass sheathing around the top also dates from this time.

The interior is more colourless than Velarde intended. His light fittings – strings of inverted cones – were damaged by the collapse of decorators' scaffolding and removed.

His reredos in chrome and two shades of red was dismantled and left outside until it became unusable.

But fascinating details remain, like the travertine chancel rail and chrome gates and trim, a semi-circular chrome and glass vestibule, and a Cubist font. The iron-framed windows with fascinating minimal colouring proved susceptible to cracking and were replaced (some survive in vestry). Recently (1977) Brian Clarke did two baptistry windows wonderfully sympathetic to Velarde but not at all imitative.

Sharpe's *Holy Trinity* has one of the most entertaining early Gothic Revival interiors in England (1837–46). Wood and stone are indiscriminately combined. Clustered piers are so spindly you suspect them of being wood. The great height is emphasized by the most gorgeous decorative feature, a panelled heraldic roof entirely filled with enormous arms.

St Mark, another Sharpe church, employs an entirely different vocabulary, Rhineland Romanesque. Here too the interior is a surprise: a single gangly space.

Lancs: Blackburn lies between Preston and Burnley. St Gabriel is on N edge of town, just E of A666; Holy Trinity NE of town centre, E of A666; St Mark on W edge, N of A674

Boltongate, with the flavour of a fortified house

little rectangular window near the top.

The effect is relentless but gratifying on this small scale. Two chapel transepts and matching porches have lean-to versions of the vault. These shorter curved segments are also in their way heroic.

Views S to snowy summits of the Lakeland hills.

Cumb: 10 miles NE of Cockermouth on B5299

Bootle

St Monica, Fernhill Road (RC)

F. X. Velarde

All things considered, this is F. X. Velarde's best work and one of the highlights of 1930s churchbuilding in England.

It is a daunting construction in brown brick and concrete, deriving about equally from Romanesque and the cinema. Down the bleak aisles, incredibly profuse roundheaded openings, and a great joke on Gothic: a series of the thinnest, most imaginary image-niches ever seen. For someone who has inspected the thousands of vacant spaces for statues on European churches, this is a wonderful last word on the subject. We are reminded of the space, but we don't have to wonder if anything will ever fill it, because nothing could.

The almost blank W tower is impressive head-on, and just a sliver from the side, like Hawksmoor in Spitalfields. Here some grotesque pictorialism is concentrated – three large angels like figures from Finnish myth on the front, streamlined eagles on the side.

In the interior, more brick, more round arches. Pevsner was repulsed by the great ersatz reredos, but it now seems a bracing effort to combine popular culture and spiritual strivings, such as one is always seeing in Italian churches. It has the sleekness of ocean liner decor.

The aisles are interestingly diverse and spatially complex. Many original fittings in Velarde's favoured materials, chrome ('stay-bright steel' it is called in contemporary accounts) and coloured mirror. The chapel of the English Martyrs (S aisle), a strait and narrow place, is a haven of atmospheric contemporary fittings.

Nearby at Clubmoor (Townsend Avenue at corner of Queen's Drive) is *St Matthew*, a slightly earlier work of Velarde's, which is light years apart. Here the tower with its Babylonian columns looks like the vulgar

appurtenance (a disguised water tank?) of a public park. But his sources in Romanesque are interestingly revealed.

The interior is much better and plays with round arches of disparate sizes. A notable ciborium and seats in the choir like Egyptian dining couches. Turquoise and chartreuse may not have been the original paint scheme, but does not seem unsuitable.

Lancs/Merseyside: just NW of Liverpool. St Monica at NE corner of Derby Park, at junction with Earl Road

Brampton

St Martin

Philip Webb

This architect's only church. Like his other major buildings it grows on the visitor, and uncovering the large amount of detailed thought in it, you understand better why Webb built so little.

Inside, more interesting than outside, feels unchurch-like at first, and a collection of spaces. Aisles are disparate: on the N, large windows and transverse tunnel vaults in wood; on the S tiny dormers and folkish truss roof. The whole is spacious yet full of unpredictable nooks, like a little glazed vestry high up in SE corner, and the great windowed space under tower, which we see into but cannot enter. Underneath,

A sample from the famous Burne-Jones windows at Brampton

the dark low baptistry with a font like an upside-down fragment.

The greatest thrill is a rich collection of William Morris glass, especially a huge E window of saints and angels with a pelican at the base and a diapering of leaves and flowers rising into the sky. Other windows contain a complete exposition of liberal (not high) church principles. Where the pink stone arcade meets pale green wooden vaults, Webb's honesty reaches a zenith of anguished awkwardness.

The rich red exterior with its witty variations on Tudoresque battlements is more curious than beautiful, but to receive the full shock of Webb's inventiveness one must go into the small raised graveyard to look at the S aisle roof.

Brampton is very pleasant and oddly laid out, with two parallel main streets.

Cumb: 9 miles E of Carlisle on A69; church lies above and S of main road not far W of market square

Brougham

St Ninian Ninekirks (CCT)
Chapel of St Wilfrid

Two small 17c churches within three miles of each other just S of Penrith.

This is a very curious pair rebuilt by Lady Anne Clifford, Countess of Pembroke, a historically minded landowner who also reinstated various castles round about, including Brougham, whose spectacular ruin you will pass on the B6262 between the churches.

About equidistant between them along A66 is the Countess's Pillar, an eccentric memorial put up by Lady Anne to commemorate her last meeting with her mother, forty years before the erection.

Velarde's exciting 1930s Catholic church in Bootle

Brougham, St Ninian Ninekirks, an unspoiled relic of the 17c, far from any road

A new road cutting renders it invisible unless you are travelling E.

St Ninian is an unspoiled relic of its time, with lovely altar rail, box pews and screen (note coat hooks on the portion which falls within the manor's pew). *St Wilfrid's* has become something much stranger through the ministrations of a 19c antiquary. Scholars may cast doubt on his jumbling of times, places and functions, but the effect of all the imported woodwork is undeniably rich. The chapel is arranged college-fashion with pews and pulpit along the sides, ruined medieval glass in the E windows, and best of all, a hefty screen unlike any other, with robust tripartite columns adorned with fish scales, spirals and diamonds, and in the tiny spandrels, grotesque medieval holdovers. It is all very odd, un-churchy and picturesque.

Westm/Cumb: St Ninian 4 miles E of Penrith, ¼ mile from nearest road (A66) down track to N across fields, skirting River Eamont to L. St Wilfrid on B6262 (N side) just E of A6

Tomb of the man who paid for rebuilding Bunbury now blocks the chancel

Bunbury

St Boniface

An out of the way place with rich remains.

The churchyard bare and atmospheric on a windswept knoll. A crowd of finials which have come down from the roof are now displayed as ornaments and look enormous at this level.

The bulky tower fronts the road, and entering under it, you are overtaken by a sensation of late Gothic airiness. This exhilarating space is framed in the usual red sandstone. A collection of worn effigies and tombs brought in from the weather are red as well.

The chancel is blocked by the rebuilder's tomb inside an iron grille. Just to the S is the best relic at Bunbury, the stone screen and wooden doors of the Ridley Chapel. The screen has early Renaissance colours and painted ornament, and the doors are miraculous, with openings carved in imitation of woven reeds, and monograms in relief. The house built for the priests who served this chantry survives to the S.

There's an outcast standing at the W end, the stone figure of a local dancing master's wife holding a bird. She looks Sumerian. This unfortunate image was buried in the churchyard by an 18c vicar outraged by its thrusting 'udders'. Pevsner calls it a 'shockingly bad upright portrait', but it is a work of authentic folk imagination.

Cheshire: 7 miles NW of Nantwich between A51 and A49

233

Cartmel

Priory Church of St Mary & St Michael

The largest medieval church which remains intact between Chester and Carlisle, with eccentric features and fittings.

The tower's top stage is turned forty-five degrees against the rest. Spidery battlements at the corners make it look even more dynamic or precarious. The nave appears semi-fortified. Basically the fabric is Norman with huge Perpendicular windows punched in it at key places, especially the E window in chancel, which has some pale 15c glass. A good Norman door inside S porch and Early English window frames on N, with snakes at the springing.

Inside, much blank wall and some rugged carving in the chancel arcade. In fact the effect throughout is of rude vigour appropriate to the region. The Harrington tomb is one of the most interesting of its date (mid 14c) in England. It has been roughly inserted in an arch between chancel and S chapel. It has its own arcading, like woodwork in its squareness. There's much bold leafage and tracery on these connecting members and stumpy figures and scenes in profusion. Pevsner praises the high quality carving, but most viewers will find it hilariously rude. In the adjacent S

Daisy Hill. This church of brick trimmed in orange terracotta is leaving Gothic behind

chapel two coarse 18c monuments intrude on Decorated tracery and eat up two of the window lights.

The other great feature is chancel stalls and screens, mainly 17c. Pierced lattices like Middle Eastern sunshades fill the spaces behind vine-clad columns and a cornice with flying robes and other emblems of the Passion. Good earlier misericords, helpfully upturned.

Fine houses frame the churchyard to NE and the fells show beyond. Cartmel village is exceedingly attractive with a stream (the River Eea), a little square, and a large chunk of priory gatehouse.

Lancs/Cumb: 2 miles W of Grange-over-Sands on unnumbered road

Daisy Hill

St James

Westleigh

St Peter

Paley and Austin

Paley and Austin's urban churches, most of which lie between Liverpool and Manchester, are a distinctive group, different from the rural ones. Many are brick, with discreet trim in terracotta or brick of another colour. H. J. Austin joined the firm in 1868 and their best work dates from the 70s and 80s. There are four Paley and Austin churches in Bolton alone.

They are remarkable for unforced variety of form, continual spatial

Cartmel. A detail from the Harrington tomb

ingenuity and sensitivity to site and materials. A prevailing sobriety and restraint veils the considerable play of imagination.

Daisy Hill is modest though not small, while Westleigh is more lavish and imposing. At Daisy Hill the external terracotta has not weathered much and remains harsh orange in tone. The tall stepped belfry aligned with the nave is a surprise. From afar it has the solidity of a tower; nearby it is seen to be flimsy.

The interior is more impressive, an aisleless space centred on a great chancel arch and the spatial enrichments beyond it, such as free-standing mullions in lateral windows. An E window by Burne-Jones forms a fitting culmination: in slightly gloomy colours, but the drawing very clear. Quite unconventionally, large figures frame smaller ones. Nearly every other window is clear glass, especially the W with moulded brick tracery.

Westleigh has a powerful tower and silhouette. Here the slightly lighter sandstone trim is recessive; you really have to look in order to see it. This building is conceived heroically inside and out. At Daisy Hill just the suggestion of a brick arcade in the N chancel. At Westleigh a wonderful eruption of arched forms around the tower. Inside, strong impressions of timber and brick.

A selection of Paley and Austin's urban churches (all in S Lancs):
Kirby, St Chad, 1869–71
Mossley Hill, Liverpool (Rose Lane),
  St Matthew & St James, 1870–75
Prestwich, St Mary, 1888–9
Waterloo, Christ Church, 1891–4

Addresses for Bolton churches:
St Thomas 1875, Eskrick St, Halliwell
All Souls 1880–81, Astley St,
  Astley Bridge
St Saviour 1882–5, Deane Road
St Margaret 1887, St Margaret's Road

Lancs/Gtr Manchester: Daisy Hill 4 miles SW of Bolton, just S of Westhoughton; church just W of Leigh Road (B5235). Westleigh 3 miles S of Daisy Hill; church W of centre, just past turning for Ince-in-Makerfield (A578)

Finsthwaite

St Peter

Paley and Austin

Paley and Austin's small churches are among the best of their date in Britain. In a confined area just south of the Lake District you can visit three of them, and with an extension westward, a couple of more elaborate ones.

St Peter, Finsthwaite (1873–4) is the simplest and in some ways the best, wonderfully placed in a hollow so that its low tower has quiet power. It is built of slate with discreet redstone dressings. Marvellous buttresses step down

twice into the roof from the tower. Inside, a smaller space than we expect, aisleless. The chancel is another world cut off by the great tower vault. Its rafters are wonderfully ornamented. A tiny lancet at the apex peeks through them. All these windows are Henry Holiday's and very good. Looking W, a satisfyingly coherent impression with a file of original iron light fittings down the centre.

St Peter, FIELD BROUGHTON (1892–4), more refined, stands beside a minor road five miles further SE. Stone banding is used astutely and the slender tower well accented by a stair turret. Again there is expressive buttressing, like a part of the landscape, at the W end. (Open on Fridays.)

St John, FLOOKBURGH (1897–1900; 3 miles SE of Grange-over-Sands, church N of square). Reputed locally to be named for the fluke, a fish which is

Paley and Austin in Cumbria. Top: Field Broughton; above: Finsthwaite

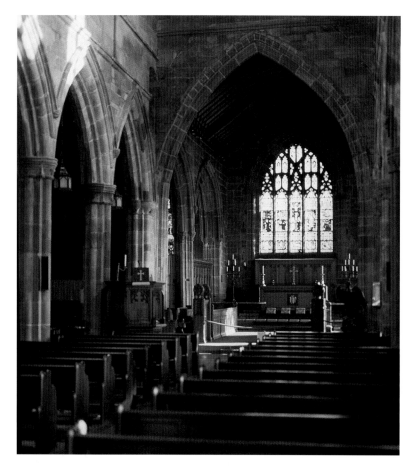

Great Budworth. Harmonious late Gothic in dark local sandstone

the town emblem, this is a place famous for shrimps caught on the sands. Here the impression is Romanesque, but many details are not. Saddleback tower, circular vestry under the raised apse. Inside, stone is powerfully present. Windows lurk under eyelids. Arcade and stairwell are massive.

Two more elaborate churches further W: DALTON-IN-FURNESS (St Mary, 1882–5, 3½ miles N of Barrow-in-Furness on A590, church at W edge), much decorative chequering in red and grey stone, an ingenious half octagon for a porch, delightful staggering of aisle windows against arcade. Its tower, looming on its bluff perch, shows wonderfully from the S. Just a mile or two in that direction lie the ruins of FURNESS ABBEY, the best medieval remains of the whole region and the inspiration for the red-grey stone combination.

At MILLOM, Cumb (St George, 1874–7; on A5093 near bottom of next peninsula W from Barrow-in-Furness),

Novel exposed roof structure at Grasmere, which makes the church like a barn

another fancy Paley and Austin job, which shows they could be uninspired. But as they built dozens of churches in the county over a fifty-year period, this is not surprising. A book about the firm is much needed.

Lancs/Cumb: 10 miles S of Windermere, 2 miles N of Newby Bridge

Gosforth

St Mary

An unattractive church in a sprawling village but the Viking remains are worth a trip to see. These include the Gosforth Cross outside, and two hogbacks and various other fragments within.

Initially the 14c cross seems rather freakish, of supernaturally spindly proportions. Like Irton's (q.v.), it is a single piece of the soft red sandstone of the district. Its perfect preservation is inexplicable. Though very slender, it is steeply tapered over its whole length. Less than halfway up it changes from cylindrical to square in section and, soon after, the figured scenes begin. These are crude and violent but haunting, like things seen in dreams. Battles between heroes and monsters or other heroes; alternate scenes are shown upside down, a bizarre convention to which one never really adjusts. Christian elements appear on one side of four and are only relatively tranquil. Though it does not at first seem a great work of art, this artefact lodges itself firmly in the memory.

The hogbacks inside have telling single figures on their ends, good tangles, and two armies behind their shields. One of the other fragments is thought to show Adam and Eve.

Cumb: 12 miles SE of Whitehaven just E of A595; church near E edge of village on road to Nether Wasdale

Grasmere

St Oswald

Wordsworth's church is just right: dateless ruggedness like a barn.

Externally there are Art Nouveau touches, melted battlements on the tower and a humpy organic roofline, which accommodates an asymmetric N aisle. Earlier writers assure us these details are medieval, and all is coated in mousy old pebbledash.

Inside, the real excitement comes in a roof structure conceptually primitive but spatially exciting. A single roof over a fairly wide span is contrived this way: down the middle of the space runs the original N wall pierced by large openings making tiered arcades. On the top of this rests the first of three gabled wooden roof structures. Its outer ends rest on the apexes of a further pair, whose inner ends meet halfway up the wall in the middle of the nave. The result is a complex lattice of timbers overhead. Much of the space the roof encloses is full of this over-complicated structure, like a lesson that goes on too long. The RCHM dates the wall 16c, the roof 17c.

A nice worn font and a fascinating memorial to Wordsworth. The inscription starts by calling him a 'philosopher' and ends making him a 'minister'. In churchyard E of the church, his (and Dorothy's and Mary's) extremely plain tombstones.

Westm/Cumb: 8 miles NW of Windermere on A591

Great Budworth

St Mary & All Saints

A regular and harmonious church in a pretty village.

It stands up well from afar and is wonderfully placed at a bend in the village street, where it turns from dense miniature urban texture to leafy but still picturesque. John Douglas built here and gave the

place some of its mellow consistency. Particularly nice his George and Dragon Inn with diminutive entrance tower.

Outside, the church looks late Gothic, with proud clerestory and battlemented tower. Inside, the great feature is the slim 15c arcade with its fascinating variety of crude faces in the interstices between the colonnettes. Nice rude bench ends, an old roof, and in the semi-distinct Lady Chapel, some lurid modern glass.

Cheshire: 3 miles N of Northwich, just E of A559

Great Mitton

All Hallows

Notable for fittings: roof, screens, and astonishing 18c monuments unique in England.

At the edge of wonderful country; the Forest of Bowland lies to the N. Not prepossessing outside, though there are an interesting sundial and a lovely 14c

cross in the churchyard. Some harsh and some attractive signs of 19c interference in the friendly, barny interior. Victorian tiles in chancel (incised on floor, embossed on step-risers) somehow fit nicely with folkish screen, iron topped, to the Shireburne Chapel. The chancel screen is finer and full of faces at waist level. It was salvaged from Sawley Abbey. The roof, with heroic frills at the points where timbers cross, can be inspected from the gallery.

Tombs are probably the most spectacular feature of all. There is one where a child out for a walk in a loose robe meets a skull and bones on the ground, at which he stares like a character in an upper-class *Pilgrim's Progress*. There are also a number of 17c gents in calf hose and buckled shoes who lie stiffly with legs demonstratively crossed, as if remembering Crusader forbears. One of these and the boy were carved by William Stanton.

W Yorks/Lancs: 8 miles NE of Blackburn on B6246; church E of road

Heysham, in a steep churchyard perched over the sea

Heysham*

St Peter, St Patrick

Important Saxon remains in a charming and unexpected coastal backwater.

St Peter's stands at the edge of the old village centre overlooking Morecambe Sands and the sea. It is diminutive like a dale chapel with squareheaded Tudor windows and a low porch.

Inside, it feels like a platform suspended over the sea in spectral light. The S arcade is granite, chunky and warm. There are bold rope-capitals on the chancel arch and in the SE corner a window formerly external has been immured by extension of the aisle. This contains a beautiful example of organic Decorated tracery, very simple.

Nearby, one of the best of all hogback tombs, with many animals and men crunched between the big beast heads at the ends. Other Saxon remains include a blocked W door, another free-standing portal in SW corner of churchyard, and a fascinating cross-base beside the path going in. On its front a little building

Irton Cross, with deeply carved patterns like the carpet pages of illuminated manuscripts

with a figure in the doorway and heads at the windows. Pevsner calls these 'busts', as if it were a columbarium or tomb of some kind.

Just a bit further W, even nearer the sea and more exposed to biting winds, are the ruins of another Saxon chapel, *St Patrick*. Blank walls rise from massive live-rock foundations. The best architectural feature is an empty doorway with ridgy arch made from one lump of stone. As often in Saxon work, though stones are massive, the treatment of form makes the result feel insubstantial. Nearby a line of six coffins has been hollowed in the cliff-slab. These are outlines of stunted jar-shape and are often full of water.

In good weather all the hills of Lakeland are visible to the N. Walking S along the forlorn cliffs, in a minute or two you are pulled up short by the surprising vision of a nuclear power station.

* Pronounced Hee-shm

Lancs: on W coast continuous with and S of Morecambe, which is 2 miles NW of Lancaster; church is in Lower Heysham, the old village

Kendal stretches on and on laterally, and finally one's orientation changes

Irton

St Paul

One of the best Norse crosses in the churchyard of a charming Victorian church.

The building is isolated at the end of a track with striking views to the NE as far as Wasdale Head. IRTON CROSS, S of the church, is a very ruddy orange on the E face, better preserved on W. Carpet patterns like those in manuscripts on E, knots on W, protrusive baubles in the centre of the lively misshapen head. A moving presence in this windswept place; an Art Nouveau imitation is located lower down to SW, with a stone rail behind.

The church is unattractive outside but lovely within. Its scale is wonderful, like a model, and there are many entertaining fittings – a painted iron screen in tower arch, rustic wooden haunches in chancel roof, lots of Victorian banners on the walls and very amusing narrative windows. These include four good late panels by Burne-Jones, of which the oddest is the Tiburtine Sibyl in a lionskin by an altar.

Cumb: 3 miles SE of Gosforth, about 1 mile E of A595, N from the unnumbered road which leaves A595 just S of where it crosses the River Irt

Lancaster, an impressive church in an impressive location by the Castle

Kendal

Holy Trinity

Topographically interesting town; the main interest of the Perp church is topographical too.

Highgate is the spine of the little stone town, and there are few other streets, at least in the older part near the river. Formerly a series of wynds or courts, still decipherable though somewhat defaced, joined the two arteries – road and waterway. This peculiarity makes for a fiendish one-way system and a hard-to-reach church.

Seen from across the river, the E end of Holy Trinity is a series of irregular units strung together. It seems to go on and on. The tower is the oldest, most authentic bit of masonry. Much Victorian renewal in aisles. Again, the W end is a remarkable agglomerate, like a neighbourhood without streets.

Inside, the effect of constantly shifting space is very powerful. Four arcades quite varied and many extended vistas, so that one's orientation tends to become lateral instead of longitudinal.

The font is a great lump of black marble with concave sides. Though the Guild windows in clerestory are garish Victorian, they hold one more strongly than such things usually do. In NE corner, a lovely Flaxman relief of a grieving family.

Westm/Cumb: 27 miles S of Penrith on A6; church S of centre, near old bridge over the Kent. Highgate, the street in which it sits, takes N-bound traffic only

Kirkby Lonsdale

St Mary the Virgin

Good Norman and Early English parts roughly cobbled together make a noble overall impression.

An exceedingly pleasant town with a curving main street has an oddly situated church, reached through impressive iron gates, off to one side from the bustle.

The tower is Norman with a good W doorway, the E end an energetic Early English composition. Although this gives the key to what we find inside, we are not prepared for the rudeness of the juncture. Instead of a Norman arcade modulating to a later one, it is as though they started from opposite ends and met in the middle.

The Norman half which begins at the tower is heroic in scale – massive circular piers incised as at Durham Cathedral, with a ragged assortment of fine carving in the capitals. At the E end a tranquil vesica-lancet group, carried rather clumsily past the arcades to the outer wall. These arcades are much higher and wider; their meeting with the massive Norman ones is oddly exciting.

A hundred yards from the NE corner of the churchyard, RUSKIN'S VIEW unfolds. This is a vista he praised as one of the world's loveliest. Now canonized by signs, pavilions and benches, it is a surprisingly mild scene. You are raised above a great curve in the River Lune which sweeps in very near the precipice on which you stand. A single old farm asserts the human presence in the foreground. Otherwise a constantly undulating hill landscape, full of subtle variation and distinctly feminine.

Westm/Cumb: 12 miles SE of Kendal on A65 (which now bypasses town); church at N edge, E of High Street

239

Lancaster

Priory Church of St Mary

In a wonderful position overlooking this seemly smallish town. It is reached by impressive steps and abuts the large castle which was tamed by J. M. Gandy so that it now sports Gothick elements.

Frank Welsh (in the *Companion Guide*) calls the church 'a decent Gothic building'. The tower is 18c and the S aisle late Perp. Inside, the best feature is a set of 14c stall canopies which look like a riot of Spanish stone carving in wood. They culminate in square finials, elaborate and inflexible at once, a morbid richness of decay.

Nearby, a memorial with the grotesque classical scene of a young girl on a bier and onlookers in Roman dress. In the churchyard another lounging female inside a railed plot and good views of the ASHTON MEMORIAL (by Belcher, 1906–9) on a distant hillock, a preposterous extravaganza of angular Baroque. Among superfluous stone piles this ranks high. In the lower town, a very good 18c church, *St John's*: dark stone and pleasingly rational shapes, now CCT.

Lancs: 21 miles N of Preston on A6; church at N end of town, W of A6

Lower Peover. Timber framed outside, and a forest of old wood within

Lanercost

St Mary Magdalene

A parish church has been contrived from the nave and N aisle of a large priory cannibalized at the Dissolution to make the former manor house strung out to the SW of it. The partly roofless ruin lies on low ground by the River Irthing about half a mile S of Hadrian's Wall, from which many stones were borrowed for the Priory. (The original charter grants the canons all the land between wall and river for a considerable stretch.) Now the precinct is entered through a large stone arch left from a vanished gatehouse, and its lawns are tended by a herd of cows.

The present E wall, erected in the 18c, looks out through high clear windows onto the visionary suggestions of a great crossing and chancel beyond. The enormous churchyard circles the ruined precincts (now in English Heritage care and open the standard hours) charily. Along all the damaged N flank runs a horizontal swathe in the pink stone which deepens to blood red and fiery orange. In fact marauding Scots burnt this establishment several times.

The W front is a rich yet masculine Early English composition, not afraid to put large forms on small (three great lancets on a blind arcade) or curvilinear next to angular (the housing for a statue high in the gable with heraldic lozenges appended). Inside, a bare and demanding impression with the welcome surprise of some Burne-Jones glass.

Lanercost. Magnificent proportions and Early English W front with monastic ruins to S and E

Cumb: 11 miles NE of Carlisle, 2 miles NE of Brampton on unnumbered road

Lower Peover*

St Oswald

A timber church of extreme picturesqueness. It is approached down a narrow cobbled lane. The little group around the church includes a stately but minute brick school founded in 1710.

Outside, St Oswald's is half-timber regularized and extended by Salvin in 1852. He also complicated a formerly simple roof into three separate ones for nave and aisles.

It's the interior we value here, with its dark arcade of octagonal posts, its varied screens – some strutted, some balustered – and the rich smell of wood. It forms an obscure webbed space, a real House of Wood. Though partly renewed, the arcades are probably 14c or even 13c in origin. But one of the most fetching details, the little lattice of open space between arcade and roof, may be a Victorian improvement.

* Pronounced Peever

Cheshire: 3 miles S of Knutsford, a turning E from B5081; church at end of cul-de-sac

Malpas

St Oswald

An atmospheric place with plenty of old fittings.

The pleasant miniature town with a steep market place lies near the Welsh border. The church makes a wonderful silhouette from afar and is placed oddly, away from the centre. Houses around it fall below the high churchyard with its fine pair of gates, which some have tried to connect with Vanbrugh. The grave markers have mostly been cleared, producing, quite unusually, a feeling of 18c gentility. On the N lies a refined brick vestry of this date and gargoyles which look like 17c folk art, including a pair of witches with dangling dugs. On the other side, a muzzled bear, also found inside on an alabaster tomb, behind a 16c screen with a big admonitory inscription which begins with a pointing hand. The main space is splendid with high arcades and a very rich roof. Here there is an abrupt contrast between dark timbers and gilded bosses.

Looking more closely at the screens, you will see gaps eked out with cast-iron replicas, a common practice in this region in the 19c.

Cheshire: 5 miles NW of Whitchurch on B5069; church is W of centre

Liverpool, Sefton Park, St Clare by Leonard Stokes

Liverpool, Sefton Park

St Clare, Arundel Avenue (RC)
St Agnes, Ullet Road
Unitarian Church, Ullet Road

A haven of interesting Victorian churches. Important works by Pearson and Leonard Stokes, and probably the most lavish and artistically accomplished Unitarian church in England.

Stokes's *St Clare* is the most exciting. It is made of brick purple and sad like a bruise, or something burnt or charred, set against the bone colour of stone trim. This is discreet, terminal Gothic; inside, more bold. Here it is unfortunate that stone piers which traverse the wall from floor to roof should now be painted; thus a subtle and precise textural contrast is lost. It can be imagined from bits which remain exposed.

Arcades continue, but beyond them, as you move E, chapels appear, seen through the forest of columns. The little door at W exactly framed by the passage through these piers makes a wonderful vista. Though much freer and cleaner, the whole effect of this space is not utterly different from Bodley's Pendlebury (q.v.).

There is a good painted reredos of the period, very saccharine, with the only stained glass window in the church, also good, above it.

Pearson's *St Agnes* is very regular, a scaled-down cathedral. Brick outside; stone, white but with a lovely fleshly tinge inside. A complete miniature ambulatory and a preposterous forest of Purbeck columns holding up the organ, one of which steps forward from its row. This interior which carries itself much bigger than it is embodies an inexplicable miracle of scale. The vicarage just behind the church is an interesting work of Norman Shaw's, 1887. To the (ritual) S a lovely garden of five years' growth (in 1990), the creation of a devoted parishioner.

Unitarian Church by Percy Worthington almost adjacent, in brick of invigorating harsh pink with dark trim. Beaten metal sea-swell doors. Very lavish meeting rooms, library, etc. In some of these, remarkable frescoes.

Lancs/Merseyside: district is SE of city centre, just N of park

Manchester

First Church of Christ Scientist, Daisy Bank, Victoria Park

Edgar Wood

Voysey never built a church. Perhaps this one of 1903 is what it would have been like if he had.

Edgar Wood, the Manchester architect who designed it, was quietly original. Unlike Frank Lloyd Wright, he never broke radically with traditional motifs. Instead he twists forms and shapes learned from vernacular structures to produce results with real personality.

Like his earlier Methodist church at Middleton this is a conglomerate building, dominated by a huge gable in the centre. This overpowering form is thin and steep like the central bony vane of a skeleton which throws out diagonal wings. An angular gate with a round opening echoes the main form, but the closer one looks, the more one finds the eccentric symmetry violated by odd stair turrets and unevenly placed doorways.

Materials are both rigorous and earthy – great expanses of pale green plaster against orange brick and stone trim the colour of wet sand. All the roofs, racing dramatically towards the ground, are slated. This is a building which never ceases to surprise, flexible past any need, combining disparate forms for the pure joy of it. Large bay windows in the L

The lavish two-storey S porch at Malpas leads to a rich late Gothic interior

wing are staggered opposite each other as if the room were a rolled newspaper being twisted. The parking lot is a perfect circle in gravel, outside a Cubist porte-cochère which conceals a saucer dome.

Inside, surprising green marble like murals on the walls, vaguely Venetian. Huge dormers in the nave letting in much light. Sad to say, the building is degraded to an examination hall for

Manchester Metropolitan University and normally locked against visitors.

Lancs/Gtr Manchester: SE of city centre just E of A34; church on S side of street

Marple Bridge*

St Martin, Brabyns Brow

J. D. Sedding, Henry Wilson

Another of the shrines of the Arts and Crafts movement, with an aisle by Henry Wilson, quirkily fitted out.

The church is modest and not entirely characteristic of J. D. Sedding, who took it over from his brother in 1869–70. Inside, some gorgeous Morris glass with flowers at the Virgin's feet and fruiting trees elsewhere.

Wilson's N aisle, of the following decades, is rich, strange and disquieting. The reredos shows an Annunciation against a wild Peak District landscape. It is surrounded by fantastic woodwork, forming low walls, thickets, etc. The vault overhead feels primitive, embossed with decadent life, including plenty of thorns. As at Brithdir in North Wales, Wilson's colour scheme was peculiar and appalling. The 'sky' is midnight blue and all the vegetable detail gold and silver leaf.[†] Some good Christopher Whall windows and a font cover which is yet another last word in vegetable decadence.

For the churchyard Wilson designed a founder's tomb of gloriously primeval character, a huge rough slab like an uneven slice of bread, with metal inlay, which appears to be suspended a few inches above the ground. The lychgate looks like Sedding's work; more like it than the church, in fact.

* Listed as MARPLE in Pevsner and LOW MARPLE in *Faber Guide to Victorian Churches*

† Or will be, after intended restoration

Cheshire/Gtr Manchester: Marple is 3 miles E of Stockport (SE Manchester); church E of town on A626, just past railway station on N side of road (W of Marple Bridge)

Middleton

Long Street Methodist Church

Edgar Wood

In this complex by Edgar Wood some of the late 19c discoveries in English domestic design are brought over into

Harmonious meeting of classical and latest Gothic at Much Hoole

church architecture for the first time. It fronts a busy road. Going through an archway, we find an assortment of buildings grouped informally around a small formal garden.

The church proper is brick with purplish sandstone trim, a subtle contrast employed both inside and out. Tracery on the W elevation is wonderful for springy organic energy, yet pared down past any literal resemblance. The single decorative effusion is a large openwork finial of tulip shape on the W gable. Wood has purified Gothic almost out of existence.

In the rest of the complex – church hall, school, etc – brick functions as enrichment of a pebbledash fabric, in buttresses and oriels, a further relaxation of decorum.

Within a few years Wood had moved further still beyond these bold simplifications (see Manchester).

Lancs/Gtr Manchester: 5 miles NE of centre of Manchester; church lies just N of centre of Middleton on W side of A6046 (Long Street)

Millom

Holy Trinity (Old Church)

A palimpsest of the centuries next to a shambling castle which is the same.

Wonderful glimpses of Lakeland hills and Morecambe Sands on the way S to Millom. The church is tucked inconspicuously behind the castle, which became a fortified house and finally just a farm; all these stages now jumbled and congested together. Church hovers on edge of the dry moat, which is surprisingly intact. There are Norman traces, an airy granite arcade, a strange vesica window in S aisle (tracery renewed), good lattice tracery in E, and two coarse tombs, one in alabaster with figures, the other in red sandstone with shields. Pews with doors, a great chancel arch, and an organ gallery which looks 18c but actually dates from 1930. Millom is one of those special places where strong flavours harmonize and nothing is dull.

Also in Millom is the Paley and Austin church of *St George*, for which see Finsthwaite.

Cumb: 6 miles SW of Broughton in Furness on B5093; church is 1 mile N of town, behind Millom Castle, on W side of road

Pleasing simplicity of untraceried windows at Mobberley

Mobberley

St Wilfrid

Notable for its woodwork, especially a magnificent screen.

Though near Knutsford, it feels quite dislocated from present patterns of settlement, away in its own tiny enclave. The overall impression mellow, with simple untraceried windows as in a Cornish church, and leaning walls.

Woodwork is the great thing, a roof whose huge beams are crusty with decoration, and above all a screen which has the peculiarity of carved frillwork on the narrower sides of the upright members. This creates an effect as of window sills or reveals.

Paintings on the N arcade give a blurred sensation of drama, and you should also look at wooden memorials high on the chancel wall. One shows the corpse laid out and various emblems flying around in the adjacent air.

Cheshire: about 3 miles NE of Knutsford; church is about ¼ mile N of B5085

Much Hoole

St Michael

A lovable chapel of 1628, semi-Georgianized.

The harmony of these two diverse styles is uncanny. One must attribute it to unusual delicacy or extreme conservatism in the later builders. Basically the brick body dates from the earlier time, and the stone frontispiece from the later. But there is some interfusion: the little brick porch sports three flaming vases, and the W front, with its pair of grand Tuscan columns supporting an arch traced across the façade, reverts to Gothic further up the tower. Surprisingly the association of quoins with pointed tracery passes off peacefully.

Inside, we find two more Tuscan columns – the tower rests on four of them. There's a gallery on the S side not matched on the N, and light filters down from two dormers in half-timbered recesses. The ceiling is a segmental vault, and there is interesting pictorial glass in the E, and some of the 1970s round the font.

The building lies in slantwise proximity to the old road now bypassed by a new one to the E.

Lancs: 7 miles SW of Preston; church on loop just W of A59, on E side of road

Nantwich

St Mary

An attractive small town with an imposing church of red sandstone.

There is a great octagonal central tower, a rich assortment of tracery, and a soaring purplish red nave. The chancel is the pride of this church. Under a stone

vault with many bosses, the stalls have wooden canopies, 14 feet high, with three big statue niches each. The full set of misericords is less wonderful, but helpfully turned up and lit by special yellow lights which make them gleam. Nantwich is altogether a church friendly to visitors.

Just before the crossing is a remarkable window of 1919 by the Irish Symbolist whom Yeats admired, Harry Clarke. It shows motherhood and sacrifice through various saints and emblems. The effect is lurid, jewel-like and, alas, a bit sentimental. In the N transept a Tree of Jesse window which is partly old, partly Kempe at his best.

Cheshire: 4 miles SW of Crewe on A534

Nantwich, an imposing town church in red sandstone with an octagonal tower at the crossing

Pendlebury

St Augustine, Bolton Road

G. F. Bodley

Bodley's greatest work and one of the highest achievements of the Gothic Revival.

The setting is surprising and the building appears to increase the awkwardness of the place. St Augustine's is a long tall vessel of brick, like some kind of industrial building when seen from afar, or like a great ship adrift on an alien sea of scrapyards, rusty fencing and high grass. It turns away from the road, and the W end takes a while to reach: only a public footpath passes there. The collegial quadrangle Bodley planned is now desolate, his vicarage demolished and the low shambles of a 1930s school risen in its place.

But the approach down an avenue of limes to the tall E end is the more impressive for the feeling of ruin on all sides. This façade is focused on the great window, from which complex panelling and a series of figures in niches radiate. The endless side wall you must then pass along is like a common experience in the modern industrial city, a power station or a railway shed, though here diversified high up with lots of Gothic perfectionism.

Inside, a single space, impossibly tall. The arcades barely detach themselves from the wall. They are internalized buttresses and soar up in unbroken strands of tawny stone. Patterns on nave walls have been whitewashed over, but the chancel is covered from head to foot in stencilling.

Spatially the most exciting experience is threading the passageway carved down the sides in those pier-buttresses. It is like walking through the wall. Overhead in each bay is a truly exquisite painting of a richly panelled saint. The glass by Burlisson and Grylls is, heresy to report, the best in any Victorian church. Bodley had a crippling idea of what glass was there for, which ruled out most pictorial narrative. So you get endless figures of saints which stay within the narrow bounds of adjacent mullions. Here the code is triumphantly justified. E and W windows are ravishing, one pale, the other rich (here a Tree of Jesse is permitted, a concession to drama). And the drawing in the aisle windows of trios of saints is lovely, very Düreresque. By contrast with the noble religiosity here, William Morris looks purely secular.

St Augustine's, practically in sight of a colliery, was donated to a poor district by a wealthy banker. It's another example of that strange Victorian philanthropic prompting represented also by St Bartholomew, Brighton, the inner city churches of James Brooks, and others.

Lancs/Gtr Manchester: NW outskirts of Manchester, N of Agecroft Road; church lies W of road

St Bees

Priory Church of St Mary & St Bega

Impressive Norman and Early English remains in an atmospheric coastal village.

St Bees is a little grim, like a mining town, in a steep hollow by the sea. The best approach to the church is from parking lot to SE. First you come on the chancel with its aisle shorn off, leaving a wonderful Early English arcade traced on the wall, the openings roughly filled with rectangular, secular-looking windows. At this point you don't know that the church has been deprived of these E parts; they are now a school music room, which does not connect, and you will see no more of them.

Passing the Victorianized nave and aisles, you are crushed between the powerful W front and nearby walls. Big buttresses, lancets above and the massive bulge of the Norman portal in red stone. Opposite is displayed the best single piece at St Bees, a gabled tympanum with St Michael fighting a worm-like dragon, the leftover space filled by disorderly snarls. This is wild early Norman. Beneath it an interesting cross head.

Inside, an impressive Norman arcade and good proportions, except that the space ends prematurely eastwards, just after the crossing. In the enormous tower opening is a remarkable painted iron screen by William Butterfield. This looks fabulous in dim light. It is just the right scale for its Herculean task (coping with truncation of the vista), in colours soft for this architect: ochre, rust, pale blue. The S aisle contains many incised tomb slabs, ruined effigies and Saxon fragments.

Cumb: 4 miles S of Whitehaven on B5345; church on W side of road and N side of town

Standish. Latest Gothic, with Tuscan columns, and a lively wooden roof

Preston

St Walburge, Weston Street (RC)

J. A. Hansom

Hansom's St Walburge is a Victorian tour de force, not tasteful but astonishing.

Preston has many interesting Roman Catholic churches, but this one stands out. Its neighbourhood of humble terraces is cut off by railway lines and has a wonderful lost feel, like an old ethnic neighbourhood in the American Midwest.

The spire, visible from anywhere in Preston, is built of an eerie white stone. It is the third tallest in England and attains an unnerving slenderness. It is fully detached from the body of the church which seems pedestrian by contrast, in rusticated and rather unattractive flesh-coloured stone. The W front is dominated by a huge rose.

Inside, a vast undivided hall with the preposterous wooden roof hanging over it. At the end of each hammerbeam stands a lifesize, brightly coloured saint. The complexity of trusses and cusps is indescribable, like matchsticks on a heroic scale. Formerly black with gold highlighting, the timbers are now painted mahogany colour.

The chancel bristles with carved images, some under good ironwork canopies. The apse extension came twenty years after the church and contains effective glass with rich blue backgrounds. St Walburge was a Jesuit foundation, which explains the large complex of buildings to the N.

Lancs: 30 miles NE of Liverpool; church lies NW of centre, S of A583

Sefton

St Helen

Sefton is one of those miraculous treasures among parish churches which appears to emerge unscathed from the centuries.

Its situation is now peculiar, in a desolate seclusion though only eight miles from the centre of Liverpool, as if its village had been emptied by some catastrophe. Externally it is ambitious Perpendicular carried out in rather battered red sandstone. The queerest feature is four pots or fused vases hemming in the spire at its base. They look like ad hoc Baroque.

Whatever the harshness or anomalies of the exterior, inside it is one of the most satisfying imaginable. High arcades, mellow roof and gorgeous screens in soft grey wood. Some of the harmony of the whole impression may be due to Caröe's tactful additions, which are indistinguishable in the upper reaches of the screen, with its lavish pendulous coving, including the magical motif of a pomegranate erupting in a sunburst. Along the dado, friezes of putti. Further variety in other screens (note pseudo-iron grilles in wood) is a never-ending delight.

Old bench ends include a complete alphabet. For the aisles Caröe copied a folkish design found in N chapel. There is further uncountable wealth of hatchments, brasses and enrichments,

Waberthwaite, a dale chapel with a complete pre-Victorian interior

and, in the E parts, lovely warrens of smaller spaces made by the screens.

Lancs/Merseyside: about 8 miles N of the centre of Liverpool in an obscure location, just N of B5422 between Litherland and Maghull

Standish

St Wilfrid

A harmonious single build in latest Gothic tipping into Tudor.

Warburton, Old St Werburgh, a lucky survivor left standing when the new church was built

Its surfaces are nicely blackened, and it sits in a huge churchyard, a boon in an urban district. The tower collapsed early in the 19c and was rebuilt in harder textured stone than the rest.

Inside, the Tuscan arcade is a delightful surprise, with unorthodox drips from undersides of capitals. The roof is spectacularly good: in each panel a criss-cross of moulded braces making a lively effect.

At the W end an exceedingly refined neo-classical monument by John Bacon Jr. It depicts two women admiring the bust of a man which is set in the face of an urn. Below, a sea port in minute relief – is it Liverpool? Plans are afoot to replace sickly yellow glass in the clerestory with clear.

Lancs/Gtr Manchester: 3 miles N of Wigan; church on S side of B5239

Stockport

St George, Buxton Road

Paley and Austin

A very impressive late Victorian church, all in dark sandstone; probably the grandest work of Paley and Austin who built a great many in the north west.

This is a building of daunting consistency on a magnificent scale. It now has an appealing sooty richness and forms a dark silhouette, culminating in the tall spire with miniature tendons of flying buttress at the corners.

Inside, lofty but a bit cold. There is little you could call decoration, yet the endless panelling on every stone surface seems fussy. Some good woodwork, notably roof beams with Art Nouveau detail, and the organ and N reredos.

By and large it is a work too anonymous to rouse much passion, except in details like the inner tracery of the E window, where bony ribs stick out and are then dissected vertically.

Cheshire/Gtr Manchester: Stockport is now joined to Manchester's SE edge; church in triangle formed by the meeting of A6 and A5102

Torpenhow*

St Michael

One of the most harmonious churches in the county, a combination of early and late, Norman and 17c.

The building is low and wide with massive buttresses on W and S. By the door, a windbreak, and within the later porch, a superb Norman portal, leaning, in tawny and iron-orange stones. A good capital with small beast heads is matched by another in the chancel arch.

Inside, the arcade is wide and hefty, of a grainy texture like granite. The felt presence of stone is exceptional in this space. One of the chancel walls is practically unwindowed and the canted vestry entrance, though chunky, is real virtuoso masonry.

Strong carved detail in chancel arch and capitals, and overhead a surprising wooden roof. It is flat, with faint decoration in its central oval. Around the edge a deep, sculptural moulding of which whole sections are thrown forward. The effect is a rustic version of a Venetian audience room.

* Pronounced Tre-penna

Cumb: about 8 miles NE of Cockermouth, 1 mile E of Bothal (and A595); church at NE edge of village

Ulpha*

St John

Notable for its simple purity and fine location.

It sits at the end (or beginning) of one of the best roads over the fells, running N to Eskdale. Behind, a stream rushes past at the bottom of the promontory on which the little harled building is perched.

Bell ropes dangle through the porch roof from the belfry above. This porch of slate looks recent, and its pointed opening frames a hill view like the ragged entrance to a grotto.

Inside, utter simplicity with deep sloping window sills and fragmentary relics of 17c wall paintings. One bit of sophistication is the Art Nouveau reredos in beaten metal; ferns in the R panel are especially good.

* The name may mean 'enclosure where wolves are trapped', from Old Scandinavian.

Cumb: 5 miles N of Broughton in Furness on unnumbered road; church on E side of road beside River Duddon

Waberthwaite

St John

Another simple dale chapel in an evocative estuarine location.

Just beyond the church the River Esk serpents its way through mudbanks. St John is a low ground-hugging building lost among a shambles of farm structures. In the churchyard the base of a Saxon cross with awkward, loopy knotwork.

A good finial on one gable, a simple belfry on the other, and a very low porch to enter by. Inside, a single simple space with box pews, text boards and a pulpit more elaborate than the

rest, its inscriptions still hidden by a fringed frontal in spite of chidings by guidebooks.

Further E, a ridiculous but likeable cast-iron altar rail of jagged pattern painted grey.

Cumb: 1 mile SE of Ravenglass as the crow flies, in Hall Waberthwaite on the River Esk

Warburton

Old St Werburgh (CCT)
New St Werburgh

Two churches, old and new, the one a marvel of preserved rusticity, the other a refined late Victorian work by **John Douglas**.

Warburton has been kept a sheltered backwater by the Manchester Ship Canal, which was meant to bring prosperity and growth. The bridge where anachronistic tolls are still collected is a high and awkward causeway over a floodplain, and its tollbooth a quaint work by Douglas.

The old church is a crazy conglomerate of stone, brick and half-timber, which was mercifully spared much regularizing improvement. A tiny brick tower with stone spikes sits incongruously at the E end. The roof inside is barn-like with lower chancel, aisles and S extension tacked on. Detailed records survive of pew assignments, but half the pews are gone.

Ulpha. Utter simplicity among the fells

Douglas located the new church a mile or so from the old in its mellow churchyard. His is a discreet building of subtle colours and unshowy details. As in many of this architect's interiors much interest centres on the roof. Gothic detail in such places as the window tracery seems on the point of giving up its historical pedigree. A glazed brick floor is the single note of strong colour.

Next door the former vicarage, now the church rooms, is Douglas's mellow picturesque at its best. More Douglas houses nearby.

Cheshire/Gtr Manchester: 7 miles E of Warrington, about 1 mile S of A57; old church 200 yds W of B5159 before bridge; new church on E side of A6144

Wasdale Head

St Olaf

In the most sublime setting in Cumbria is found the region's most exquisitely humble church.

The only paved approach takes you down the whole length of Wastwater. Hills press in on the L, dark water of the deepest and wildest of the Lakes on the R, with the famous screes forming the other shore. At the end of the journey is a flat valley-head, surrounded by high peaks including Great Gable.

The church looks forlorn, a low shed, sunken in the earth and shrouded by a

Rich wooden textures at Whalley, which include stalls from the abbey

little crowd of yews which stick up in an emptiness marked by low stone walls.

Windows are scarce, and posts and beams of the roof come very near overhead. Electric light and a patron saint (Olaf, a Norse king) new since 1977. This church still had a dirt floor, unglazed windows and a hurdle at the door early in the last century. Only then was a graveyard allowed. Previously corpses were carried across the hill into Eskdale for burial at Boot.

By comparison, the modest church at NETHER WASDALE is very spruce and

Wasdale Head, a humble building at the head of Wastwater

civilized (4 miles E of Gosforth; church just W of point where roads to Eskdale and Wasdale Head split). It has an octagonal arcade, making for pleasant spatial complexity, and some nice woodwork. The farm landscape at this end of the lake seems soft and effete after the rigours of the upper end.

Cumb: Wasdale Head about 8 miles NE of Gosforth on unnumbered road which goes at first directly E; church is short distance SE of inn at Wasdale Head

Whalley

St Mary All Saints

Whalley has one of the richest, most interesting interiors in the county, the sediment of many centuries.

The tiny town is extremely pleasant, and the churchyard makes a kind of close or precinct away from the High Street. Externally the church has a mellow 16c or even 17c appearance brought on by the secular-looking tower placed sideways to the body. Outside the S door, a Saxon cross surprisingly thin for its width, with bold patterns like an impressionistic translation of acanthus, which could almost be Arts and Crafts. Two other crosses, one by chancel door, one further S, on which some detect the Scandinavian 'Dog of Berser'.

Inside, later dormers bring a hint of 18c freshness to the high narrow nave, which is basically Early English. The roofs are notable: prickly lacework in the nave, and barn-like simplicity in the chancel. To the R is a large pew with its own carved screens like a small room, called The Cage. It is inscribed with various dates and is essentially 17c. Other pews and screens, and in the chancel a magnificent set of stalls and misericords from the Abbey, whose ruins may be inspected to the SE (especially an Early English doorway with giant wide-spaced bosses).

Pevsner rates the misericords among the best in England. Good neo-classical monuments in chancel. A beautiful Hepplewhite altar table with cups, grapes and grain in N chapel. Over it, a pleasant surprise: the window of 1918 in sultry enamel style by a pupil of Christopher Whall. In S aisle there is a window by Whall himself.

Lancs: 6 miles NE of Blackburn between A59 and A671

Whitehaven

St James

The best 18c church in the county raised above one of the most interesting planned towns in England.

Whitehaven is a unique example of 17c town planning. Basically, a grid layout has been attached to a small tangled core. Now the streets are only intermittently harmonious because of depletions in the old fabric, but to some viewers this variety will make the place all the more interesting. Whitehaven is not a museum and still enjoys a certain amount of dereliction. The harbour too is a unique survival of 17c forms, with later additions.

St James sits apart from the old core, surrounded by grey council housing of the 1960s instead of the Georgian terraces which framed it originally. It ends a vista at the top of a gentle slope, its squat ashlar tower forming a centrepiece between pebbledash aisles.

Inside, too, proportions are comfortably squat, after the stair-vestibule which is probably the most elegant space. Galleries carry Ionic columns; architrave composed of plaster roses looking in different directions. A low segmental arch in the apse, and an unjustly celebrated Italian painting in the reredos. Most of the windows are framed in narrow bands of red glass with short Scriptural texts written in yellow across them.

Cumb: 8 miles S of Workington on A595; church at N end of Queen Street (N edge of old core)

Wreay, one of the most original in England, the brainchild of a local bluestocking

Wreay*

St Mary

Sara Losh

One of the most original buildings in England, the brainchild of a local bluestocking, Sara Losh, who meant it as a memorial to her dead sister and their Continental tour of 1817. She rediscovers the spirit of Romanesque carving via, of all things, early 19c science.

The W front displays various primitive species – horsetail, coral, ammonite fossils – rudely carved by local workmen. The whole complex exhibits a voracious ransacking of the past and love of odd corners of vegetable and animal creation (huge insects, palm trees and flowers are everywhere). One would dearly love to see Sara Losh's garden, but this homely building with cosmic ambitions is perhaps an approximation. Pulpit and reading desks are monstrous growths, half stump, half carved bog oak. Fossil silhouettes let in light through twelve lunettes around an apse of early Christian flavour. Beneath them are seven 'lamps of the spirit' – mysterious orange and yellow glass spheres inserted in the wall above ritual seats, and burning with the unexpected fire of daylight. The font cover is a lily pond made of mirror with stone leaves and blooms 'floating' in it.

To the N of the church is the culmination of Miss Losh's symbolic vision: a family graveyard like an archaeological site, where one walks among toppled stones as if back at Palmyra. You might almost mistake the bumpy carvings for fossils and the cross stump nearby for a Saxon or Greek relic. It shows Miss Losh had studied Bewcastle (q.v.), but is a memorial to her parents. The locked mausoleum adjacent lets us peer in at the seated marble figure of her sister holding another pine cone, one of many here preaching the doctrine of death bursting with seeds of further life.

Nearby are little Romanesque cottages in stone, still other signs of Sara Losh's intellectual energies.

* Pronounced Wree-a

Cumb: about 7 miles S of Carlisle between M6 and A6

Whitehaven, the best 18c church in Cumbria in a 17c planned town

Glossary

achievement heraldic term for coat of arms

Agnus Dei (Latin: Lamb of God) Christ depicted as a lamb holding a flag, an emblem of sacrifice

ambulatory continuous walkway at E end, between chancel and outside wall, or chancel and chapels further E

ashlar dressed stone which is given a smooth surface, as against undressed stone or rubble, which is left rough

baldacchino tent-like canopy over a freestanding altar, generally supported by four columns

ballflower a type of Decorated decoration: small, widely spaced spheres in a concave moulding, minimally characterized as flowers

barrel vault simple vault in form of continuous round arch; also called tunnel vault

battlement ornament on parapet, imitated from fortification, consisting of alternating higher and lower sections, in later examples sometimes elaborately pierced

beakhead Norman decorative feature, a zigzag-like fringe in the form of birds' beaks, found around doorframes, internal aisles and, more rarely, windows

black letter or Gothic script; the form of writing with thick black vertical strokes characteristic of many 13–17c inscriptions

boss a decorative termination in wood or stone, a bulge or finial at crossing or meeting point of members

box pew a form of seating with relatively high, thin wooden walls separating one set of seats from another

broach spire where octagonal spire modulates direct from square tower (rather than from within parapet) by means of conical segments; Early English

buttress generally a stone support perpendicular to the wall it supports; it may be stepped, angled from a corner, or so thoroughly pierced it seems to be 'flying'

chamfer softening of a right angle in stone or woodwork by shaving off edge

chancel part of a church E of nave and crossing, where the Eucharist is celebrated; formerly the patron's responsibility (as opposed to nave, which was parishioners')

chantry a small chapel-like space for recital of masses for the soul of the benefactor, added to the body of church or inserted into existing fabric, often between chancel and chancel aisle; the institution was outlawed by Henry VIII in 1545

chapel of ease dependent, usually smaller branch of a parish church set up for convenience of remote parishioners

clerestory higher storey of nave above aisles, which allows the entry of plentiful light; often a Perpendicular addition to existing church

clunch a soft white limestone or hard chalk; not good building material but used decoratively

college a group of priests or lay clerics paid by endowment to say masses for the donor and his family; a church which houses a college is called **collegiate**

corbel a small support, generally a single stone, which projects from a wall. On it rests a superstructure, often of wood, perhaps a roof; ordinarily occurs in series

corona a metal lighting fixture of round or crown-like form

crocket protruding bumps or knobs of leaf-form spaced regularly on a sloping moulding or edge

crossing meeting point between transepts and main body in plan of a large church; often vaulted, with central or crossing tower above

cusp, cusped in Gothic tracery and other enrichment, an internal prong or excrescence along edge of a form

Decalogue the Ten Commandments; from the Reformation required by law to be posted at E end of all churches. Many 18c examples survive

dogtooth a form of Early English decoration like a row of Xs with their centres pulled away from the wall

east end where ritual activity and therefore architectural complexity is concentrated in churches. In England unusual care is taken to make church buildings face as near true E as possible (cf **ritual directions**)

entablature in classical architecture everything above the capital, which might be a complex cornice of several stages

entasis correction for optical distortion applied to columns by the classical Greeks: instead of straight lines the profiles of columns are slightly convex

fan vault a late Gothic system peculiar to England where upward-spreading cones of stone replace ribs emanating from piers; the aim is to conceal structure under rich surface pattern

flamboyant a phase of French late Gothic which resembles English Perpendicular in papery brittleness, but favours interwoven curves ('flames') as the main formal motif

flushwork a kind of exterior variegation on flint buildings, common in East Anglia, where interstices of a flat pattern in whitish stone – frequently of monograms or tracery – are filled with dressed flint

gargoyle grotesque human or animal form as exterior ornament, usually craning outward and carrying rainwater spout

grisaille a nearly monochrome design in tones of grey, in painting or stained glass

hall church plain spatial organization of barn-like effect, resulting from aisles equal in height to nave. The form developed in Germany; a partial parallel in Franciscan preaching boxes in Italy

hammerbeam wooden roof-type, in which short beams are linked by vertical strut to the pitched members. These short beams often have carved or decorated ends

hatchment heraldic arms on diamond-shaped board, hung outside a dead person's door, carried in the funeral and then lodged high on interior wall of church

header a brick laid so its short face shows in the wall

herringbone a feature common to Anglo-Saxon masonry, in which alternate courses are laid at rightward- and leftward-sloping angles

hogback distinctive Anglo-Danish tomb form found in Northern England: a long humped shape which looks like an animal's arched back

Jesse Tree Christ's ancestry depicted as a tree sprouting from the sleeping Jesse's navel, showing the generations of kings leading to Christ

Lady chapel dedicated to the Virgin Mary and an important focus in many English churches, often extending E of chancel

lancet plain tall window with pointed top, common in Early English period

lantern top stage of dome or tower, often a windowed polygonal pavilion

lights separate windows joined in larger whole; a five-light window will have five main divisions, separated by thin stone mullions (q.v.)

long and short work a method of quoining at external corners, characteristic of Anglo-Saxon building, in which large, irregular stones are laid first horizontally, then vertically, in series

lucarne window-like opening in side of spire, treated like a miniature dormer; essentially decorative

lunette half-moon shape, either window or decorative panel

lychgate (from Old English *lich*, corpse) an elaborate churchyard gateway which originally provided shelter and slab rest for coffin on its way to burial. In later examples the roof remains but not the resting place

misericord (from Latin *misericordia*, compassion) now refers to carved support beneath a half-seat which shows when stall-seats are turned back; these could be leant upon during services

mouchette ornament in interstices of tracery, a drooping lozenge with pointed end

mullion vertical divider in a window

narthex porch-like W antechamber which in Western Christianity has lost its original ritual significance as waiting place of non-communicants

ogee pointed arch incorporating a double curve so the top appears pulled or stretched; common in Gothic design from early 14c

orders in classical architecture, elaborated forms of post and lintel, of five canonic varieties: Doric, Tuscan, Ionic, Corinthian, Composite. An order consists of entablature, column (capital, shaft) and base, all of whose forms are highly regulated

pediment end or section of gable, originally marking the presence of a roof but now often confined to a triangular embellishment over a window or frame

pilaster a flat column half incorporated in a wall

piscina a little niche with a drain in wall beside an altar, for washing of Communion vessels

plate tracery an early method of combining glazed sections within one design; the stone dividers are so heavy that the glass looks punched out in a solid medium

poppyhead (from French *poupée*, doll) the elongated carved top of a wooden benchend

porticus (sing. and pl.) a porch-like extension entered from main space; a feature of Anglo-Saxon churches, sometimes used for burial

pulpitum solid divider between nave and chancel which might incorporate rood loft, chantries and other functions

quatrefoil a four-lobed shape; a common Gothic motif

quoin treatment of corner of a wall, which emphasizes the stones by rustication, colouring or patterning

reredos panel, often painted or carved, rising behind an altar

reveal surface between glass and wall plane, within a window frame: horizontal, it is the sill; vertical, the reveal

ritual directions the orientation of Christian churches on an E–W axis, with main altar in E and entrance at or near W end, dates back extremely far. It signals a link between Christ and the rising sun and echoes pre-Christian practice

rood, rood loft a large figure of Christ on the Cross, usually accompanied by Mary and John, placed over the entrance to the

chancel, mounted on a beam or on top of the screen; such features were removed from English churches at the Reformation but revived by Anglo-Catholicism last century

rood loft a passage across top of screen with its own stair in adjacent pier

rubble undressed or semi-dressed fieldstone left irregular on surface plane (as against **ashlar**, q.v.)

scraped internal walls from which plaster was scraped by Victorian restorers seeking (erroneously) the primitive medieval state of the fabric. William Morris's conservation group, the SPAB (Society for the Protection of Ancient Buildings), was popularly known as 'anti-scrape'

sedilia (Latin: seats (pl.); sing. *sedile*) three seats generally hollowed in thickness of chancel S wall, for three participants in the service: priest, deacon and sub-deacon. An ornamental focus in many churches

segmental arch or arcade a flat arch formed from a segment of a larger circle

spandrel roughly triangular space left over at each side above an arch, often a focus for decoration

springing the point at which an arch or vault begins to depart from the vertical course of column or wall

squint small, tube-like passage made through wall to enable celebrant at side altar to watch main altar and to co-ordinate his elevation of the Host

stops decorative termini of mouldings, for example around windows or other apertures, often in form of heads, leaves, etc

stoup bowl containing holy water, usually recessed in wall just inside entrance

strapwork rustic classical decoration of maze-like straps

and ornamental placards; Elizabethan and Jacobean

string course a simple moulding consisting of an extruded thread of stone; seen on Gothic wall planes

thermal window semi-circular opening derived from Roman baths, commonly divided by two mullions and sited well above eye level

tracery the ornamental pattern traced in windows or on other flat surfaces by narrow dividers

transept arm perpendicular to nave in a cruciform church; ordinarily occurring in matched pairs

transom horizontal divider in a window

tunnel vault the simplest kind, a continuous round arch; also called **barrel vault**

tympanum the panel above a door between the round or pointed arch and the lintel beneath; especially in Norman period, often filled with sculpture

undressed stone left rough, not given smooth (or other) finish

vault arched ceiling of stone, more durable and graceful alternative to flat wooden ceilings; occasionally stone vaults are imitated in wood, as at York Minster and Warminghurst, Northants.

vernacular (from Latin *vernaculus*, domestic) local, usually rustic, building tradition as opposed to sophisticated academic or courtly forms

volute scrolly classical ornament often in three-dimensional form as part of broken pediment or trimming on frames

voussoir one of the tapered stones making up the curve of an arch

Index

Bold numbers indicate
photographs.